Praise for *How to Survive and Prosper as an Artist*

"Provides the best overview of political and other aspects of the art world that I have ever come across . . . It is a bible that every artist should have."

—Shannon Wilkinson, president,
Cultural Communications, New York

"This self-help career book is the pick of the litter. . . . Every page is filled with practical advice and imaginative ways to build your career." —Donna Marxer, *Artists' News*

"Michels is well versed in the business aspects of an artist's career. Her enjoyable book is filled with valuable information and sound advice. . . . Highly recommended." —*Library Journal*

"This is a definitive guide to self-promotion and solid business planning for artists of all disciplines. . . . The best guide I have seen . . . it gives thoughtful, practical advice."

—Matthew Brown, *ArtsInk,* Mid Atlantic Arts Foundation

"Michels is an optimistic . . . and supportive ally, someone who dismisses the old cynic's saw that 'you can't make a living as an artist.'"
—Marion Wolberg Weiss, *Southampton Press*

"Encourages the pioneering spirit of artists to apply their creativity to the practical aspects of their dreams . . . Caroll Michels has a unique insider's view." —Tess Elliott, *The Arts Journal*

"A successful artist friend said that pretty much everything she knew about making a living as an artist came from this book."

—Greg Dixon, shared-visions.com

"An excellent orientation to the artist's life and the art marketplace." —*FYI*, New York Foundation for the Arts

"Michels provides information on art world politics that artists really need. She also gives a lot of straightforward advice on strategizing." —Barbara Schreiber, *Art Papers*

"This book can serve as the bible of marketing for visual artists. . . . It has the best practical and honest information. . . . This is the book you should have on your shelf if you are a visual artist."

—Mary Bowmar Richmond, *Creative Women Networking*

"The best guide I've found that looks at creating fine art as a career."

—Chris Farrell, *Right on the Money*,
Twin Cities Public Television (TPT), Minneapolis

"Michels is a tough but compassionate advocate, savvy in the ways of the world and the demands on artists in this materialistic society."

—Richard Pachter, *The Miami Herald*

"*How to Survive and Prosper as an Artist* is the very best book I've found to demystify the artist's process of dealing with the fine art/ gallery world."

—Diana Bryan, *Graphic News*, Graphic Artists Guild

"Caroll Michels' book . . . is a must for any serious artist desiring to be more than a Sunday painter."

—Martha Boynton, *The Palette*,
Mid-Atlantic Plein Air Painters Association

CAROLL MICHELS

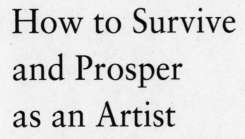

How to Survive and Prosper as an Artist

SELLING YOURSELF WITHOUT SELLING YOUR SOUL

· SIXTH EDITION ·

A HOLT PAPERBACK

HENRY HOLT AND COMPANY | NEW YORK

Holt Paperbacks
Henry Holt and Company, LLC
Publishers since 1866
175 Fifth Avenue
New York, New York 10010
www.henryholt.com

Library of Congress Cataloging-in-Publication Data
Michels, Caroll.
     How to survive and prosper as an artist : selling yourself
without selling your soul / Caroll Michels.—6th ed.
     p.   cm.
     Includes bibliographical references and index.
     ISBN-13: 978-0-8050-8848-9
     ISBN-10: 0-8050-8848-2
     1. Art—Vocational guidance—United States.
2. Art—Marketing.   I. Title.
     N6505 .M46   2001
     706'.8'8—dc21   2001039307

Henry Holt books are available for special promotions
and premiums. For details contact: Director, Special Markets.

Sixth Edition 2009

Designed by Victoria Hartman

Printed in the United States of America

10   9   8   7   6   5

To dance instructors Dwayne Biggs of The Ballroom of Sarasota and Gina "Ballerina" Wexler of SRQ Dance, Inc., and the West Coast Civic Ballet in Sarasota, Florida. With immense gratitude for helping me carve out a new edition of life.

A very special thanks for helping me get the sixth edition off the ground to Patrick Clark, former assistant editor of Henry Holt and Company, Monika Verma of Levine Greenberg Literary Agency, Inc., and Tad Crawford of Allworth Press.

Contents

Introduction: An Overview

In 1978 I began counseling visual and performing artists and writers on career management and development. I set up my own business and called myself an "artist's consultant." Today, I refer to my profession as a "career coach and artist advocate," a job title that better describes the work that I do.

Ranging in age from twenty-one to eighty-five, clients have included painters; sculptors; printmakers; fiber artists; poets; playwrights; novelists; cartoonists; journalists; photographers; craft artists; theater and film directors; film and video artists; performing artists; choreographers; dancers; classical, jazz, and pop musicians and composers; and opera singers. They have included well-known artists, unknown artists, beginning artists, self-taught artists, midlife career changers, artists fresh out of school, and college dropouts. My clients have also included groups of artists, artist couples, arts administrators, curators, gallery dealers, art consultants, critics, arts service organizations, and theater and dance companies. I have assisted a rabbi, a retired executive of Macy's department store, a retired host of a television variety show, a gossip columnist, ex-offenders, corporate executives, physicians, surgeons, architects, psychiatrists, psychologists, lawyers, and editors.

When I first began working with artists, the majority of my clients lived in the New York City area. However, today, through phone consultations I help artists nationwide, as well as those who live in Canada, Europe, Japan, and South America. I also meet with many artists in person in Sarasota, Florida.

I have advised and assisted artists in developing such basic career tools as résumés, artist statements, biographies, and brochures. I have provided information and advice on exhibition, performance, and commission opportunities. I have advised and assisted in the preparation of exhibition proposals, book proposals, and grant proposals, and public relations campaigns. I have advised artists on how to negotiate with art dealers and to prepare for studio visits.

I have also counseled artists on complex and seemingly less tangible career problems such as developing goals and helping artists learn to see themselves in relation to the world at large and as participants in the specific world of art and its various components. I have also counseled artists on handling rejection as well as success and on maintaining momentum and overcoming inertia.

However, the most significant aspect of my work is helping artists to take control of their careers.

Calling myself an artists' consultant and "hanging out a shingle" was not an easy task. For valid and comprehensible reasons, deep-rooted skepticism was intrinsic to all arts communities. Initially, it was difficult to reach artists and convince them that what I had to say and offer was worthwhile.

I jumped this major hurdle when a writer from the *Village Voice* wrote an article about me and why my services were needed and necessary. It was only one journalist's opinion, but the endorsement was set in type, and I was deemed legitimate!

Literally an hour after the *Voice* article hit the newsstands my life changed drastically. I was swamped with phone calls from artists eager to set up appointments.

Nevertheless, after more than thirty years of counseling artists, I still find it is not uncommon to be questioned about why I am qualified to give artists advice. Some of my specific accomplishments are sprinkled throughout this book, cited to make or emphasize a point or convey an experience. Although I am no longer doing artwork, I have always been proud that I was able to live solely off my earnings as an artist. I exhibited at museums and cultural institutions throughout the United States and in Europe. I established a solid track record for winning grants and corporate contributions. I developed and implemented all of my own public relations and publicity. And I was regularly published in newspapers and periodicals.

Managing my own career was something that *no one person* taught me. I learned from several individuals, positive and negative encounters, trial-and-error experiences, and personal intuition.

My father was an artist and studied at the Art Institute of Chicago. He earned a living as a graphic designer for the U.S. government. Early in his career he also worked as a freelance political cartoonist. In the evenings and on weekends he would design all sorts of "products"—ranging from a line of greeting cards with rather offbeat messages to T-shirts and other paraphernalia with messages that espoused his political point of view. Although he was jubilant about each and every project and would go as far as having everything *printed* without a marketing plan, he "froze" when it came time to make business contacts and organize sales. Some of the cards and T-shirts were distributed free of charge to friends and relatives, but basically our basement became a huge repository for what might have been.

When he retired, he started painting profusely. And although he read every word in each edition of my book, he never asked me for advice on how to get his watercolors beyond the walls of his house nor did I ever hear him mention that he submitted his work for exhibition consideration.

Only in recent years did I finally make the connection between the work I do with artists and my family background—that I am helping artists achieve what my father was unable to do: enter the marketplace.

This book contains information and advice derived from all of my experiences when I was working as an artist, as well as those of my clients, and most certainly some subliminal messages that I received from my childhood and adolescent years. I have offered perceptions, observations, and advice that would have been invaluable to me when I first started to make a career as an artist.

What artists need most is objective advice, but what they usually receive is reinforcement of a myth of what it is like to be an artist. All too often artists are characterized as underdogs, and accordingly this image is reinforced throughout their careers. I can't promise that all of my advice is objective, since my personal experiences come into play, but the original incentive to write this book came from realizing how much underdog philosophy was being published under the guise of "nuts and bolts" career management. Much of the reading material published in the 1970s and 1980s flatly stated that the way the art world operates will always remain the same, and it is naive to try to change it. Other publications were more subtle, but the tone was patronizing: "Yes, artists, you might be creative, talented, and have a lot to give to the world, but there are 'others' who *really* know what is going on, *others who know best.*"

A book published in 1970 used the sexist title *The Artist's Guide to His Market.* Although the title of subsequent editions was changed to *The Artist's Guide to the Art Market,* the author advised that it would be unrealistic for artists to believe that they can earn a living through art sales.[1]

Although, in the 2000s, books on career management for artists are more plentiful and some publications emit tones that are more optimistic and empowering, the attitudes displayed by artists and many members of the art world continue to reek of the master/slave and victim/victimizer mentality.

This book addresses artists' roles in advancing and bettering their lot, taking control of their careers, learning to market their work, learning to exercise self-motivation, and approaching and managing their careers as other professionals deal with theirs. In other words, artists should apply many of the same techniques that other self-employed professionals use to make their careers work.

You will rarely find the word *talent* used in the forthcoming pages. The belief that an artist has talent is a subjective judgment, and there is no guarantee that a talented artist will be successful or that a successful artist is talented. When I use the words *success* and *successful,* I am referring to the relative level of achievement within a specific category, not the inherent talent of an artist.

Measuring my success as an artists' career coach is very similar to measuring my success as an artist. In both professions I have achieved immediate success, long-range success, and no success. I have received direct feedback, indirect feedback, and no feedback. I have felt successful in my work when my clients have followed up and used the leads, information, and advice that have enabled some of them to win grants from foundations and government agencies, fellowships to artist-in-residence programs in the United States and abroad, and invitations to exhibit and perform. Clients have received press coverage and have had their work published. In some instances I have been successful in providing information and advice that was put to immediate use, and in other cases it has taken several years to see any new development.

Although many of the examples and anecdotes I use to illustrate or make a point involve visual artists, performing artists and writers will also be able to identify with many of the situations. All artists in all disciplines will get something out of this book.

This book will not provide all of the answers an artist is seeking, nor does it contain everything an artist needs to know about the art world. However, it fills in the gaps that have been omitted, overlooked, or ignored in other publications; it elaborates on subjects that have been inadequately covered and challenges some basic notions about what an artist's career is all about. It contains advice, opinions, and impressions that will not be particularly palatable to members of the art world—*including artists,* the media, funding agencies, patrons, art dealers, administrators, curators, and critics— because it also explores the ills and injustices of the art world and sheds some light on who is responsible.

The art world is in dire need of reforms and structural changes. These changes will not happen overnight, but they *will* happen if more and more artists take control of their careers, reject the image of artists as sufferers, and refrain from practicing a dog-eat-dog philosophy when it comes to competing with other artists.

Some time ago I shared these views with a client who has been seeing me since I began counseling artists. He had been represented by a dealer for more than three years, during which time his work substantially increased in sales and in value.

From the beginning of their relationship, much against my judgment, the artist refused to have a written contract with the dealer drawn up. However, the artist accepted and acted upon my advice to learn to market his work, independent of the annual one-person show he received at the gallery. Eventually, he became highly skilled in initiating new contacts and following up on old ones. Both initiatives resulted in many sales.

When the dealer saw what was happening, she added some new stipulations to their oral agreement, which originally set forth a specified commission on all work sold through the gallery. She began charging "special commissions" for special circumstances, circumstances in which she was not directly involved either in initiating a sale or in doing the legwork or paperwork to make it happen. The artist, who was afraid to challenge the dealer because he felt that it would jeopardize their relationship, acceded to her demands.

I pointed out to the artist that, apart from money, a principle was at stake, and that each time an artist compromises a principle, his or her career and the status of artists in general, now and in the future, are set back another notch.

I advised the artist to confront the dealer with a proposal that was more equitable. If the artist must give the dealer a commission on every work sold, even if the sale did not originate with the gallery, the dealer should give the artist something in return, such as a monthly advance against future sales. I pointed out that if the artist had a written contract, chances are the dealer would never have tried to impose an arbitrary commission formula. I also pointed out that the artist had adequately proved his market value and selling power to the dealer, who was deriving steady revenue from the sale of the artist's work, a situation that the dealer would not want to give up easily. *It had not occurred to the artist that he had bargaining power.*

Such occurrences are common in the art world—unnecessary dilemmas and frustrations created by middlepeople who have usurped power from artists and by artists who allow their power to be usurped.

Artists, by the fact they are artists, have power. *Artists provide thousands of nonartists with jobs!* Examples of nonartists who depend on artists for jobs include dealers; gallery staffs; curators; museum staffs; arts administrators; critics and journalists; corporate art consultants and advisors; federal, state, and municipal employees; teachers; framers; accountants; lawyers; and art suppliers.

Yet more nonartists than artists make a living from art, and nonartists make *more* money from art than artists! This inequity exists, as do many others, because artists, the "employers," individually and collectively have not yet recognized their power.

Another problem among artists is a diffusion of power. Although there are more artists than ever before, as the community of artists multiplies, it simultaneously divides into different factions, movements, self-interest groups, and trends. There are artists who segregate themselves into pockets of racial, sexual, and ethnic identity. Everyone is vying for the same bone; no one wants to share it.

On the other hand, some aspects of the art world are in good shape and are getting better all the time. Much headway has been made in art law, legislation, and artists' rights.

More colleges and universities are providing fine-art students with career development information through courses, seminars, and workshops. And more art dealers and arts administrators are entering the art world with degrees in arts administration, and they are better prepared than many of their predecessors with the marketing and business aspects of art. They are also, one hopes, more sensitive to the needs of artists and the public's understanding of art.

If I didn't believe that there is a lot of room in the art world for many artists to make a decent living, I certainly never would have started a consulting service or written a book about art-career management. There is ample opportunity for artists, even within the still imperfect art world.

Most of the structural changes in the art world will come about only through artist pressure, artist initiative, and artist participation. While the prospects of radically changing the art world might seem overwhelming to any one artist, one of the most important contributions that any artist can make is to *restructure and take control of his or her own career*. The following chapters will elaborate on why this is important and provide options, suggestions, and advice on how to make it happen.

Keep in mind that it took me *several years to build a career* as an artist. It also took a lot of time to learn, master, and apply the skills that are described in this book. I mention this to help readers counteract sensations of being *overwhelmed* by all of the suggestions and information that are provided in the forthcoming chapters. My career did not develop overnight; it was a slow but constant buildup. I absorbed information that I needed to know at the time when I needed to know it. When I listened to my inner voice, I moved forward; when I didn't, I stumbled.

In this edition a new chapter has been added titled "Art Marketing and the Internet," and because the Internet is impacting artists' careers in many ways, reference to the Internet is also dispersed throughout the book.

The addresses of organizations, programs, publications, software, audiovisual components, and Web sites referred to in the text are listed in the appendix of resources at the back of the book.

An adjunct to the appendix of resources is a Web site that I created, the Artist Help Network (www.artisthelpnetwork.com). It was launched in conjunction with the fifth edition of this book and is a free resource service to help artists *take control of their careers*. The Web site contains most of the contacts listed in the sixth edition's appendix of resources. Readers can use the Web site to receive updated contact information and listings of new resources that have come to my attention. The Artist Help Network is a work in progress with new information being added on an ongoing basis.

For readers who wish to contact me, I have included my address, phone and fax numbers, email address, and Web site addresses (see "About the Author" at the end of the book).

Launching or Relaunching Your Career: Overcoming Career Blocks

As an artist you have experienced the exuberance of creating something you like, which might be the culmination of a direction in your work or might articulate something new. It felt good. The goodness screamed out. You mastered and controlled. The power felt good. Your expectations were rewarded.

However, producing something you like and believe in does not resolve the question of how to use your creation to survive and prosper. For artists, the question is particularly complex because of the difference between survival and prosperity as defined by artists and those in other professions. For an artist, *survival* often means bare-bones existence; *prosperity* may be keeping your head above water. In other professions, *survival* is keeping your head above water; *prosperity* is success.

Being an artist means believing you are an artist; making a living as an artist requires mastering many of the skills and professional attitudes shared by successful self-employed persons engaged in other occupations. Equally important, it is necessary to overcome the career blocks that are particular and indigenous to the fine-arts field.

In the book *A Life in the Arts: Practical Guidance and Inspiration for Creative & Performing Artists,* the author and psychotherapist Dr. Eric Maisel pinpoints twenty types of creative blocks that artists often experience:

Blocks from parental voices, personality blocks, personality trait blocks, self-censorship, self-criticism, world criticism, world-wariness, existential blocks, conflicts between life and art, fatigue, pressure paralysis, environmental blocks, social blocks, skill deficits, myths and idealizations, self-abuse, anxieties, depression, and incubation and fallow periods.[1]

Although these problems and limitations are presented as *creative* blocks, they are the very same obstacles that encumber *career* development.

REJECTING THE MYTH OF THE ARTIST

Over many years our society has created a myth about what it means to be an artist. Perpetuated consciously and subconsciously by artists and nonartists, this myth is based on trading off many of the things that other people value for the right to be an artist.

For example, the myth tells us that struggle, complexity, and suffering are necessary components of creativity, and without these key elements an artist will stagnate. The myth tells us that the desire for comfortable lives and financial success will ultimately poison and distort art, that a true artist is concerned *only* with art and anyone else is a dilettante. The myth tells us that *real* artists do not discover themselves. Other people do, preferably when the artist is dead!

The myth warns us about *selling out,* although the majority of artists who are concerned about this issue are not in a position to sell out, nor are they quite sure what it means.

The myth says that artists are expected to be flamboyant, provocative, moody, weird, or antisocial. Writer and social critic Tom Wolfe suggests that this stereotyped image of the artist was formed in the nineteenth century, based on the style and behavior of writer and art critic Théophile Gautier. Wolfe writes:

[W]ith Gautier's own red vests, black scarves, crazy hats, outrageous pronouncements, huge thirsts, and ravenous groin . . . the modern picture of The Artist began to form: the poor but free spirit, plebeian but aspiring only to be classless, to cut himself forever free from the bonds of the greedy and hypocritical bourgeoisie, to be whatever the fat burghers feared most, to cross the line wherever they drew it, to look at the world in a way they couldn't *see*, to be high, live low, stay young forever—in short, to be the bohemian.[2]

Many of the basic problems of artists trying to enter the art world and sustain a career there are created by their feelings of insecurity and helplessness. There is a direct correlation between how artists see themselves and where art-world power is currently centered. For example, the term *stable of artists* is commonly and casually used by both artists and dealers alike. It refers to the artists who are represented by a gallery, but it implies much more, and, unfortunately, as a metaphor it works well. It suggests that artists are like herds of animals that need to be contained in an environment where their master can control their lives. *Starving artist* is another demeaning and frequently used phrase that contributes to the stereotypical image of how artists are perceived and how they see themselves. The lingo is used in advertising, on Web sites, in URL titles, and in products, and even as the name of art galleries.

PERCEIVING "FINE ARTIST" AS A VALID PROFESSION

In our society, there is a myth that suggests that to be antibourgeois, a free spirit, and classless, one should not have an occupation. The myth implies that being an artist is a state of mind and casts great doubts on whether being an artist is a valid profession.

Seeds of doubt suggesting that fine art is not a valid occupation are planted and reinforced, for example, by educators who, under the guise of providing career advice, emphasize *alternatives to fine art* and steer students into applied arts fields. Medical and fashion illustration, set design, graphic design, industrial design, and commercial photography are viewed as viable alternatives to painting, sculpture, and fine-art photography. Students in art school are encouraged to take a lot of education courses to have something to fall back on. If we were educated to believe that being a fine artist is a valid profession, there would be fewer artists needing an occupational backup. Has a law student ever been advised to take a lot of education courses to have something to fall back on?

Although the cautious advice given to artists comes from people who are trying to be helpful, it is advice based on other people's experiences, as well as on hearsay and myths. Other people's reality should not be your reality, nor can it be.

Believing in other people's perceptions is a disastrous trap. However, artists sometimes find it attractive, hoping that it can be a shortcut on the road to success or shield them from confrontations. Ralph Charell, author of *How to Make Things Go Your Way,* observes:

> If you filter the perceptions you receive through mediators, you deprive yourself of a direct encounter with the event itself. The more you come to depend on the perceptions and opinions of others, the less of yourself you are able to put into the equations of various experiences of your own life. Soon, if the process continues, your life becomes dim and pale and you are eventually at sea, tossed and buffeted, alone under a starless sky, without an internal compass of your own.[3]

DUAL CAREERS AND
LOW-INCOME EXPECTATIONS

Art educator Ronald H. Silverman clearly sees the correlation between how artists are viewed as low-income producers and the low priority art is assigned in school curriculums. Pointing out that substantial evidence indicates that more than 90 percent of school-age children do not connect art with a means of acquiring money or earning a living, Silverman goes on to say:

> While these figures may reflect pervasive cultural attitudes which stereotype artists as starving Bohemians, they may also be the consequence of current art education practices. Teachers are either ignoring the economic impact of the arts or they are telling their students that an interest in art has little if any economic career implications. Although these approaches may be the honest view of well-intended teachers, they do not square with the

facts. They may also be the key deterrent to art becoming a part of the basic school curriculum.[4]

Low expectations of artists' earning power have given rise to the practice of dual careers. While few question its symbolic implications, the concept of dual careers for artists is a widely accepted norm that is readily encouraged and propagated. For example, the academic dean of an art college condones the practice of dual careers:

> We are teaching [artists] that having a dual career does not necessarily mean that you make less art. After all, what's the point of having all your time free to make art if you have no money for materials and supplies? This no longer means that artists have to wait on tables. There are many more opportunities and diverse choices for the artist today than ever before. They may go into arts administration or arts-related services.[5]

The phrase *dual career* is a euphemism for *holding two jobs,* and under the work ethic of many cultures and religions it is emblematic of fortitude, stamina, dedication, and responsibility. But in reality, and in most cases, anyone engaged in a dual career for any length of time understands that it creates a life-style of frustration, confusion, stress, chaos, exhaustion, and guilt.

INSUFFICIENT TRAINING OF FINE ARTISTS

Even when students persevere and select fine arts against all odds, they may enter their careers questioning the propriety of earning a living as a fine artist. Moreover, they usually haven't the foggiest notion of how to begin.

The late artist and author Jo Hanson believed that

> artists are set up for difficult career adjustments by the omissions from art education, and by the self-image projected through the art sub-culture that discourages, and even scorns, attention to business management and competence in it. In attitudes and preparation, I believe most of us begin with several strikes

against us. We find, through difficult experience, that we must work our way up to zero to get in a position to go forward. I speculate that "successful" artists are the ones who figured things out early in their careers and could follow a clear line toward their goals.[6]

In previous editions of this book I described my experience in the mid-1980s when the College Art Association held its annual conference in New York City. Responding to an open call for panel discussion topics, I submitted a proposal suggesting that the conference include a panel focusing on the importance of including career management courses in fine-arts college and university curriculums. Although the response to the idea was less than enthusiastic, I did not receive a total bum's rush, and was given fifteen minutes to state my case at a session called "Special Projects," a potpourri of topics not valued enough to warrant panel discussions.

Five of the fifteen minutes had to be used to establish my credentials to this particularly credential-conscious audience. With a limited time allotment I managed to make the point that hundreds of students are being graduated each year ill-equipped to handle the realities of life after art school or navigate the maze of confusion surrounding the art world.

There was polite clapping, and a few members of the audience later told me they were in agreement with my position. But it was apparent that career courses for fine artists were not on most educators' list of priorities.

In many schools even the mention of "career" and "life after school" is discouraged—or, as one recent graduate of an art school in an Ivy League university complained, "My teachers made me feel guilty when I asked questions that were in any way related to the business aspect of art or how to go about finding a gallery. I was chastised for admitting that I was concerned about making a living from photography."

Some academics who discourage career advice at the college level believe that students should be sheltered from real-life survival issues while in school. But many fine-arts faculty members are opposed to career development courses for selfish and self-serving reasons: they are aware that today's student artists will become tomorrow's practicing artists, and eventually artists with whom they will compete for gallery, museum, and press attention, so there is much resistance to imparting any sort of information that could possibly give these future peers a career edge or jeopardize their own pecking order in the art world. Even long after I started doing artist career development workshops at colleges and universities, my presence was so threatening that I was considered a "witch"—and not a good witch! Invitations to conduct workshops were generally extended by well-intentioned career counselors at academic institutions who would enthusiastically announce my visit to the art department faculty, who in turn chose either not to inform students about the workshop or adamantly suggested that the workshop be boycotted.

In 1999, I conducted a workshop at the Savannah College of Art and Design that was organized by a faculty member who had read my book. She rallied all of her students to attend the workshop and persuaded a few other faculty members to urge their students to attend. Word quickly spread to the college career counselors about the success of the workshop, and a few years later they invited me back for a repeat performance. However, the faculty member who had enthusiastically organized the original workshop had left the college. Without the support of the faculty, and without exaggeration, in the morning session only a handful of students attended, and in the afternoon session only one student showed up!

Career development information is not only opposed by academia for self-serving reasons, but it has also been used as a scapegoat to explain the ills of the art world. For example, the book *Has Modernism Failed?* by Suzi Gablik contains a reprint of a brochure announcing a series of workshops called "The Business of Art and the Artist," sponsored by the Maryland Summer Institute for the Creative and Performing Arts, the University of Maryland, and the U.S. Small Business Administration. Gablik concludes that the workshop was

> another telling example of how much career progress, even in art, now depends on making organizational values an intrinsic

part of one's life. . . . The assumption is that success in the higher corporate world of art requires training in the techniques of business administration, and it leaves no doubt that the principles and practices of corporate management now produce the psychological model shaping even the lives of artists.[7]

The development of a program on survival skills for artists—one that covers such topics as health hazards, contracts, copyright, estate planning, insurance, and record keeping—is hardly an indication that artists are motivated by corporate institutional and organizational values. But Gablik is not the only misguided individual who believes in the myth that it is far nobler for artists to drive a cab to support their art than to derive a living from creating art!

SCHOOLS THAT ADDRESS REAL-LIFE ISSUES

More and more headway is being made to help fine-art students prepare for the transition from art school to real life.

In 1996, when I was preparing the fourth edition of this book, I contacted 156 schools in the United States with four-year fine-art programs, most of which were accredited members of the National Association of Schools of Art and Design. A letter was sent to each school to inquire whether a required or elected credit or noncredit course or workshop was offered on professional practices and career planning that were specifically geared for *fine-art students*.

Forty-one of the schools responded, a bit over 25 percent, and out of the forty-one respondents sixteen of the schools *required* students to take a career development course as a prerequisite to graduation. Another sixteen of the respondents offered courses in professional practices as electives. All of the schools that conducted mandatory and elective professional practice courses awarded credit hours ranging from one to four credits. An additional five schools offered noncredit workshops or seminars specifically for fine artists.

In 2001, when preparing for the fifth edition of my book, I contacted 175 schools in the United States with four-year fine-art programs to inquire whether a required or elected credit or noncredit course or workshop was offered on professional practices and career planning specifically geared for fine-art students. Most of the schools were accredited members of the National Association of Schools of Art and Design.

Eighty-five of the schools responded, or nearly 49 percent, and out of the eighty-five respondents, thirty-nine of the schools *required* students to take a career development course as a prerequisite to graduation, and twenty schools offered courses as electives. The majority of schools in both groups offered courses that specifically focused on professional practices; other schools integrated a career development curriculum into courses that dealt with other issues and topics.

All of the mandatory and elected professional business practice courses awarded credit hours, ranging from one to six credits.

Most of the required and elected courses covered a range of topics, including marketing, presentation materials and documentation, grant writing, résumés and artist statements, art law and copyright, applying for graduate school, publicity, exhibition installation, and gallery relations.

At the Cleveland Art Institute, Professor Matthew Hollern is the dean of faculty and teaches Professional Practices, a course that he designed several years ago. Originally an elective, in 2004 it became mandatory for all graduate students. The course focuses on three main themes: presentation and communication; participation and professional activity; and planning, business goals, and career goals. It has a three-track career emphasis: entrepreneur; industry; and studio, gallery and exhibitions. In addition, the institute requires all graduates to take a professional writing course devoted to grant-writing, proposal-writing, contracts, and cover letters.

The University of North Texas in Denton offers a course called Professional Practices for the Studio Artist. It is described in the graduate catalog as a "study of theoretical and practical aspects of succeeding as a practicing artist outside the academy. Survey of protocols and common practices expected of the artists [sic] as a productive member of the business community where fine art is the commodity."

Every two years at the University of Texas at San Antonio, Kent Rush, professor of art and chairperson of the art and art history department, teaches the elective Professional Practices and Survival Skills, a graduate seminar course. In addition to covering career development basics such as copyright issues, income and sales tax, and résumé development, the course includes office organization, mailing lists and databases, and health and safety. Rush also plans to invite a psychologist to discuss issues regarding self-esteem, stress, rejection, and career versus family.

In 1999, at the University of Wisconsin-Madison, graduate students Sophia Allison and Dan LaValley created the Web site Professional Practices in the Arts. It was designed as a final project for a seminar on professional practices conducted by Professor Leslee Nelson. With the assistance and support of Professor Nelson, Allison and LaValley received grants to maintain the site. When Allison and LaValley left school, the site was reorganized and administered by other students and renamed artUW.com. The site continues to provide career-related information and Professor Nelson continues to teach elective professional practice courses for graduate students, "but I allow motivated seniors to take them too."[8]

In 2000, Professor Michael Warrick, who for several years taught the required course Professional Skills in the Visual Arts at the University of Arkansas in Little Rock, organized and moderated a two-session panel, "Teach Them to Swim or Let Them Sink," for the joint meeting of the Southeastern College Art Conference and Mid-American College Art Association.

One of the panelists, Stephen Driver, associate professor of art at Brescia University, presented the paper "Teach Them to Swim . . . ? How Long Can They Tread Water?" In his presentation Driver pointed out that he developed the seminar "as a response to the lack of preparation for a career in the arts that I received as a student."[9] He went on to say, "Many of my peers who no longer make or teach art fell by the wayside because they just couldn't see their way past all the obstacles."[10]

Driver teaches a mandatory professional practices seminar for seniors in the fine-arts department. "It is a valuable course on several levels. Students for the most part find it as a wake-up call to just how competitive the art marketplace is and . . . as an opportunity to get their act together."[11]

As college faculty and academic career advisors see the large impact a career development curriculum can have on fine-art students, Professor Gary Keown at Southeastern Louisiana University points out clear reasons why career development also benefits schools:

> It should be understood that, with university budget cuts, this system is streamlining its various programs. In light of this, we as art studio faculty should realize that upper-administrations look very closely at student success rates after graduation through exit reports. As a result, art departments have a vested interest in the success of their students through career achievement after graduation. Preparing these students is of utmost importance during these pragmatic times.[12]

In the article "Art Schools: A Group Crit" published in *Art in America,* thirteen educators, artists, and scholars discussed, among other issues, the skills young artists should acquire. Out of the thirteen participants only a few people raised the importance of business and professional practices. Bruce Ferguson, a former dean of the School of the Arts at Columbia University in New York and an independent curator and critic, believes that

> the issue of "success" is a much more interesting and complicated one than the issue of failure . . . therefore . . . instruction that stresses professional preparation, from the conceptual and theoretical to the legal and administrative, has a place in contemporary pedagogy. To send students out into the world to re-invent the wheel, as was often the case, is both depressing and condescending.[13]

Dave Hickey, who taught art criticism and theory and ran a graduate program in studio art at the University of Nevada in Las Vegas (where he is a professor of English), points out that

> teachers of art practice have one overriding obligation to their students: to be intimately familiar with the contemporary stands of art practice, discourse, trade and exhibition against which their students' work will be measured—so their students will know the unspoken rules they are choosing to break or not to break. The art market itself should be dealt with evenhandedly and explained in detail. It is a fact and an option from which students should not be cloistered. Demonizing the art marketplace

does more damage to students than exposing them to collectors
and dealers who are irrevocably a part of the art world.[14]

Although many more art schools are acknowledging the importance of preparing students for real life, artists who are planning to
enter B.F.A. or M.F.A. programs should consider application only
to those colleges and universities that offer professional practice
programs for fine artists.

CONFRONTING MONEY ISSUES

How much do you want to earn as an artist, and how much are you
willing to spend in order to earn it? Thoughts of money are ever
present and, depending on one's situation, the thoughts are in the
forefront of one's mind or are nestled in the subconscious.

How much is my work worth? How much am I worth? How
much do I need this year, this month, this week? What can I afford?
How much should I be earning?

There are artists who have identified with poverty for so long that
when money finally comes their way they are consumed with enor-
mous guilt, a theme that dominates their existence. There are artists
who become Little Johnny One-Notes, churning out whatever made
money in the past, in fear that venturing in new directions will
bring them back to Poverty City. And there are artists who attach so
many stigmas to the concept of prosperity that they undervalue
their work, riding the train to martyrdom. And as psychotherapist
Annette Lieberman and writer Vicki Lindner state in their book *The
Money Mirror: How Money Reflects Women's Dreams, Fears, and
Desires,* "Money Martyrs think it is 'morally superior' to ignore
their financial needs and often become the victims."[15] They also
point out that "artists believe, often with validity, that financial
rewards are bestowed on artistic products that are not the best.
They say that they have not earned much money for their work
because it is 'good' or 'pure.'"[16]

Carol Lloyd, a writer, performer, and author of *Creating a Life
Worth Living,* describes the attitudes of many artists who have con-
flicted relationships with money: "They want a luxurious life but no

signs of filthy lucre passing through their hands. They want stability without savings. They want to be poor and righteous and generous of spirit on the one hand and they want to be rich and fabulous on the other. They want to do wonderfully healthy things for the world for free and, at the same time, work in high-powered prestigious fields and get paid by the truckload."[17]

Lloyd goes on to say that "if you have this internal battle with greed and guilt, hedonism and morality, you may be suffering from the effects of extreme thinking. From this black-and-white perspective, the middle ground of getting paid for good, hard work reverberates with negative connotations: borrowing, staid, conventional, capitalist, careerist."[18]

"Almost all of us have struggled at one time or another with money shortfalls and found ourselves face to face with overwhelming fears,"[19] writes author Tad Crawford in another very good book, *The Secret Life of Money: How Money Can Be Food for the Soul*. Through stories and myths from around the world Crawford helps us understand why money is so much more than the useful tool we may think it to be. He discusses how money secretly influences our lives, why money is so easily worshiped, and why money sometimes feels more important than life.[20]

The most common money-related mistake artists make is a reluctance to invest in their own careers. Although artists are willing to spend relatively large amounts of money on work materials and equipment, they are miserly and skimp when it comes to other important aspects of career development, such as travel, presentation tools, publicity, and mailing lists, and such preventive medicine as using contracts, hiring lawyers and accountants, and engaging the services of other professionals. Subsequent chapters discuss why these expenditures are important. But it simply boils down to this: *If you are not willing to invest in your career, who is?*

An artist's reluctance to make crucial career investments is sometimes spearheaded or aggravated by the attitude of a nonartist spouse or mate, particularly if the artist does have a separate bank account. If "family funds" are being used for career expenditures, an artist might experience subtle or not so subtle pressure to generate art sales in a relatively short amount of time or provide some sort of *tangible* justification that career investments are not a waste of time and money. Although it is not always possible, it is important for artists to sensitize their mates to the reality that earning a decent part-time or full-time income from sales and commissions is certainly possible, but it can take time. Help them understand that when instant gratification occurs, it most likely happens during the process of creating work and not in the early stages of launching a career.

INTIMIDATION OF VISUAL ART

Many people are intimidated by visual art, including many of those who buy and sell art.

The fear of visual art is perpetuated throughout our schooling, beginning as early as kindergarten, as we are bombarded with conflicting messages about the importance and relevance of visual art in our culture. Often visual art is presented as a "filler" subject—not in the same league, for example, as science, mathematics, or history. But by adulthood visual art is perceived as a discipline that can only be appreciated and understood by someone possessing a high IQ or a substantial background in art history.

On the other hand, random interviews with members of the public inquiring about preferences in music will produce immediate and confident responses. People are eager to tell you that they like jazz, country and western, classical, or rock and roll!

But ask the same public about their preferences in visual art, and their responses are laced with hesitation and discomfort. Often defensive platitudes are offered such as "I don't know anything about art but I know what I like."

Art historian and lecturer Carol Duncan described an experience with a department of motor vehicles inspector during a test for her driver's license:

> Upon discovering that I taught art history, he felt compelled to tell me of his dislike for Picasso, probably the only modern artist he could name. For a good fifteen minutes, while I did my turns and stops, he complained steadily about modern art. "I'm not stupid," he kept saying, "but that art doesn't say anything to

me." Indeed, there was nothing stupid about him. But he felt that someone was telling him he was stupid by holding up for admiration expensive and apparently meaningful objects he could not comprehend. Students in the state college I teach often indicate such resentment—or else they are full of apology for not liking modern art.[21]

Educational systems that give mixed messages about visual art have contributed to the shaping of a society of individuals who do not value or trust their own opinions and feelings about visual art.

As a result of the public's intimidation by visual art and insecurity about their beliefs and feelings, a power structure has developed within the art world comprised of intermediaries whom we have come to depend on as sources of truth. We actually believe that *good* art can only be determined by the judgments and decisions of art dealers, critics, curators, academics, and art administrators. Unfortunately, many people within the art world believe this myth, including artists!

If members of the public were self-confident about their preferences in art, the strength of the power structure would diffuse. For example, art dealers would be acknowledged as sales personnel, a title that reflects their *real* occupation versus the messiah-like image currently awarded. Arts-related professions would be recognized as occupations that were created around artists, and not, as it often seems, the other way around! Or as arts administrator Ted Potter pointed out: "Curators, administrators, directors and art dealers are all really flight attendants for this thing called art. . . . Art and the creative artists are what it's all about."[22]

VALIDATION AND ARTISTS' INSECURITY

Self-validation has great staying power compared to the type of validation that artists often seek from the art world. Validation awarded from the art world is fickle, volatile, often irrational, and usually short-lived.

When external validation is bestowed, the recipient might feel ecstatic, making one conclude that whatever sacrifices were made, and whatever time and money were spent, it had all been worth it. But for some people, it doesn't matter how much praise, press, exhibitions, commissions, and sales they receive, it will never be enough.

The ability to validate your own artwork does not always come easily nor does it come quickly. When I am called upon to validate an artist's work, I point out that in my capacity as a career coach and as a human being, it is not my role to assess whether an artist has talent. And when put in this position, I pose the question: How would you respond if you showed your work to six artists and half of the group said you are talented and the other half disagreed?

Emphasis on gaining approval from the art world has become so commonplace that few artists question the negative implications of looking for validation from external sources. For example, in her book *The Practical Handbook for the Emerging Artist,* Margaret R. Lazzari, who is an artist, earnestly writes that

> there are two ways to have your artwork validated, that is, recognized as significant and meaningful by others. One way, the "mainstream" method, is to have your work recognized by people within the museum/gallery system, such as curators, dealers, and critics. These people are art professionals who are entrusted by society at large with evaluating, displaying, buying, selling, and preserving artwork.[23]

For artists not seeking mainstream validation, Lazzari goes on to say that "validations for these artists cannot come through the traditional gallery-museum system, but through alternative means. Artists must identify the audience who is interested in what they make, and find ways to bring the work to them."[24]

The types of validation that Lazzari describes encourage artists to give away their power in deference to "those who know best."

Contrary to Lazzari's message, David Bayles and Ted Orland, authors of the book *Art & Fear,* take a much healthier approach to the issue of validation, reminding us that

> courting approval, even that of peers, puts a dangerous amount of power in the hands of the audience. Worse yet, the audience is seldom in a position to grant (or withhold) approval on the one

issue that really counts—namely, whether or not you're making progress in your work.[25]

Other issues regarding artist insecurity are discussed in chapter 11, "Rationalization, Paranoia, Competition, Rejection, and the Overwhelm Factor."

AWE OF NEW YORK AND
SELF-IMPOSED REGIONALISM

Artificial barriers and provincial attitudes about the art market can deeply restrict artists' career development. Preoccupation with regionalism has given rise to the expression "regional artist," a self-limiting phrase that, unfortunately, some artists use to describe their status.

I lived in Manhattan for twenty-five years. In 1995 I moved to East Hampton, New York, a small town at the end of Long Island, where I lived until 2004 when I moved to Sarasota, Florida, a small city. In East Hampton and Sarasota I witnessed firsthand an obsessive desire of many *local* artists to *only* exhibit in *local* venues.

Some artists adhere to a self-imposed hierarchy of believing that you have to "start small and work your way up." Other artists believe that their market is limited to their town or city of residence, or that some sort of universal censorship is imposed, illogically concluding that there is no market *anywhere* for their work if they are unable to find a receptive audience in their hometown. (Artists living in large cities such as New York, Chicago, and Los Angeles, for example, are as likely to engage in this form of provincialism as artists living in towns and small cities.) Other artists earnestly believe that hometown exposure leads to national recognition; should a hometown be a city with a vibrant contemporary art community this is sometimes true. However, this is the case of neither East Hampton nor Sarasota. More often than not the motivating force of many artists to exhibit work in local galleries and cultural centers is a deep-seated need based on anger and rage to prove to local folks that "I'm somebody."

Sadly, for most artists who pine for national or international recognition, but limit their horizons to local or regional resources, their longings will go unfulfilled because the artists have yet to understand the universal law that national and international recognition and support usually comes your way from venues and audiences *outside of your neighborhood.*

The myth of equating career success with exhibiting work in a New York gallery is highly imbued in the minds of artists and nonartists. In all of the many years I have traveled throughout the United States and in Canada to conduct workshops on career development, the question always arises: *"Do I have to show in New York to make it in the art world?"* Although my answer is always an ardent "no," in most instances members of the audience do not hear me or want to hear me because they have been brainwashed to believe that being represented by a New York gallery is pivotal to career success.

Because of the importance that has been attributed to exhibiting in New York, some artists will *pay anything* to have a show in a New York gallery. Naive attitudes, feelings of neediness, and the extraordinary pervasiveness of the belief of the myth of New York have contributed to the growth of vanity galleries in New York (and in other cities, see page 135).

ADOLESCENT CAREER GOALS

The phrase *successful artist* loosely describes a person who has achieved some degree of fame and/or fortune. Depending on whom you ask, the definitions of fame and fortune can vary considerably.

Although, as previously discussed, some artists equate success with having a show in New York, other artists equate success with being reviewed in a leading art trade publication, while other artists equate success to being featured on the publication's front cover! Some artists describe success as having their works included in the "right" private collections, and other artists believe that success is being represented in the "right" *museum* collection. Some artists define success as having a solo show at a museum, while others view success as nothing less than an invitation to exhibit in the Whitney Biennial or Documenta. To some artists the sale of a work at $5,000 is a sign of success; to other artists anything above $50,000 is an impressive number.

Although attainment of these goals is not insurmountable, it is *naive to believe that achieving any one of these goals, or a combination thereof, will lead to career success that spans a good portion of adult life.* Yet an astonishing number of artists' belief systems is centered around adolescent aspirations, and for many such artists these aspirations have become obsessions.

In practical terms the meaning of the phrase *successful artist* could describe, for example, an artist who earns a living doing what he or she loves doing best: creating fine art. Many artists are able to derive a healthy part-time or full-time income doing what they love doing best without being swept away with all of the illusions surrounding the mystique of how to be successful in the art world. But because these artists' names are relatively unknown, the existence of alternative forms of career success is also relatively unknown, and adolescent attitudes prevail.

THE MYTH OF SCARCITY

Nancy Anderson, in her powerful book *Work with Passion,* points out:

> There are two ways to look at the Planet Earth: (1) It is contracting and shrinking—therefore my chances are scarce. Colloquially put, "there ain't enough to go 'round so I've got to get mine!" (2) It is expanding and growing with opportunity—my chances are based on abundance. The choice is mine, and time is my ally.[26]

Unfortunately, many artists have adopted the philosophy that "there ain't enough to go 'round so I've got to get mine!" The "shrinking" mode of thinking is also reinforced by other members of the art world. The foolish platitudes that *there are too many artists* or *there are too many artists for the number of commercial galleries* throw artists into panic attack or a chronic state of anxiety; some artists develop sharp elbows. A belief in scarcity is played out in many areas of an artist's career. Some artists sell their work at low prices because they have come to believe that the *only buyer* for their work is the buyer who makes himself or herself known at that given time. Some artists exhibit at galleries under unfavorable terms or circumstances because they believe it is their *only chance* to show their work and they must seize the moment. Many artists withhold from fellow artists introductions and referrals to art world contacts because of a *fear there that isn't enough to go around.*

In the long run, if the "community of artists" were truly functioning in a healthy capacity, whether on a national, regional, or local level, my occupation would be deemed obsolete because artists would be exchanging information and banding together to change the many basic inequities in the business of doing art. Unfortunately, a *fear of scarcity* has created a lack of a sense of community among artists. A fear of scarcity is largely responsible for why artists often feel isolated from one another.

DENYING ART IS A BUSINESS

Another stumbling block in career development for artists is not realizing or coming to terms with the fact that if you want to sell and/or exhibit work, art becomes commerce and it is a business. The next chapter, "Launching or Relaunching Your Career: Entering the Marketplace," looks at the business aspects of art and examines some of the ways in which artists can successfully enter the marketplace and sustain a career.

To launch or relaunch a career that is earmarked for success, artists must learn to transcend career blocks and emphatically reject the myth of the artist. The myth, like racial and religious prejudice, is subtle and sneaks up without warning. Do not underestimate the extent to which aspects of the myth can affect, influence, and limit an artist's career.

If artists go along with the myth, they must accept the consequences of leaving their careers in the hands of others. If artists do not develop and expand meaningful goals and act on these goals, their careers will be formed, manipulated, and eventually absorbed by people who have goals that are meaningful only to them. Artists become a means to the ends of others.

Launching or Relaunching Your Career: Entering the Marketplace

If you walk, just walk, if you sit, just sit,
but whatever you do, don't wobble.
—*Zen Master Unmon*

An artist who wants to sell work must enter the marketplace, a highly structured world made up of many networks. There are two ways to enter—haphazardly or with a plan. Unfortunately, most artists enter haphazardly, which means short stays and unhappy endings.

As the late artist and author Jo Hanson pointed out: "Artists have the same need as other people to set goals and plan their careers, and attend to the business of their work—and be good at it."[1] Hanson goes on to say that if artists "fumble through too much of their working life before discovering the need to plan and focus, the possibilities of choice and decision can close down significantly."[2]

Entering the marketplace with a plan means that your tools are lined up (see the next section) and your psyche is tuned up. How well you tune up your psyche depends on how thoroughly you have rejected the myth of the artist, have developed personal goals, and have been willing to act on these goals and get yourself moving. A good plan also includes having a well-thought-out philosophy about money: how much you want to earn as an artist, and how much you are willing to spend in order to earn it.

Albert Einstein is attributed to having defined insanity as doing the same thing over and over again and expecting different results.

Artists who are reentering the marketplace must be willing to abandon strategies that didn't work or change attitudes that got in their way during their last incarnation in the art world.

HOMEWORK: DOWN TO BASICS

The following homework includes basic investments necessary to launch, relaunch, and sustain an artist's career. Some investments require money, some require time, and some require both.

Read, Note, File, and Retrieve

During the last twenty-five years the art trade publications field has expanded and diversified, with each of the art disciplines having newspapers, tabloids, magazines, ezines, and Web sites that focus on *real art news* rather than reviews and critical essays. These resources contain valuable information on numerous aspects of the business of art and the business of being an artist, including grant, exhibition, and employment opportunities, legal and accounting advice, health hazards related to the arts, and arts-related legislation.

There are publications with a regional focus, such as *Artweek,* devoted to artists living in the Northwest, Southwest, Alaska, and Hawaii; *Art New England,* geared to artists in the Northeast; and *Chicago Artists' News,* for artists in the Midwest. There are also publications of national interest, such as *Art Calendar* in the United States and *Agenda* in Canada. In addition, there are periodicals that specialize in various disciplines, such as *The Crafts Report, Sculpture, Art on Paper, Fiberarts, Afterimage,* and *Surface Design.*

The Artist Help Network is a Web site that I developed that lists most of the resources in the appendix of this book. The site is updated on an ongoing basis; new resources are added and contact information is amended.

State and municipal agencies can also be good sources for information on career development and career opportunities. For example, the Web site Resources for Individual Artists is sponsored by the Division of Cultural Affairs, Florida Department of State. ArtsOpportunities is sponsored by the Southern Arts Federation.

Chicago Artists Resource is sponsored by the Chicago Department of Cultural Affairs. One of the most comprehensive sites is NYFA Source. Although it is sponsored by the New York Foundation for the Arts, it includes artist career opportunities throughout the United States. The Western States Arts Federation (WESTAF) sponsors CaFÉ™, a user-friendly online system that provides open call information on public art commissions, exhibitions, grants, and awards. Users create a profile with contact information and upload digital images of their work, and CaFÉ™ allows you to apply to the respective open call entries *directly from its Web site*.

Art Opportunities Monthly, available by email in PDF format, lists grants, exhibition and public art commission opportunities, and residencies. Art-Support is a Web site that offers photographers career advice, and TextileArts.net is devoted to career-related information and opportunities for artists working in the textile and fiber art fields. A-N: The Artists Information Company is an invaluable source of information for artists interested in establishing contacts in the United Kingdom and in Europe. It contains online career guides, resources on a variety of arts-related subjects, and career advice. The addresses of these Web sites and publications can be found in the appendix sections "Career Management, Business, and Marketing," "Periodicals," and "International Connections."

Become aware of the numerous local, regional, national, and international arts service organizations, and take advantage of their various programs, services, and publications. Throughout the appendix, many service organizations are listed that have a regional, national, or an international focus. In addition, the appendix section "Arts Service Organizations" lists various national and regional organizations.

Many arts service organizations serve the needs of special-interest groups. Examples include the Asian American Women Artists Alliance; the Society for the Arts in Healthcare; the Arts and Healing Network; the Disabled Artists' Network; and En Foco, a national organization that supports contemporary fine art and documentary photographers of diverse cultures who are residents of the United States and are of Latino, African, and Asian heritage, and Native Peoples of the Americas and the Pacific. The addresses of these and other arts service organizations are listed in the appendix sections "Arts Service Organizations" and "Artists with Disabilities."

With the plethora of information available, there is no excuse for artists not to be well versed in what is going on in their own profession.

Read, note, file, and retrieve—or practice what authors Judith Appelbaum and Nancy Evans refer to as the "pack-rat process."[3] Set up a file and contact system that is imaginative and considers the present and the future. Contacts and information that might not necessarily be of interest or apply to your career now could be important and relevant in the future.

Review the files on a regular basis. Unless you have a photographic memory, you will forget a lot of information that has been clipped and stored away.

Set up paper or computer files for various categories, choosing those that make sense and have meaning for you. For example, a file system could include the following categories: fellowships and grants; artist-in-residence programs and art colonies; museum and independent curators; art consultants and art advisors; art service organizations; legal, accounting, health insurance, and studio insurance information; contracts and business forms; mailing lists; press contacts; public-art programs; artist registries; vendors that provide services to artists; software programs; and health hazards in the arts.

Mailing Lists—The Usual and the Esoteric

Starting, developing, and maintaining a good mailing list requires a lot of time and energy, but it is well worth the effort. Like a file/contact system, a mailing list can and should be used over and over again. It should be updated on a regular basis to reflect the changes you are making in your career (new contacts) and the ever-changing scene in the art world (the names usually stay the same, but the institutions and organizations might fluctuate). A good list implies quality more than quantity, meaning that your list should include the names and addresses of people who can do something for your career—directly or indirectly—now or in the future.

Do not wait until you need to use a mailing list to put one together. Develop a list when "nothing's happening" so that when something happens it will not become one of the thousand other chores you have to do in connection with exhibition/performance planning.

When artists are having an exhibition, it is common practice to use the mailing lists of the gallery. Unfortunately, gallery lists tend to include everyone who has signed the gallery guest book, which does not necessarily mean that all of the names are of interest to you. Many gallery lists and lists compiled by arts organizations are not updated on a regular basis. In some cases the lists are shortsighted and they do not contain a comprehensive representation of an arts community.

Following are the major categories that should be included in a comprehensive arts mailing list:

Directors of galleries
Directors and curators of alternative spaces
Museum and independent curators
Directors of college and university galleries
Curators of corporate art collections
Art consultants and advisors
Directors of public-art programs
Interior designers and architects
Art critics
Web sites and blogs that contain news and feature articles about
    artists and exhibition reviews
Editors of international, national, regional, and local arts publi-
    cations, including online magazines
Editors of interior design and architecture publications
Arts and culture editors of magazines and newspapers
Producers of local and national arts-related television and radio
    programs
Assignment editors of local and national television and radio pro-
    grams
Editors of trade publications
Fans and collectors

Mailing lists in the categories cited above can be purchased or rented. For example, the company Mailing Lists Labels Packages offers various mailing-list packages pertaining to public-art and percent-for-art programs. ArtNetwork in Nevada City, California, rents mailing lists in various arts-related categories. Art-Support offers a photography gallery mailing list that includes galleries, private dealers, and nonprofit photography organizations. It is available in Excel, Word, and PDF formats. And I have mailing lists available for purchase that are updated on a regular basis. These lists include art consultants; regional, national, and international arts press contacts; New York City area press contacts; art critics; museum and independent curators; and interior design, architecture, and landscape architecture press contacts. Some of my lists are available on a CD-ROM. The addresses of mailing list resources are listed in the appendix sections "Mailing Lists" and "Press Relations and Publicity."

If you are using mailing lists to write *cover letters* (see page 54), make sure that the lists you purchase or rent *include the names of specific individuals*. It should not be a list that is addressed to such generic titles as "gallery director" or "curator."

Purchasing or renting arts-related lists will save a lot of time and energy, but if you are determined to compile your own press and museum lists, the following resources will be of assistance:

The names of museum curators are listed in the *American Art Directory* and *The Official Museum Directory*. Both of these publications are listed in the appendix under "General Arts References."

Ulrich's Periodicals Directory is an online subscription service that provides contact information on thousands of international magazines, newspapers, and ezines, including art publications. The Web site NewsDirectory.com links more than sixty-five hundred English-language print and broadcast media from around the world.

The online editorial staff of newspapers, consumer magazines, and television, radio, and cable network stations and shows can be found in *Bacon's Internet Media Directory*. The names and addresses of arts publications and interior-design and architecture publications can be obtained in *Bacon's Newspaper/Magazine Directory*.

The names of newspaper feature and news editors and of journalists who write about the arts can be obtained in *Editor & Publisher Directory of Syndicate Services* and *Bacon's Newspaper/Magazine Directory*.

For those interested in key press contacts in California and/or New York City, the directories *Bacon's Metro California Media* and *Bacon's New York Publicity Outlets* are excellent resources. Information about these publications and the ones listed above can be found in the appendix section "Press Relations and Publicity."

The names of interior designers and architects can be obtained through local chapters of the American Society of Interior Designers and the American Institute of Architects (see "Corporate Art Market" in the appendix). The names of interior design and architecture publications are listed in the appendix section "Interior Design and Architecture."

One of the most underexplored areas of an arts-related mailing list is the inclusion of trade publications. Trade publications often include articles about new and unusual uses of the materials that they promote. For example, if you are a sculptor working with glass, the names of trade publications in the glass industry can be obtained from the *Writer's Market*. Or, by using the Web site Mediafinder .com, you can link to target market trade publications, newsletters, magazines, and directories. Articles in trade publications that feature the work of an artist can lead to corporate commissions, acquisitions, and sponsorships.

If you are living in a place other than where you were born or raised, include the names of newspapers in your hometown. The names of alumni publications issued by the college or university you attended should also be on your mailing list. Always write a cover letter to accompany any material that is sent, pointing out, for example, that you are a native of the area or an alumnus or alumna.

A comprehensive mailing list should also include the names of local publications that offer free listings to announce an exhibition, performance, or cultural event.

Career Coaches

An artist's career coach is a relatively new occupation, and as in the case of many emerging fields it is still going through the growing pains of defining itself and establishing boundaries. During the past thirty years I have kept abreast of some of the activities and business practices of those people who have shared my occupation. Since I have been credited for pioneering in this field and I have had the benefit of observing how other artist's career coaches operate, what we share in common, and where we differ, I offer the following pointers and advice:

An artist's career coach assists artists with various aspects of career planning. A *good* career coach should be knowledgeable about the many facets of the art world and the many options and opportunities available to artists.

Specifically, an artist's career coach should be able to provide advice, guidance, and support for a wide range of career-related issues and tasks. This can include, for example, assistance in the development of effective presentation materials such as brochures (see page 59) and Web site fine-art portfolios (see page 74); public relations and press relations; and establishing prices for artwork. An artist's career coach should be able to provide an overview of the various art markets and provide assistance with marketing strategies, grant proposals, exhibition proposals, and proposals for commissioned work. And an artist's career coach should know how to proceed once a dealer makes a verbal commitment to represent an artist.

Unlike an art consultant or art advisor, an artist's career coach or *anyone with job titles related to artist career development,* should not also serve in the capacity of an artist's agent and sell artwork. In order to serve artist clients most objectively and ethically, artist's career coaches should not represent any one artist or be involved in any endeavor that is a conflict of interest.

Because conflicts of interest should not happen, it does not mean that they do not happen! Out of all of the services an artist's career coach should provide, the most important is the role of *artist-advocate.* However, the ability of an artist's career coach to perform an advocacy role is the crux of the problem that involves issues related to conflicts of interest. Artist's career coaches who are *also* art dealers cannot serve artists in an advocacy capacity because they are influenced by factors that they perceive to be in their best interests as dealers. Moreover, artist's career coaches who are *also* publishers who solicit paid advertising from artists, or charge fees to be included in artist sourcebooks (see page 151), cannot serve artists in an advocacy role because they must be looking out for their best interests as publishers whose livelihood relies, in part, on artist-paid advertising.

Some artist's career coaches provide their clients with competent advice and services and rigidly avoid areas where there are conflicts of interest. However, other advisors straddle the gray areas or plunge way over the fence. Other artist's career coaches might not have an impeccable code of ethics but their advice follows more traditional lines, and it tends to encourage artists to maintain a status quo and give away their power to the "powers that be."

There are also artist's career coaches who have had very little experience in the art world, and although their intentions might be honorable, the advice and services they provide reflect their limitations.

Before working with an artist's career coach, learn as much as you can about the person's background. Most artist's career coaches have Web sites with information about services, fees, and their credentials.

Do not be afraid of changing artist's career coaches or of using different coaches for different purposes, depending on their strengths and fields of expertise. Do not expect an artist's career coach to solve a problem overnight that most likely you have spent the better part of your life creating.

Know the Law

In the early 1960s a friend of mine lost approximately 150 paintings in court. He gave his work to a Washington, D.C., gallery owner on consignment without a receipt or any form of written agreement.

After six months he asked to "borrow" some of his paintings in order to enter a juried show. The dealer said that she didn't have his paintings and didn't know what he was talking about.

The artist hired a lawyer. It took another six months for the case to go to court. On the day of the trial, the dealer brought a majority of the lost paintings to the courtroom. She had a simple explanation: she told the judge that the artist had given her all of the paintings as a *birthday present*. The judge believed her. She was free to keep the paintings and do with them what she wished. Case dismissed.

With new legislation and changes in laws that protect artists from being victimized, much has changed in nearly fifty years. But undoubtedly a day does not pass that some artist is ripped off by an opportunist or discovers a hitch in what seemed a straightforward deal. *The majority of new legislation will not do an artist any good unless he or she bones up on the legal rights of artists and understands how these rights affect or may affect an artist's work and career.*

"Artists should never feel intimidated, helpless or victimized. Legal and business considerations exist from the moment an artist conceives a work or receives an assignment. While no handbook can solve the unique problems of each artist, the artist's increased awareness of the general legal issues pertaining to art will aid in avoiding risks and gaining benefits that might otherwise pass unnoticed,"[4] writes Tad Crawford in his book *Legal Guide for the Visual Artist,* which should be on the top of your list of books to buy. This book is written in down-to-earth language and covers a comprehensive range of subjects that should be near and dear to an artist's heart, including copyright, wills and estates, sales by galleries and agents, income taxation, studios, and leases. It includes examples of sample contracts and agreements for a vast number of situations that an artist might and probably will encounter.

The fourth revised edition of *Legal Guide for the Visual Artist,* published in 1999, addresses issues relating to multimedia art, including work that combines still pictures, text, music, and film or video; digitization of information; delivery of new media, such as CD-ROM, computer networks, and cable television; and interactive projects. It also includes a chapter that is devoted to copyright and the digital revolution.

Legal Guide for the Visual Artist is among several publications available that zero in on the nitty-gritty of art law. It would be superfluous for me to paraphrase or try to cover the ground that has already been covered by people far more experienced and knowledgeable on the subject. However, the "Law" sections of the appendix provide solid lists of references, both publications and organizations. Many of these publications and organizations provide sample contracts, as well as advice for numerous arts-related legal situations. If you require additional information before a contract is signed, or if you find yourself in the unfortunate situation of needing legal advice after an agreement has been consummated, or for whatever reasons, there are many excellent places to turn to.

Not being able to afford a lawyer specializing in art law is no longer a valid excuse! For example, Volunteer Lawyers for the Arts (VLA) in New York City offers free legal consultation and legal services, at minimal administrative fees, to artists and nonprofit organizations. Volunteer Lawyers for the Arts offices are located throughout the United States and in Canada, some of which were created by arts councils, arts organizations, state bar associations, law firms, and law schools. Services offered, eligibility requirements, and administrative fees vary. In addition to offering legal assistance to individuals, many VLA groups offer seminars on various art-law-related topics and publish resource books, such as *An Artist's Guide to Small Claims Court,* which is applicable to artists in New York City. The "Law: Organizations" section of the appendix lists Volunteer Lawyers for the Arts groups and other resources.

COPYRIGHT

Copyright protection is available to artists working in every medium, including prints, photography, painting, sculpture, drawing, graphics, audiovisual works, video and film, and recordings and compositions.

The 1978 Copyright Act made copyright procedures very simple, automatically protecting a work of art when it is created. Up until March 1, 1989, the use of a copyright notice was mandatory but after that date use of a copyright notice is optional. Although you are not required to formally register your copyright with the Copyright Office of the Library of Congress, there are certain advantages that mainly concern your rights if anyone tries to infringe on your copyright. And particularly with the advent of the Internet, copyright registration has become more important. Registration forms can be downloaded from the Web site of the Copyright Office or you can request a Copyright Information Kit from the Copyright Office. Be sure to specify that you are requesting the kit for visual artists.

The ins and outs of copyright and how it affects the visual and performing arts are covered in many publications, including *Legal*

Guide for the Visual Artist, and *The Copyright Guide: A Friendly Guide to Protecting and Profiting from Copyright.* The appendix section "Law: Copyrights, Patents, and Trademarks" includes contact information about these publications and Copyright Office registration forms.

CONTRACTS

Most visual artists do not use contracts. Performing artists and writers use contracts as regular parts of their professional lives. Why are visual artists reticent about using contracts?

Some artists are averse to the use of contracts because they naively believe that people who sell, buy, and exhibit art are good, kind, and trustworthy by virtue of their involvement with art. However, most artists who resist using contracts are struggling with the issue of psychological leverage and erroneously believe that they have not achieved a level of recognition or success that permits them to ask for what they want.

Requiring art dealers, art consultants, exhibition sponsors, and clients to use contracts is not a sign of mistrust. Rather, it shows that you take yourself and your work seriously, and you are demonstrating good faith in wanting to maintain a smooth working relationship by ironing out in advance any possible conflicts or misunderstandings.

If an art dealer, art consultant, exhibition sponsor, or client is opposed to using a contract, it usually indicates either that the individual is extremely naive and unenlightened in professional business practices, or that he or she is engaged in unethical business practices and does not want anything in writing that could be used against him or her in court. Another reason dealers and art consultants resist using contracts is that they prefer to see themselves as mentors rather than as business professionals, and they find the use of contracts is not in keeping with their self-image.

If your dealer dies, is your artwork protected from becoming part of his or her estate? If your dealer files for bankruptcy, is your work protected from being used to pay creditors? Is your work insured while it is in a dealer's possession, and is it insured for the full retail value? Is a dealer entitled to a commission on studio sales under all, some, or no circumstances? Should artists split dealer/client discounts? Is an artist required to pay advertising expenses for an exhibition? If so, how much? A good contract should be comprehensive and farsighted.

Protect yourself and your artwork by using contracts when you deal with galleries, art consultants, collectors, exhibition sponsors, and clients. Specific contracts such as consignment agreements, exhibition agreements, and agreements for commissioned work will be discussed in subsequent chapters. The appendix section "Law: Contracts and Business Forms" lists publications that provide sample contracts, including *Business and Legal Forms for Fine Artists, Business and Legal Forms for Crafts,* and *Business and Legal Forms for Photographers.* Each of these publications also includes instructions for preparing contracts for a variety of situations and a kit of tear-out contracts. A great advantage is that each also comes with a CD-ROM.

ARTISTS' ESTATES

On a number of occasions I have been contacted for advice by family or friends of deceased artists who left no instructions regarding the disposition of their artwork. Particularly when many pieces of artwork are involved, it can be an overwhelming responsibility to make decisions without guidance, instructions, or suggestions from the artist. On the other hand, if a deceased artist's friends and relatives are not conscientiously seeking a solution that is in the best interest of the artist, there is a good chance that the artwork will not long survive the artist's death.

In the publication *Future Safe: The Present Is the Future,* published in 1992 by the Alliance for the Arts, the authors point out:

> As an artist, you are used to being your own best resource, so it will come as no surprise that you must take the initiative in planning for the survival of your work. You must give yourself time. The process of making a will and planning for the care of your work can be seen as an act of self-respect. The commercial success of your art should not be a factor in your planning—you have spent a lifetime making this art and it deserves to survive.[5]

It is important to come to terms with estate planning, preparing a will, deciding on a beneficiary or beneficiaries, and providing the beneficiary with instructions or guidelines on the disposition of your artwork.

Depending on various career-related factors, estate planning for artists can be relatively simple or quite complicated. It is wise to consult an attorney and/or an accountant who is experienced in estate planning for *artists*.

To learn more about the subject of artists' estates there are good resources available. In addition to *Future Safe,* the Marie Walsh Sharpe Art Foundation has published *A Visual Artist's Guide to Estate Planning* with a *2008 Supplement Update* that includes new information on changes in tax and copyright laws as they pertain to artists' estates. Both publications are only available online. In *Legal Guide for the Visual Artist* an entire chapter is devoted to the artist's estate.

Volunteer Lawyers for the Arts in New York City has initiated the Artist Legacy Project, which provides free and specialized estate-planning services to visual and performing artists and writers. The Alliance for the Arts sponsors the Estate Project for Artists with AIDS. Organizations and publications cited in this section and other resources are listed in the appendix under "Law: Estate Planning." In addition, suggestions for handling the dissemination of deceased artists' artwork are discussed in the chapter "Exhibition and Sales Opportunities: Using Those That Exist and Creating Your Own." See page 144.

Artists and Income Taxes

Closely allied to the subject of law is your income tax status, or lack of status, whichever may be the case.

A few years ago I was invited to speak at a conference dedicated to the business of being an artist, sponsored by a college in an afflu-ent suburb of New York City. The audience was comprised of artists from the area, and from the tone of questions and concerns I quickly ascertained that this was not a group of full-time artists but rather of "Sunday painters." The college had also invited guest speakers from the visual and performing arts and from the publishing indus-try. During the discussion period I was surprised to find that the per-son who received the most questions was the guest accountant, and from the level and content of questions it was easy to tell that this audience was abreast of tax laws governing artists, particularly those related to deductions. It is ironic that the artists who probably have the hardest time proving themselves "professional" versus "hobby" artists in the eyes of the IRS are the ones most up-to-date and knowledgeable on tax issues.

I am not going to expound on the morality or virtues of paying or not paying taxes, but what is of concern is that too many artists are spending too much energy agonizing over taxes, energy that takes them away from being artists.

One of the reasons artists are squeamish about taxes is the deep-seated myth that being an artist is not a valid occupation and the government will tax an artist in an arbitrary way. The fact is that the occupation of artist has been duly recognized by the IRS for a number of years, most specifically in the 1969 Tax Reform Law.

"An artist actively engaged in the business or trade of being an artist—one who pursues art with a profit motive—may deduct all ordinary and necessary business expenses, even if such expenses far exceed income from art activities for the year,"[6] writes Tad Crawford in *Legal Guide for the Visual Artist*. "The regulations set forth nine factors used to determine profit motive. Since every artist is capable, in varying degrees, of pursuing art in a manner which will be considered a trade or business, these factors can create an instructive model. The objective factors are considered in their totality, so that all the circumstances surrounding the activity will determine the result in a given case. Although most of the factors are important, no single factor will determine the result of a case."[7] (The nine factors are listed in Crawford's book.)

"The working artist who is not yet making a profit from art activity has an alternative to being taxed as a hobbyist,"[8] wrote Jo Hanson in the preface of the excellent publication *Artists' Taxes: The Hands-on Guide* (see "Accounting, Bookkeeping, and Income Taxes" in the appendix). Hanson, who endured five tax audits in the 1980s, parlayed her experiences into a book that presents clear and detailed advice to artists.

Federal tax laws frequently change, and many of the changes directly affect artists. The Tax Reform Act of 1986 is having an adverse effect on artists in many ways. For example, income averaging (which was very helpful to artists whose income varied widely from year to year) has been abolished. Under the old law a business had to be profitable two out of five years to avoid being treated as a hobby. Under the new law the business has to be profitable *three out of five years;* and the new law makes it tougher for self-employed artists to take their home-office expenses as a deduction. This deduction cannot exceed an artist's net income from the art business, as opposed to the gross income limit under the old law, and the portion of home space claimed as an office or studio must be used *only* for the art business, and on a regular basis.

Some business-related tax deductions artists should be aware of include insurance premiums; studio and office equipment; telephone bills; telephone answering service (on a separate business line); attorney's and accountant's fees; dues in professional organizations; books and professional journals; admission charges to museums and performances; protective clothing and equipment as well as associated laundry bills; commissions paid to dealers and agents; promotion expenses, including Web site design and hosting fees, photographs, ads, résumés, and press releases; repairs; training and education expenses and tuition for courses that improve or maintain skills related to the profession; shipping and freight charges; the cost of business meetings (such as meals) with agents, patrons, professional advisors, dealers, et cetera, regardless of whether the relationship is established or prospective; business gifts; and automobile expenses for traveling to an exhibition or performance, delivering or picking up work at a gallery, purchasing supplies, driving to courses and seminars, et cetera.

These are only some of the tax deductions that affect artists. The list certainly is not all-inclusive, and there are special rules and regulations governing the application of many of the deductions listed above. Because of the intricacies involved in knowing tax regulations and tax-law changes, if you personally do not keep abreast of the ins and outs and changes, it is very important to *maintain a relationship with an accountant who specializes in the tax problems of artists.*

Art tax law is a special field, and not all accountants are familiar with the various intricacies. Case in point: Barbara A. Sloan, the author of the *Do-It-Yourself Quick Fix Tax Kit* and other related publications, is an artist, an attorney, and an art business consultant.

Although she is *not* an accountant, she was called upon so often by certified public accountants for advice on behalf of artist-clients that she started writing *Tax Kits*. During the last thirteen years, tax preparers, attorneys, and artists throughout the United States have purchased Sloan's publications.[9]

Many accountants who specialize in the arts are affiliated with organizations such as Business Volunteers for the Arts (see appendix under "Accounting, Bookkeeping, and Income Taxes"). Some accountants who specialize in the arts often advertise their services in art trade publications, such as the ones listed in the "Periodicals" section of the appendix. If you are unable to find an accountant through a good recommendation, do not hesitate to ask the accountant you do find for a list of references of artists whom he or she has helped in the past. Check out the references to make sure that the clients have been satisfied customers.

Insurance: Insuring Your Health, Work, and Future

HEALTH INSURANCE

One of my clients broke his leg. He was in the hospital for three weeks and then was an outpatient for several more weeks. During the first week he was hospitalized he learned that he had won an art competition with a cash award of $5,000. But his jubilation over the award was eclipsed when he also learned that his barebones hospitalization policy (a so-called fringe benefit of the college where he was teaching) would pay only meager benefits toward his hospital bills and doctors' fees. Thus, he had to use his entire cash award to pay the bills.

One could elaborate for pages about similar and even worse stories involving artists who do not have health insurance or who are not adequately covered. For many years artists were subjected to exorbitant *individual* rates for health insurance. They were ineligible for *group* rates because of the nature of being a self-employed artist, a unit of one. However, times have changed and many organizations offer group plans. Some of the national and regional organizations that offer group rates to members are listed in the appendix section "Health Insurance and Medical Plans."

STUDIO AND WORK INSURANCE

"All-risk" insurance policies are specifically designed for artists and their particular needs. "All-risk" policies cover insured work on your premises, on exhibit, and in transit. The nonprofit organization Fractured Atlas offers liability insurance to members, and the American Craft Council offers members property/casualty insurance.

In addition, the Fireman's Fund Insurance Company offers a fine-art policy that provides coverage to individuals in the fine arts and entertainment fields. The companies Huntington T. Block and K&K Insurance Group, Inc., also offer various forms of studio insurance.

The addresses of the above-mentioned organizations and companies are listed under "Studio Insurance" in the appendix.

PENSION PLANS: INSURING YOUR FUTURE

Not everyone is going to retire. Some of us reject the notion on principle, and others will not have any choice in the matter because they will not have stored up a nest egg. If you are heading for the latter category, or if you fall into the first category and are forgetting that bad health might necessitate a change in your plans, or if you are in neither category and basically haven't thought about retirement because you are just getting started, consider this: artists can now participate in pension plans, a fringe benefit once bestowed only on members of society who were willing to devote most of their lives to working for someone else. Now there are pension plans for self-employed persons that *offer financial security for your future*.

Keogh plans are pension plans for the self-employed. However, even if you are employed by a company with a retirement program, you may maintain a Keogh plan and make an annual contribution of up to 20 percent of your net self-employment income, or $46,000 (whichever is less), to the plan. Your money can be invested in a trust, an annuity contract from an insurance company, a custodial account, a special U.S. government retirement bond, or one of certain face-amount certificates purchased from investment companies. Money contributed to a Keogh plan is tax deductible and no taxes are levied on the growth of your investment until the funds are withdrawn. There are penalties if you withdraw the money before the age of 59½, unless you are disabled.

Another kind of pension plan, an Individual Retirement Account

(IRA), is available to anyone who is not covered by a company retirement plan, or anyone who is covered by a company plan but has an adjusted gross income of less than $53,000 ($85,000 for a married couple). In an IRA you can invest up to $5,000 per year until the year you turn 70½ ($6,000 if you are 50 years of age or older). Married couples filing a joint federal tax return can contribute up to $10,000 to each spouse's IRA subject to earned income limitations and eligibility requirements. Married couples who are both 50 years of age or older and file a joint federal tax return can contribute up to $12,000 to each spouse's IRA subject to earned income limitations and eligibility requirements. If one spouse is younger than 50, the spouse 50 years or older can contribute up to $11,000.[10] As in a Keogh plan, the money you place in an IRA is tax deductible. There are penalties if you withdraw the money before the age of 59½, unless you are disabled. A Roth IRA is another type of personal savings plan that provides tax advantages for setting aside money for your retirement. If you satisfy certain requirements, distributions from a Roth IRA, unlike a traditional IRA, are not subject to income tax. You can contribute to a Roth IRA regardless of your age (even after the age of 70½) if you are receiving compensation and your adjusted gross income is under $116,000 if you are single or under $165,000 if you are married and filing a joint return. However, unlike contributions to a traditional IRA, contributions to a Roth IRA are not tax deductible.

For further information on self-employment retirement plans, visit the Internal Revenue Service Web site or contact your local IRS office. Web site information and contact information of other pension-plan resources are listed in the appendix under "Pension Plans and Savings and Loans Programs."

Credit Unions

Credit unions are financial cooperatives that are owned and controlled by their members and offer a range of services. For example, the Artists Community Federal Credit Union (ACFCU) is a federally insured credit union that offers artists secured and unsecured loans. The art service organization Arthouse in Austin, Texas, has a credit union for members. The Craft Emergency Relief Fund provides craft artists with interest-free loans. The Artist Loan Fund sponsored by

Springboard for the Arts in St. Paul, Minnesota, offers low-interest loans to Twin City area artists.

In addition, the Artist Pension Trust (APT) is a for-profit company with programs dedicated to the needs of beginning and mid-career artists. In lieu of cash, participating artists invest works of art. When a piece of artwork is sold, the artist receives 40 percent of the net proceeds of the sale, and 32 percent of the net proceeds accrue to the collective benefit of all participating artists. The remaining 28 percent of the net proceeds are retained by APT to cover management and operating costs. The addresses of the above organizations are listed in the appendix section "Pension Plans and Savings and Loans Programs."

Artists' Health Hazards

Health hazards to artists is a relatively new area of study, because it has only been recognized in recent years that various materials used by artists are directly responsible for a multitude of serious health problems, including cancer, bronchitis, and allergies.

Solvents and acids used by printmakers are responsible for many health problems; dirt and kiln emissions have created problems for potters; resins and dirt in a sculptor's working environment and gases and vapors used in photography are also responsible for various ailments. Toxic chemicals in paints are directly linked to cancer, including pigment preservatives used in acrylic emulsions and additives such as those used to protect acrylic paints during freeze-thaw cycles. In addition, improper ventilation is a common abuse, and its side effects are directly responsible for temporary discomfort as well as permanent damage.

Performing artists are also directly affected. Toxic chemicals are found in concert halls and theaters, onstage, in dressing rooms, in makeup rooms, et cetera. Health problems are created by such things as poor ventilation; certain types of aerosols, acrylics, and plastics used in sets and costumes; photographic chemicals; asbestos; sawdust; gas vapors; dust; and machine oil.

If you are not already aware that the materials you might be using in your studio or work environment are considered taboo, it is time to investigate.

The Art and Creative Materials Institute, Inc., is an international organization comprising art material manufacturers. It was organized to assist its members in producing nontoxic art materials. All products in the program undergo extensive toxicological evaluation and testing before they are granted the right to bear the ACMI certification seal. The institute also provides information on hazardous products. Arts, Crafts and Theater Safety (ACTS) is a not-for-profit organization that provides information on health and safety in the arts. ACTS answers inquiries and provides copies of educational and technical materials. It also publishes a newsletter. ACTS was founded by Monona Rossol, a chemist, industrial hygenist, and artist, who wrote the very informative book *The Artist's Complete Health and Safety Guide*.

The Center for Safety in the Arts, founded by Dr. Michael McCann, pioneered the dissemination of information on health hazards in the arts. Dr. McCann is also the author of the important book *Health Hazards for Artists*. Due to funding cutbacks, the center no longer exists.

Various Web sites are devoted to exposing arts-related health hazards. These sites include Health Hazards in the Arts, produced by the Rochester Institute of Technology, and Health Hazards for the Artist, produced by the Gund Library of the Cleveland Institute of Art.

Information about the above-mentioned organizations and the names of other excellent publications that are available on the subject of health and safety in the arts are listed in the appendix section "Health Hazards."

MINIMIZING EXPENSES

There are many ways to keep expenses low in order to afford the necessary initial financial investments to launch and sustain your career. Some of the ways are described below.

Bartering

Bartering has been in existence for thousands of years. Artists can trade their artwork and special skills for career-related supplies, materials, and equipment. You can also save money on various daily living expenses so that you can allocate more funds for your career.

Some of my clients have bartered with doctors, dentists, printers, restaurants, food stores, plumbers, carpenters, and electricians.

The bartering phenomenon has expanded into big business, and barter organizations and clubs exist throughout the United States. The names of barter organizations can be found in the Yellow Pages Business-to-Business Directory under "Barter and Trade Exchanges."

In addition, the Web site Gigafree lists barter exchanges in the United States, Canada, and other parts of the world. *BarterNews* is a quarterly publication that includes information and ideas about bartering, along with contacts. For information about Gigafree and *BarterNews* and other bartering resources, see the appendix section "Bartering."

Using Apprentices

You can save money and time by using the services of an apprentice. Apprenticeship programs provide artists with students who want studio or work experience. Some apprenticeship programs are structured as a barter: free assistance in return for learning and developing new skills; other programs require an artist to pay an apprentice a reasonable hourly wage.

Local and state arts councils can provide information on apprenticeship programs. In addition, the New York Arts Program, sponsored by Ohio Wesleyan University, provides students with opportunities for one semester to serve as apprentices to established professional artists or arts institutions in New York City.

The *National Directory of Arts Internships* lists the names of artists throughout the United States who use apprentices. Each listing describes eligibility requirements, applications procedures, and a description of what the position entails. On the Internet, the Web sites that list internships include Artjobonline, Arts Opportunities, hireCulture, and NYFA Source.

For additional information about apprenticeship programs, see the appendix section "Apprenticeships and Internships."

Materials for the Arts Programs

You can save money on materials, supplies, and equipment by participating in materials for the arts programs that are sponsored by municipal government agencies. The Materials for the Arts program in New York City provides artists who work with a registered New York City cultural organization with free office equipment and supplies, furnishings, art materials, and other items. For information about these and other programs, see the appendix section "Materials for the Arts Programs."

Presentation Tools
and Packages

The first chapter of this book, "Launching or Relaunching Your Career: Overcoming Career Blocks," covers some of the difficulties artists encounter in career development, including the cause and effect of the public's fear of visual art. It points out that many people *in the art world* are also intimidated by visual art, although they are unlikely to admit it. Consequently, presentation materials such as résumés (see below), press clippings or excerpts (see page 52), artist statements (see page 53), and cover letters (see page 54) are important props because they help insecure people determine that it is okay to like your work!

This chapter will present guidelines for preparing presentation materials and suggestions for maximizing their effectiveness. A new chapter, "Art Marketing and the Internet," provides guidelines and suggestions for integrating presentation tools into an artist's Web site.

AN ARTIST'S RÉSUMÉ

The specific purpose of an artist's résumé is to impress gallery dealers, curators, collectors, grant agencies, juries, and anyone else in a position to give an artist's career upward mobility. However, since an artist's résumé has purposes other than seeking employment, it requires its own special structure.

A résumé should reflect your achievements in the arts field. It should not be a thesis about what you hope to achieve or an explanation of the meaning of your work. Keep résumés pure—free of narratives that justify or describe your work's inner meanings.

Keep in mind that the *intrinsic purpose of a fine-arts résumé* is to impress people with your credentials. Therefore, if your achievements amount to more than can be listed on one sheet of paper, use another sheet or several sheets. *Who said that our lives have to be limited to one page?* One-page résumés were created for the purpose of obtaining employment, giving a potential employer an overview of one's employment history prior to a personal interview. However, obtaining employment is not the purpose of a fine-arts résumé.

On the other hand, if you have substantial achievements, consider a résumé as a tool that highlights your accomplishments and eliminates minor credits. Use such phrases as *exhibition highlights* or *selected exhibitions, selected collections,* and *selected bibliography* to convey that this is only a sampling.

If you use the format of exhibition highlights or selected exhibitions, make sure that you keep for your own use a complete résumé that lists *all of your accomplishments*. This documentation is important to a curator, for example, who is preparing a catalog to accompany a retrospective exhibition.

If you are applying for a teaching job in the art field, a fine-arts résumé should accompany your teaching résumé.

The following are suggestions for structuring a résumé and the order in which categories should be listed:

NAME, POSTAL ADDRESS, PHONE NUMBER, EMAIL ADDRESS, AND WEB SITE.

PLACE OF BIRTH. Your place of birth can be a good icebreaker. You might share a regional or local background with the reader.

BIRTH YEAR. Some artists object to putting their birth year on a résumé in fear of the stigma of being considered too old or too young. If a person is negatively influenced by your age, it is a strong indication that his or her judgment is poor, and you wouldn't want to be associated with that person under any circumstances.

EXHIBITIONS/PERFORMANCES. List the most recent exhibitions/performances first. Include the year, exhibition/performance title, name of the sponsor (gallery, museum, or organization), city, and state. In addition, list the name of the curator and whether it was an invitational or a juried show. (If you won an award, mention it in the "Awards and Honors" category described below.)

If you have had three or more one-person shows, make a separate section for "Solo Shows" and begin the résumé with this category. Make another category for "Group Exhibitions." If you have had fewer than three one-person shows, include the shows under the general heading "Exhibitions/Performances," but code the one-person shows with an asterisk (*) so they stand out, and note the code on the résumé. For example:

EXHIBITIONS. (*Solo Shows)
   2009   *Objects and Images,* Alternative Space Museum, New York City. Curated by Charlie Critic. Invitational.

   *Smith Wheeler Gallery, Chicago, Illinois.

   Spring Annual, Hogan Gallery, Detroit, Michigan. Juried by Peggy Panelist and Joe Jurist.

COMMISSIONS. List projects or works for which you have been commissioned, including the name of the project or medium, the sponsor (institution, company, or person), and the date.

COLLECTIONS. List the names of institutions that have purchased your work, as well as corporations and well-known collectors. If you haven't been "collected" by any of the above, omit the category (unless you need to pad the résumé with the names of relatives and friends).

BIBLIOGRAPHY. List all publications in which you have been mentioned or reviewed and any articles that you have written related to art. Include the name of the author, article title, name of the publication, and publication date. If you have been published in an exhibition catalog, include the name of the exhibition and the sponsor. If something was written about you in the catalog, credit the author. Include in a bibliography articles on the Internet in which you have been featured or cited. A Web site bibliography entry should include the name of the author, the date the Web site was created or when the particular online source was published (if known), the name of the Web site, the title of the article, the date the Web site was accessed, and the Web site URL. An example of a Web site bibliography entry is included in the sample résumé on page 49.

AWARDS AND HONORS. Include grants or fellowships you have received. List any prizes or awards you have won in exhibitions or competitions. Include artist-in-residence programs or any other programs that involved a selection process. If you won an award that was associated with an exhibition, repeat the same information that was listed in the "Exhibitions/Performances" category, but begin with the award. For example:

First Prize, SPRING ANNUAL, Hogan Gallery, Detroit, Michigan. Juried by Peggy Panelist and Joe Jurist, 2009.

LECTURES/PUBLIC-SPEAKING ENGAGEMENTS. Use this category to list any lectures you have given and/or radio and television appearances.

EDUCATION. This should be the *last* category. Many artists make the mistake of listing it first. This suggests that the biggest accomplishment in your life was your formal education!

The following is a sample résumé:

Terry Turner
15 West Main Street
Yourtown, U.S.A. 12000
Born: Washington, D.C., 1974
www.yourwebsiteaddress.com
terry@yourwebsiteaddress.com

*Selected Exhibitions (*Solo Shows)*

2009   WINTER INVITATIONAL, Whitehurst Museum, Whitehurst, Illinois. Curated by Midge Allen.

OBJECTS AND IMAGES, Alternative Space Museum, New York City. Curated by Charlie Critic. Invitational.

*Smith Wheeler Gallery, Chicago, Illinois.

SPRING ANNUAL, Hogan Gallery, Detroit, Michigan. Juried by Peggy Panelist and Joe Jurist.

2008   ILLUSIONS, Piper College, Lakeside, Pennsylvania. Curated by Abraham Collins.

2007   *Pfeiffer Gallery, Düsseldorf, Germany.

*Limerick Gallery, San Francisco, California.

TEN SCULPTORS, Kirkwood Park, Denver, Colorado. Sponsored by the Denver Arts Council. Invitational.

2006   PITTSBURGH BIENNIAL, Pittsburgh Cultural Center, Pittsburgh, Pennsylvania. Curated by Mary Clark and Henry North.

HANNAH, WRIGHT, AND TURNER, Covington Gallery, Houston, Texas.

2005   THE DRAWING SHOW, traveling exhibition organized by the Southwestern Arts Center, Tempe, Arizona: Seattle Museum, Seattle, Washington; Minneapolis Museum, Minneapolis, Minnesota; Virginia Museum, Richmond, Virginia; and Miami Museum, Miami, Florida.

Commissions

Plymouth Airport, Plymouth, Massachusetts. Sponsored by the Plymouth Chamber of Commerce, 2009.

Bevington Department Store, New York City. Sponsored by the Bevington Corporation, 2009.

Hopewell Plaza, Chicago, Illinois. Sponsored by the Downtown Citizens' Committee in conjunction with the Chicago Arts Council, 2008.

Public Collections

Whitehurst Museum, Whitehurst, Illinois.
Pittsburgh Cultural Center, Pittsburgh, Pennsylvania.

Corporate Collections

Marsh and Webster Corporation, New York City.
Avery Food Corporation, New York City.

Bibliography (*Reviews)

*Chris Mellow, "Terry Turner Show at Smith Wheeler," *Art Around Chicago,* June 1, 2005, http://www.artaroundchicago.com (accessed February 1, 2008).

*Bradley Mead, "Terry Turner Opens at Smith Wheeler Gallery," *Chicago Artist's Monthly,* February 2009.

*John Short, "Emerging Artists Featured at Whitehurst Museum," *Whitehurst Daily News,* January 16, 2009.

Nancy Long, "Winter Invitational at Whitehurst Museum," *Museum Quarterly,* Winter 2009.

Midge Allen, *Winter Invitational Catalog,* Whitehurst Museum, Whitehurst, Illinois, 2009.

Beth Ryan, "Ten Sculptors Show at Kirkwood Park," *Sculptor's Monthly,* June 2007.

Mary Clark and Henry North, *Pittsburgh Biennial Catalog,* Pittsburgh Cultural Center, Pittsburgh, Pennsylvania, 2006.

Awards and Honors

First Prize. SPRING ANNUAL, Hogan Gallery, Detroit, Michigan. Juried by Peggy Panelist and Joe Jurist, 2009.

Fellowship. Denver Arts Council, Denver, Colorado, 2008.

Fellowship. Minerva Hills Artist Colony, Minerva Hills, Montana, 2007.

Second Prize. International Sculptor's Competition, Essex, Ontario, Canada, 2006.

Project Grant, Pittsburgh Cultural Center, Pittsburgh, Pennsylvania. Juried, 2005.

Lectures/Public-Speaking Engagements

Lecture, Pratt Institute, Brooklyn, New York, 2009.

Lecture, Art Department, University of Colorado, Boulder, Colorado, 2009.

Interview, "Culture Hour," WRST-TV, Detroit, Michigan, 2008.

Lecture, Covington Gallery, Houston, Texas, 2007.

Interview, "The Drawing Show Artists," WXYZ-Radio, Tempe, Arizona, 2005.

Education

Art Department, Ross College, Huntington, Iowa, B.F.A., 1996.

Thin Résumés

Few of us can begin careers with heavyweight résumés full of fancy exhibition/performance credits and citing articles and reviews in leading publications. But the anxiety of having a thin résumé should not prevent you from putting a résumé together. I like the reaction of a painter whom I was assisting with a résumé. She studied the various category headings and replied: "How exciting. I can't fill in all of these categories, but look at all of the things I can look forward to."

While it is not advisable to pad résumés with insignificant facts and data, a few things can be done to fill up a page so that a résumé does not look bare. For example, double-space between each entry and triple-space between categories. Use "Collections" to list the names of any well-known people or institutions who have your work, even if they did not purchase it. Include student shows in the "Exhibitions/Performances" category and use "Awards and Honors" to list any scholarships or teaching assistantships you have received in graduate or undergraduate school. If you have teaching experience in the arts, list this experience in a new category, "Career-Related Experience" or "Teaching Experience."

Less Than Thin Résumés

Over the years I have had many clients who had no formal art training, and/or when they first came to me they had no exhibition history, nor had they sold any work. In other words, when they were in the beginning stages of marketing their work, none of the suggested categories in a fine-arts résumé would have been applicable.

In such cases I always recommend dealing with the dragon head-on! Abandon the use of a formal résumé and prepare a narrative entitled "Background Information" that states that you are self-taught. The narrative should combine a biographical statement (see page 52) and an artist statement (see page 53).

This format was used by one of my clients, a self-taught artist who began painting at the age of forty. His "background information" narrative contained three short paragraphs, or a total of sixty words. It stated that he had no formal training; it mentioned where and when he was born; and it included a few sentences about his work.

Once he began a focused effort to gain exposure, his lack of academic and art-world credentials was of no consequence. As a result of his first group show, he received an enthusiastic review from an art critic in *The New York Times*. By the end of the second year he had a one-person show in an alternative space in New York City, and by the third year he had a two-person show in a New Jersey museum.

Updating Résumés

The following advice might sound silly, but artists are often negligent about résumés: as career changes and accomplishments occur, update your résumé. If you have been invited to participate in an exhibition/event in the future, add a new category to the résumé, "Forthcoming Exhibitions." If an article is planned in the future, add a new category, "Forthcoming Articles." Suggestions for presenting a résumé on your Web site are included in chapter 4, "Art Marketing and the Internet" (see page 75).

Excerpts from Publications

If you have received good reviews, excerpt the most flattering quotes on a separate sheet of paper and attach it to your résumé. Credit the author, article, and publication, and give the date. If you have not been reviewed in a periodical, but an exhibition catalog contains prose about your work, include the relevant quotes on a separate sheet of paper, credit the author, and give the exhibition title, sponsor, and date. Although many artists present an entire article, unless the key phrases about you are *underlined* or *highlighted*, chances are the article will not be read.

Biographies

A biography is a synopsis, written in prose, of your career accomplishments. It highlights various credits listed on your résumé. A biography has many uses. In certain instances, it is used in lieu of a résumé, as described in the section "Less Than Thin Résumés" on page 51. It can also be integrated into cover letters (see page 54), press releases (see page 104), on Web sites (see page 75), in exhibition catalogs, and in various presentation packages. Following is an example of a biography, based on the sample résumé on pages 47–50.

> Terry Turner's paintings have been exhibited in solo and group exhibitions in galleries and museums throughout the United States and abroad, including the Whitehurst Museum in Whitehurst, Illinois; the Smith Wheeler Gallery in Chicago; the Limerick Gallery in San Francisco; and the Pfeiffer Gallery in Düsseldorf, Germany.
>
> In addition, her work is in public and corporate collections, including those of the Pittsburgh Cultural Center and the Avery Food Corporation in New York City.
>
> Ms. Turner is the recipient of numerous awards and honors. She received fellowships from the Denver Arts Council and the Minerva Hills Artist Colony in Minerva Hills, Montana.
>
> Terry Turner was born in Washington, D.C., in 1974. She received a B.F.A. from Ross College in Huntington, Iowa.

Like a résumé, a biography should not be a thesis that explains the meaning of your work. Save such explanations for an artist statement.

ARTIST STATEMENTS

Many artists assume, somewhat naively, that everyone is automatically going to "get" or comprehend their work on the exact level on which they intend it to be perceived. Although an artist statement can be an effective tool in helping insecure people better understand your work, one does not have to be insecure about visual art to appreciate the aid of an artist statement.

But translating visual concepts into clear prose is an exercise that often meets with much resistance. For several years, I have conducted workshops on a variety of career-related subjects, including developing artist statements. Many workshop participants anticipate preparing an artist statement as eagerly as they might a tooth extraction. And I often find the task of getting artists to describe their own work in a meaningful and interesting way not unlike pulling teeth!

As a warm-up exercise, participants are asked to describe the work of an artist whom they admire. For the most part, passionate adjectives and poetic phrases flow with unrestrained ease. But after the warm-up, when artists are asked to describe their *own* work, dry abstractions and clichés fill the page.

Although artists vehemently criticize the overintellectualized style of writing used in leading art magazines, many believe that their work will not be taken seriously unless they *imitate what they despise.*

An artist statement can be used as a tool to help dealers, art consultants, and advisors sell your work, and as background information in helping writers, critics, and curators prepare articles, reviews, and exhibition catalogs. In addition, an artist statement can be incorporated into a cover letter (see page 54), on your Web site (see page 75), and into grant applications (see chapter 9).

An artist statement can focus on one or more topics, such as symbols and metaphors, materials and techniques, or themes or issues underlying or influencing your work.

Avoid using weak phrases that reflect insecurities, confusion, or doubt, such as "I am attempting," "I hope," or "I am trying." The statement should be coherent, direct, and energetic. Here are some examples:

My paintings are landscapes that twist and turn and are tossed about and split apart. Sometimes they merge into sky or water, or disappear off the edge of a cliff. Flooding is a regular occurrence. I view the painting process as a portal to my interior life and responses to environmental and global events; it has evolved out of a deep fascination with the metaphor of landscape and the expressive possibilities of oil paint. In moving paint over and around a surface, weather and geological processes become agents of change, acting on landforms that are repositories of memory and accumulated experience. I meander through a landscape versus describing it, and capture not a moment but a process—forms, elements and events, moving and changing over time. *Dorothy Robinson*

I create photographs of assemblages constructed from pieces of ordinary paper. Twisting, tearing, and crumbling paper into various shapes, I produce visual imagery that forms intriguing illusions and relationships between my objects when light, shadow, and forms merge. At first glance, a photograph might appear as an exotic flower, but on taking a closer look viewers will see the familiar scalloping and rippling of a paper plate. *Leonard Morris*

When a piano is beyond repair I rescue it from the trash. I detach the parts from their original role in this instrument of sound and combine them into another reality. The forms have organic and sometimes creaturely characteristics. In this series, "Piano Revival," I am influenced by my father who began a twenty-two-year career as a piano technician at the age of seventy. *Bea Mitchell*

My portraits are another way of telling stories of people, about their optimism or introspection, their innocence or wisdom, their grace and complexity. They also speak about me—and how I read the world and the people in it. More than just a likeness, they are my interpretation of a unique individual using the language of sculpture. *William Hanson*

COVER LETTERS

The use of a cover letter is more than a courtesy; it can provide a context to help people view your work. Some people need the context of art-world validation, such as the information provided in a résumé (see page 44). Some people are not concerned with glitz but want to know what your work is all about. Others need a combination of glitz and substance. An effective letter can cover all grounds.

It should include the following:

(1) *An introductory paragraph* stating who you are and the purpose of the letter. For example:

I am a sculptor and am writing to acquaint you with my work. Enclosed are recent examples.

(2) *A short artist statement.* For example:

My portraits are another way of telling stories of people, about their optimism or introspection, their innocence or wisdom, their grace and complexity. They also speak about me—and how I read the world and the people in it. More than just a likeness, they are my interpretation of a unique individual using the language of sculpture.[1]

(3) *A brag paragraph* that plucks from your résumé a few credentials. For example:

My sculptures have been featured in solo and group exhibitions in museums and galleries, including the Contemporary Art Museum in Fairfield, Arizona; the Ridgemont Museum in Spokane, Washington, and the Wallace Gallery in Chicago. In addition, my work is in public and corporate collections, including those of the Whitehurst Museum in Whitehurst, Illinois, and the Marsh and Webber Corporation in New York City.

(4) *A concluding paragraph.* For example:

If you find my work of interest, I would be pleased to send additional visual materials and background information. You can also visit my Web site at www.nameofsite.com.

Or:

If you find my work of interest, I would be pleased to arrange a studio visit in the near future. You can also visit my Web site at www.nameofsite.com.

If applicable, include a paragraph listing the reasons you are contacting a particular gallery or curator. For example:

"I have visited your gallery on several occasions and believe my work shares an affinity with the work of the artists featured."

Or:

"I have visited your Web site and believe my work shares an affinity with the work of the artists featured."

Or:

"I attended the exhibition *Modern Dreams* and, judging by the selection of artists featured in the show, I thought that you would be interested in my work."

Depending on your career stage, it might not be possible to include a brag paragraph, but an artist statement can be integrated into the letter regardless of whether you have been working as an artist for ten months or ten years.

Writing a cover letter and including any one or all of the elements outlined above is no guarantee that you will get what you want. However, with a well-written cover letter you have a better chance of making an impression and setting yourself apart from the hundreds of artists who send packages to dealers, curators, collectors, and exhibition sponsors with form letters, insipid letters, or no cover letters at all.

VISUAL PRESENTATIONS

Since few dealers and curators will consent to an appointment to actually view your artwork without receiving visual information in advance, for many years artists have been stuck with the slide package system. This system was designed for the convenience of dealers and curators, but not in the best interest of artists.

Thanks to technology, I can almost speak of the slide package system in the past tense. Slides are being replaced with CD-ROMs, DVDs, computer-generated reproductions, high-quality photocopies, and various types of graphic files transmitted over the Internet. (However, for an initial introduction to your work, before sending imagery over the Internet, I recommend using brochures (see page 59) and postcards (see page 62).

The slide package is an absurd method of presentation. With few exceptions, your slides are examined without the aid of a slide projector, light box, or hand viewer, and while glancing at a group of tiny images the person viewing your slides makes a decision in about fifteen seconds on whether your work is of interest.

Thus, after completing a work, you must create an artificial viewing situation that will present the work advantageously in a slide or photograph. Unless the work happens to *be* a photograph, this is not the way it was intended to be viewed or experienced. (The idiocy of the slide system is further heightened when photographers are requested to present slides of their prints!)

Often, because of the importance placed on good photographs, an artist is guided and influenced during the creation process by how well the work will photograph!

Slides are not completely relics of the past. For example, they are still requested in some grant applications, proposals, and by some art dealers and art consultants. *To be on the safe side, when photographing artwork it is a good idea to shoot slides.*

Photographing Artwork

When artists photograph their own artwork, there are some advantages, namely, saving money, documenting work on your own schedule, and not relying on another person's vision of how the work should appear in photographic form. However, only photograph your work yourself if you can really do it justice. Books that present guidelines and tips for photographing artwork are listed in the appendix section "Photographing Artwork."

If you are unable to take professional-quality photographs, use a photographer experienced in *fine-art* photography. Decide before the shooting how you want the work to look in a photograph and what features you want emphasized. If the final result falls short of your expectations, reshoot, and, if necessary, continue to reshoot until you have what you want. If your work contains details that get lost when the piece is photographed as a whole, shoot separate photographs of the details you want emphasized or clarified.

Since you are going through the time and expense of a photography session, use a film camera and a digital camera, and shoot in color and black-and-white. Color photographs can be used for all types of presentations, and black-and-white and color prints can be

used for exhibition announcements (see page 115) and public relations campaigns (see chapter 6, "Public Relations: Keep Those
Cards and Letters Coming In and Going Out").

If you have never had your work photographed, shoot all of
the work, but reserve the older work for personal documentation and
future use. Dealers and curators are interested in your current direction and do not want to see a retrospective in the initial presentation.

Since photographs are the lures to get art dealers, art consultants,
and curators interested in your work and possibly see your work in
person, if they are unimpressed with the work as it appears in photographs, it is unlikely a dialogue will begin. For photographic purposes, do not glamorize a piece of work with special effects that
misrepresent what the viewer will actually see in person. Ultimately,
the deception will catch up with you.

Additional information about various forms of photographic presentations, along with submission guidelines and tips, are discussed
in the following section, "Rethinking Presentation Packages."

RETHINKING PRESENTATION PACKAGES

When I began keeping track of the number of presentation packages
my clients annually sent to galleries, art consultants, and curators, I
learned that generally it takes *fifty* exposures of the *same body of
work* to generate *one* positive response.

This means that on the average, fifty people must see a presentation package of the same work in order for an artist to receive an
invitation to exhibit or spur interest in establishing a consignment
relationship, sale, or commission opportunity. Although artists have
sent fewer than fifty packages and received good feedback (in one
case three packages led to the sale of three paintings), such experiences are by far the exception rather than the rule.

The *good news* is that the number of initial packages most artists
send—between twelve and fifteen a year—does not even begin to
approach an effective market penetration level that justifies any
sense of defeat or rejection if the response is unfavorable.

On the other hand, preparing fifty packages that contain a visual
presentation and support materials such as a résumé, an artist state-

ment, press clippings, a cover letter, and a self-addressed stamped envelope can be unwieldy, costly, and time-consuming.

There are better ways of doing a marketing outreach to large groups of art-world contacts that are cost-effective, time-effective, and visually effective. The following sections discuss the use of brochures and postcards for an initial introduction to your work. They also describe other types of support materials once you receive a nibble. When considering visual alternatives to traditional presentation packages, be prepared for negative criticism from peers as well as others in the art world who suffer from petty jealousies or a lack of understanding of basic marketing principles. Many artists, as well as dealers, are afraid of making a move outside of the archaic and illogical rules of art-world etiquette. But there are also many people in the art world who are looking for fresh, imaginative, and effective ways to find new audiences.

Brochures

In the 1980s one of my first clients to publish a brochure did so in conjunction with an open-studio event (see page 163).

One thousand brochures were printed, one-third of which were used to accompany an invitation to her open studio. The brochures were sent to New York area galleries, private dealers, art consultants, curators, friends, and people who had previously expressed interest in or purchased her work. In the months following the open studio she sent brochures to galleries, private dealers, art consultants, and curators nationwide. With each brochure she sent a cover letter in which she offered to send support materials if the recipient found her work of interest.

I asked the artist to keep track of the response generated from the brochure for a twelve-month period. Here are the results:

- Brochures were sent to 329 art consultants, private dealers, and galleries. She received 48 responses.
- Out of 48 responses, 12 people requested slides; 7 people retained the slides for future consideration.
- The artist developed consignment relationships with two galleries in California and one gallery each in New Jersey, Connecticut, and Alabama.

- She was invited to have a one-person exhibition at an alternative space in New York City.
- Two paintings were sold at the open-studio event, another painting through the art dealer in New Jersey, and another piece at the one-person show.
- In addition, several copies of the brochure were sent to dealers and art consultants with whom she had previously worked, resulting in the sale of two additional paintings and a corporate commission.

Translating the results into dollars and cents, in one year the artist quadrupled her income from the sale of artwork as a result of using a brochure.

The cost of the brochure, including printing, layout, and design for one thousand copies and envelopes, was $2,392. The artist spent another $533 for the design and printing of a letterhead for cover letters, making the total cost of the project $2,925. The brochures were sent via first-class mail, which, at the time of the mailing, came to a postage rate of fifty-two cents each. Thus, the final cost of each package was $3.44.

If the artist had continued to use traditional slide packages, which cost her $25 each, she would have spent $8,225!

A few years ago, an artist who published a brochure as a result of reading my book sent me an email summarizing the results. He used some of my mailing lists (see page 26) and sent 650 brochures to galleries, museums, curators, and art consultants. Within six months he received 40 positive responses, a 16 percent response rate. He was offered two solo shows in public museums; two corporate curators in Los Angeles and California expressed interest in selling his work; he developed a consignment relationship with a gallery in the Midwest; and he received feedback from several museums stating that they would consider him for inclusion in future exhibitions.

Various factors will determine the cost of a brochure, including the number of color images, the paper stock, the size and shape, and the print run. Another consideration is where the printer is located. (Generally printers located in cities where real estate is expensive tend to charge higher prices because of their high overhead.)

In addition to drastic cost savings, there are other important benefits of using a brochure rather than a slide package:

- Compared with a slide package, which generally pulls a 2 percent response rate, the response rate of a brochure is generally between 6 and 14 percent.
- A brochure allows work to be reproduced in a larger format. The visual impact is much more effective than the tiny image of a slide.
- The use of a brochure also resolves the problem of having to wait for materials to be returned for recirculation. Often several months pass before material is returned, creating false hope that you have won someone's interest, when in reality the package is accumulating dust, the victim of a forgetful or disorganized dealer.
- Brochures are easier to handle and quicker to assemble, though each brochure must be accompanied by a cover letter (see page 54). It is likely that you will follow up on more leads or contacts and send out more large mailings when your time involvement is minimized.
- Brochures can also serve as sales tools for dealers and consultants.

For many artists, career advancements and art sales can be attributed to the use of a brochure. For example, a painter who had been employed as a legal secretary for many years gave her brochure to the law firm's partners. Although the partners knew that she was an artist, interest in her work was spurred when they saw her work "in print." One partner purchased three paintings.

As a result of a brochure, another painter received invitations for eight solo and group exhibitions at galleries throughout the United States during a twelve-month period.

For another painter, the brochure helped a collector make a decision in the artist's favor. Trying to decide between the work of two artists, the collector asked the dealer if she had any written information available on the artists. When the dealer presented the collector with my client's brochure, he was thoroughly impressed and made a quick decision in favor of the artist with the brochure.

POINTERS AND TIPS FOR
CREATING A BROCHURE OR POSTCARD

It has now been well over twenty-five years since my clients began using brochures and postcards to make initial contacts with dealers, curators, corporations, potential collectors, and the press. Through a process of trial and error and tracking the results, I offer the following pointers:

Design and Format

An understated brochure or card is as *effective* as one that has been lavishly designed. Although *I highly recommend* using a graphic designer, the layout, background colors, and fonts should not compete or distract from your artwork. Sometimes graphic designers tend to overdesign and need to be reminded that the purpose of brochure or card is to feature your work—not theirs!

A basic brochure should have a minimum of two visual images with one or two folds. If you select a printing company's standard size, such as 5 by 7 inches, it will be much less expensive than a custom-size format. An advantage of using a 5-by-7-inch format is that the brochure can fit into a standard greeting card envelope. Brochures and cards should be printed on sturdy paper.

Many of my clients have used a postcard, approximately 4 by 8 inches. The format lends itself well to including two or three visual images on one side of the card and text on the other side. This format also has the advantage of fitting into a regular number ten envelope.

Brochures and cards should express visual sensitivity and sophistication. Avoid the "home grown" look. Although some artists use their computer to design and print brochures, unless you have a talent for graphic design, get some help from a professional. Printing off of your computer is not necessarily cost-effective. The cost of inks and appropriate paper can be very expensive, particularly if you are doing large mailings.

Visual Images

A brochure or card should contain at least two visual images from the *same body of work*, and the images should reflect your most current direction. Do not mix disciplines, series, or themes. Select visual images that will translate well in a printed format. If you are inexperienced in having your work reproduced, a good printing company will be able to advise you of the suitability of the images you have selected and the likelihood of technical problems.

Text

Include a short biographical text (see page 52) in lieu of a résumé. A biography is a good way to avoid the use of dates (which ultimately can *date* the brochure or card), and more information can be packed into a prose format. A biographical narrative is also a helpful tool for those artists who are at the beginning stages of their career and have a limited number of career-related credits.

Also include a short artist statement (see page 53) that pertains to the artwork featured on the brochure or card. Avoid "kiss of death" phrases or information in the biography and artist statement that can sabotage your efforts. Such "no-no's" can include, for example, mentioning that you are *currently* taking art courses, or comparing your work to other artists'. And if you have a dual career that has no bearing on the work you are doing as a fine artist, do not refer to your other occupation.

Make it easy for people to contact you and provide all of the options. Include your snail mail address and phone number, and, if applicable, your email and Web site addresses.

As a design consideration, the text should be placed on one or two panels of a brochure, separated from the visual images so that it does not compete with the artwork. If you are using a postcard, the artwork should appear on one side of the card and the text on the other side.

If space allows, a brochure can also include a photograph of the artist and excerpts from reviews (see page 52).

Some artists are under the false impression that a brochure needs the validation of an art critic. In fact, some artists have actually resorted to paying critics to write an essay for their brochures. If the notion were true that it is imperative for a brochure to contain a critical essay, this would imply that a brochure lacking an essay is ineffective. *This is most definitely not the case!*

Shannon Wilkinson, president of the New York–based Cultural Communications Corporation, a public-relations firm that promotes creative and cultural clients, points out that some of the critics who are commissioned to write essays for artists are "becoming highly overexposed."[2] The negative consequence of this overexposure is that dealers and curators are able to recognize quickly those artists who are participating in the distasteful syndrome of paying for a review, otherwise known as "vanity press."

Ill-advised artists are spending large amounts of money to secure the seal of approval from critics, and, as Wilkinson also points out, some critics and artist marketing consultants "are making substantial profits from artist-commissioned essays . . . and will have far easier retirements because of artists."[3]

Keep in mind that the recipient of the brochure is most interested in *visual information,* and in most instances long essays are distractions and they go unread.

Cover Letters

Brochures and cards *must* be accompanied by a cover letter (see page 54). Without a cover letter the brochure or card can easily be misconstrued as an exhibition announcement that requires no response.

Print Run

If you are contacting galleries, art consultants, and curators, order a minimum of two thousand brochures or cards. To maximize the effectiveness of a brochure or card, keep the momentum going and send them out on a continuing basis. Do not get discouraged if you do not receive an instant response. As previously mentioned, a brochure or card can bring a higher response rate than a slide package, but responses can sometimes be immediate or come in dribbles and drabs over a long period of time. Brochures and cards have an amazing longevity. Clients have reported that they have received a response as much as three years after an initial mailing.

Slide Packages

If you are not ready to publish a postcard or brochure to make *initial* contacts with dealers, curators, and potential collectors, limit the number of slides that you send to three. Your package should also include a résumé (see page 44), an artist statement (see page

53), and a cover letter (see page 54). In the cover letter, offer to send additional slides if the recipient finds your work of interest. Depending on the price of the slides, it may or may not be cost-effective to enclose a self-addressed stamped envelope.

Web Site Fine-Art Portfolios

A full discussion about creating a Web site designed as a fine-art portfolio can be found in the chapter "Art Marketing and the Internet."

Follow-up Support Materials

After the initial mailing, when you receive requests for support materials, this is the time to assemble a comprehensive presentation package. If the person does not specify a particular format, inquire whether they would like to receive a CD-ROM, a DVD, computer-generated copies, color photocopies, image files transmitted over the Internet, photographs, or slides. If you have a Web site, in some instances a dealer, art consultant, curator, et cetera, will obtain all of the information they need from your site.

Include in the package a copy of the brochure and card that originally piqued their interest and a short letter reminding the person that he or she requested the material.

Although, as mentioned earlier in this chapter, requests for slide packages are diminishing, if slides are requested it is a good idea to resubmit the brochure or card because often there is an incongruity between the image portrayed in a slide as compared to an enlarged version in the printed format. The viewer might not recognize that it is the same piece of artwork.

Regardless of the format, visual presentations should be a cohesive presentation of your most current direction and not a retrospective of all of your work. Include a minimum of six images and a maximum of twenty images. Do not bombard people with images of vast amounts of work. To avoid criticism or the accusation of being unfocused or a dilettante, it is important to only feature *one medium* in *one body of work* that expresses a *unifying theme*. In other words, if you paint and draw, present paintings or drawings, but not both. If you paint landscapes and figures, only submit landscapes or figures, but not both. If you paint landscapes of rolling green hills and barren farmland, submit rolling green hills or barren farmland, but not both. Once you develop a relationship with dealers and curators, there will be time at a later point to inform them that you work in various mediums or themes.

All photographs should be labeled with the dimensions of the work, the medium, the title, and your name. Keep a personal record of dates when all work was created, but do not include this information on presentation materials. What you consider your most recent body of work, perhaps a series that spans a period of five years, could very well be considered *old* by subjective art-world standards.

Eliminate any possibility that a viewer will not understand the correct direction in which artwork should be viewed. It is an intimidating situation for a viewer to have to hem and haw over the right way to view work. The viewer's embarrassment can create a negative atmosphere, meaning that your work is not being viewed under the best circumstances, and this can lead to a negative response. Depending on your presentation media, small and subtle directional arrows might be necessary.

Include in your support package a résumé and an artist statement, and if applicable, reviews and exhibition catalogs. Submit a retail price list (see page 95) to gallery dealers and art consultants.

Snail Mail or Email?

I receive approximately one-hundred "look at me" emails a week from artists who erroneously think I am an art dealer or an artist-agent. In such situations, due to time constraints (and a concern for computer viruses), *I never open the attachments.* Being on the receiving end has given me insight into how many unsolicited emails with attachments are being sent to art dealers and art consultants to gain representation, and how many must go unread.

Although there are exceptions, and a discussion of snail mail versus email will be revisited in the next chapter, "Art Marketing and the Internet," generally, I recommend sending initial presentation packages by snail mail.

No Apologies

Prepare presentation materials with tender loving care, and do your best to make the experience pleasurable for recipients. In an interview on the Web site Chicago Artists Resources, sponsored by the

Cultural Planning Division of the Chicago Department of Cultural Affairs, artist Lynn Basa shared wise advice that she had received: "One of the best pieces of advice I've ever gotten . . . came from a (successful) artist friend who told me: Never send out materials that you have to apologize for—as in, 'The color in this printout isn't right,' or, 'I have a Web site but it's way out of date,' etc."[4]

STREAMLINING PAPERWORK

This chapter and the previous chapter, "Launching or Relaunching Your Career: Entering the Marketplace," outline various tasks, tools, and homework assignments for career development. One of the surest ways to set yourself up for defeat is to become overwhelmed by administrative work.

In the book *Conquering the Paper Pile-Up: How to Sort, Organize, File, and Store Every Piece of Paper in Your Home and Office*, author Stephanie Culp describes a situation that is shared by many artists:

> They say we are living in the Information Age, and indeed, there does seem to be a staggering amount of information to be gleaned from every imaginable source. . . . This abundance of information has given rise to the phrase "information anxiety." . . . As the paper arrives, the information-anxious folks adjust their level of anxiety upward several notches with every few inches of papers that get added to the existing piles of papers with information yet to be absorbed. The overworked and understaffed small business watches the papers multiply at a frenzied rate.[5]

You can avoid a state of inundation if you aim to accomplish one goal or task at a time, if you do not attempt to do everything simultaneously, and if you learn to streamline paperwork. Computers have made this possible.

Computers have radically reduced paperwork and repetitive chores. Résumés, cover letters, mailing lists, and artist statements can be stored on a computer and updated in a matter of minutes. A computer can be used to store a variety of information and perform many services, from storing inventories and price lists to creating invoices and contracts.

Special software programs are also available that are tailored to the needs of artists. For example, WorkingArtist: The Artist's Business Tool is a Windows program that was created to help artists manage the business side of art. It catalogs artwork, creates consignment invoices, mailing lists, price lists, price grids, and labels, and provides other services. GYST Software for Artists tracks artwork, prices, and sales and provides sales invoices. It also includes a database for creating a mailing list, an artwork checklist for exhibitions, and many other business-related functions. A special feature includes a guide with detailed instructions to help users write grant proposals and other proposals.

In addition to Stephanie Culp's book *Conquering the Paper Pile-Up,* there are books available that specialize in time management and organization for creative people, including *Organizing for the Creative Person* by Dorothy Lehmkuhl and Lee Silber's books *Time Management for the Creative Person* and *Organizing from the Right Side of the Brain: A Creative Approach to Getting Organized.*

The use of business forms, specially designed for artists, is another good time-saving tool. Attorney and publisher Tad Crawford has produced a series of books containing business and legal forms for artists for varied circumstances. These include *Business and Legal Forms for Crafts, Business and Legal Forms for Fine Artists, Business and Legal Forms for Illustrators,* and *Business and Legal Forms for Photographers.* The most recent editions of each book include a CD-ROM.

And, yes, artists can have secretaries! Once a system is developed for disseminating presentation materials and reaching various markets, an assistant can take over. A workable system does not require full-time energy. This is something that can be accomplished in a few hours a week.

The subject of experiencing overwhelming sensations when trying to balance studio work with the business of art is also discussed in chapter 11, "Rationalization, Paranoia, Competition, Rejection, and the Overwhelm Factor." For additional information about publications, computer software programs, and the other organizational aids cited above, see the appendix sections "Organizing Paperwork" and "Law: Contracts and Business Forms."

4

Art Marketing and the Internet

Since the mid-1990s when arts-related Web sites were first developed, a few pioneering artists had their own Web sites, but most sites were in the form of online galleries that featured the work of many artists. Online galleries were hailed as the most promising vehicle for the direct sale of artwork between artists and the public. Many art dealers felt threatened by this new form of competition and prohibited the artists they represented to sell work online. In some cases, when artists created their own sites, they were dropped by galleries for listing their own contact information and not the gallery's.

As time passed, the initial excitement about commercial online galleries subsided and during the mid-2000s there was a tremendous surge in the number of artist-owned sites, and traditional galleries joined the bandwagon.

The question of whether technological developments will eventually and completely replace traditional art-marketing venues will be answered in the future. At present, the Internet can be used as an effective adjunct to traditional art-marketing efforts. This section offers advice and information about using the Internet to make your vision better known and let people know that you exist.

DEFINING WHAT YOUR SITE SHOULD BE

Generally Web sites developed by artists fall into two main categories: consumer-oriented sites and fine-art portfolios. A consumer-oriented Web site usually incorporates ecommerce with the use of a shopping cart and/or credit card services. The purpose of a site aimed at the general public—versus the art public—is to sell artwork *directly online—and appeal to the widest possible audience.* Given the goal of attracting the widest possible audience, a successful sales record is dictated by *the amount of money the general public will spend on art.* Realistically this amount usually equates to what they will spend on a widget. Although articles have been posted on the Internet about artists who have been successful in selling work directly to the general public *through their own Web sites,* the price range for their artwork can be as low as $9.95 for a print. In many cases consumer-oriented sites offer a potpourri of artwares that include, for example, T-shirts, coffee mugs, and magnets. This is not to say that there have not been instances when artists have sold work online directly to members of the general public at much higher prices, but most examples of pricier online sales have been the result of work that is featured on online galleries (see page 83).

The purpose of a site designed as a fine-art portfolio is to gain exposure and introduce artwork to various art-world factions. The anticipated results are that the Web site will lead to career recognition, invitations to participate in exhibitions, invitations for gallery representation, and eventually sales and commissions.

Artists who develop Web sites that are designed as a fine-art portfolio have seemingly unlimited opportunities to have their work seen by gallery dealers, art consultants, collectors, curators, public-art agencies, architects and interior designers, and the press. A fine-art portfolio can also function as an educational tool to help people better understand an artist's work, concepts, and ideas. In addition, a fine-art portfolio can serve solely for the purpose of paying tribute to an artist's career, a topic that is discussed on page 144, in the section "Posthumous Exhibitions."

Unfortunately, *many* artists make a *big mistake of combining* a consumer-oriented with a fine-art portfolio. They naively believe that a multipurpose site will attract the general public for the purpose of generating mega sales and also gain the interest of the art world. However, it is highly unlikely that members of the art world are impressed with a Web site that drools of advertising hype, or that offers paintings for sale that are categorized as "extra large, large, medium, and small." Nor will members of the art world be impressed with Web sites that include a gift shop featuring magnets, T-shirts, mugs, stickers, and buttons.

Regardless of whether you are selling art or "widgets," *consumer-oriented Internet marketing is a field unto itself* with its own special requirements, guidelines, and lists of dos and don'ts. However, this chapter addresses the development of Web sites that are specifically designed as a *fine-art portfolio.*

If you are planning a *consumer-oriented site,* there are resources listed in the appendix section "Internet Art Marketing." These include the Web site Empty Easel, which posts many articles about selling art online, and Artists Web Wiki, which publishes articles related to art marketing on the Internet. Also of interest is Marcia Yudkin's book *Poor Richard's Web Site Marketing Makeover: Improve Your Message and Turn Visitors into Buyers.* Although it is not specifically addressed to art marketing on the Internet, it delves into the details that make or break a Web site and how to transform a site to generate more interest and more orders. It includes sample makeovers and a commentary on ten different kinds of sites, including multiproduct sales.

Two books that specifically focus on art marketing on the Internet include *Marketing and Buying Fine Art Online: A Guide for Artists and Collectors* by Marques Vickers and *Internet 101 for the Fine Artist* by Constance Smith and Susan Greaves. The second edition of *Internet 101 for the Fine Artist,* published in 2007, contains a special guide to selling work on eBay. Although these resources are specifically designed for *Internet* art marketing, *make sure* that the advice you follow is clearly aimed for *either* a consumer-oriented site or a fine-art portfolio. Often boundaries are blurred and confusion exists.

WEB SITE DESIGN AND DESIGNERS

"Many people have unrealistic expectations about having a well-designed site that can really show off their work,"[1] said William Lombardo of Skyhook Studios, a Web site designer in New York City who designed the Artist Help Network site (see page 253). "Do you have the skills to build it yourself? Unless you are *really* a designer as well as a photographer, the consequences may be very dated and boring."[2]

If you decide to hire a Web site designer, keep in mind that although the word *designer* is used in a job title, in many cases, a Web site designer is not a graphic designer. And although the designer has the technical skills to create a Web site, it is not necessarily indicative that he or she will have the graphic skills or visual sensitivity to successfully handle the design of a fine-art portfolio.

Work with a designer who *specializes* in Web site design *for artists*. Although many designers might be experienced in designing sites for businesses and corporations, designing a fine-art portfolio is a completely different challenge.

William Lombardo points out that "too many sites fail because visitors are presented with design bells and whistles overpowering the artwork on the site. You want the artwork to be the star, not hectic graphics, music, or sound effects. If you make a visitor listen to Beethoven's 9th before they can access your artwork or if they must wait for an animation to reload each time they hit the back button to your home page, they will not be happy."[3]

Work with a designer who encourages your participation so that you are comfortable articulating ideas, concepts, and the atmospheric feeling that you want your site to convey. It is a good idea to interview several designers before you take the plunge to ensure that your personalities are compatible and that you are not working with a dictator.

In planning a site and selecting a Web site designer, Lombardo offers the following pointers:

- Bookmark artists' sites that you like and make a note of the links to the Web designers who designed them.

- Also bookmark the sites that you dislike—so that once you select a Web site designer, you can refer to the sites that are appealing and not appealing to give the designer a good idea of how you would like your site to look.
- Find a designer who "understands" you. Make sure that you get the feeling that he or she is interested in *your work being the center point* of the site—*not their design.*
- Once you have selected a Web designer, use a contract that contains specific information about the cost of the design from start to finish and specifies the site's content and visual presentation. For example, an agreement should include the number of photographs that will be used, the number of menu sections, the navigation style, what information and materials the artist is expected to provide, a design fee payment schedule, how many designs will be provided before incurring add-on charges and what the add-on charges will be, how long it will take to launch the site, who will update the site in the future, and if you will be supplied with all files that generate the site. Always think in terms of the future. For example, what happens if you want to change designers—are you going to have to get a U.S. marshal to get back the source files?[4]

Once a Web site has been completed and is up and running, William Lombardo suggests that it is a good idea to make notes about any positive or negative feedback you receive from Web site visitors and friends. Also, keep tabs of any bugs. Obviously bugs should be reported to the designer as they are found. After you have lived with the site for a while, you may have some ideas on how the site can be improved. Keep notes on ideas for future changes and let this list accumulate for a few months to warrant one major site update. Otherwise, updates made every now and then can get expensive, and the designer will not appreciate being asked to make minor changes if they are not his or her fault.[5]

PLANNING A WEB SITE FINE-ART PORTFOLIO

In planning a virtual fine-art portfolio, think in terms of planning a traditional fine-art portfolio. In other words, when you have an appointment to present your work, what materials will you bring? Focusing within this framework will rule out a lot of extraneous materials. Following are suggestions for content development of an online fine-art portfolio.

Home Page

The design of a home page is very important because it provides visitors with a *first impression* of your work. The goal of the home page is to achieve maximum visual impact to entice visitors to look at more artwork.

Avoid a "busy" home page with many images and text. Although it is very usual for artists to be involved with more than one medium and/or more than one theme, the home page is not the place to sprinkle a sample of everything you are doing. The "sampler" approach can easily lead visitors to conclude that your work is unfocused, that you are all over the place, or that you are a dilettante.

I recommend featuring *one large image* of artwork on the home page with a caption that identifies the title, dimensions, and medium. The home page should also include your name and a menu.

Menu

A basic site menu might include the following sections: Gallery or Galleries, About the Artist, a Price List, and Contact Information. Optional pages can include a formal résumé (see page 44), press excerpts (see page 52), and a blog (see page 77).

Web Site Gallery or Galleries

Creating a gallery or galleries for a Web site should be approached with a "curatorial eye" and reflect a discerning and focused point of view. In selecting images for your Web site, follow the same guidelines as those suggested for designing brochures and cards (see page 59). Do not overwhelm viewers with a retrospective of your own art history. The gallery should feature only current work. If you have a need to feature older work or work unrelated to your current body of work, use a "secret link" system for access to a special section of your Web site (see page 76).

Keep in mind that you are inviting visitors to view your site for the primary purpose of seeing your artwork. The photographs of your artwork should be top-notch (see page 57). Artwork should be presented in a consistent manner in terms of style and medium. If you are working on more than one series or in more than one discipline, separate the work into respective galleries so that each gallery has a strong sense of focus. If you are a painter but are experimenting with sculpture, start a sculpture gallery section when you have completed five or six visually consistent pieces.

Artwork should be labeled with the title, dimensions, and medium. Do not post prices next to the artwork. Prices posted next to artwork are a distraction. You want people to look at the work and not the price. A price list should be handled in a separate manner (see below).

About the Artist

An artist statement (see page 53) and a biography (see page 52) can be posted under a Web page titled "About the Artist." A biography can be presented in lieu of a formal résumé (see page 44). However, if you want to include both, provide a PDF link from the biography to a formal résumé. In the section "About the Artist" you might also include a head shot or a photograph of you working in your studio.

Price List

Including a retail price list (see page 95) on a Web site has the following advantages: It serves as a filter to eliminate people from contacting you who have unrealistic and usually low expectations of artwork prices. And for artists who have some blocks and inhibitions about talking about money, posting prices online offers a comfort zone knowing that when someone contacts you as a result of seeing your Web site, the person is already familiar with your price structure, and there is less of a chance that you will be thrown into a defensive position. As previously mentioned, a price list should be posted on its own Web page far away from the gallery of artwork.

Contact Information

Make it easy for people to get in touch with you and include full contact information, including a snail mail address, phone number, and an email address. If you do not want to include a home address, rent a post office box.

Press Excerpts

A Web page can be devoted to excerpts from exhibition reviews, exhibition catalogs, and articles that have been written about you. If an article or review is particularly insightful, reproduce it in its entirety.

Secret Links

Using a "secret link," artwork can be posted on your Web site that is meant to be viewed for "special eyes" and not by everyone who visits your site. A secret link is not included in a Web site menu, but it can be advertised on a business card or on stationery, or passed on to people verbally or through email and snail mail.

A secret link can be used in various situations. For example, it will be of support to artists who subsidize their income through painting commissions that stylistically and/or thematically are *unrelated to the body of work featured on their Web site*. A secret link can be used by artists whose Web sites reflect their current direction but also want to present an online retrospective of their artwork for the benefit of curators, art historians, critics, and collectors. It will be helpful to artists who have bodies of work they want to sell that are *unrelated to their current direction*.

USING WEB SITES TO SUPPLEMENT
SNAIL MAIL MARKETING TOOLS

When the Internet was relatively new and a small minority of artists had their own Web sites, gallery dealers, curators, and art consultants honored email requests to preview sites. But over the years email requests to preview Web sites have grown considerably, and many recipients of "look at me" emails are overwhelmed to put it mildly. One of my clients told me that her gallery receives four thousand email requests a month to preview artist Web sites.

Some galleries and art consultants state specifically on their Web sites for representation consideration that they only accept online submissions or CD-ROMs. However, in most cases there are no directives, and unless you have *already* established a relationship with a gallery dealer, curator, or art consultant, and you are *coming in cold,* the best way to attract people to your Web site is to communicate using snail mail. Send a brochure (see page 59) or a card (see page 62) that includes examples of your artwork. Cards and brochures *should be accompanied by a personalized cover letter* that announces the Web site and provides background information about yourself and your work (see page 54). If you do not include a cover letter, there is a good chance that your mailing piece will be construed as an exhibition announcement that requires no follow-up. Into the wastebasket it will go!

Your Web site address should be included on the brochure or card and on your résumé (see page 47). Reference to Web sites can be incorporated into cover letters (see page 54). For example, in the concluding paragraph you could write: "If you find my work of interest, I would be pleased to provide further visual material and background information. Additional images of my work can be seen on my Web site www.whateveritis.com.

In many cases, recipients of brochures and cards are no longer requesting support materials via snail mail and are using an artist's Web site to obtain all the information they need.

OTHER MEANS OF INTERNET PRESENCE

Blogs

A blog has the potential of substantially increasing traffic to a Web site by giving you more search engine prominence. A blog can also be a very effective way of connecting with collectors and potential collectors. It can also be of interest to critics and writers for use in reviews and articles. A blog can serve as an effective tool in helping people transcend their intimidation of visual art (see page 14). And it can add a much needed *human* dimension to the art-world planet, giving artists more visibility and reminding people that a real person has created the artwork. Also, a blog can play a large role in counteracting the intense feelings of isolation that so many visual artists experience.

There are advantages to hosting your blog through your Web site instead of using an outside blog network. Hosting your own blog gives you complete control over content, keeping it advertisment-free, if this is your choice, and it adds search engine value to your Web site. For additional information about the ins and outs of blog hosting, see the suggested resources in the appendix section "Internet Art Marketing."

Nadine Robbins is a portrait painter who creates full-scale unconventional and nontraditional paintings. She uses her blog[6] in several ways: It serves as a running commentary about her painting process, both the highs and the lows. She also provides interviews with her subjects and biographical information. From time to time she provides insights into her artwork and advice about studio maintenance—from ventilation issues to keeping brushes clean. She also shows the evolution of a portrait from preliminary sketches and drawings through completion.

Cassandra Tondro, a painter in Santa Monica, California, started a blog[7] to get more people to look at her artwork, increase traffic to her Web site,[8] and obtain a high placement in search engine rankings. She accomplished all of her goals. Her blog averages 120 visitors a day, and as of this writing, her Web site ranks number twenty-five on a Google search using the keyword phrase "contemporary abstract painting." "One unexpected side effect of having the blog is that I get a lot of email from people thanking me for explaining techniques, asking questions about my work, and just writing to chat. I enjoy hearing from these people knowing that someone is benefiting in some way from my efforts."[9]

Tondro often struggles with the question of how much to reveal about herself on her blog. "On the one hand, I want to appear professional to gallery owners and art consultants. On the other hand, a blog is usually the place where you can be more chatty and informal. But how chatty and informal? I go back and forth on this issue, and this is reflected in my blog archives. There have been times when I've posted pictures and commentaries about my cats, friends, and family. Then I went through a phrase where I was posting daily about anything art-related—movies, exhibits, et cetera. Now I mostly post new work. I'm not sure if I've yet found the right balance between providing personal and professional information."[10]

Susan Kapuscinski Gaylord has spent part of her career, which started in the late 1970s, creating artists' books. In 2005, she ended that part of her journey having completed a thirteen-year project of meditative books called the Spirit Books series. She is currently working with poetry and manipulated photographs, and indoor and outdoor installations. She also conducts artists' books workshops. To encompass her past, present, and future in the visual arts, Gaylord developed a primary Web site[11] with interconnected blogs and an email newsletter.

She uses the blog "in good spirit"[12] to post photographs of work in progress, make observations, post information about her upcoming exhibitions, and announce other exhibitions and Web sites that have come to her attention. She sporadically uses the blog "The Creative Year"[13] and thinks of it in terms of being a book proposal in progress.

"Making Books with Children"[14] includes information about the workshops that she conducts, ebooks that she sells, and resource materials. "My blog is one more layer to my presence on the Web that has definitely helped build my reputation. For example, in 2007 I was invited to exhibit my books and give a workshop in South Korea."[15] "Making Books with Children" has made it much easier for people to contact her and they have a better idea of what her workshop is all about, resulting in less time spent on the phone with organizational details.

Gaylord points out that "a blog is a good starting point for someone who does not yet have a Web site. It gets you out there until you have the time and money to develop a site and helps organize your thinking about your work and how to present it."[16] In order to develop a viewership, she advises blog owners to post consistently. "Being featured by other blogs brings readers to your blog, and this is more likely to happen if you post frequently."[17]

Gaylord uses Google Analytics, a free service that generates detailed statistics about the visitors to Web sites and blogs, including how they discovered the site, the time spent on a site, their geographic locality, what they searched for, and other information.

A blog can lead to some interesting outcomes. For example, in 2007, Laurel Ptak, a photographer, started a blog[18] that featured the work of young and unknown international photographers. Word quickly spread about the blog's existence and sparked the interest of Daniel Silverstein and Kim Bourus, the former head of cultural projects at Magnum Photos, who invited Ptak to curate an exhibition based on her blog at their gallery Higher Pictures in New York City.

The blog titled "How's My Dealing?" provides a well-organized venting and feedback service, inviting artists to share their positive and negative direct dealings with galleries, curators, and critics. The blog also invites current and former gallery employees to contribute comments that will be useful to artists. In addition, galleries are invited to comment on various arts-related topics.

Video Podcasts

Artist Leslie Fry, who is known for public art projects and installations, has made good use of incorporating videos into her Web site. Her one-minute video, *Lists and Dreams,* can be viewed through two links in a section of her Web site titled "News and Media." One of the links goes to YouTube.

The video explores daily life and features a sculpture consisting of two parts that face each other on the walls of Fry's living room. The sculpture "is made out of to-do lists, lottery tickets, and written-down dreams. We try to give shape to our lives, which are often opposing elements of what we have to do (our lists) and what we dream of. In this sculpture, the two become one."[19]

The "News and Media" page also includes links to two public art projects: a six-minute video *Wild Life Sculpture Search* about a six-piece sculpture installation for the Boca Ciega Millennium Park in Seminole, Florida, commissioned by Pinellas County Cultural Affairs, and a two-minute video, *Art Park Seasonal Changes,* that shows the effects the four seasons have on Fry's sculptures at the Pomerleau Park in Burlington, Vermont. In addition, one of Fry's Web pages lists the book *Wild Life: A Public Art Project* about the Boca Ciega

Millennium Park, which was produced by an Internet print-on-demand publisher (see page 86).

Video presentations can be useful for showing three-dimensional work that is difficult to photograph. Videos can also be quite effective in portraying or enhancing an ambiance or mood, and in a very short amount of time provide viewers with a lot of information.

In conjunction with a solo exhibition of paintings at the Schomburg Gallery in Santa Monica,[20] Atanas Karpeles commissioned filmmaker Patricia Cunliffe of Joie de Vivre Productions to produce a video. Although the video is only three minutes and forty-seven seconds long, it is packed full of upbeat material and information capturing the very celebratory atmosphere of the exhibition opening, with close-ups of the artwork, and on-camera statements by Karpeles, his collectors, and art critic Peter Frank. It also includes studio shots of work in progress. The video is linked to the home page of Karpeles's Web site.[21]

Social and Business Network Services

Wikipedia describes the purpose of online social networks as "communities of people who share interests and activities, or who are interested in exploring the interests and activities of others. . . ." They "provide a collection of various ways for users to interact, such as chat, messaging, e-mail, video, voice chat, file sharing, blogging, discussion groups, and so on."[22] Wikipedia also points out that "social networking has revolutionized the way we communicate and share information with one another in today's society. Various social networking websites are being used by millions of people every day on a regular basis."[23]

The online social network phenomenon has evolved not without controversy involving various privacy issues ranging from the harvesting of email addresses from users' email accounts for spamming purposes, which I have personally experienced, and the availability of personal information that is used to the advantage of people with sinister intentions. Much has also been written about the psychological ramifications of online social networking, questioning whether it is *really* "social," suggesting that we are building a new society that lacks the skills to interact face-to-face. Social network sites are also being used by thousands of people for the purpose of reinventing themselves with personal profiles that have absolutely no relationship to reality. On the one hand, fantasy profiles might indicate that they were designed by people with creative minds, but they can also be indicative that there are thousands of people who are very unhappy in their own skins and have taken a passive route to try and make things better.

Although there are many negatives, social network sites have added to the vast dimension of possible uses of the Internet and offer artists creative and pragmatic communication and marketing opportunities.

In 2008 I asked 125 visual artists who subscribe to my newsletter whether anyone was using social networking Web sites as an art marketing tool. Only one person responded to my inquiry, but New York City artist Merrill Kazanjian[24] responded with great enthusiasm and gusto, and provided details of his experiences using MySpace where he subscribes to more than three hundred gallery blogs. "When there are calls for art, I jump on it. This strategy has gotten me in my first gallery."[25]

Kazanjian taught himself how to do animations and created a very humorous video podcast series called "The Art Gallery Alpha Males," which originated as a parody of the New York City art world. He uses MySpace to contact galleries and offers them free advertising in the way of a video critique of the work of gallery artists, using the characters developed in "The Art Gallery Alpha Males" series. The first gallery that he contacted, which was randomly selected, the Art Slave Gallery[26] in Los Angeles, consented to his proposal. One of Kazanjian's goals is to build the "Art Gallery Alpha Males" brand, and in an ironic sort of way, he is using art galleries to achieve what he wants.

A group of artists and art professionals called True Art Professional[27] is registered with the business networking site LinkedIn. Membership categories include fine arts, photography, music, virtual, and entrepreneur. Most of the members are from Europe and the United States. Individual members are required to be LinkedIn members, but they also have direct email access to other members and do not have to go through LinkedIn to contact one another.

Artist Adrienne Fritze of Portland, Oregon, established a page on MySpace for her company Working Artists, LLC, which offers a variety of programs and services. She uses her MySpace page to re-post entries from her blogs.[28] She also posts press releases, exhibition announcements, videos from YouTube, and information from other sources that pertain to artists and performers. In an Internet article titled "How to Use Social Networking Sites to Help Your Business Grow,"[29] Fritze wrote a step-by-step guide for using social network sites and about the various benefits she has derived.

Exhibiting Work on Not-for-Profit Online Galleries

Many state arts commissions and art service organizations have initiated online galleries that encourage potential collectors to contact artists directly. For example, ArtistsRegister.com sponsored by the Western States Arts Foundation (WESTAF) is a juried site that showcases the work of artists who are United States residents. The Ohio Online Visual Artist Registry also features the work of artists throughout the United States. The registry is a joint project of the Ohio Arts Council's Individual Creativity Program and the Humanities, Fine Arts and Recreation Division of the Columbus Metropolitan Library. The Maryland State Arts Council's Visual Artists Registry features the work of more than 2,300 artists in the region. The Pittsburgh Artist Registry, sponsored by the Greater Pittsburgh Arts Council, includes artists in southwestern Pennsylvania.

Not-for-profit art service organizations also sponsor online galleries that are available to members for a fee or free. For example, the American Print Alliance, a nonprofit consortium of printmakers' councils, sponsors an online gallery open to members and subscribers of the publication *Contemporary Impressions*. The Chicago Artists' Coalition offers members access to an online gallery.

Exhibiting Work on For-Profit Online Galleries

For-profit online galleries have various types of fee structures: Some only receive compensation in the form of sales commissions; others charge an annual or monthly fee. There are also some for-profit online galleries that charge an annual or monthly fee *in addition* to receiving a sales commission. Other for-profit online galleries charge a one-time application fee and sales commissions.

Commission-based galleries are either juried or nonjuried.

Although some of the fee-based galleries vow that their sites are also juried, this is questionable. Since the main goal of fee-based galleries is to register as many artists as possible to collect hundreds of monthly or annual fees, with the exception of eliminating artwork that is perceived as pornographic, it is likely that their aesthetic standards are very broad.

The big advantage of using commission-based galleries is that the sponsors of these Web sites have a sales incentive to conduct ongoing advertising campaigns to direct people to their sites. A correlation between successful sales and effective publicity, and press and advertising campaigns is very clear. Commission-based online galleries that held the belief that just being on the Internet was *enough* were short-lived.

A big drawback of participating in fee-based online galleries is that the sponsors are compensated with artists' fees, regardless of whether sales are made or not made. As with vanity galleries (see page 135), fee-based online galleries do not have a sales incentive to spend time and money conducting marketing campaigns on behalf of participating artists.

Sales commissions charged by commission-based online galleries vary, from as little as 20 percent to as much as 60 percent. It would be ill-advised to work with an online gallery that charges more than 50 percent, just as it would be to work with a traditional gallery or art consultant that charges more than 50 percent.

Be careful about working with an online gallery that requires exclusive representation of *all* Internet-exhibited artwork. Some online galleries might consent to having your work exhibited on not-for-profit Web sites as long as commerce is not involved but would require exclusivity for all Internet sales. An online gallery might also perceive a conflict of interest if you are represented by a traditional gallery that features your work on its Web site.

Although you might agree to give an online gallery an exclusive arrangement for a *limited* number of works that are being featured on the gallery's Web site, and for a *limited* amount of time, having all of your work tied up with one online gallery means that you are putting all of your eggs in one basket and receiving little in return. This type of broad-based exclusive arrangement rarely makes sense, regardless of whether you are working with an online gallery or a traditional gallery.

You should be free to work with as many online galleries and traditional galleries as desired. In selecting online galleries, only agree to terms that are in your best interest. You might be willing to agree to a limited type of exclusive arrangement if the sponsor is consistently engaged in advertising and promotion campaigns. Unfortunately, some of the for-profit online galleries were modeled after the greedy philosophy of traditional galleries, offering artists a minimum of services while charging high sales commissions. Examples of for-profit and not-for-profit online galleries are listed in the appendix sections "Online Galleries" and "Artists Registries."

INTERNET MARKETING SERVICES

Using Email for Marketing and Public Relations

The Web sites of some galleries, art consultants, museums, and other exhibition venues post specific instructions about the format of materials they would like to review when considering an artist for representation. This might include, for example, CD-ROMs, JPEG files, and Web sites. On the other hand, as previously mentioned in this chapter (see page 76), many galleries, art consultants, and curators are being flooded with "look at me" emails that call attention to artists' Web sites. Unless you know for sure that *new* contacts are willing to preview your Web site, referenced in emails, the best way to attract people to your Web site is to communicate via snail mail using a brochure (see page 59) or a card (see page 62) accompanied by a cover letter (see page 54).

However, for other types of art marketing projects, emails and email attachments can be effective. Constant Contact is an email marketing service predominantly used by the business world. Clients pay a monthly fee for various email marketing services. Some of the services offered can be adapted for low-key art marketing projects. For example, Constant Contact provides a variety of templates that can be used for press releases, newsletters, invitations, cards, and other communication vehicles. The company also provides mailing list management and delivery services, and tracking and reporting services. According to its Web site Constant Contact, it "employs strict anti-spam policies and procedures and enforces them rigorously."[30]

Even before the advent of email, many of my clients used newsletters as a marketing tool and an effective way to stay in touch with collectors, potential collectors, and other art world contacts. Some newsletters are published annually, quarterly, monthly, or sporadically. In some instances, the newsletters are similar to a blog and contain information about upcoming exhibitions and exhibitions that already took place, work in progress, commissions, new collections, et cetera.

Use of the Internet for press release distribution has gained much momentum because it offers a substantial savings of money on postage and certainly shortens destination arrival time. However, not all members of the press are open to receiving press releases by email. The arts-related press lists that I maintain (see appendix section "Mailing Lists") include email addresses of press contacts that are *willing* to receive a press release via email, although I have observed that some members of the press retract the email offer within a year after experiencing a barrage of press releases. A full discussion of press releases, including content and when to issue a press release, can be found in chapter 6, "Public Relations: Keep Those Cards and Letters Going In and Going Out."

In addition to Constant Contact and other paid services, there are Internet companies that distribute press releases free of charge. These include I-Newswire.com, PR.com, and Free Press Release.com.

For assistance in planning publicity campaigns on the Internet, the following book will be helpful: *The New Rules of Marketing and PR: How to Use News Releases, Blogs, Podcasting, Viral Marketing and Online Media to Reach Buyers Directly* by Steve O'Keefe. (See the appendix section "Internet Art Marketing.")

Print-on-Demand

As pointed out by Ellen Lupton, curator of contemporary art at the Cooper Hewitt National Design Museum, "Self-publishing used to be denigrated as 'vanity press,' but a new generation would rather call it 'independent.' Self-published books are ready to take their place alongside indie music, film, theater, and more."[31]

The self-publishing movement escalated during the 2000s as a result of print-on-demand technology, making it possible for artists and writers to bypass traditional publishing houses to launch projects and get them out into the world. This autonomy affords artists and writers protection from the whims, fads, idiosyncracies, and naysayers of the corporate publishing world.

Print-on-demand technology offers artists the opportunity to publish creative books and art books ranging from paperback publications that can also serve as exhibition catalogs to hardcover "coffee table" books. The technology has also made its ways into the field of artists' books (see page 229), which has a well-established national and international distribution system. Print-on-demand technology has other applications, including calendars, posters, cards, et cetera. Giclée prints (see page 229) is another form of print-on-demand technology.

Artists can use the print-on-demand technology to produce books that are sold through niche market bookstores and museum shops. Books can be sold to corporations for use as executive gifts to business associates. Print-on-demand publications can be sold by museums and galleries in conjunction with exhibitions, and they can be used as gifts to collectors. There are numerous possibilities.

With the advantage of printing on an "as need" basis, print-on-demand technology eliminates the problem of having to pay in advance for large print runs. It also eliminates storage problems. With letterpress and offset printing, the traditional forms of printing, it is cost-prohibitive to print single copies of any type of document because setup costs are much higher than those of print-on-demand technology. Although with print-on-demand, the unit price of each physical copy printed is higher than with offset printing, the average cost is *lower for small print runs*.

Unlike offset printing services, print-on-demand publishers, such as Lulu.com and Blurb.com, also provide distribution channels and marketing support through the Internet. However, it is very much advised that you plan and execute an auxiliary marketing plan and press campaigns even though you are using a print-on-demand service that provides marketing support. For assistance with marketing and publicity ideas, I recommend the book *How to Get Happily Published* by Judith Appelbaum. Although it was written for book projects directed at traditional publishing houses, Appelbaum urges authors to develop marketing and press strategies independent of the publisher. I have been using and recommending the book since 1983 when the first edition of *How to Survive and Prosper as an Artist* was published.

Publications that specifically deal with marketing and publicity for print-on-demand books include *Best in Self-Publishing & Print on Demand* by David Rising and *Aiming at Amazon: The New Business of Self-Publishing, or How to Publish Books for Profit with Print on Demand by Lightning Source and Book Marketing on Amazon.com* by Aaron Shepard, and *Print-on-Demand Book Publishing: A New Approach to Printing and Marketing Books for Publishers and Self-Publishing Authors* by Morris Rosenthal.

For additional resources pertaining to various topics addressed in this chapter, see the appendix section "Internet Art Marketing."

5

Pricing Your Work:
How Much Is It Worth?

Within the same week, two artists called me for appointments. Marsha was in her forties and had a successful career as a real estate agent, but planned to leave her job to paint full-time. She arranged to have a one-day weekend exhibition at a suburban library located outside of New York. In one afternoon she sold $18,000 worth of work. The highest-priced painting sold for $6,000. Prior to the library show, she had never had an exhibition or sold work.

Katherine was also in her forties, but had worked full-time as an artist for more than twenty years. She had exhibited in many well-known museums and was represented by galleries on the East and West Coasts. She had received grants and fellowships from federal and state agencies and private foundations. Her work had been reviewed in leading American and international arts magazines. Katherine's paintings ranged in price from $5,000 to $7,500.

Why is an artist new to the art world and without art-world recognition able to sell work in the same price range as an established artist whose six-page résumé is filled with impressive credentials?

Marsha brought to her new career the philosophy and concerns she had learned in the business world. She recognized the value of her time and valued her talent. Her goal was clear: to derive a decent income from doing what she liked doing best. It was inconsequential whether her work found a home on the walls of a museum or over a living-room couch. Unlike Katherine, she was naive about the criteria used by the art world in pricing work. In this case, ignorance was definitely bliss!

Fear-based thinking is responsible for the difficulties artists have in establishing prices for their work. Establishing prices for artwork in which you compensate yourself fairly has everything to do with self-confidence and a willingness to defend your prices and take some risks.

In the book *Creating a Life Worth Living,* author Carol Lloyd asks readers to "consider for a moment the positive aspects of doing work you love and value in return for fair compensation. Money, when coupled with genuine interest, can give you permission to do something well. In fact, it often *demands* that you do."[1] Lloyd also points out:

> The transition from being a wage slave (making money from things you don't like to do) to a self-employed creative person (making money from things you love to do) is the most difficult transition for many people to make. Exiled from the small, protected space of a conventional job, it's often hard to comprehend the expansiveness of the new terrain. Just as chemicals in the brain block perception to prevent sensory overload, you may unknowingly avoid the idea of earning a living from your creative work as a way of defending yourself against the vertigo of possibilities.[2]

CONFLICTING AGENDAS AND CONFLICTING ADVICE

Setting a price on a work can be a grueling task. Many artists tend to undervalue their work, with the belief that their careers haven't measured up to the criteria necessary to justify charging higher prices or a fear that, by setting prices that compensate them fairly, their work will not sell. Unfortunately, these myths are reinforced by some artist career advisors and the advice contained in artist career management books. But when artists set low prices on their artwork, it is a public declaration of their insecurities and lack of confidence.

The tendency of advising artists to sell work at low prices is also reinforced by dealers and art consultants whose pricing agendas are rarely in an artist's best interest. Unfortunately, the "price low philosophy" is embraced by many academics, art marketing and art business advisors, and artist career coaches, who might be well-intentioned but in actuality perpetuate a long-standing myth that equates low prices with high sales volume.

Some artists who have the courage to establish prices that correspond to *fair compensation* versus slave labor compensation can become unnerved by reactions to their *healthy* prices by members of the public and other artists. Often members of the public and artists convey either verbally or through body language "Who does he think he is?"

One of my clients experienced this type of episode. She had a solo exhibition at a college gallery. The show was hung with the assistance of a lab assistant who worked for the college for many years. The lab assistant complimented the artist on her artwork. She also received kudos from a department secretary and a slide librarian. However, the attitude of all three staff members immediately changed when they inquired about the artist's prices. In defense of the prices, the artist volunteered that I had helped her establish a price list. The librarian requested my email address (I assume for the purpose of asking "Who do you think you are?" but she did not contact me).

The same day the artist attended the opening of another exhibition at the college where the lab assistant joked in front of the artist's colleagues that her work was "terribly overpriced." The comment threw the artist off guard, putting her in a defensive position, and she attempted to justify herself. But when she returned home that evening, although she was sorry that she had felt obligated to explain and defend herself, she was not sorry about her prices. She sent me an email telling me about the incident and said: "They can talk all they want behind my back—even that doesn't matter much to me anymore. Impressing the department secretary, slide librarian, or lab assistant is not my goal, and I am not holding a gun to anyone's head to buy anything either."

A primary concern of many dealers is to move work quickly, and, unfortunately, low prices are correlated with making a fast buck. The pricing policies of the majority of dealers basically reflect the amount of money *they think* their constituencies will spend on art.

One of my clients received an email from an art dealer requesting a price list so that she would "be able to consider your work in all its context. I have to see if the price you ask is in accordance with the quality of the work and with your artist's curriculum vitae." In addition to putting herself in a position of authority, reading between the lines, the dealer was also telling my client that she wants to know whether his prices coincide with what her clients will pay—and in case they don't, she will attack his résumé, and tell him that he does not have enough credentials to warrant the prices he is charging.

Few dealers understand that they could sell more work, and at higher prices, if they took the time to help the public understand an artist's vision and the multilayered process and rigorous discipline involved in creating visual art—from conceptualization to actualization.

Most dealers establish a price range based on the hearsay of other dealers or fall into the trap of believing the myth that the work of unknown artists has little value. Reluctant to move out of established parameters, few dealers will admit that they are vying for a particular price market. They camouflage the "fast buck" philosophy and adherence to a pricing system based on the status quo by using various gimmicks aimed at undermining an artist's work and/or career. For example, there is the scenario described above when an artist is told that his or her résumé does not have the "right" credentials to justify selling work at a higher price. Or the work is attacked on the basis of size, materials, or subject matter. One of the typical ploys used to weaken an artist's self-confidence is an accusation that the work is derivative.

More often than not, artists heed a dealer's self-serving pricing advice, erroneously believing that dealers know best.

PRAGMATIC PRICING, MARKET VALUES, AND SELF-CONFIDENCE

Setting a price on artwork necessitates homework. You need to consider and integrate three factors: *pragmatic pricing,* understanding how much it is really costing you to create a work of art; *market value* considerations; and *confidence* in the price you set. Self-confidence is of paramount importance if you hope to get what you want and negotiate with strength.

You can achieve pragmatic pricing by maintaining careful records and keeping tabs on the amount of time you spend creating work, from conceptualization through development to completion. Pragmatic pricing must also include the cost of overhead and materials, prorated accordingly.

For example, if work-related costs, such as studio rental, utilities, professional fees, transportation, dues and publications, postage, documentation, and materials, total $10,000 per year, and you create an average of fifteen pieces of work each year, the overhead expense per work is approximately $667.

In many instances, after determining the costs of time, overhead, and materials and comparing the proceeds of a sale, artists discover they are working for less than a dollar an hour!

The process of determining overhead can be simplified by including in the equation only art supplies, art materials, and art production costs (e.g., foundry fees, digital scans, other printing costs, et cetera). After calculating an overhead cost per piece, assign an hourly value to your time and estimate an *average* number of hours it takes to create a piece. For example, if it required twenty hours and you want to be paid $50 an hour, assign a labor charge of $1,000. Total the overhead cost and labor cost. In the examples cited above, the total cost of overhead and labor costs is $1,667.

At this point, the size (or sizes) of your artwork becomes an important factor. *All work should be priced the same if they are of the same size and in the same medium.* Many artists make the mistake of setting prices based on subjective criteria such as how much they like each piece. However, this type of pricing system can easily backfire. For example, if you are charging $5,000 for a painting that is 36 by 48 and $6,000 for another of the same size and medium, a price discrepancy can easily undermine the confidence of a potential collector who might like the lower-priced painting best but because it costs less, makes an assumption that the higher-priced painting is a *better* painting. Once a potential collector begins to lose confidence in his or her "taste," it is almost a sure bet that you will also lose a sale.

Devising a price list based on square inches or cubic inches sounds crass, but it can make the task of pricing work easier. The following are some guidelines in using a square-inch pricing formula:

To ensure that you are *not* paying a sales commission to art dealers for labor costs and overhead costs, the price set for your work should include a 100 percent markup. Therefore, using the above example, when the amount of $1,667 is doubled, the minimum selling price of the painting becomes $3,334. A painting that is 36 by 48 has 1,728 square inches (multiply 36 by 48). To determine the square-inch value of a painting with 1,728 square inches, and using $3,334 as a *minimum* selling price, divide 1,728 square inches into $3,334. The painting has a per-square-inch value of $1.93.

Although a square-inch value of $1.93 can sometimes be used to establish a *minimally acceptable* price for some paintings that are smaller or larger than 1,728 inches, if there is a substantial change in the size of paintings the formula will throw prices out of whack, creating prices that are way too low or much too high. When this happens, to counteract the dilemma, assign a flexible square-inch-value system so that paintings with fewer square inches have a higher square-inch value and paintings with more square inches have a lower square-inch value. For example, paintings that are 144 square inches might be priced at $7.64 per square inch; paintings that are 1,728 square inches might be priced at $1.93 per square inch.

If you are selling work through an art dealer and are using minimally acceptable selling prices, you are being compensated only for labor and overhead costs. If the work sells through your studio, you are being compensated for labor and overhead costs as well as receiving a profit.

Set prices that build in a profit margin, regardless of whether you sell through a dealer. The amount of profit is a personal decision and should have some relationship to the art market, although art market values are elusive and include an abundance of illogical rules and regulations.

You can determine a seemingly elusive market value by visiting many galleries, finding work that is allied to your own, looking at prices and the artists' résumés, and comparing their career levels to your own. But keep in mind that *other artists' price ranges should serve only as guidelines, not as gospel, because many artists make the mistake of letting dealers determine the value of their work.*

Knowing the amount of labor, materials, and overhead spent on creating work and becoming familiar with market values can help you build confidence for establishing prices. But, of course, the process of gaining self-confidence is quickly accelerated when work is sold at the price you want.

On several occasions I have assisted artists in negotiating prices with dealers. In one case, although a dealer thought the artist was overcharging, the artist would not budge from her position. The dealer passed, only to return to the artist's studio six months later with a client who paid the original asking price.

I also advise artists to set a value a few hundred dollars over the price they actually want. This way there is bargaining leverage and dealers believe they are participating in pricing decisions.

NO MORE REGIONAL PRICING

Artists sometimes wonder if they should charge certain prices in large cities but lower the prices if the work is shown in the boondocks. The answer is an emphatic no. Regional pricing is insulting. It penalizes your market in large cities and patronizes your market elsewhere. It also supports elitist notions that people in small cities or rural areas are incapable of valuing art.

The chances are, if you are an artist in a rural area or small city and are affiliated with a local gallery, you have been persuaded to price work at what the dealer thinks the local market will bear. If you also connect with a gallery in Chicago, for example, make sure the prices in the local gallery are in accord with what the dealer in Chicago is charging. Prices must be universally consistent, whether your work is sold in Vienna, Virginia, or Vienna, Austria.

DEVELOPING PRICE LISTS

When assembling a price list, *always* state the retail price, and make sure the word *retail* appears on the price sheet. The danger in stating a "wholesale price" or "artist's price" is that it gives dealers carte blanche to price your work in any way they see fit. The "wholesale price" is construed as an artist's bottom line, and many dealers feel justified in selling work for as much as several hundred percent above the wholesale price and pocketing the difference. This happened to an artist who signed a consignment agreement with a gallery in New York that required artists to state their wholesale prices. The gallery sold a sculpture for $25,000. The artist received $2,500! The transaction was completely legitimate because the artist stated in writing a wholesale price of $2,500.

Another problem with wholesale pricing is that it prevents artists from establishing a *real* market value. For example, if you are using wholesale prices and have relationships with more than one gallery or art consultant, it is highly conceivable that your work will sell for vastly different prices in different cities or within the same city.

When establishing a retail price, assume a dealer will take a 50 percent commission. Do not adjust the retail price if a dealer's commission is lower. Do not work with dealers who require a commission higher than 50 percent.

A price list should state the name of the artwork, medium, size, and retail price. A dealer's commission is generally based on a percentage of the retail price. However, in some instances it is imperative that large overhead expenses are separated out on the price list so that an art dealer or consultant is not paid a commission on your overhead. When fabrication or production costs are high, these costs must be deducted before a dealer's commission is calculated (see page 97). This "understanding" should not be left to an oral agreement. It must be stated in a contract (see page 32).

For example, some forms of sculpture involve expensive foundry fees. One pricing solution is to set a retail price on a piece by multiplying the foundry costs by three, with the gallery receiving one-third. Gallery dealers who are experienced in selling sculpture have no problem accepting this formula. Dealers and consultants who are not experienced create problems when they insist on receiving a commission based on 40–50 percent of the retail price.

For photographers, laboratory processing fees can be high. Dealers knowledgeable about photography take these high overhead fees into consideration and accept a commission based on the retail price of a print less overhead. But more often one encounters dealers who balk at this proposal. For example, a photographer submitted a detailed price list that separated out his overhead costs for various-sized color prints. He outlined the consultant's commission after the overhead costs were deducted from the retail price. When she saw that her 50 percent commission was not based on the retail price, she threw a tantrum. After she cooled down, the artist explained that his lab fee on a 72-by-96-inch color print was $1,000. The retail price of the photograph was $6,000. If he agreed to give her 50 percent of the retail price, she would receive $3,000, the lab would receive $1,000, and he would receive $2,000. The consultant finally understood the logic of why a traditional commission based on the retail price would not be equitable.

For artwork that has a high overhead, a special type of price list is required. In such instances, a suggested price-list format follows:

Artist's Name
Retail Price List and Commission Policy
Medium: Color Photographs

Title	Size	Lab Fees	Base Price*	Retail Price
Untitled 1	40"x60"	$350	$1,950	$2,300
Untitled 2	48"x60"	$400	$2,300	$2,700
Untitled 3	72"x96"	$1,000	$5,000	$6,000
Untitled 4	72"x180"	$1,800	$8,400	$10,200

*Commissions are paid on base price.

A price list can also state your discount policy. Guidelines for developing a discount policy are described in the following section.

DEVELOPING A DISCOUNT POLICY

Shortly after beginning a consignment relationship with a gallery, an artist named Steven was informed by the dealer that a client was interested in buying one of his paintings. The client had previously purchased work from the gallery, and the dealer offered a 20 percent discount, which she asked Steven to split.

New to the gallery world, Steven was unfamiliar with discounts, an issue that had not been addressed in a consignment agreement issued by the gallery. Steven was confused and talked to a friend with more gallery experience. The friend confirmed that artist/gallery discount splits are usual occurrences.

Steven complied with the dealer's request. The painting was sold and he received a check equaling 40 percent of the retail price—the dealer had deducted a 50 percent commission and another 10 percent that represented Steven's share of the discount.

Many artists split discounts without analyzing what discounts actually symbolize or represent. For a gallery, the main purpose of giving discounts to a collector is to reward loyalty and patronage, and to create an incentive for the collector to remain a client. As a token of gratitude, awarding a discount is a public-relations gesture. But is it logical or ethical for artists to be required to share or absorb public-relations expenses of a gallery, and if so, under what circumstances?

Steven was a new gallery artist, and the discount he allowed was a public-relations token that directly rewarded the collector's *previous* patronage of the gallery and of *other* gallery artists. How would Steven have responded if he had been required to contribute 10 percent of the painting's sale price toward exhibition announcements for other gallery artists, or toward a generic brochure tooting the horn of the gallery?

If the 50 percent commission charged by most dealers can in any way be justified, this hefty amount provides a very adequate cushion that enables dealers to offer clients discounts without infringing on an artist's profit. It also provides enough flexibility for dealers to split commissions with art consultants and interior designers.

The time to discuss discount splitting is *before* beginning a gallery relationship. This means *before* any work enters the gallery for exhibition and/or consignment and *before* an agreement has been signed. If a dealer insists on splitting all discounts, you have the option of not working with the gallery or suggesting a compromise of splitting discounts only if (1) the client has previously purchased *your* work and/or (2) the client is simultaneously purchasing more than one piece of *your* work. If a dealer is in agreement with this arrangement, it *must* be stated in writing.

Some dealers have been known to deduct a discount from an

artist's share of a sale when in actuality a discount has not been given. A step in the right direction to protect yourself from this situation is to require a copy of a bill of sale or invoice or use an artist sales contract. As I mention in chapter 8, "Dealing with Dealers and Psyching Them Out," there really isn't a foolproof way of shielding yourself from art dealer fraud. But one sure way to begin to protect yourself is to *make the decision not to work with art dealers that do not provide a bill of sale or sales documentation*. An artist sales contract is a contract between an artist and a collector that not only covers important copyright issues but also states the purchase price of the artwork. Examples of a bill of sale, an invoice, and an artist sales contract can be found in *The Artists' Survival Manual* by Toby Judith Klayman, with Cobbett Steinberg. The forms are also included in the following books by Tad Crawford and are available as tearout sheets and on a CD-ROM: *Business and Legal Forms for Crafts, Business and Legal Forms for Fine Artists, Business and Legal Forms for Illustrators,* and *Business and Legal Forms for Photographers*. These resources are listed in the appendix section under "Law: Contracts and Business Forms."

Of course, an unscrupulous dealer overpowered by greed can always find ways of deceiving both artists and clients even when a sales contract or bill of sale has been used. Once the deed is discovered, however, it is much easier to go to court with a good contract in hand than with a handshake or spoken understanding.

Discounts on Studio Sales

Awarding discounts on studio sales is another issue about which there is much confusion. Over the years a strange protocol has developed according to which artists are *expected* to offer clients a 50 percent discount on work sold from their studios. It is one of those chicken-or-egg situations: which came first, artists volunteering a 50 percent discount or clients demanding a 50 percent discount because the artwork was not being sold in a gallery or through an agent? Regardless of how this precedent started, it should be abolished with haste.

When a studio sale is imminent, it is easy for an artist, seduced by the excitement of the moment, to abandon powers of logic and reason and succumb to some rather unreasonable requests concerning the terms of a sale, such as granting a large discount. To avoid being caught off guard, vulnerable, or tongue-tied, always keep a price list on hand that states *retail* prices and your *discount policy*. For example, your policy could be the same as that offered to dealers: 10 percent if more than one piece of work is simultaneously purchased, and 10 percent for clients who have previously purchased work.

Or you can give discounts based on a sliding scale according to the retail value, say, 10 percent for work priced up to $2,000 and 15 percent thereafter. Or you can have a policy of offering no discounts under any circumstances!

A discount range of 10 to 15 percent provides the flexibility needed to negotiate with clients who insist on a larger discount. Whether or not you acquiesce is a personal decision, but studio discounts should not exceed 25 percent.

Clients who expect a 50 percent discount on studio sales and balk at a lower rate need to be reminded that artists have overhead expenses just like all other businesspeople—and just like art dealers. Consequently, granting discounts of 50 percent is unrealistic and impracticable.

Unfortunately, within the art world, guidelines regarding discounts do not exist. Much of the time, dealers' policies are based on hearsay or greed, and artists' policies are manifestations of confusion and feelings of powerlessness.

Set the same high standards for pricing work as you do for creating the work. Do not be afraid to negotiate. The extent to which you compromise is a personal decision and greatly depends on the status of your ego and bank account, and how well you are able to exercise powers of logic.

Odds and Ends

Questions regarding pricing also arise when artists are presented with opportunities to have photographs of their work used in periodicals, annual reports, books, posters, calendars, and other print media. *Pricing Photography: The Complete Guide to Assignment & Stock Prices* by Michal Heron and David MacTavish is an excellent resource for establishing prices for a multitude of situations. Although it is geared for photographers, art directors, and graphic designers, the book can be very helpful to fine artists for establishing prices and fees for various circumstances when a photograph of their artwork is used for commercial purposes.

Closely aligned to the subject of pricing are commissions paid to dealers for the sale of work. This topic is discussed in chapter 8, "Dealing with Dealers and Psyching Them Out." Resources for additional information about pricing can be found in the appendix section "Pricing Artwork."

6

Public Relations: Keep
Those Cards and Letters
Coming In and Going Out

In 2007, Shelly Bancroft and Peter Nesbett, copublishers of the magazine *Art on Paper* and codirectors of the alternative space Triple Candie in Harlem, New York, issued a press release announcing a solo exhibition of the work of Lester Hayes:

> Lester Hayes (1936–2004) is an American artist of African descent who was a vital force in the downtown New York art scene during the 1960s and early 1970s. Working primarily in sculpture and installation, Hayes pioneered a form of racially conscious abstraction. . . . The fact that Hayes' work has remained unknown is in no small part due to his disappearance from the New York art scene in the mid-1970s when he took a teaching position at Carnegie Mellon University in Pittsburgh. Friends and colleagues describe his departure as fueled by disappointment at the lack of critical and commercial interest in his work.[1]

The press release concluded with the surprising information: "Note: The artist Lester Hayes is a fictitious creation of Triple Candie. When the exhibition closes, all the 'artworks' will be destroyed, never to be recreated."[2]

Although the text of the press release did not provide an explanation of why Bancroft and Nesbett mounted an exhibition by a fictitious artist, the show generated a "buzz." The press release resulted in articles that analyzed and interpreted the purpose and meaning of the show. Press coverage was extensive and included national publications, blogs, and art-related and non-art-related Web sites.

Although more and more artists have come to understand the importance of publicity and self-promotion, in some circles it is still considered controversial. Some artists are offended by self-promotion because they believe it taints their work and self-image. Others are offended by some forms of publicity but accept other forms that they consider in good taste. Still others are averse to publicity only because they are not receiving it. And some artists are offended by self-generated publicity but do not question publicity generated by an art gallery, museum, or organization on their behalf. Often, in such cases, an artist does not believe that the gallery, museum, or organization is doing enough.

Writer Daniel Grant gives two perspectives on the publicity issue:

> Publicity has become a staple in the art world, affecting how artists see themselves and how dealers work. On its good side, this publicity has attracted increasing numbers of people to museums and galleries to see what all of the hullabaloo is about and, consequently, expanded the market for works of art. More artists are able to live off their work and be socially accepted for what they are and do.
>
> On the other hand, it has made the appreciation of art a bit shallower by seeming to equate financial success with artistic importance. At times, publicity becomes the art itself, with the public knowing that it should appreciate some work because "it's famous," rather than because it's good, distorting the entire experience of art.[3]

The questions that Grant raises about what constitutes art appreciation and good art and what distorts the art experience have been asked for hundreds of years, many years before the great media explosion came into being. They are questions that will continue to be debated and discussed, within the context of publicity and without. In the meantime, this chapter will discuss basic public-relations tools and vehicles for developing an ongoing public-relations program for your career.

Public appearances, demonstrations, and lectures are vehicles that offer excellent exposure and can also provide income. They are discussed in chapter 10, "Generating Income: Alternatives to Driving a Cab."

THE PRESS RELEASE

A press release should be written and used to announce and describe anything newsworthy. The problem, however, is that many artists are too humble or too absorbed with aesthetic problems or the bumps of daily living to recognize what about themselves is newsworthy, or they view the media as an inaccessible planet that grants visas only to famous artists.

A press release should be issued when you receive a prize, honor, award, grant, or fellowship. It should be issued if you sell your work to an important local, regional, national, or international collector. Use a press release to announce an exhibition, regardless of whether it is a single show in a church basement or a retrospective at the Whitney Museum or a group exhibition where you are one of two or one of one hundred participants. A press release should be issued to announce a slide and lecture show, demonstration, performance, or event. It should also be issued to announce a commission and the completion of a commission.

A press release should also be issued if you have a new idea. New ideas are a dime a dozen, particularly if you keep them to yourself. What might seem humdrum to you could be fascinating to an editor, a journalist, a host of a radio or television interview program, or a filmmaker looking for a subject. Personality profiles also make their way into the news.

Internal Press Releases

A press release has many uses. It *does not have to be published to generate a response.* In some instances, distributing a press release to friends, acquaintances, collectors and potential collectors, gallery dealers, art consultants, and curators is more appropriate than sending it to the press. I refer to this type of press release as an *internal* press release. Events that might warrant the publication of an internal press release include the announcement of an award or honor, a public or corporate commission, acceptance as an artist-in-residence or at an art colony, and sale of work to a public or corporate collection.

Although the press might not consider any of these events newsworthy, an internal press release can be of interest to others. For example, an internal press release can lead to an invitation from a curator to participate in an upcoming theme show, or it can generate a response from an art consultant interested in commissioning you for a project. This internal use of a press release can bring tangible and intangible rewards by reminding people that you exist and that your career is moving forward.

Why Bother?

Press releases can lead to articles about you. Articles can help make your name a household word, or at least provide greater recognition. Articles can lead to sales and commissions. Articles can lead to invitations to participate in exhibitions or performances, and to speaking engagements. Articles can help you to obtain fellowships, grants, honors, and awards.

Keep in mind that recipients of a press release should not be limited to national art trade publications. Certain consumer publications, television and radio programs, Web sites and blogs should also be included in your mailing list.

Resources for obtaining arts press and consumer press mailing lists are included in the appendix sections "Mailing Lists" and "Press Relations and Publicity." In addition, you can use a press release distribution service. For example, I-Newswire.com, PR.com, and Free Press Release.com are free email press release distribution services. Contact information about these services are included in the appendix section "Press Relations and Publicity."

Press releases that I wrote and distributed concerning some of my own projects generated an interview on *Bloomberg Radio News* and led to articles in the *New York Times,* the *Washington Post, Life, House and Garden, Playboy, Metropolis, New York* magazine, the *Crafts Report,* and the *Village Voice,* and syndicated articles in more than one hundred newspapers throughout the United States (via the Associated Press and United Press International). In Europe, my press releases generated articles in the *International Herald Tribune,*

Paris Match, Der Spiegel, Casabella, and *Domus.* These articles then generated invitations to exhibit at museums and cultural centers throughout the United States and in Europe. In addition, some articles led directly to commissions and sales.

Prior to the advent of the Internet, to keep track of whether your press release generated press coverage, it was necessary to use a press monitoring service known as a clipping bureau. Today, search engines provide this service.

Dos and Don'ts

A press release should whet the appetite of the reader, inspire a critic to visit the show, inspire an editor to assign a writer to the story, inspire a writer to initiate an article, inspire television and radio stations to provide coverage and interviews, and get dealers, curators, collectors, influential people, and the general public to see the exhibition or event.

The fact that an exhibition or event is taking place is not necessarily newsworthy. What the viewer will see and who is exhibiting can be. A press release should contain a *handle,* a two-sentence summary that puts the story in the right perspective. A handle does not necessarily have to have an aesthetic or intellectual theme. It can be political, ethnic, scientific, technological, historical, humorous, and so on. Editors and writers are often lazy or unimaginative about developing handles. Give them some help.

Although a reporter might not want to write an article exclusively about you or your show, your handle might trigger a general article in which you are mentioned.

Press releases have an amazing longevity. Writers tend to keep subject files for future story ideas. Although your release could be filed away when it is received, it could be stored in a subject file for future use. My releases have resulted in articles or mentions in books as much as six years after they were issued!

If writing is not your forte, do not write a press release. Get someone to do it who is good with words, understands the concept of handles, likes your work, and finds the experience of writing in your behalf enjoyable. *You serve as editor.* Too often artists are so excited about a press release that they relinquish control of its content and let a description pass that understates or misinterprets their intentions. On its own, the press has a field day in this area. It does not need any encouragement.

Many artists believe that they do not have anything to say. Use a press release to articulate your thoughts about your work and motivations (see "Artist Statements," page 53). Learning to do so is particularly useful for preparing grant applications and for face-to-face encounters with people who are in a position to advance your career. It is also a good way to prepare for interviews.

A press release should be written in an appropriate journalistic style so that it can be published verbatim. In fact, many press releases that meet professional standards are published word-for-word in newspapers and magazines and on Web sites. "Meeting professional standards" means that your press release is grammatically correct and contains no spelling or typographical errors. It should be free of critical content or boastful prose about your work. Although it is completely acceptable to include a quote or quotes from critics and art-world personalities that praise your talents, this type of information should appear *in quotation marks* along with the name of the quoted source. Do not list the artists that have influenced your work. Naming names distracts from you and leaves yourself wide open to be accused of creating derivative artwork. A press release should also be free of flat sentences that are empty in content such as the popular phrase that all too often appears at the very beginning of some press releases: "The Ajax Gallery is pleased to present the work of John Doe." And as a courtesy, a press release should be double-spaced so that, if necessary, it can be easily edited if the release is being submitted by snail mail versus email (see page 110).

Do not use a press release to exercise your closet ego or show off your academic vocabulary. Who wants to read a press release with a dictionary in hand? Avoid using art criticism jargon and long sentences that take readers on a wild-goose chase. Writing over the heads of readers is guaranteed to breed intimidation. This kind of release ends up being filed under "confusion"—in the wastebasket. Here is an example:

> The . . . exhibition presents the work of six differently motivated artists. . . . They each arrive at their own identity through an approach based on the dynamic integration inherent in the act of

synthesis, synthesis being the binding factor which deals compre-
hensively with all the other elements involved in the creative
process, leading ideally to an intuitively orchestrated wholeness
which informs both the vision and the process.[4]

What to Include

The headline of the release should capture the handle and announce
the show, award, commission, or event.

The average arts-related press release that I receive is destined for
the wastebasket because it loses my attention in the first paragraph.
For example: "A group exhibition featuring the work of sixteen
abstract artists opens at Highgate Gallery on June 1, 2009. The
exhibition features paintings, drawings, and sculpture." Although
this opening paragraph provides basic information, it does not spur
interest in attending the show, except perhaps for the sixteen artists'
parents, relatives, and friends.

The first paragraph should contain the handle; use strong sentences that capture reader interest. For example:

> They are dark, dangerous places where you are warned not to
> go. But for photographer Xavier Nuez, bleak urban settings are
> his inspiration and second home. For many years late at night he
> has ventured into some of the country's most threatening corners
> that frequently lead to trouble. Whether it is an eerie alley in
> Compton, California, an inner-city ruin in Detroit, or a dead-end
> backlot in Brooklyn, his pilgrimage has a purpose.[5]

> Do you think you can tell the difference between a photograph
> and thousands of pieces of fabric and paper? Wife and husband
> team Laura Breitman and Michael Needleman collaborated on
> their first joint exhibition entitled "Seeing Double," which opens
> June 1, 2008, at the Port of Call Gallery in Warwick, New York.
> For ten years, Needleman has been taking photographs of the
> Hudson Valley, imagery that Breitman uses as models for her real-
> istic collages. When viewed close up, the tiny hand-cut compo-
> nents of the collage can clearly be seen. As viewers back away, the
> photograph and collage appear so alike it's like seeing double.[6]

> From a distance it looks like a huge floral-patterned Cinderella
> gown—but upon closer look it is a sculpture with flowering vines

growing over a welded steel surface. Look longer and one can see an image of a cat's head in the bodice area—eyes and ears in strategic garment areas. The sculpture titled *Big Dress* is the work of artist Leslie Fry and is currently on loan to the Gulf Museum of Art in Pinewood Cultural Park.[7]

The lead or second paragraph should also contain information known in journalism as the "five Ws": who, what, when, where, why, and sometimes how.

Subsequent paragraphs should back up the first paragraph. They should contain quotes from the artist and, when possible, from critics, writers, curators, and others. Let them toot your horn.

A short biography should also be included (see "Biographies," page 52). The biography should highlight important credits such as collections, prizes, awards, fellowships, exhibitions, and other significant accomplishments. In addition, it can mention where you were born and/or where you went to school.

Press Release Letterhead

When possible, a press release should be issued by the sponsor of your exhibition, event, prize, award, or commission. If the sponsor routinely issues press releases, provide the sponsor with resource materials including an artist statement (see page 53), a biography, a résumé (see page 44), and, if available, press excerpts about your work (see page 52). If the press release focuses on an upcoming exhibition, provide a description of the work that will be included in the show. If the press release focuses on a commission, provide a description of the project. Ask the sponsor to provide you with a draft of the press release before it is issued.

However, if the sponsor does not issue press releases, request permission to use its letterhead with an understanding that the sponsor can approve the final copy. The release should include, as a courtesy, a paragraph about the sponsoring organization or gallery—for example, a historical sketch and a description of its activities or purpose.

If the sponsor does not have a qualified person to handle public relations, provide your name and home telephone number and identify yourself as the press contact. To determine whether the sponsor's public-relations representative is qualified, use the following criteria: the person is willing to cooperate and is not threatened by your aggressive pursuit of good press coverage; you have a good rapport with the person; and he or she *really* understands your work.

   If you are unable to use the sponsor's letterhead, issue a press release using your own stationery, and identify yourself as the press contact.

Visual Support Materials

When announcing an exhibition, installation, commission, or an award for a particular piece of artwork, a photograph or photographs should be included with the press release. Visual support materials are equally as important as a press release, and sometimes more important, in winning the interest of the press. When a press release is distributed by snail mail or email (see below), photographs can be scanned directly on to the press release. Or when a press release is distributed by email, photographs can be submitted as an attachment.

Listing Releases

Many publications offer a free-listings section. A special release should be written for these publications and a listings release should be sent to the attention of each publication's listing editor. Free-listings columns use very few words to announce an exhibition or event. Therefore, your release should contain the basic who, what, where, and when information. Why and how can be included if you can succinctly explain the information in one or two short sentences. Otherwise, the description will not be used.

Snail Mail Versus Email

Some members of the press prefer to receive press releases by email; others insist on snail mail. The various press lists that I make available (see the appendix section "Mailing Lists") provide email addresses for each person who prefers to receive correspondence electronically. If you do not know a person's preference, send the press release and visual support materials by snail mail.

Press Kits

A press kit is similar to presentation packages that are described in chapter 3 (beginning on page 44). *A press kit should not be sent to everyone on your press list.* It should be sent to a select group of prime press contacts. It can also be used to fulfill requests for support materials from members of the press.

A traditional press kit consists of a package of material that is enclosed in a sturdy folder with pockets. It includes, for example, a biography; a glossy 5-by-7 or 8-by-10 photograph of the artist with caption and photo credit; a glossy 5-by-7 or 8-by-10 photograph or photographs of your artwork with captions and photo credits; if available, a brochure (see page 59); copies of articles by you or about you; copies of reviews that you have received; a quote sheet with press excerpts; and a business card.

You can also use a CD-ROM as a press kit and include, for example, a biography; a photograph of the artist with caption and photo credit; photographs of your artwork with captions and photo credits; copies of articles by you or about you; copies of reviews that you have received; and a quote sheet with press excerpts. In addition to a CD-ROM, the package should include a business card and, if available, a brochure (see page 59).

A press kit is a flexible tool that can be adapted for many purposes. For example, it can be used to publicize an exhibition, performance, or commissioned project. It can also be used to publicize a lecture series or workshop (see page 227). If a press kit is being used to publicize a particular event, it should include a press release (see page 104) devoted to that event. The press release can also be used to help generate a feature article about you and your work.

If the press kit is being used to generate publicity about a particular event or if it is being used to generate interest in a feature article about you and your work, it should be accompanied by a special cover letter known as a "pitch letter" (see page 112).

Other Types of Press Packages

Most of the names on your mailing list should receive a basic promotion package that contains an exhibition announcement and a press release. Although many artists only send out an exhibition announcement, accompanying it with a press release is very important, particularly when contacting people who are unfamiliar with your work.

The basic press package can be enhanced and customized for specific markets. For example, along with the press release and exhibition announcement, you might want to send photographs and/or a brochure (see pages 56–64) to a select group of critics and curators.

Pitch Letters

Pitch letters are easier to compose after a press release has been written because it can incorporate the "handle" (see page 108) that has been prepared for the press release. To illustrate this point, excerpts from a press release succeeded by a pitch letter follow:

"CHOCOLATE THROUGHOUT THE LAND!"
FEATURING ARTIST PETER ANTON
OPENS AT THE BRUCE R. LEWIN GALLERY,
NEW YORK CITY

The United States ranks 10th in chocolate consumption with the average American consuming approximately ten pounds a year. Artist Peter Anton's passion for chocolate far exceeds the national average. Through his sculptures he pays homage to his addiction by dedicating his next one-person exhibition to "the food of the gods" at the Bruce R. Lewin Gallery in Manhattan. Entitled CHOCOLATE THROUGHOUT THE LAND! the exhibition opens April 26.

"Chocolate is rich in taste and equally rich in history," said Anton, pointing out that the Aztec Emperor Montezuma drank 50 goblets of cocoa a day. Louis XIV discovered chocolate when he was given a wedding gift of cocoa imported from Mexico. He was so enthusiastic he created the official court position of "Chocolate Maker to the King."

"CHOCOLATE THROUGHOUT THE LAND!" will present a selection of familiar chocolate forms that are sculpturally interpreted with ceramic-like plaster material. It will include giant boxes of assorted chocolates, approximately 4′ x 3′ x 9″. The character and properties of each boxed chocolate are portrayed in Anton's sculptures. Some of the candies are randomly pinched or bitten open to reveal various centers including creams, nuts, jellies, and caramels.[8]

The following is a pitch letter that evolved from the press release:

Dear (name of editor):

The United States ranks 10th in chocolate consumption with the average American consuming approximately ten pounds a year. My passion for chocolate far exceeds the national average. I am an artist and through my sculptures I pay homage to my addiction by dedicating my one-person exhibition at the Bruce R. Lewin Gallery in Manhattan to "the food of the gods." Entitled CHOCOLATE THROUGHOUT THE LAND! I believe the exhibition will be of interest to your readers.

Chocolate is rich in taste and equally rich in history. For example, the Aztec Emperor Montezuma drank 50 goblets of cocoa a day. Louis XIV discovered chocolate when he was given a wedding gift of cocoa imported from Mexico. He was so enthusiastic he created the official court position of "Chocolate Maker to the King."

"CHOCOLATE THROUGHOUT THE LAND!" will present a selection of familiar chocolate forms that are sculpturally interpreted with ceramic-like plaster material. It will include giant boxes of assorted chocolates, approximately 4' x 3' x 9". The character and properties of each boxed chocolate are portrayed in my sculptures. Some of the candies are randomly pinched or bitten open to reveal various centers including creams, nuts, jellies, and caramels.

Enclosed is a press release that describes all of the work that will be featured in the exhibition, and other background materials.

I have participated in exhibitions in museums and galleries throughout the United States, including the Austin Museum of Art in Texas; the Castellani Art Museum in Niagara, New York; the Aldrich Museum of Contemporary Art in Ridgefield, Connecticut; and the Allan Stone Gallery in New York City. I have also had a one-person show at the Henri Gallery in Washington, D.C. This is my second one-person show in New York City.

Please let me know if you require additional information.

Sincerely,
Peter Anton

Keep in mind that if you are preparing a pitch letter to entice a publication, Web site, or television program to do a feature story about your work (when an exhibition, performance, or other event is not the focus), a pitch letter can be sent without an accompanying press release. However, it would be appropriate to include visual support material or a press kit with the pitch letter.

Additional sources of information about press releases, press kits, and pitch letters can be found in the books *Six Steps to Free Publicity* by Marcia Yudkin, *Fine Art Publicity: The Complete Guide for Galleries and Artists* by Susan Abbott and Barbara Webb, *The Fine Artist's Guide to Marketing and Self-Promotion* by Julius Vitali, *Sell Yourself Without Selling Your Soul* by Susan Harrow, and *Writer's Guide to Queries, Pitches & Proposals* by Moira Allen. For assistance in planning publicity campaigns on the Internet, the following books by Steve O'Keefe will be helpful: *The New Rules of Marketing & PR: How to Use News Releases, Blogs, Podcasting, Viral Marketing & Online Media to Reach Buyers Directly* and *Publicity on the Internet: Creating Successful Publicity Campaigns on the Internet and the Commercial Online Services*. The above-mentioned books and other resources are listed in the appendix "Press Relations and Publicity."

PUBLICITY FOR UPCOMING EXHIBITIONS AND PERFORMANCES

If you are invited to exhibit or perform, do not rely or depend on the sponsoring organization to do your public relations. Create an auxiliary campaign (which might end up being the primary campaign). Try to persuade the sponsor to cooperate with your efforts. If the sponsor agrees to collaborate, volunteer and *insist* on overseeing the administration.

Doing your own public relations or taking control of the sponsor's operation is important because of the following: (1) For various illogical reasons, sponsors can be lax, disorganized, and unimaginative in the public-relations area. Many sponsors do not realize that if they develop an effective, ongoing public-relations program they not only promote their artists but also make their institution or gallery better known—both of which can offer prestige and financial rewards in the present and future. (2) If you are in a *group* show or performance, the sponsor will probably issue a "democratic" press release, briefly mentioning each participant, but little more. Your name can get lost in the crowd. Sometimes participants are not even mentioned. (3) Sponsors' mailing lists are usually outdated and full of duplications, and very few lists show any imagination for targeting new audiences. (4) Sponsors can be negligent in timing press releases and announcements so that they coincide with monthly, biweekly, weekly, and daily publication deadlines. Sometimes they do not take advantage of free listings, or if they do, they send only one release prior to the opening of the exhibition or performance, even though the show runs for several weeks.

Designing Announcements

Several years ago Braintree Associates of New Jersey, a company that uses Jungian symbolism in fund-raising, placed a small broken-egg symbol on a direct mail solicitation to raise money for a charitable organization. As a result, the dollar amount of contributions its client received increased 414 percent. The broken egg was not mentioned in the fund-raising letter, and, according to a follow-up poll, donors claimed not to have noticed it.

Each month I receive hundreds of exhibition announcements from artists nationwide. But the vast majority of communiqués contain neither a subliminal nor a conscious message that would stimulate my interest in attending the show or inspire me to pick up the phone to request additional information.

This is not to suggest that symbols of broken eggs should be incorporated into exhibition announcements, but the results of the Braintree campaign illustrate the importance of visual information in getting a message across.

The use of exhibition announcements as an extension of an artist's creativity and very special way of looking at the world is all too often a neglected aspect of public relations. For various reasons, artists, curators, dealers, and other exhibition sponsors do not analyze the purpose of an announcement, the results it should achieve, or what it should communicate.

There is a direct correlation between announcement design and exhibition attendance. Well-executed announcements can stimulate interest in an exhibition, and the more people that are in attendance, the greater the chances are of increasing sales and commission opportunities. Creative announcements can also generate press coverage and invitations for more exhibitions.

Generic invitations, those that omit visual information and merely list the name(s) of the artist(s), exhibition title, location, hours, and dates, are frequently used for group exhibitions to resolve the problem of selecting one piece of work to represent all of the exhibiting artists. A generic solution may also be used because some artwork is not photogenic and loses its power when reproduced in photographic form. But the most common reason generic announcements are used is to save money.

Granted, generic announcements are less expensive than four-color cards, but a successful announcement does not need to be in color or contain a photograph of actual work. For example, for an exhibition entitled *Reflections,* organized as a memorial to artist Jane Greengold's father, a square of reflective paper was attached to a card accompanied by a text describing *reflections* as a metaphor for her feelings and thoughts after her father's death.

For an exhibition entitled *Paintings at the Detective Office,* artist Janet Ziff's announcement contained a drawing of a mask to which two actual sequins were attached.

Taking a more minimal approach, for the exhibition entitled *Lost Watches,* artist Pietro Finelli's announcement contained only basic who, when, and where information, but the intriguing exhibition title and text were printed in silver ink on a thick piece of gray cardboard that was pleasurable to read and touch.

To announce the group exhibition at the Educational Testing Service in Princeton, New Jersey, entitled *Myth America: Selling the American Woman: Through Her, to Her, and Short,* artist Debora Meltz, who also served as the show's curator, designed a black-and-white announcement shaped as a reminder tag for a doorknob, with a string inserted into the hole.

In each of the above examples, without using photographs of actual exhibition artwork or costing a lot of money, the invitation did more than announce a show. Each invitation also gave the recipient a sense of the artist and was in itself an *invitation to respond to the artist's message* with intellect, humor, compassion, pleasure, or whatever emotions and sensations were evoked.

Exhibition announcements should be given tender loving care. Cutting corners might ease time and money pressures in the short run, but short-term thinking can backfire. Boring publicity tools usually bring boring results.

Advertisements

Dealers pour thousands of dollars into advertising each year. "The art magazines . . . are publicity brochures for the galleries, sort of words around the ads, and [they create] total confusion between editorial and advertising," observes writer and critic Barbara Rose. "The only way you can really get your statement, your vision, out there to the public is to put it up on the wall. And to be willing to be judged."[9] If Rose's observation is correct, and I am convinced it is, it implies that whoever is buying or exhibiting art on the basis of seeing it published in art magazines cannot differentiate between a paid advertisement and a review or article. Thus, everything that is in print becomes an endorsement.

But according to Nina Pratt, a former art-marketing advisor, many dealers are misguided when choosing advertisement content and design and when selecting publications where advertisements are placed. She criticizes the use of "tombstone" ads, those without visual information (what I have referred to as generic advertising), and she believes that many galleries lack an overall or specific advertising strategy and rarely employ important target marketing concepts. Dealers repeatedly place ads in the same art periodicals without analyzing whether the readership is actually the primary market or the only market a gallery wants to reach. There is an excellent potential market in non-arts-related publications. For example, a dealer who already has collectors from the business community, or wants to develop such a clientele, would find it advantageous to advertise in publications that businesspeople read, such as the *Wall Street Journal*.[10]

If you have to pay for your own advertising space to announce an *exhibition,* think twice about spending your money. (Paid advertising to announce a performance or event for which tickets or reservations are required is entirely different.) Unless you are willing and able to buy multiple ads, month after month, bombarding the public and art world with your name (just as an ad agency launches a campaign to promote Brand X), I am not convinced that paid advertising is a worthwhile investment for an *individual artist.*

In recent years an unfortunate precedent was established with galleries requiring artists to split the cost of an advertisement or pay the entire amount. In most instances galleries have an annual contract with one or two art trade publications. Therefore, an ad *with the gallery's name* appears month after month. The gallery benefits from the name repetition, but an artist, whose name only appears once in an ad (during the one month the exhibition is up), derives no benefit from the multiple-insertion approach.

However, if you have no qualms about participating in bribery, sometimes an ad will guarantee that your show will receive editorial coverage. Some of my clients have had firsthand experience in this area. For example, a sculptor telephoned a weekly New York paper about getting press coverage for a group exhibition. She was transferred from department to department until someone in advertising told her that if she bought a display ad there was a good possibility the show would be covered. Another client was approached by the editor of an art publication after he had written an excellent review of her work. He asked her for a payoff. Instinct told her no, and she politely turned down his request, but she had many misgivings about whether she had done the right thing. And another client was told by the editor of a newspaper based in the Hamptons, New York, that he would write an article about her upcoming exhibition if she gave him a painting. She declined the offer.

On the other hand, if your gallery or sponsor is willing to buy advertising space on your behalf, by all means tell them to go ahead. As I previously mentioned, many galleries have annual advertising contracts with arts publications (and some publications make sure that their advertisers are regularly reviewed, a corrupt but accepted practice).

Publicity Step by Step

An ideal situation is to have twelve months to plan a publicity campaign. Following are scheduling suggestions if you have the luxury of having a full year to plan and execute publicity. If you only have two months or three weeks before the actual opening to get your plans together, the schedule will have to be condensed and compressed.

TWELVE MONTHS BEFORE OPENING

ESTABLISH A PUBLIC-RELATIONS BUDGET. Find out what the sponsor is doing about public relations so that your efforts are not duplicated. Try to coordinate efforts. Make it clear what the sponsor is paying for and what you are paying for. Budgetary considerations should include postage, printing (press releases, press kits, photographs, duplication of mailing lists, invitations, posters, catalogs, or any other printed materials), and the cost of the opening. If you are involved in a group show, try to coordinate your efforts with other participants. If the sponsor has little money to appropriate toward public relations, take the money out of your own pocket. Don't skimp. But squeeze as many services out of the sponsor as possible (administrative, secretarial, and clerical assistance; photocopying; use of tax-exempt status for purchasing postage, materials, and supplies).

PREPARE MAILING LISTS. (See "Mailing Lists—The Usual and the Esoteric," page 24.) Study the mailing lists and decide how many press releases and invitations you need. (See "Six Months Before Opening.")

DETERMINE WHETHER YOU WILL HAVE A CATALOG. If the exhibition sponsor is providing a catalog, inquire about the support materials that are required and the deadline.

DETERMINE THE CONTENTS OF PRESS KITS AND PROMOTION PACKAGES. (See the sections "Press Kits" and "Other Types of Promotion Packages" earlier in this chapter.) Determine the materials to include in the press kit. Also select the names on your mailing list to which to send press kits and those to which to send promotion packages.

Accompany the press kit and promotion package with a short note to a select group of people with whom you have been in contact. Remind them of who you are and where you met or how you know them, and tell them that you hope they can attend the exhibition.

PLAN AND DESIGN INVITATIONS, POSTERS, AND CATALOGS. (See the section "Designing Announcements" earlier in this chapter.)

SELECT PHOTOGRAPHS OF YOUR WORK. Choose photos that you want disseminated to the press (see "Photographing Artwork," page 57). Many free-listings columns and gallery guides also publish photographs, so include these publications in your photo mailing.

RESOLVE THE ISSUE OF PAID ADVERTISEMENTS. (See the section "Advertisements" earlier in this chapter.) If you are planning to buy advertising space, decide on the publication(s) and obtain all of the relevant information pertaining to closing dates for text and artwork.

PREPARE A MAILING SCHEDULE. Decide who gets what and when. Use the guidelines listed in the following sections to establish mailing dates, but it is important to check with the publications to confirm their closing-date schedules.

SEVEN MONTHS BEFORE OPENING
WRITE A PRESS RELEASE. (See the section "The Press Release" earlier in this chapter.)

WRITE FREE-LISTING RELEASES. (See the section "Free Listing Releases" earlier in this chapter.)

COMPOSE A "PITCH LETTER." (See the section "Pitch Letters" earlier in this chapter.) Compose a pitch letter for appropriate publications and determine the visual support materials that will accompany the letter.

SIX MONTHS BEFORE OPENING
GO TO PRINT. Print press releases and invitations. Print and/or scan photographs.

SEND PITCH LETTERS AND/OR PRESS RELEASES OR PRESS KITS TO PUBLICATIONS THAT HAVE A SIX-MONTH LEAD. Send materials to select monthly publications *so they will be able to cover your exhibition or performance prior to the opening and/or while the exhibition or performance is in progress.* For this type of press coverage, monthly publications usually have a deadline of five to six months before the cover date, but check with each publication. (Invitations and press releases to critics and staff members of monthly publications that *review work* should be sent *three weeks* prior to the opening.)

SIX WEEKS BEFORE OPENING
SEND PITCH LETTERS AND/OR PRESS RELEASES, FREE LISTING
RELEASES, OR PRESS KITS TO WEEKLY PUBLICATIONS. Send materials
to select weekly publications *so they will be able to cover your exhibition or performance prior to the opening and/or while the exhibition or performance is in progress.*

THREE WEEKS BEFORE OPENING
SEND PITCH LETTERS AND/OR PRESS RELEASES, FREE LISTING
RELEASES, OR PRESS KITS TO REMAINING PRESS CONTACTS. Send
materials to select daily publications, television and radio stations,
Web sites, and blogs. Invitations and press releases to critics and
staff members of monthly publications that *review work* should also
be sent at this time.

SEND INVITATIONS AND/OR PRESS RELEASES TO EVERYONE ELSE ON
YOUR LIST. Include curators, art consultants, gallery dealers, collectors, friends, and relatives.

Press Deadlines

The above schedule is a general guide, and it is very important to
check with the various publications regarding their copy deadlines.
For example, some weeklies require listings releases to be submitted
ten days before an issue is published, while other weeklies have
deadlines as much as twenty-one days before publication.

Generating a Feature Article in Consumer Publications

If you are aiming to generate a feature article in a monthly consumer
publication to coincide with the opening of an exhibition, this task
should begin a year before the exhibition opens. Time and planning
are required to solicit the interest of a freelance journalist or to have
an editor assign a journalist the story. Once a writer is selected, an
interview or series of interviews will be conducted, and the writer
will prepare a draft of the article and will usually have more questions to ask. Photographic sessions will also need to be arranged.

The names of freelance writers are published in various media
directories. For example, *Bacon's New York Publicity Outlets* lists
the names of freelance writers who are based in New York. The

listing includes contact information, a description of topics of interest, and the names of publications for which they write.

OPENINGS

Many artists would rather have open-heart surgery than go to their
own openings, or to any openings for that matter, and many guests
feel the same way. Most openings are lethal: cold, awkward, and
self-conscious. But they don't have to be that way. You worked hard
to open. Your opening should be your party, your celebration, and
your holiday. Otherwise, why bother?

Do not look at the opening as a means to sell your work or
receive press coverage. If it happens, great, but many critics boycott
openings, and rightfully so, for with all of the people pressing themselves against the walls (hoping they will be absorbed in the plaster),
how can anyone really see the art? And many serious buyers like to
spend some quiet time with the work, as well as with the artist and
dealer, and an opening is not the time or place to do it. Some openings are planned around a lot of booze to liven things up, and while
things can get peppy, often in the high of the night people make buying promises they don't keep.

When the exhibition *11 New Orleans Sculptors in New York*
opened at the Sculpture Center, the eleven New Orleans artists surprised their guests with a creole dinner. It was an excellent opening,
and some of the best openings I have attended (including my own)
involved the serving of food (other than cheese and crackers). The
menus were not elaborate, but something special, which indicated
that the artists actually liked being there and liked having you there;
that the artists were in control and were "opening" for reasons
other than that it was the expected thing to do. In addition, the
breaking of bread among strangers relieved a lot of tension.

Choreograph your opening and be involved in the planning as
much as possible. Not all dealers are willing to relinquish control
and try something new, but push hard. The opening shouldn't be a
three-ring circus structured for hard sell with a little goodie (glass of
wine) thrown in as a fringe benefit. This is your show, and the opening should be structured accordingly.

CRITICS AND REVIEWS:
THEIR IMPORTANCE AND IRRELEVANCE

Many idiosyncrasies, ironies, and irrationalities surround art reviews and art criticism, beginning with the "words without pictures" approach used by newspapers and periodicals. Although a publication might publish as many as ten reviews, in most instances nine of the reviews are unaccompanied by photographs of the artwork being described. Paintings, sculptures, drawings, and other visual media, unlike other art forms, such as concerts, can be reproduced in print! But for illogical reasons most reviews about visual art are unaccompanied with *visual* documentation, a less than subtle message that the words surrounding the artwork are more important than the work itself!

"All these years . . . I had assumed that in art, if nowhere else, seeing is believing. Well—how very shortsighted!" wrote author Tom Wolfe. "Not 'seeing is believing' . . . but 'believing is seeing,' for *Modern Art has become completely literary: the paintings and other works exist only to illustrate the text.*"[11]

Pontificating about art is not a new phenomenon. The smug and pretentious prose that is published in magazines, newspapers, and catalogs has become a norm in art-world communication.

In 1986, *The New Yorker* published an interview with Ingrid Sischy, who was then the editor of *Artforum*. The interview was conducted by *The New Yorker* staff writer Janet Malcolm. Said Sischy:

> Even now, if I wasn't forced to edit them I probably wouldn't read some of the things we publish. . . . It's always been a problem, this troublesome writing we print. . . . That is probably why I was brought in as editor—because I found much of *Artforum* unreadable myself. . . . An object lesson I keep before me all the time is that of my mother, who picks up *Artforum,* who is completely brilliant, sophisticated, and complex, who wants to understand—and then *closes* it.[12]

"[Criticism] adopts its own mechanistic modes," wrote art critic Nancy Stapen, "and all too often produces its own sectarian dialect, resulting in the sort of obfuscated, impenetrable verbiage that, as we have seen, even a mother cannot love."[13]

Through layers of verbose ramblings, filled with obscure meanings, symbols, and theories, art is stripped of its own visual language. And although most artists agree that this form of writing is incoherent and repulsive, many artists would not be averse to having their artwork dissected in the press in a similar manner. Even gibberish is viewed as a source of validation!

Although not all critics choose to write in a style of opaque discourse, the emphasis on the importance of being reviewed has grown out of proportion to the intrinsic value of art criticism.

Granted that some artists have gained more "recognition" as a result of their work being praised by the arts press, there is an unfounded perception among artists that having an exhibition reviewed is tantamount to career success.

Critic and curator John Perrault comments:

> I know that artists in general will do almost anything to get a review. I have had artists tell me, "Please write about my show. I don't care if you hate it but write something about it." It's very important for artists to have that show documented in print somehow. Often artists don't think that they exist unless they see their names in print.[14]

The fact of the matter is that an artist can have a substantial and sustaining career with or without reviews.

Artists are not alone in equating reviews with career success. Some dealers, curators, and collectors don't think an artist exists unless the artist's name is in print.

Recognizing that the art world contains a preponderance of insecure individuals who depend on the printed word to form their opinions or convictions about artwork and to decide whether or not you're a good bet and someone to watch in the future, artists should consider the pursuit of a review a *routine* task using some of the public-relations channels suggested in this chapter. *Pursuing a review is not worthy of obsession.*

My own good breaks came from several different circles: insecure people with power, secure people with heart, and those with both heart and power. Ultimately, I have to take credit for putting this kind of constellation together because dealing with the review system also means putting together a backup system so that *your career can flourish with or without reviews*.

CRITICS AND ETHICAL ISSUES

In 2003 the *New York Times* issued a fifty-two-page code of ethics that included several provisions directed at the newspaper's art critics, art journalists, and their editors. *Ethical Journalism: Code of Conduct for the News and Editorial Departments* was designed to protect the paper's impartiality by avoiding conflicts of interest or the appearance of impropriety. (A year later the newspaper incorporated the code into a manual titled *Ethical Journalism: A Handbook of Values and Practices for News and Editorial Departments*.) Under the code, the newspaper's art critics, art journalists, and their editors are prohibited from recommending artists to galleries, serving on advisory boards, juries, committees or panels organized by people they write about. In addition, the code specifies that if the arts writers and arts editors own art, qualified as "exhibition quality," they are required to annually provide an associate managing editor with a list of acquisitions and sales.[15]

In 2008 the art critic Christian Viveros-Fauné was dismissed by the *Village Voice* after he accepted the positions of managing director and curatorial advisor of New York's Volta Art Fair and curatorial advisor to Chicago's Next Art Fair. In an interview by Tyler Green published in his blog Modern Art Notes[16] on the Web site Arts Journal: The Daily Digest of Arts, Culture & Ideas, Viveros-Fauné was asked whether his involvement in art fairs was a conflict of interest with his position as an art critic, a writer, and a journalist. Viveros-Fauné responded by saying: "I believe you can wear a lot of hats in the art world, and one needs to because, among other things, critics can't survive on the money that they make from writing. Very few critics can. And, not only that, but I'm interested in curating, and I firmly believe that there is no interest in the art world without a conflict of interest."[17]

Christian Viveros-Fauné's philosophy that "everyone's doing it, why not me" is symbolic of the ethically dubious activities and commerce that permeate the art world. The sense of entitlement expressed by Viveros-Fauné is the basis of justification for writers who participate in the various sleazy "rent-a-critic" schemes. Each year more and more art critics are added to the payroll of companies that offer artists marketing and public relations services.

MAKING NEW CONTACTS AND KEEPING IN CONTACT

Making new contacts and keeping in touch are very important aspects of public relations. Establishing new contacts and reviving old contacts can begin with a few first-class stamps and emails.

It is also important to keep your contacts warm and remind people that you exist. For example, at my urging, a client who was literally destitute, out of work for several months, and being evicted from his apartment contacted a music critic at the *New York Times*. Two years before, the critic had written a highly enthusiastic and flattering review about the musician. He reminded the critic of who he was and laid on the line his current dilemma. Consequently, the critic was instrumental in finding the musician work, which not only helped him over a huge financial crisis, but also helped him restore faith in himself, in his work, and in humanity.

Set aside time each week to make new contacts, by using the telephone or sending presentation packages and letters to solicit and generate interest in you and your work. The more contacts you make, the greater the chances that you will find yourself at the right place at the right time.

Do not underestimate the value of this phenomenon. For example, a sculptor who had recently moved to New York from the West Coast asked me to assist her with contacts. I provided her with a list of exhibition spaces that I thought would be interested in her work. The first alternative space she contacted immediately accepted her work, as it precisely fit into the theme of an upcoming show. Both the sculptor and the show received excellent reviews. The sculptor was then invited to participate in a group exhibition at a museum (as well as another alternative-space gallery); a dealer from a well-known gallery saw the museum show and singled out the sculptor and invited her to exhibit at his gallery. This all took place in less than three months!

Once a rhythm is established for a consistent approach to public relations, the job becomes easier and less time-consuming. The letter that once took you hours to compose will become a snap. And if you keep up on your homework (see "Read, Note, File, and Retrieve," page 22), you will never exhaust the list of people, organizations, and agencies to contact.

Keeping in Touch

There are many ways to keep in touch. Press releases and exhibition/performance announcements are two such ways. But there are other vehicles. Some of my clients send newsletters a few times a year to collectors, people who have expressed interest in their work, and contacts in the art world that they know personally. Other clients have created blogs (see page 77). The newsletters and blogs announce upcoming exhibitions and recap recent activities.

The use of an internal press release described earlier in this chapter (see page 104) is another effective way of keeping in touch. It can bring tangible and intangible rewards by reminding people that you exist and that your career is moving forward.

The Law of Averages

One of the most important factors about the effectiveness of public relations and marketing is that it is based on the *law of averages*. Regardless of your talents, abilities, and vision as a fine artist, no one will know about you unless you contact many people and do it on a continuing basis. The more contacts you make (and reestablish) and the more opportunities you create to let people know that you and your work exist, the greater the chances that events and situations will occur that accelerate your career development.

As previously mentioned, a presentation package that is based on a brochure generally produces a 6 to 14 percent response; a slide package averages around a 2 percent response. Much less predictable is the response rate of a press release that is targeted to generate press coverage. But what is predictable is that if you do not issue a press release, it is unlikely that press coverage will transpire.

Each time you receive a letter of rejection (or of noninterest), initiate a new contact and send out another package. The "in and out" process feeds the law of averages and increases your chances of being at the right place at the right time. It also wards off rejection and puts it in a healthier perspective (also see chapter 11, "Rationalization, Paranoia, Competition, Rejection, and the Overwhelm Factor").

Exhibition and Sales Opportunities: Using Those That Exist and Creating Your Own

More than ever before, there are many opportunities to exhibit and sell work. This chapter describes various exhibition and sales markets, including national and international resources, available to artists outside of the commercial-gallery system (which is discussed in chapter 8, "Dealing with Dealers and Psyching Them Out").

ALTERNATIVE SPACES

During the 1970s the *alternative-space movement* emerged in reaction to the constrictive and rigid structure of commercial galleries and museums. Artists took the initiative to organize and develop their own exhibition spaces, using such places as abandoned and unused factories and indoor and outdoor public spaces that previously had not been considered places to view or experience art. Some alternative spaces acquired a more formal structure, such as artists' cooperatives, and became institutionalized with tax-exempt status.

Alternative spaces mushroomed throughout the United States under such names as the Committee for Visual Arts, the Institute for Art and Urban Resources, and the Kitchen, all in New York City; the Los Angeles Institute of Contemporary Art; the N.A.M.E.

Gallery in Chicago; the Washington Project for the Arts in Washington, D.C.; and the Portland Center for the Visual Arts in Oregon.

The alternative-space system continues to spread, providing general exhibition and performance opportunities, as well as exhibition opportunities for specific artists. For example, there are alternative spaces dedicated to African American artists, women artists, African American women artists, Hispanic artists, and artists born, raised, or living in specific neighborhoods of cities. There are alternative spaces dedicated to mixed media, photography, performance, sculpture, and so forth.

When the original alternative spaces were established, their goals were simple and direct: to "provide focus for communities, place control of culture in more hands, and question elitist notions of authority and certification."[1] While on the surface the goals of the newer alternative spaces might appear to be in harmony with those of their predecessors, many, unfortunately, have other priorities. Although some spaces are still being run by artists, others are being administered by former artists who have discovered that being an arts administrator or curator is a quicker route to art-world recognition and power.

Consequently, some alternative spaces are being administered and operated with a hidden agenda that is not in the best interests of artists or the communities they were originally intended to serve. An *alternative elite* has arisen, so it should not surprise an artist that the reception he or she receives when contacting an alternative-space gallery could well be reminiscent of the reception encountered at a commercial gallery.

Of course, there are alternative spaces that remain true to the ethic and purpose of what an alternative space is, and generally the alternative-space system has many good attributes.

The biggest and most important difference between an alternative space and a commercial gallery is that the former is nonprofit in intent, and therefore is not in business to *sell* art or dependent on selling for its survival. Basically, its survival depends on grants and contributions, which impose another kind of financial pressure. But without the pressure of having to sell what it shows, the alternative space is able to provide artists with exhibition space and moral support, and feature and encourage *experimentation* (a word that can cause cardiac arrest for many dealers). This is not to imply that work is not sold at alternative spaces, for it is, but an artist is not obligated to pay the ungodly commissions required by commercial galleries. If an alternative space charges an artist a commission, it is usually in the form of a contribution.

Alternative spaces have many other good points. For example, they offer an artist a gallery-like setting in which to show his or her work. This can help a dealer visualize what the work would look like in his or her gallery. Do not underestimate the value of this opportunity: many dealers have remarkably little imagination. Also, alternative spaces are frequented by the media and critics, providing artists with opportunities for press coverage, which, as discussed in chapter 6, can often be an important factor in career acceleration. And alternative spaces provide artists with a chance to learn the ropes of what exhibiting is all about.

Curators and dealers include alternative spaces in their regular gallery-hopping pilgrimages, for glimpses into *what the future might hold* as well as to scout for new artists. Some of my clients' alternative-space experiences skyrocketed their careers or took them to a new plateau.

Many artists have misconceptions about the value and purpose of an alternative space and regard it as a stepchild of the commercial-gallery system. They think that it should be used only as a last resort. This is not true. While alternative spaces provide valuable introductory experience into the art world and exhibition where-withal, *it is counterproductive to abandon the alternative-space system once you have been discovered by a gallery.* Balance your career between the two systems. Until a commercial gallery is convinced that your *name alone* has selling power, you will be pressured to turn out more of what you have thus far been able to sell. You might be ready for a new direction, but the dealer won't want to hear about it. Those offering an alternative space do!

Alternative spaces are not closed to artists who are already with commercial galleries. In fact, including more established artists in alternative-space exhibitions adds to the organization's credibility, and for an alternative space whose survival depends on grants and contributions, there is a direct correlation between reputation and financial prosperity.

The names and locations of alternative spaces throughout the

United States are listed in the *Art in America Annual Guide to Galleries, Museums, Artists* (see the appendix section "Exhibition and Performance Places and Spaces").

Other Alternative Sites and Spaces

In addition to the traditional types of exhibition spaces in commercial galleries and museums, there are many other kinds of spaces available for artist-initiated exhibitions. Mimi and Red Grooms's *Ruckus Manhattan* exhibition opened in a warehouse in lower Manhattan and ended up at the Marlborough Gallery. Artist Richard Parker turned the windows of his storefront apartment into an exhibition space for his work and received a grant from the New York State Council on the Arts to support the project. Bobsband, a collaborative of artists, convinced New York City's Department of Transportation to let them use the windows of an unused building in midtown Manhattan to exhibit their work and the work of other artists. They started the project with their own money and eventually received financial support from federal and state arts agencies. Banks, barges, restaurants, parks, alleys, rooftops, building facades, and skies are only a sampling of other alternative sites and spaces that artists, dancers, performers, and musicians have used as focal points, props, and backdrops for projects.

In a blog sponsored by an artists' organization in New York City, a painter reported that she had a two-day exhibition at a yoga center; it would be the first exhibition the yoga center sponsored. Although she was skeptical that a show held within a very short time span at a non-art-related venue would produce tangible results, she sent out emails to her network of professional contacts and friends. She was pleasantly surprised that the yoga center also participated in publicity efforts. A day after the show closed, she sold a painting for $4,000 to a person who had seen the exhibition.

In the same blog another artist wrote that she had reluctantly agreed to exhibit two paintings in a breast imaging center. As a result of the show she sold a painting for $26,000. A third artist reported that she was invited to organize a new exhibition space for local artists in the lobby of a New York hospital. An art consultant visited the show and purchased three pieces of work for a project she was doing at another hospital.

Cooperative Galleries

Cooperative galleries are based on artist participation. Artists literally run a cooperative gallery and share in expenses (in the form of a monthly or annual fee) in return for a guaranteed number of one-person shows and group exhibitions within a specified period. Gallery artists make curatorial decisions and select new artists for membership.

Because of its participatory structure, the cooperative system, at its best, offers artists a rare opportunity to take control, organize, and choreograph their own exhibitions and be directly involved in formulating goals, priorities, and future directions of the gallery. At its worst, since a member must accept group decisions, you might find yourself in compromising situations, having to abide with decisions that are in conflict with your own viewpoints. And you might also find yourself spending more time squabbling and bickering over co-op-related matters than on your artwork!

It is always difficult to know what you are getting yourself into, but before rushing into a cooperative, talk to the members to ascertain whether you are on the same wavelength. Obviously, if you receive an invitation to join a co-op, the majority of members approve of you and your work. You should determine whether your feelings are mutual.

Co-op memberships are limited and correspond to the single-show policy and space availability of the gallery. For example, if the co-op agrees that members should have one-person shows for one month every eighteen months, the membership will be limited to eighteen artists. Or if the gallery has the facilities to feature two artists simultaneously, the membership might be limited to thirty-six artists. Some co-ops have membership waiting lists; others put out calls for new members on an annual basis or when a vacancy occurs. In addition, some co-ops have invitationals and feature the work of artists who are not members.

Some cooperatives do not take sales commissions; others do, but the commissions vary and are far lower than those charged by commercial galleries. If commissions are charged, they are recycled back into the gallery to pay for overhead expenses.

In *On Opening an Art Gallery,* Suzanne K. Vinmans describes with refreshing honesty and humor the evolution, trials, and tribulations of a co-op gallery, as well as the events leading up to its demise. Although problems with a landlord were a contributing factor to the closing of the gallery, most of the difficulties were created by the gallery's artists, many of whom shirked responsibility, suffered from an acute case of stinginess, and were overpowered by negative attitudes. "If I had it all to do again, I would . . . make myself the director from the outset. As the person who did most of the work and made most of the decisions, I should have received that recognition," writes Vinmans. "I would search for more committed artists. . . . A gallery such as ours could have worked if each member was committed to the fullest degree."[2]

If you join a co-op gallery, it is important to *know when it is time to leave*. Since artists are guaranteed a set number of single and group exhibitions within a specific time frame, all too often a co-op serves as a security blanket for members afraid to venture out into the world and risk the possibility of being rejected.

To subsidize the operating costs of a gallery, many cooperatives sponsor "invitationals." It is a juried procedure, and artists who are selected are also required to pay some sort of fee. Although some artists have had positive experiences participating in cooperative-sponsored invitationals, artist Donna Marxer's ordeal in New York was less than positive:

> I got an "invitational" to show in the secondary room of one of the best co-ops around—one that was frequently reviewed and well-located. I also had to undergo rigorous review of my work to be accepted. The cost of that back room was $2,000 for three weeks.
>
> The director and committee were adamant about their standards. They insisted on hanging the show, leaving out a third of my work. They rewrote my perfect news release in their one-paragraph format—fine for someone with nothing to say, but dear reader, that is not me. They gave me a huge out-of-date mailing list that yielded nothing. $4,500 later, I had not made even one sale, had lured no one of importance into the gallery (in spite of promises), and went unreviewed. The only thing I got out of that show was one line on my resumé."[3]

VANITY GALLERIES: ARTISTS BEWARE

Vanity galleries are *for-profit* galleries that require artists to pay an exhibition fee and sometimes an assortment of other exhibition-related expenses. In addition, many vanity galleries also require a commission on work that is sold. For the most part there are no exhibition standards as long as an artist is willing to pay for an exhibition.

Cooperative galleries are often confused with vanity galleries because in co-ops artists are required to contribute to the galleries' overhead and administration costs through monthly or annual dues or fees. And as previously mentioned, cooperative galleries also sponsor "invitationals" that require artists to pay exhibition fees.

Adding to the confusion, some alternative spaces also require artists to contribute to exhibition overhead. And, of course, as discussed in chapter 8, "Dealing with Dealers and Psyching Them Out," some commercial galleries are also requiring artists to contribute to exhibition expenses.

Although all too often there are some fine lines between the practices of a vanity gallery and a nonvanity gallery, keep in mind that, unlike cooperative galleries and other alternative spaces, a vanity gallery has no exhibition standards, it is not in business for educational purposes, and it does not have an artist's best interests in mind.

Vanity galleries that are located in large cities are particularly seductive. They appeal to naive, and often desperate, artists who believe, for example, that having a show in a New York gallery, even if you have to pay for it, provides the path to fame and fortune. Many foreign artists also resort to using a vanity gallery in New York to seek validation in their home countries.

Through advertisements in regional and national art publications, vanity galleries entice artists with tempting come-ons such as "New York gallery looking for artists." Artist sourcebooks (see page 151) are also used by vanity galleries to locate potential prey. For example, the Agora Gallery in New York contacts artists with a form letter stating that "we have noticed your work in the *Encyclopedia of Living Artists* and are very impressed."

Vanity galleries use an assortment of schemes and methods for getting artists to spend vast amounts of money to exhibit. For example, *in addition* to exhibition fees ranging from $2,000 to $15,750 for one- to three-week solo exhibitions, the Caelum Gallery in Manhattan charges extra for postcard printing and mailing, catalog production and mailing, advertising, framing, and a reception. They also charge a sales commission of 30 percent.

Once, when a gallery dealer deflated the ego of one of my clients, he trod over to a (now-defunct) vanity gallery, much against my advice, like the guy who discovers his mate has been unfaithful and marches off to a prostitute. He signed up for a show, signed the dotted line on the contract, and wrote a check for several hundred dollars. In addition to the "exhibition fee," he had to pay for all of the publicity, including invitations, announcements, press releases, and postage, and for the wine served at the opening. Although the show did nothing for his career, he felt victorious. He had shown the dealer!

Although exhibiting in a nonvanity New York gallery does not guarantee recognition or financial success, the Herculean strength of the mythology surrounding the importance of exhibiting at a New York gallery enables vanity galleries to flourish. In New York and elsewhere, stay clear of vanity galleries and related schemes that place all of the financial risks on artists. If artists made a concerted effort to boycott vanity galleries, these galleries would disappear.

JURIED EXHIBITIONS

Hundreds of local, regional, national, and international juried exhibitions are held each year. If you were so inclined, you could enter a juried exhibition every day of the year.

But there are drawbacks, one of which is the expense involved in entering juried exhibitions. Most shows require entry fees, and these fees continue to increase dramatically.

"What would you think of a theater that charged the performers rather than the audiences?" asked art critic Joan Altabe in an article about juried shows in the *Sarasota Herald-Tribune*. "Crazy, right! Behold the crazy art world. The arrangement described above is one of the ways many exhibit halls support themselves. . . ."[4]

In the article Altabe interviewed various not-for-profit arts organizations who justify charging entry fees because the fees pay for
the group's overhead. "We couldn't survive without entry fees,"[5]
declared a representative of one of the organizations. Altabe
responded by offering a practical and intelligent suggestion: "Charge
the audience, not the artists."[6]

The issue of charging fees and other related matters made juried
shows so controversial that in 1974 the National Artists Equity
Association adapted Guidelines for Juried Exhibitions stating that:

> National Artists Equity is unalterably opposed to artists bearing
> the cost of exhibitions in the form of entry fees. Furthermore,
> Equity expects exhibiting sponsors will provide insurance and
> adequate security while juried work is in sponsors' possession.

> The selection of judges and jurying of exhibitions should be
> accomplished so that aesthetic considerations are maximized and
> extraneous biases are minimized. To this end, judging should be
> done in terms of the work itself. Neither age, sex, religion, nor the
> race of the artist should be a qualification or deterrent for the
> work submitted to any government-supported exhibition. In gen-
> eral, local judges should not be selected because of possible bias.[7]

Unfortunately the National Artists Equity's guidelines are
enforced by a minority of organizations and it is more likely than
not that most juried shows not only charge entry fees, artwork is not
insured.

CARFAC Ontario, a branch of Canadian Artists Representation/
le Front des artistes canadiens, a national art service and artist advocacy organization, also published a set of Guidelines for Professional
Standards in the Organization of Juried Exhibitions. The guidelines
are more precise and comprehensive than those that were endorsed
by the National Artists Equity Association. CARFAC Ontario states
that it "considers the payment of entry fees inappropriate to the
exhibition of works by professional artists," and that "the collection
of commissions on sales of work inappropriate to the activity of a
public gallery."[8] The guidelines also include a specific list of responsibilities by juried exhibition organizers including, for example,
insuring artwork for its full declared value from the time of receipt

to its return to the artist; the task of unpacking and repacking of art-work done by professional packers; paying for all exhibition costs, including publicity, catalogs, and jurying fees and per diem; and pro-viding artists with copies of all printed publicity, including catalogs, posters, press releases, and exhibition reviews.[9]

Art critic Joan Altabe's suggestion to charge the audience a fee to attend an exhibition instead of charging artists a fee to participate[10] brings to mind how convoluted the justification actually is for artists to pay for an organization's overhead.

Sponsors of juried shows that are for-profit and not-for-profit organizations have overhead costs related to juried exhibitions. But because the sponsors experience little resistance from artists to pay entry fees, they have not been forced to develop more creative ways of keeping their organizations and businesses alive. In most instances, in addition to entry fees, sponsors also receive a commis-sion on work that sells during a juried exhibition.

Some juried shows that are sponsored by *for-profit* enterprises use only a small percentage of fees for legitimate expenses, with the bulk of the money going directly into the pockets of the organizers.

For example, one New York gallery sponsors a juried competi-tion in which artists are required to pay a registration fee of $35 for up to four slides, $5 for each additional slide, a $10 nonrefundable fee for repacking and handling artwork "even if hand-delivered," and a 40 percent commission on all sales!

The artist Richard S. Harrington was so outraged after reviewing the prospectus of a national juried competition sponsored by the NoBIAS Gallery in North Bennington, Vermont, he sent a letter to the gallery's executive director pointing out:

> In addition to generating income by the charging of entrance fees you are also benefitting by charging a 25% commission on all sales. While it is not uncommon for galleries to charge a commis-sion on sales it is excessive to expect an artist to pay twice to be included in an exhibition. Your prospectus states that you are ". . . devoted to strengthening the dialog between artist and audience." Shouldn't this include having the "audience" share part of the financial demands of organizing a juried exhibition from which they directly benefit. . . .[11]

Harrington believes that artists should always be thinking on a larger scale of how they can make their voices heard, and he sent copies of his letter to the executive directors of the Vermont State Arts Council and the National Artists Equity Association. All three letters went unanswered.

As I mentioned earlier in this chapter, another drawback of juried shows is that many of their sponsors do not insure artwork, and many sponsors take little or no precautions to protect the work from theft, vandalism, and loss.

Some juried shows *appear* to be very prestigious because the jury is composed of art-world personalities. But keep in mind that *jurors are paid* to lend their name to exhibitions. The fact that a famous critic, curator, or gallery dealer is on the jury is *absolutely no indication* that the show has been organized with high standards and that it is in the best interest of artists.

I have not seen any overwhelming evidence to support a correlation between juried shows and meaningful and lasting career development. In fact, the biggest illusion about juried shows is that award-winning artists benefit in ways that provide tangible career acceleration. For example, many artists who have won awards in shows that were judged by art-world figures are astonished and disappointed to discover that in most instances a juror's interest in the artist ends after the awards have been given. Although there are a few exceptions, rarely will a juror follow through by providing an artist with some sort of entry into the art world.

The majority of artists who benefit from juried shows are those not particularly concerned with long-range career development. They approach a juried show as a means to an end in gaining respect and recognition in their *local communities*. But for artists who have more ambitious and professional goals, there are many more productive and effective ways in which to use time, energy, and money.

In some arenas the juried show is such a common appendage of the art world that it will take quite a while to change thinking about the relevance of juried exhibitions. If you are convinced that juried shows will help provide a means to your end, use the following guidelines before plunging in.

Before submitting work to a juried exhibition, even if it is sponsored by a museum or reputable institution or organization, do your homework. Make sure the sponsor will provide a contract or contractual letter outlining insurance and transportation responsibilities, fee structures, submission deadlines, and commission policies. If you pay an entry fee, you should not have to pay a commission on work that is sold, and you should not participate in exhibitions that do not insure work while it is on the sponsor's premises.

The appendix section "Competitions and Juried Exhibitions" includes a list of resources from which you can obtain additional information on juried exhibitions.

ARTIST REGISTRIES

Artist registries are sponsored by artists' organizations, museums, alternative spaces, and public-art agencies throughout the United States. An active registry is used by many people: by curators and dealers to select artists for exhibitions, by collectors for purchases and commissions, by critics, journalists, and historians for research, and by federal, state, and municipal public-art agencies to purchase art and select artists for site-specific commissions.

The majority of online artist registries have replaced slide registries. This is a positive development, guaranteeing greater accessibility and use of registries. Prior to the advent of the Internet, some slide registries were inactive and were rarely used.

Municipal and state arts agencies sponsor registries featuring the work of regional artists, including the Arkansas Arts Council, the Connecticut Commission on Culture and Tourism, the Maryland State Arts Council, the New Jersey State Council on the Arts, the Greater Pittsburgh Arts Council, and the Southern Arts Federation. Some arts agencies sponsor registries that are open to regional and national artists, including the City of Las Vegas Arts Commission and the Western States Arts Federation (WESTAF).

Artist registries are also sponsored by arts organizations and alternative spaces. For example, The Irving Sandler Artists File is a digitized image database and registry sponsored by Artists Space in New York City. It is one of the largest and most comprehensive registries in the United States and is regularly used by curators, artists, art dealers, collectors, art consultants, and students. White Columns in New York City is an alternative space that sponsors a registry open to artists *worldwide.*

The Drawing Center in New York City sponsors the Viewing Program Artist Registry, a curated registry that features the work of national artists. Artists who are not attending school and do not have New York gallery representation are eligible to submit a portfolio for consideration. International artists living in the United States are also eligible to apply. Twice a year The Drawing Center presents "Selections," a group exhibition of artists curated from the Viewing Program. Information about the above-mentioned organizations and other artist registries can be found in the appendix section "Artists' Registries."

My first encounter with a registry occurred when I was preparing an exhibition at a museum in New York City and spent a lot of time in the curatorial chambers. The curators meticulously went through their registry, on the lookout for artwork that would fit into a theme show they were preparing (eighteen months in advance). When they found something they liked, regardless of whether the artist lived in Manhattan, New York, or Manhattan Beach, California, they invited the artist to participate.

It is very important to *continually update the images you submit so the registry reflects your most recent work.* A person reviewing the registry will assume that whatever is there represents your current work, but, unless your images are up-to-date, this might not be the case. For example, one of my clients was invited to participate in a museum exhibition by a curator who had seen her work in a registry. It would have been her first museum show, but she learned that the curator wanted to show only the work that she had seen in the registry. The artist was mortified: a year earlier she had destroyed the entire body of work, and the curator was not interested in her recent work. It was a big letdown, and the artist was depressed for weeks.

MUSEUMS

My first exhibitions were sponsored by museums, *contrary to the notion* held by many artists that one must be affiliated with a commercial gallery before being considered by a museum. In many instances, what initially led to an invitation from a museum was a résumé, visual support materials, and an exhibition proposal (see the section "Develop and Circulate a Proposal" in this chapter). Many of my clients have followed suit and their outreach to curators has been rewarded.

Other exhibition invitations came as a result of both long- and short-term professional relationships with museum directors and curators.

My own experience in gaining museum shows is not unlike the steps Patterson Sims outlined when he was associate curator of the Whitney Museum:

> On the basis of slides and exhibition notices the curators will call for appointments with individual artists for studio visits. . . . Calls from friends, collectors, and gallery owners about the work of an artist are another means of introduction. . . . Conversations with artists, art writers, and museum personnel will bring an artist's name to a curator's attention.[12]

Sims also described how artists are actually invited to exhibit at the Whitney: "Decisions . . . [are] made at curatorial staff meetings. It is up to the individual curators to promote the work of an artist they feel has a fresh style, a sense of quality, and a provocative outline. If a curator can convince others . . . the group will decide to invite an artist to participate."[13]

The unilateral support system that Sims describes is one of the biggest snags in the exhibition process of some museums. It is debatable whether the artist who is presented for consideration on the basis of a visual presentation and a studio visit has the same leverage as an artist who was brought to the attention of curators by "friends, collectors, and gallery owners." Many artists believe that the Whitney, for example, is a closed shop to artists not affiliated with well-known commercial galleries. Judging from who *is* invited to participate in the Whitney Biennials, this is a logical conclusion. On the other hand, one of my clients who had no particular gallery affiliation was invited to participate in a Whitney Biennial. She concluded that she was a "small fish that slipped through the net!"

There are curators who have autonomous power and are able to make their own decisions rather than succumb to peer or dealer pressure. Do not let hearsay discourage you from contacting curators, nor should you be fooled by the myth that only artists connected to prestigious commercial galleries can exhibit in museums.

Curators organize exhibitions, assemble collections, and write catalogs and articles. They are under pressure to put contemporary art into a historical context, discover "new movements," and develop thematic exhibitions, and they cannot rely solely on well-known artists to accomplish their goals. And if they are aggressively pursuing a reputation in the art world, they are on a constant quest to discover artists who will reinforce and support a particular point of view.

Curators select artists whose work thematically falls within the parameters of future exhibitions through the use of artist registries (see page 140). In many instances curators have their own personal registries, which are developed, in part, through artist initiative: artists send letters and presentation packages to introduce these curators to their work.

A young artist who was having a one-person exhibition at a suburban library couldn't understand why a museum would possibly be interested in her work. But I convinced her to include curators in the mailing to announce the show. She sent a cover letter, a color postcard featuring a piece of her work, and a press release to curators nationwide and was utterly amazed that the mailing elicited a response from curators at the Hirshhorn Museum and the Guggenheim Museum. Both curators requested a set of slides to keep for their files.

I maintain a list of museum and independent curators that is available as a printout and on a CD-ROM. Information about this list can be found in the appendix section "Mailing Lists." In addition, *The Official Museum Directory* includes the names of museum personnel (see appendix section "General Arts References").

COLLEGES AND UNIVERSITIES

Colleges and universities are often receptive to sponsoring exhibitions and performances, and their interest is not necessarily limited to alumni, although approaching a college or university of which you are an alumnus or alumna is a good beginning.

The first step is to send college and university gallery directors a presentation package and cover letter or a proposal. This process is described in the section "Develop and Circulate a Proposal" in this chapter (see page 162).

Exhibiting at colleges and universities can also offer other rewards. Sometimes, as a result of an exhibition, artwork is purchased for the school's collection, and artists are commissioned to do projects for particular campus sites. In some cases, exhibiting artists are invited to present a lecture about their work, for which they receive a fee and travel expenses. On the other hand, many college and university galleries have small operating budgets and expect artists to pay all exhibition-related expenses.

The names and locations of some college and university galleries throughout the United States are listed in the *Art in America Annual Guide to Galleries, Museums, Artists.* In addition, the ArtNetwork rents a mailing list of college and university galleries. These and other resources can be found in "Exhibition and Performance Places and Spaces" in the appendix.

POSTHUMOUS EXHIBITIONS

From time to time I am contacted by a family member of a deceased artist requesting advice and suggestions for the disposition of large quantities of artwork they inherited. Unfortunately, many artists do not address artwork disposition issues in a will, and this daunting responsibility is delegated to a spouse, life partner, or children.

There are organizations that can be of assistance, but not nearly enough to tackle the vast amounts of artwork available. The Art Connection in Boston sponsors an art donation and placement program for artists and collectors who want to donate artwork to public and nonprofit organizations. The organization serves as an art clearinghouse, simplifying the donation process and offering a wide range of original works to qualifying nonprofit agencies. The Art Connection offers assistance to organizations in other cities to use their model to launch similar programs. Art for Healing in San

Francisco lends artwork donations free of charge to health-care facilities, including Ronald McDonald House, cancer projects, AIDS hospices, general hospitals, and homes for the aged. Information about these organizations can be found in the Appendix of Resources section in "Art and Healing" and "Law: Estate Planning."

In addition to distributing artworks through nonprofit agencies, some relatives in charge of an artist's estate have devised creative solutions to ensure that deceased artists continue to receive career recognition. After the death of Elizabeth Delson in 2005, her husband, Sidney Delson, created a Web site devoted to her artwork.[14] "It is vitally important to me that my beloved Liz not be one of those forgotten artists whose work is much later discovered in some warehouse sale as a human-interest story."[15] The Web site, which was designed as Elizabeth's catalogue raisonné, includes more than 400 paintings and prints. The site is organized into a painting gallery and a print gallery with thematic subgroups. It also includes a biography and a list of solo exhibitions, group exhibitions, collections, and a bibliography. In addition, Sidney Delson was successful in placing 33 of Elizabeth's etchings in the Fine Print Collection of the Newark Public Library in Newark, New Jersey, and two etchings in the Smith College Museum of Art.

Maxine Rosen, the widow of painter and poet Bruce Rosen, sent a catalog from his posthumous exhibition at the Guild Hall Museum in East Hampton, New York, to museums and cultural centers throughout the United States. The catalog was used in conjunction with a cover letter that proposed a traveling exhibition of paintings and poems. Her inquiries led to seven exhibitions held between 2000 and 2007. As of this writing, an eighth exhibition is being planned. Maxine Rosen's ultimate goal is to find the right permanent homes for her husband's artwork and papers.

Soon after the death of John Regis Tuska in 1998, his son Seth Tuska began thinking about the ways in which he could pay tribute to his father's life and artwork. Seth spent three years developing an exhibition concept and proposal that spanned his father's career demonstrating the diverse media and expressions used in his work. In 2007, the exhibition "Tuska: The Human Condition" was accepted into the touring exhibition program of ExhibitsUSA, a nonprofit organization and an arm of the Mid-America Arts

Alliance. Seth also prepared a large catalog that showcased the sixty works featured in the exhibition. In addition, he received a grant from Kentucky Educational Television (KET) to create a thirty-minute documentary about John Regis Tuska's life and career. The documentary *Tuska: Non Basta Una Vita* was completed in 2008. Seth was also successful in placing his father's papers and research archives in the Special Collections and Digital Programs of the University of Kentucky. John Regis Tuska's home was converted into The Breakers: The Tuska Museum, in Lexington, Kentucky. Seth Tuska is also working on a biography of his father.

THE CORPORATE ART MARKET

The corporate art market offers artists many sales and exhibition opportunities. Although some corporations buy art primarily for the purpose of investment, the majority buy art to attain a prestigious image, for decorative purposes, or even for the far nobler reason of improving employee morale. Although some of the motives behind corporate collecting are basically self-serving, the corporate market has become a viable arena for many artists to sell and exhibit work.

Generally, corporations steer away from work that is political, overtly sexual, religious, or negatively confrontational. Otherwise, the field is open.

The term *corporate market* encompasses a wide range of institutions, ranging from financial corporations and law offices to hospitals and restaurants.

There are several ways to reach the corporate market: through art consultants and art advisors, through galleries that work with corporations, through architects and interior designers, through real estate developers, and by directly contacting corporations, usually through staff curators and facilities managers. I maintain an annotated list of art consultants and art advisors that is updated several times a year. It includes the names, addresses, telephone and fax numbers, email addresses, Web sites, and, if available, information about art disciplines and markets of interest. The list is available as a printout and on CD-ROM. *The International Directory of Corporate Art Collections* lists hundreds of corporate art collections throughout the United States and abroad. Each listing contains the names of the people responsible for assembling the collection, such as in-house curators, art consultants, or advisors. It also describes each collection and its review procedures and policies. The directory is available as a spiral-bound printout and on CD-ROM from the International Art Alliance, Inc.

Another way of reaching art consultants is to advertise in the *Sourcebook of Residential Art,* which is published by the Guild. Each edition contains color photographs of artwork, contact information, and a biography of each participating artist. *The Guild Sourcebook* is distributed *free of charge* to more than 7,000 art consultants, high-end consumers, residential design firms, architectural firms, and galleries.

The book *Corporate Art Consulting* by Susan Abbott provides a thorough overview of the corporate market. Although it was written primarily for art consultants, gallery dealers, architects, and interior designers, artists will glean ideas and advice on how to approach corporations. For additional information about the above-mentioned resources, see the appendix section "Corporate Art Market."

Art Consultants and Art Advisors

Art consultants are agents who sell work to corporations and individuals. If work is sold or commissioned through the efforts of an art consultant, the artist must pay a commission.

Anyone can become an art consultant. Like gallery dealers, art consultants are unregulated. The occupation of art consultant is often confused with *art advisor,* and often these job titles are used erroneously and interchangeably. Some art advisors are members of the International Association for Professional Art Advisors (IAPAA), a nonprofit organization that has stringent regulations regarding business practices and professional qualifications. The IAPAA Web site lists qualifications for becoming a member. The qualifications include:

a thorough knowledge of art history, with at least one area of specialization; on-the-job experience with a museum, gallery, or other arts organization that teaches correct curatorial skills and art-handling procedures; knowledge of the art market and a good working relationship with members of the art community; personal integrity and ethical working procedures.[16]

Art advisors do not receive commissions from artists on work sold or for projects commissioned. They are *paid by their clients* (individuals, organizations, and businesses) to provide information, advice, and related services *without any conflict of interest*. This means that, unlike many art consultants, art advisors do not maintain permanent inventories of art, so they are not "pushing" only the work of artists they have on hand. Also, art advisors accept work on consignment only for the purpose of presentation or approval.

Expect to be asked to pay art consultants between 40 and 50 percent on work that has already been created. Some consultants charge less but they are very much in the minority. Commissions can be negotiated, and since I have the benefit of having many clients who are represented by the *same* consultant, I know firsthand that some artists pay the same consultant less of a commission because they negotiated. A logical argument for paying an art consultant less of a commission than what a gallery receives is that theoretically a gallery provides artists with gallery services. And I say "theoretically," because as pointed out in chapter 8, "Dealing with Dealers and Psyching Them Out," the quality and amount of services galleries offer artists have drastically diminished.

Under no circumstances should you pay more than 25 percent of the artist's fee for *commissioned* projects obtained through an art consultant, a gallery dealer, or any form of an agent. In other words, do not pay a commission on the overhead expenses of the project. Additional advice and discussion about commissions and fees are included in chapters 5 and 8, "Pricing Your Work: How Much Is It Worth?" and "Dealing with Dealers and Psyching Them Out."

If an art consultant or art advisor requests work on consignment, do not let any work leave your studio *before* an artist/agent contract is signed. If a commissioned project has been arranged by an intermediary, you should use an artist/agent contract *in addition to* the commission contract between yourself and the client. The appendix section "Law: Contracts and Business Forms" lists publications that discuss contracts, such as *The Artists' Survival Manual,* which provides an artist/agent agreement, and *Business and Legal Forms for Fine Artists*, *Business and Legal Forms for Crafts*, and *Legal Guide for the Visual Artist*, which include a contract for commissioned work. For further information on contracts, refer to pages 199–204.

When approaching an art consultant or art advisor, submit a basic presentation package (see chapter 3).

Corporate Curators

Generally, corporate curators have the same professional qualifications as museum curators and function in a similar capacity as art advisors, but they are on the staffs of corporations and receive salaries for their services instead of fees.

Corporate curators should receive a basic presentation package (see chapter 3). The names and addresses of corporate curators are listed in *The International Directory of Corporate Art Collections* (see the appendix section "Corporate Art Market").

Architects and Interior Designers

Many architectural and interior design firms commission artwork or purchase work in behalf of their clients. Some firms delegate a project manager or project designer to select work and/or maintain an artists' registry. In some instances a registry is organized by a staff librarian.

Architects and interior designers should receive a basic presentation package (see chapter 3).

The names and addresses of architects and interior designers can be obtained in several ways. For example, *The Dodge Report* is a quarterly publication that provides information on every construction project nationwide, including the name of the design firm in charge and whether a budget has been allocated for the purchase or commissioning of artwork. Individual state reports are also available.

Architect Finder is an online database sponsored by the American Institute of Architects. Architects can be located by country and state, areas of speciality, and services provided.

In addition, you can obtain the names and addresses of architects and interior designers in your area by contacting local chapters of the American Institute of Architects (AIA) and the American Society of Interior Designers (ASID), or through the national headquarters of the AIA and ASID.

Develop a more personalized list of firms by studying architectural, architectural landscape, and interior design publications, Web sites, and blogs to look for designers whose work is aesthetically compatible with your own. The names and addresses of these publications in the United States, Canada, and abroad are listed in the appendix section "Interior Design and Architecture."

Another way of reaching architects and interior designers is to advertise in the *Sourcebook of Architectural & Interior Art* which is published by the Guild. Each edition contains color photographs of artwork, contact information, and a biography of each participating artist. *The Guild Sourcebook* is distributed *free of charge* to more than 10,000 architects, interior designers, public art specialists, landscape architects, liturgical consultants, art consultants, and other professionals.

The results of a survey of 161 design professionals conducted by the Guild about why artists are selected for commissioned projects provided interesting findings that challenged some popular misconceptions.[17] These misconceptions include the belief that artists must be well known, or they must have had prior experience in executing a similar project, or that local artists or artists who submit low-cost project budgets have a better chance of being selected.

A copy of the survey was sent to design professionals who actively use the Guild to commission art. Fifty-nine people responded to the survey, including 24 interior designers, 15 architects, 8 art consultants, 3 developers, and 2 art brokers.

Addressing the question "What were the most important factors in selecting the artist?" Forty-three percent of the respondents said that it was the quality of an artist's portfolio; 16 percent stated that it was the artist's track record with similar projects; 13 percent of the respondents stated it was on the strength of the project proposal; 11 percent stated that it was the personal chemistry with the artist; 10 percent stated that it was an artist's prominence; 4 percent stated that it was an artist's unique style; 2 percent that it was the low cost of proposal; and 1 percent of the respondents said that it was an artist's location.

Not all artists' sourcebooks are as reputable as those published by the Guild or used as frequently by art consultants, architects, and interior designers. Before advertising in a sourcebook, do your homework and request information about the number of copies that will be printed, how the book will be distributed, and if copies are distributed free of charge to target markets that would be in alignment with the type of artwork you create. Also request sample tear sheets to ascertain the printing quality and paper stock that are used.

For additional information regarding the Guild sourcebooks and other resources related to the corporate art market and architecture and interior design, see the appendix sections "Corporate Art Market," "Interior Design and Architecture," and "Artist Sourcebooks."

Publicizing and Generating
Corporate Sales and Commissions

If your work is purchased or commissioned by a corporation, use public-relations tools such as press releases (see page 104) and photographs (see page 56) to generate publicity and new contacts. *Past accomplishments should always be used as a springboard to solicit new clients and projects.*

Issue a press release to announce a corporate commission or sale. Press releases should be sent to collectors, clients, potential collectors and clients, and people in the art world with whom you are in contact, or people in the art world whom you have always wanted to contact.

Send a press release and photograph to *Public Art Review,* a biennual publication that contains the column "Recently Completed Projects." Each announcement contains the artist's name, the title of the artwork, a project description, the year the work was completed, medium, and the name of the sponsor. If a commission or sale involved the *services of an art consultant or art advisor,* send a press release and photograph to *Art Business News,* a monthly publication that announces recent corporate acquisitions and commissions. The address of *Public Art Review* is listed in the appendix section "Public Art," and the address of *Art Business News* is listed in the appendix section "Corporate Art Market."

A press release issued by an artist announcing the acquisition of three photographs by a Canadian bank led to a feature article in a major New York newspaper. A press release issued by an accounting firm, in behalf of a sculptor, announcing the completion of a commissioned piece was sent to various trade publications read by accountants. An article in one such publication announcing the commission led to a commission for the sculptor from another accounting firm.

THE HEALTH-CARE INDUSTRY

Within the health-care field, many opportunities exist for artists to exhibit and sell work, and create special projects. In the article "Getting Better: Art and Healing," published in *Sculpture* magazine, the author Anne Barclay Morgan pointed out:

> As our concern with healing the earth has received widespread attention, there is also a renewed interest in healing ourselves. With health care reform now at the foreground of national debate, health services, alternative medicine and other forms of healing are receiving broader public scrutiny. Directed toward health care facilities, such as hospitals and hospices, the burgeoning field of art and healing is creating venues and modes of interaction for artists, health care givers and patients.[18]

The Society for the Arts in Healthcare is a national membership organization that is dedicated to the incorporation of the arts as an appropriate and integral component of health care. Toward this goal, the society is engaged in programs that serve many purposes: to demonstrate the valuable roles the arts can play to enhance the healing process; to advocate the integration of the arts into the planning and operation of health-care facilities; to assist in the professional development and management of arts programming for health-care populations; to provide resources and education to health-care and arts professionals; and to encourage and support research and investigation into the beneficial effects of the arts in health care.

The society's membership includes physicians, nurses, arts administrators, medical students, architects, designers, and artists of all disciplines. It sponsors an annual conference and publishes a membership directory.

To supplement the healing work of hospital staffs, the Foundation for Hospital Art provides original artwork to hospitals, nursing homes, and correctional facilities throughout the United States. The Healing Arts Initiative, a program of the Massachusetts Cultural Council, is active in Massachusetts, Vermont, and New Hampshire, and uses the arts as an innovative new treatment method for patients living with chronic disabling diseases at participating heathcare sites. RX Art, Inc., in New York City is a nonprofit organization that selects and installs original works of art in patient rooms, treatment rooms, and public areas of health-care facilities. The Shands Arts in Medicine program at the College of Medicine University of Florida in Gainesville combines standard medical practices with innovative healing methods that include a program involving artists, patients, and their families. Shands Arts in Medicine also sponsors an artist-in-residence program.

The Web site of the Arts and Healing Network is a comprehensive resource about the healing potential of art. Updated on an ongoing basis, it lists publications, organizations, and related Web site links. It also features the work of many artists. Other Web sites of interest include Artslynx that provides information on international programs dedicated to healing individuals and communities through the arts, and the North Carolina Arts for Health Network, an organization formed to promote, sustain, encourage, improve, and expand the incorporation of the arts in healing and well-being in North Carolina. Contact information about the above-mentioned resources can be found in the appendix section "Art and Healing."

PUBLIC-ART PROGRAMS

In addition to private and corporate clients, there is a wide range of commission and sales opportunities available to artists through public-art programs sponsored by federal, state, and municipal agencies and independent organizations.

There is also a wealth of information available about public-art programs. For example: *The Artist's Guide to Public Art: How to*

Find and Win Commissions by Lynn Basa provides guidance on how to start and build a career in public art. It includes information on how to find, apply for, compete for, and win public art commissions. It also contains interviews with experienced public-art artists and arts administrators. And it gives suggestions for cutting through the red tape and winning commissions that are financially and artistically rewarding. The excellent semiannual magazine *Public Art Review* publishes practical articles about public-art programs and provides lists of opportunities in the public-art field. The *Directory of Percent-for-Art and Art in Public Places Programs* is a comprehensive resource that is updated on an ongoing basis. Published by Mailing Lists Labels Packages, the directory lists public-art programs sponsored by city, county, state, and federal agencies, including transit and redevelopment agencies, private and not-for-profit organizations, colleges and universities, and sculpture gardens and parks. The directory, related mailing labels, and postcards for use in contacting the various programs are available separately or as packages.

The Public Art Network (PAN) is a program of Americans for the Arts. It offers a range of professional services and networking opportunities for public-art professionals, visual artists, design professionals, and organizations planning public-art projects and programs.

Web sites of interest related to public art include Art-Public, a membership organization that documents thousands of public art projects throughout Europe. Art in Cities documents the work of artists who are using cities as outdoor exhibition spaces throughout the world. Public Art Online, hosted by the Glasgow School of Art, is a comprehensive site that includes advice, opportunities, and dialogues about public art. Public Art on the Internet includes various types of information about the field of public art, including essays, articles, projects, links to other related sites, and an email group for those interested in public art.

Contact information about the organizations, publications, and Web sites mentioned in this section, along with other resources, can be found in the appendix section "Public Art."

Federal Public-Art Programs

Through the Art in Architecture Program sponsored by the General Services Administration (GSA), the federal government commissions artists to produce large-scale works of art for new federal buildings.

One half of 1 percent of a building's estimated construction cost is reserved for commissioned work. A panel consisting of art professionals, civic and community representatives, and the project's lead design architect meets to discuss opportunities for artists to participate in the building project. The panel reviews diverse work of many artists and nominates finalists.

The GSA maintains a large registry of artists interested in being considered for federal commissions. The registry is the primary source used in selecting artists for each new project.

Municipal, State, and Independent *Public-Arts Programs*

The precedent of allocating a certain percentage of the cost of new or renovated public buildings for art, as described in the GSA's Art in Architecture Program, has also been legislated by many cities, counties, and states throughout the United States. Canada, England, France, and Australia have similar programs.

The Art and Community Landscapes Program, administered by the New England Foundation for the Arts and the National Endowment for the Arts, supports site-based public art projects. FORECAST Public Art Works in Minneapolis is a nonprofit organization that supports the development and appreciation of public art by creating opportunities for artists and communities in the Twin Cities area. The Public Art Fund, Inc., sponsors installations in public spaces throughout New York City. The Social and Public Art Resource Center in Venice, California, is a multicultural arts center that produces, exhibits, distributes, and preserves public artwork; it also sponsors murals and workshops.

Public-Art Programs for Transportation Systems

Other public-art projects have been initiated in conjunction with public transportation providers and airport administrators. For example, in New York City, the Metropolitan Transportation Authority Arts for Transit program commissions artwork for its family of agencies: MTA New York City Transit, MTA Metro-North Commuter Railroad, MTA Long Island Rail Road, and MTA Bridges and Tunnels. Arts for Transit places permanent art throughout its network through its Percent for Art program. It installs photographic work through its Lightbox Project, and brings music to subway stations through its Music Under New York initiative. MTA Metro Art is sponsored by the Los Angeles Metropolitan Transportation Authority, which commissions artists to create artwork for a wide variety of transportation projects throughout Los Angeles County, including bus stops, rail stations, streetscapes, bus interiors, and construction fences. The Art in Transit Program in St. Louis, Missouri, commissions artists to create temporary and permanent public art works at MetrolLink stations, at MetroBus centers, and at bus shelters. Artwork projects also include vehicle interiors. The TriMet Public Art Program in Portland, Oregon, incorporates artwork in various transit stations, in bus shelters, and in the commuter line that connects passengers to Portland's airport.

The names and addresses of organizations and resources cited in this section are listed in the appendix section "Public Art."

MAKING NATIONAL CONNECTIONS

A recent edition of the *Art in America Annual Guide to Galleries, Museums, Artists* lists 5,487 galleries, alternative spaces, museums, university galleries, private dealers, corporate art consultants, and print dealers throughout the United States, from Anniston, Alabama, to Rock Springs, Wyoming.

Not counting museums and university galleries, the *Annual* lists 709 commercial and not-for-profit galleries in New York City, 110 in Chicago, 89 in Los Angeles, 67 in San Francisco, 47 in Miami, 36 in Boston, 34 in Atlanta, and 33 in Dallas. Although many consider New York to be the art capital of the world (and also make the erroneous assumption that New York artists are more talented than artists elsewhere), the main reason New York is deserving of its title is the large number of exhibition opportunities that are packed into the small island of Manhattan. However, thousands of exhibition and sales opportunities are available throughout the United States and outside of the United States, resources that are consistently overlooked and neglected by the majority of artists.

As discussed in chapter 1, the main reason these resources are overlooked is that many naive artists believe that their market is limited to their area of residence; or that some sort of universal censorship is imposed, illogically concluding that there is no market *anywhere* for their work if they are unable to find a receptive audience in their hometown or city.

In addition, many artists fail to make national contacts because they ponder trivial details and dwell on the logistics of transporting work to other cities and working with out-of-town dealers.

It is important to keep in mind that regardless of the varied philosophical or altruistic reasons dealers give to explain their involvement with art, the bottom line is *money*. If someone believes *money can be made from your work,* geographic considerations become inconsequential.

Venue Viewer is an excellent resource for locating galleries in the United States and abroad. The online database was created by artist Brian David Dennis of the Visual Art Management Project (VAM-P). For a very reasonable annual fee, nearly 8,200 galleries in 87 countries can be accessed; 4,800 of the galleries are in the United States. When possible, the database includes a contact person's name (not a generic title), along with a postal address, phone number, and email address. To qualify for inclusion, a gallery must have a Web site. VAM-P started as a contact and inventory management database and grew out of Dennis's need as an artist to stay organized and grow.[19]

The *Art in America Annual* can be a helpful tool in locating out-of-town exhibition resources. On a state-by-state, city-by-city basis, it lists the names, addresses, phone numbers, email addresses, and Web sites of gallery dealers, alternative spaces, university galleries, and museums. In most cases it provides a short description of the type of art and/or medium of interest and the names of artists represented or exhibited.

Although some of the descriptions that are provided in the *Annual* are vague or very general, since most galleries have Web sites, by previewing the sites in the *Annual* or in the Venue Viewer database you can quickly ascertain if your work is appropriate for a particular gallery. If you are using a brochure (see page 59) or other forms of printed matter (see page 62) to contact a gallery, the cost-effectiveness of these presentations eliminates the need to spend a lot of time researching each gallery.

Publications that are more regional in scope offer more detailed information about exhibition resources. For example, *The Complete Guide to New York Art Galleries* lists galleries and alternative spaces in New York City. It describes each gallery's area or areas of interest, the selection process, philosophy, price range, and whether artists are required to contribute exhibition expenses or pay exhibition fees. The *Artists' Gallery Guide to Chicago and the Surrounding Area* lists exhibition opportunities in the Chicago region; and the *Ontario Association of Art Galleries Directory* includes contact information for 457 key individuals in 183 art galleries and organizations throughout Ontario. *The Ontario Gallery Guide* published by Visual Arts Ontario lists commercial galleries, nonprofit galleries, and artist-run galleries and cooperatives. The names and addresses of the publishers of these resource guides are listed in the appendix section "Exhibition and Performance Places and Spaces."

When an out-of-town gallery expresses interest in representing your work, the most effective way to determine if the gallery is appropriate is to visit it in person. (For guidelines on helping you determine whether a gallery is right for you, see page 187, and for advice before making travel plans, see page 192.)

You can also make national contacts by writing to out-of-town museums, alternative spaces, public-art programs, art consultants, and university galleries and museums.

Developing markets beyond your home city offers many rewards. You should also consider extending your horizons beyond the United States.

MAKING INTERNATIONAL CONNECTIONS

If you are interested in exhibiting and selling work abroad or participating in international arts programs, there are several resources that are available:

A-N Magazine is a monthly British publication with a comprehensive listing of exhibitions, residencies, competitions, and other opportunities for artists primarily in the United Kingdom. Its publisher, A-N, The Artist Information Company, sponsors an excellent Web site that contains hundreds of resources on exhibitions, organizations, and professional contacts in the United Kingdom and in other countries.

Many Web sites are devoted to the international arts' community. For example, Art Beyond Borders was initiated by a group of artists who use the Web to exchange ideas and information and organize exhibitions in members' respective countries; Art Forum is a chat room where career and resources are exchanged between Australian artists.

Artist Elizabeth Bram of Long Island, New York, contacted many of the resources provided by A-N, The Artists Information Company. As a result, her artwork was exhibited in five galleries in England and Scotland during a two-year period. Keeping detailed notes about her transatlantic adventures, she composed a journal under the title "Zero Gravity: Diary of a Travelling Artist." She wrote: "Why spend your life feeling rejected by the New York art scene when there are millions of other people on the planet who might enjoy your art work?"[20].

The artist realized how fortunate she was to have cultivated professional contacts outside of the United States, contacts who did not look to New York for validation of her talents.

The Venue Viewer online database, described on page 157, includes international galleries. *The International Directory of Corporate Art Collections,* published by the International Art Alliance, Inc., contains information on hundreds of corporate art collections, including the collections of Japanese and European corporations.

The London-based organization Visiting Arts publishes several directories that list cultural agencies, art venues, and resources in specific countries, including the publications *Angola Arts Directory, Hungary Arts Directory, Israel Arts Directory, Norway Arts Directory, Quebec Arts Directory,* and *South Africa Arts Directory.* Visiting Arts also has a free email newsletter published monthly with international arts and culture news and information, including funding opportunities, calls for artists, exhibitions, and more.

Artists Communities, compiled by the Alliance of Artists Communities, features a special section on artists' communities, art agencies, and key contacts that support international artist exchanges. Res Artis, The International Association of Residential Art Centres and Networks, is an organization consisting of arts centers and artists' organizations that encourage the development of contemporary art and artists through residential exchange programs. Trans Artists is a foundation that provides artists working in all disciplines with information about international artist-in-residence programs and other opportunities.

In addition, there are many organizations that provide opportunities for artists to work, study, and/or exhibit abroad. For example, the American Academy in Rome sponsors the Rome Prize Fellowship and other residency programs. The American Council on Germany awards professional fellowships annually to promising young Germans and Americans in a variety of fields, including the arts. The American Scandinavian Foundation awards fellowships and grants to professionals and scholars, including those in the creative and performing arts, who were born in the United States or in Scandinavian countries. The Bellagio Study Center, sponsored by the Rockefeller Foundation, sponsors Creative Arts Residencies, a program for artists, composers, and writers in Como, Italy. CECArtsLink, Inc., sponsors exchanges between American artists and artists from Central Europe, Russia, and Eurasia. The U.S./Japan Creative Artists' Program sponsored by the Japan/U.S. Friendship Commission provides six-month residences in Japan for artists in all disciplines.

By scanning periodicals that review and/or advertise international galleries you can get an idea of the type of work certain galleries exhibit. International periodicals can be found in bookstores and libraries that have extensive art sections.

After compiling a list of museums and galleries, send each contact person a presentation package (see chapter 3), and include a cover letter stating that you are planning a trip to that person's city and would like to arrange an appointment if the person finds your work of interest. If you receive positive responses, make the trip a reality!

The same guidelines for selecting and working with domestic galleries are applicable to galleries in foreign cities (see page 187). The contacts cited in this section and additional resources for making international connections, including funding organizations, artist-in-residence programs, and studio-exchange programs, are listed in the appendix section "International Connections."

CREATING YOUR OWN EXHIBITION OPPORTUNITIES

Even though your presentation packages are circulating in registries, museums, commercial galleries, alternative spaces, and so forth, don't sit around waiting to be asked to exhibit and don't depend on someone to suggest a context in which to exhibit your work. Create your own context and exhibition opportunities.

Theme Shows

Curate your own exhibitions or performances, based on themes that put your work into a context. Theme shows can feature your work exclusively or include the work of other artists. At their best, theme shows increase and enhance art-viewing consciousness, demand the participation of many of our senses, and help the public as well as the art community understand and learn more about what an artist is communicating and the motivating influences revealed in the work. For example, the group exhibition *Empty Dress: Clothing as Surrogate in Recent Art* featured the work of thirty contemporary artists. It focused "on the use of clothing abstracted from the body as a means of exploring issues of psychological, cultural and sexual identity."[21] The group exhibition *A, E, Eye, O, U, and Sometimes Why* contained two-dimensional pieces that used "a variety of media to express the concerns and reactions to different social, informational, and psychological situations, through the combined use of words and images."[22] The theme show *Top Secret: Inquiries into the Biomirror*[23] featured the work of artist Todd Siler and consisted of a "32-foot, 3-dimensional sketch of a Cerebreactor, drawings and detailed studies which introduce Siler's theories on brain and mind, science and art."[24]

Another asset of theme shows is that it is far more likely you will obtain funding for a theme show with *broad educational value* than for a show called *Recent Paintings*.

DEVELOP AND CIRCULATE A PROPOSAL

A proposal should describe your idea, purpose, intentions, and audience. It should tell why the theme is important, how you plan to develop it, and who will be involved. Supporting materials should include information about the people involved (résumé, visual materials, etc.) and indicate your space or site requirements. Depending on the intended recipient of the proposal, it could also include a budget and ideas on how the exhibition will be funded.

The proposal should be circulated to museums, colleges, galleries, alternative spaces, cultural organizations, and funding organizations. It could very well be that you will need only one of these groups to complete the project. On the other hand, you might need all of these groups, but for such different reasons as sponsorship, endorsement, administration, facilities, funding, and contributions.

ExhibitsUSA, a national division of the Mid-America Arts Alliance, is a not-for-profit organization that organizes traveling exhibitions. Although it does not accept proposals directly from artists represented in an exhibition, it considers proposals submitted by independent curators, museums or museum affiliates, and community cultural organizations.

Once a proposal is accepted, it is listed in an online catalog that is announced to museums, colleges and universities, and cultural centers throughout the United States. Each exhibition that is described in the catalog includes such information as the exhibition fee and what expenses the fee covers, shipping arrangements, availability dates, and the type of security required.

Curators and participating artists in the ExhibitsUSA program receive a fee.

Smith Kramer, Inc., has a traveling exhibition program similar to ExhibitsUSA and does not accept proposals directly from artists represented in an exhibition. Smith Kramer, Inc.'s exhibitions encompass a variety of themes, including those related to paintings, ceramics, photography, graphics, and textiles. Contact information for Smith Kramer, Inc., and Exhibits USA is listed in the appendix section "Exhibition and Performance Places and Spaces."

A book published by the American Museum Association titled *On the Road Again: Developing and Managing Traveling Exhibitions* is a good resource for artists interested in curating exhibitions.

It covers a range of factors that need to be taken into consideration, including development of an exhibition concept and budget, and crating and shipping. It also includes pointers for dealing with foreign custom officials when shipping work abroad. For further information see "Exhibition and Performance Planning" in the appendix.

ARTIST FEES

Often artists let the excitement of an exhibition opportunity interfere with clear thinking, and overlook various exhibition costs. The most neglected item in budget planning is an artist's *time*—for example, the time spent conceptualizing an exhibition, researching and contacting galleries and museums, and preparing and sending proposals and/or presentation tools. Then there is the time spent preparing, installing, and dismantling the exhibition. The list could go on and on.

Although some alternative and nonprofit galleries pay artists a fee to help offset exhibition expenses, this practice has not been widely adopted, nor is it widely recognized by artists that they have the right to request a fee, particularly a *realistic* fee.

Canada is far ahead of the United States in acknowledging the need for realistic artist exhibition fees. For example, the Canadian arts service organization Canadian Artists' Representation Ontario (CARO) recommends minimum exhibition fees that artists should charge when exhibiting in public or nonprofit museums and galleries. Recommendations take into account a wide variety of exhibiting situations, including single, two-person, three-person, four-person, and group shows; regional, interregional, national, and international touring and nontouring shows; and juried and nonjuried shows. CARO's recommended fees are published in the document *CARFAC Recommended Minimum Exhibition Fee Schedule,* which is posted on the CARFAC Web site (see the appendix section "Exhibition and Performance Planning").

Open-Studio Events

You can generate exhibition and sales opportunities by opening your studio and/or home to the public. However, a successful open-studio event requires careful planning: You must develop an imaginative guest list with many *new* names and have a clear idea of what you want to achieve. Is your main goal exposure, sales, or a combination of both?

Following are guidelines for open-studio planning:

DATES. An open studio should be held on a *minimum* of two (not necessarily consecutive) days, preferably including at least one weekend day and one weekday evening.

INVITATIONS AND MAILING LIST. This paragraph dealing with invitations pertains to invitations to an open studio event—versus a group or solo exhibition in a gallery or museum (per pages 115–16). For an open studio, the invitation should include a photograph of the artist's work versus a generic announcement. Invitations should be sent to collectors, potential collectors, contacts within the art world, family, and friends. But most important, *invitations should also be sent to new people.* One way to do this is by telling friends and associates *who admire your work* and are *not* necessarily part of the art world that you want to increase your contacts for the purpose(s) of sales and/or exposure. Ask if they would be willing to write a personal note on the invitation, inviting their friends and associates to attend. If ten people send ten invitations in your behalf, one hundred new contacts will be generated. Another way of generating new faces is to send invitations to members of the business community in your area. Mailing lists can be obtained from local chambers of commerce or mailing list companies. Of interest to New York artists is the *New York Business Online Directory* compiled by *Crain's New York Business.* It contains hundreds of New York–based companies and identifies decision makers by occupation. It is also available as a printout (see "Mailing Lists" in the appendix).

USE AN ASSISTANT. All too often, open studios resemble gallery openings, with guests self-consciously glued to the walls. Uncomfortable environments are not conducive to generating sales or exhibiting work; people want to leave as soon as possible. It is important to create a warm and energizing atmosphere. Guests should be introduced to one another. But if you are serving beverages, answering the door, asking people to sign a guest book, and taking care of other activities, you will not have time to meet people in an effective way, introduce guests, talk about your work, or answer questions. Hire a person or ask a friend to help out with all of the various tasks associated with an open studio so that you are free to spend time with people.

PROVIDE PRINTED MATERIALS. Prepare multiple copies of printed materials (as many copies as the number of guests expected), including a résumé (see page 44) or biography (see page 52), an artist statement (see page 53), press clippings (if applicable), and a price list (see page 95). These materials should be placed in a central location.

MUSEUM STORES

Museum shops offer a viable venue for the sale of certain types of one-of-a-kind objects and multiples, including ceramics, sculpture, photography, prints, woodworking, fiber arts, graphic products, and jewelry. There are literally thousands of museums shops throughout the United States and abroad.

Museum buyers decide which objects and multiples will be sold through their respective museum shops. Large museums usually have several buyers, some of whom are responsible for product selection, and others for product development.

Kathy Borrus, formerly a merchandise manager at the Smithsonian Museum Shops, recommends that "before you send information to a museum shop or call the buyer, understand the museum's mission. Learn as much as you can about the museum and the shop's products and price points. Remember that education and museum relatedness drive a buyer's selection."[25] Contact the museum shop's buying office to inquire about the presentation tools they require for an initial introduction to your work, and whether they prefer a CD-ROM, photographs, or actual samples. Borrus also advises artists to "be prepared to wait for a response. Buyers are inundated with calls and unsolicited samples."[26]

Museum buyers are also interested in working with artists on product development. Borrus points out that "product development is more time consuming [than] selling your basic line. . . . The process is often lengthy. Several prototypes and numerous stages of approval are the norm before an item is ready for sale."[27]

A list of museum shops can be obtained from the ArtNetwork, which rents a list of museum store buyers. The Museum Store Association also sells a list of museum shops nationwide and in other parts of the world. However, the list is only available to Museum Store Association members. Affiliate memberships are offered to artists who are already selling work to museum shops at a wholesale price. The addresses of both of these organizations are listed in the appendix section "Art Sales and Commissions."

Selling from Your Studio

Most artists find the experience of selling work directly to the public gratifying on several levels. The intimacy of a studio and direct contact with an artist can create a positive environment, and for many people direct contact with an artist is a chief factor in buying art.

But people buy art for many different reasons. Increasing studio sales requires an understanding of basic sales skills particular to selling art, and an understanding of individual buying styles. In her book *How to Sell Art: A Guide for Galleries, Art Dealers, Consultants, and Agents* (see the appendix section "Career Management, Business, and Marketing"), Nina Pratt, a former art market advisor, offers the following advice:

> Learn your own buying style, because it influences your selling style. . . . There are as many different buying styles as there are people. But there are a few main categories that most people fall into . . . [for example,] impulsive versus calculating buyers. . . . There are also people who hate to be told anything . . . as opposed to the ones who want a full biography of the artist; the ones who have to tell you their life stories before they are ready to buy; the apparently timid, docile client with a will of steel; [and] the bargain hunters [who] will ask for a discount at the drop of a hat. Learning how to distinguish each type comes with time and practice. Until your instincts develop, rely on . . . skillful questions to find out which sort of person you are dealing with.[28]

The questions Nina Pratt recommends include: Does this person buy art? What kind of art? In what price range? Is your work appropriate for this person? Does this person have the authority to buy, or will a spouse have the final say?[29] Pratt points out, however, that "most visitors . . . would be turned off if you boldly grilled them on these subjects. So you must learn to probe delicately but precisely for the information that you need."[30]

There are a number of books available that provide tips and advice on acquiring collectors and selling artwork out of your studio, including *The Art of Creating Collectors* and *The Art of Selling Art* by Zella Jackson; *Selling Art Without Galleries: Toward Making a Living from Your Art* by Daniel Grant; and *Selling Art 101: The Art of Creative Selling* by Robert Regis Dvorak. Although the books *The Art of Selling to the Affluent* by Matt Oechsli and *Marketing to the Affluent* by Thomas J. Stanley do not focus on fine art, they provide information on the buying and patronage habits of the wealthy, along with tips and advice on reaching this market. Information about these resources can be found in the appendix section "Art Sales and Commissions."

Dealing with Dealers
and Psyching Them Out

Somewhere between the mid-1990s and mid-2000s, art dealers in New York reinvented themselves and changed the title of their occupation to "gallerist." Although an article in the *New York Times*[1] suggests that the advent of this new appellation happened in the mid-2000s, a blog reader who responded to a posting about the *Times* article said that he first heard the term used in Europe in the mid-1990s.[2]

The new title arrived with a set of rules regarding who can use the title and who cannot. In an attempt to explain the difference between an art dealer and a gallerist, a gallery owner interviewed in the *Times* described an art dealer as one who buys and sells art but does not represent artists. The *Times* article also suggested that a gallerist nurtures artists.[3] The *Artlex Art Dictionary* offers a broader definition of *gallerist* and an explanation from where the term derived:

> A professional artist's representative, who may or may not also be an art dealer—someone involved in the buying and selling of art. This term might have been derived from the French *galeriste,* long used by top gallery workers in France to distinguish themselves from the mere marchand de tableaux, or picture merchant. Alternatively, perhaps it came from Germany, where *galerist* or *galeristin* denotes, respectively a male or female gallery owner.[4]

Nina Pratt, who for many years served as a New York-based art marketing advisor to art dealers and art consultants very accurately observes that many dealers believe the myth that art and business do not mix. "Dealers are terrified of being viewed as used-car salesmen. They go to great lengths to dissociate themselves from the 'business' aspects of art."[5] Consequently, in an effort to reinvent themselves and ward off their worst fear, American art dealers gave themselves a new title. Although the new title is pretentious and a less-than-subtle embellishment of the occupation of "sales person," it can also be interpreted that the "ist" at the end of "galler-ist" symbolically represents yet another encroachment into an "art-ist's" territory. It can be compared to the 50 percent sales commissions art dealers receive, an implication that they are major contributors to the creation of artwork!

Although this chapter is primarily about gallery dealers, much of the information and advice and most of the perspectives and views are also applicable to people in other arts-related occupations, including art consultants, curators, critics, administrators, collectors, and artists. Some of my impressions and characterizations might seem severe, but it is not my intention to throw all of the blame for the ills and injustices in the art world on dealers, curators, and the like. *Artists must also accept responsibility for the way things are,* mainly because most artists, overtly, covertly, or inadvertently, participate (or try to participate) in the dog-eat-dog system. Few are trying to change it.

If I had my way, I would replace commercial galleries with a system in which artists exhibited work in their studios and sold it directly to the public. But such a system could work only if artists acquired enough self-confidence not to need gallery validations, and if the public, likewise, had the self-confidence necessary to buy work without gallery validation. Since there is a very remote chance that these events will occur in my lifetime, the next best thing for changing the system is to regulate the business practices of galleries nationwide, including policies affecting commissions, discounts, insurance, payments to artists, and the use of contracts. For the time being, since the gallery system is still very much intact and is virtually unregulated, the following opinions, advice, and observations are aimed at helping artists acquire more business savvy, more control over their careers, and more control in their relationships with those who are currently running the show.

LIES, ILLUSIONS, AND BAD ADVICE

Artists are constantly bombarded with erroneous, irresponsible, and unethical advice about the art world and art galleries. While some advice is exchanged through word of mouth, much of it is disseminated through articles in trade publications. Some of these articles are written by well-meaning but naive individuals who are connected to the art world in some capacity; others are written by less-than-well-intentioned art-world figures whose motives are self-serving. For example, in an article from *Art in America,* a dealer assures readers that "a minority of dealers are strictly concerned with commercial success."[6] However, he then condones the greedy practice of awarding dealers a commission on *all* studio sales:

> An artist may on occasion sell a work directly from his studio to a friend or to a collector he has known before his gallery affiliation. It is the artist's ethical obligation to report such transactions to his dealer and to remit a reduced commission, commonly 20 percent, to compensate the dealer for a work he cannot offer under the usual terms of their agreement.[7]

Another dealer advises *ARTnews* readers that the fastest track into the art world is to work for a famous artist.[8] In an article in *American Artist,* a political scientist *cum* art collector advises beginners to exhibit only in small local or regional galleries.[9] An arts administrator encourages artists to retreat for a few years if they are rejected by galleries.[10] And a career consultant to artists (who later became an art dealer) states that it is important to dress presentably to give the impression that you are making money through artwork sales.[11]

Artists also give each other peculiar and bad advice. For example, in a book profiling contemporary artists, an artist discusses how she uses sex to get ahead: "I've been propositioned a lot: 'I'll give you a show if you sleep with me.' It happens often. Would I do it for a show? Now I would, but when I was younger I wouldn't. I wouldn't because I was a jerk."[12] And another artist tells beginners that "one of the necessary qualities of being an artist . . . is to not expect an awful lot, to be somewhat dense about any thoughts of what you will get out of being an artist."[13]

If you believe everything you read you would conclude that, in order to find a gallery and succeed in the art world, you must sleep with dealers, and dress as though you have a lot of money. You should work for a famous artist, and when beginning your career, you should have low expectations and exhibit in small, local galleries. You should avoid large cities at all costs. And if you are rejected from galleries, you should retreat and wait a year or two before trying again!

Although in composite form these recommendations sound very silly, many artists, unfortunately, believe the advice to be true.

DEALERS: THEIR BACKGROUNDS AND PERSONALITIES

The Complete Guide to New York Art Galleries[14] includes a profile of the various galleries listed in the publication. Some galleries limited their profile to contact information and business hours; others provided more substantial information such as how the gallery selects artists, the gallery's philosophy, and the type of work exhibited. Art dealers were also given the opportunity to provide information on their "background."

I read the profiles of 363 mainstream commercial galleries in Manhattan that specialize in contemporary art. Two hundred and thirteen of the galleries opted not to include "background" information. Since the majority of dealers omitted the information, it was not possible to formulate a typical profile about the backgrounds of dealers in Manhattan. However, one conclusion that can be drawn is that most dealers in Manhattan are unwilling to share biographical information.

Of the dealers that provided information, 57 described their background as having worked in other galleries, were directors of other galleries, owned other galleries, or were art consultants; two were art advisors. Eleven dealers had a background or degree in art history; three had been museum curators and another three had "museum experience." Eight dealers described themselves as artists or former artists; four dealers said they had a business background. Four dealers were attorneys, one was an attorney with a public relations background in financial services, and another described himself as an attorney, artist, and professional tennis player. Other dealers had an assortment of backgrounds, including a cultural journalist, a bond sales person on Wall Street, an architect, an artist/architect, a director of an art school, and an arts administrator. Some people described their background by listing a university degree or the college they attended. Only one person had a master's degree in arts administration! (See page 186.)

Allowing for a handful of elderly dealers who most likely exempted themselves from answering the question because they had been dealers for most of their working lives, one can speculate that the reason dealers were unwilling to share details of their backgrounds is that their backgrounds have nothing to do with visual art. They fear that such a discovery will diminish their power and credibility, and even worse, it will cause them to lose the mystique that envelops their occupation: the mystique of possessing a "golden eye," which gives them the right to determine "good" art and "good" artists.

Although a background in fine arts does not ensure that a dealer will be effective in art sales and capable of running a gallery, for many dealers who do not have such a background fear of exposure of what they *perceive* to be their "dirty little secret" has become a major factor in the molding of their personalities.

Relating to people who possess a fear-based psyche, whether an artist or a dealer, is very difficult, and the difficulties are manifested in several ways. For example, *arrogant* and *temperamental* are adjectives frequently used to describe both artists and dealers. Was it the arrogance of an artist that forced a dealer to retaliate with the same weapon? Or was it a temperamental dealer who elicited the same response from an artist? Is it a chicken-and-egg situation or a matter of simultaneous combustion?

Arrogance is a self-defense tactic to disguise insecurities. Some artists and dealers suffer from the same basic insecurities about their past, present, and future. The fear that causes a dealer to conceal biographical information originates in the very same place as the fear that makes it painful for an artist to compile a résumé because he or she lacks an academic background in the fine arts or enough exhibition experience. The fear that causes a dealer to cut gallery expenditures in all of the wrong places is the same fear that causes an artist to be miserly about investing financially in his or her career. The fear of a dealer that he or she will never attain art-world recognition is comparable to the fear of an artist who experiences a panic attack when a fortieth, fiftieth, or sixtieth birthday begins to approach.

Many dealers are frustrated artists who did not have the tenacity, perseverance, and fortitude to stick it out. Consequently, they are jealous of anyone who did. The wrath of some dealers pours forth when they spot weak work or weak personalities. A weak artist reminds them of themselves, and the memories bring little pleasure. Other dealers behave like bulls that see red: they believe all artists are threatening. They do not differentiate.

Because many dealers are unable to produce provocative work, and *showing* provocative work does not gratify their frustrated egos, they compensate by cultivating provocative personalities. Some dealers are so skilled in verbal delivery that they lead others to believe they know what they are talking about. These dealers begin to believe that their reputations give them the right to make outrageous, irresponsible demands and give outrageous, irresponsible advice. These dealers also believe that reputation alone exempts them from the requirements of morality or integrity, let alone courtesy.

A painter once came to me for advice about his dealer, with whom he had worked for several years. The dealer gave him single shows on a regular basis, and the artist sold well at all of them. However, the dealer, one of the better known in New York, had been badgering the artist for months to stop doing freelance work for a national magazine. The dealer contended that if the artist continued to work for the magazine he would not be taken seriously as a fine artist. The artist began to question the dealer's judgment only when it infringed on his financial stability. Until then, he let the dealer's opinions influence and control his life.

In response to his problem, I simply stated that it was none of a dealer's business how an artist made money; the artist looked at me as if this were the biggest revelation of the century!

Another client was told by a dealer who had just finished rejecting him to be careful about showing his work to other artists because they might steal his ideas. The artist didn't know what to do with the backhanded compliment. On the one hand, the work wasn't good enough for the dealer. On the other hand, the ideas were good enough to be stolen. Up until that point the artist had not been paranoid about other artists stealing his ideas, but the dealer successfully instilled a fear: beware of the community of artists!

Dealers take great delight in giving artists advice on how their work can be *improved*. The lecture begins with a critique of the artist's work that quickly transforms into an art history class based on tidbits of jargon they have picked up from listening to artists and other dealers pontificate. And artists listen. They listen in agony, but they listen.

It Takes Two to Tango

Many artists have an "attitude" about dealers and anyone else in the art world who is perceived as an authority figure. In the years that I have worked with artists, I have had to remind clients on several occasions that I am not the enemy!

I am reminded of an artist who called me to make an appointment to discuss her career. She called back a few days later to cancel, saying her slides weren't ready, then quickly changed her mind about the excuse she had offered and lashed into a tirade that ended with: "And who in the hell are you to judge my work? I don't want to be put in a position to be judged."

It took me a while to regain composure, but when I did, I told her that, in my capacity as a career coach to artists, I did not judge work, and even if I did, I hadn't called her, *she had called me* and set up the situation!

Once, at a cocktail party where artists were in the majority, a painter used the opportunity to verbally abuse a dealer he had just met for the first time. At the top of his lungs he held the dealer personally responsible for the hard time he was having selling his work, and he tried, unsuccessfully, to goad his colleagues into joining his tirade. The scene served no other purpose than to add some excitement to what, up to that point, had been a very dull party. The dealer left in a huff, followed by the artist, who was angry that he had received no support or encouragement from his peers.

On another occasion, a meeting I had with a client and his dealer centered on the artist's career. As long as this was the case, the artist was enthusiastic and amiable. However, when we finished with the subject at hand and drifted on to other topics, the artist began yawning, squirming in his chair, and nervously rapping on the table. When he saw that neither the dealer nor I intended to respond to his body language, he started ranting that he was bored with our conversation. With one conciliatory sentence the dealer placated the artist so easily and skillfully that I realized how familiar and experienced he was with this kind of behavior.

Artists have been known to engage in the shady practice of secretly selling artwork to a dealer's client at a highly discounted rate. Although it does not happen often, it does happen, and once a dealer experiences a broken trust, he or she begins to suspect *all* artists of participating in such schemes.

I recently learned of an artist who had been asked by his dealer to crate and pack a painting that had been sold through the gallery. The artist did not know the name or address of the collector, but in the packing crate the artist left a note saying that if the collector wanted to buy the painting at a substantial discount, he should return the work to the gallery and contact the artist directly. The proposal appealed to the collector, and he informed the dealer that he had changed his mind about buying the painting. When the collector returned the painting to the gallery in the packing crate, he inadvertently included the artist's letter. When the dealer unpacked the crate and found the letter he received quite a shock. And so ended the artist's relationship with the gallery.

Dealers can also be cruel or even sadistic, heaping abuse on artists while the artists masochistically allow it. The following episode illustrates the point loud and clear.

A painter took slides to a dealer. While he was viewing her work, he lit up a cigar. After examining the slides he said that he wasn't interested—her work was "too feminine." He then proceeded to give the artist a lecture on the history of art, all the while dropping cigar ashes on her slides.

The artist watched in excruciating pain, but didn't say a word. When the dealer finished the lecture, the artist collected her slides and left the gallery. But she was so devastated by the symbolism of the ashes on her work that she put herself to bed for three days.

Regardless of whether the dropping of ashes was sadistic or inadvertent carelessness, the question remains, Why didn't the artist say something? For example, "Excuse me, but you are dropping ashes on my slides!"

One wonders: if the dealer had been pressing his foot on her toe, would she have allowed him to continue? When the dealer said that her work was "too feminine," she should have immediately left the gallery (with a curt "Thank you for your time") or stayed to challenge his idiotic statement. As Mark I. Rosen, author of *Thank You for Being Such a Pain,* points out:

> The decision to tough it out or take a hike is one of our most difficult choices. There is no wrong choice, because we learn from both. Either choice may help us to become a better person or offer us experiences that will help the next time we find ourselves in a similar situation.[15]

Just as artists tend to forget that, to a great extent, a dealer's livelihood depends on an artist's work, dealers also forget, and they need to be reminded. Reminding them won't necessarily mean that they are going to like your work any more, but it can give you some satisfaction and put things in perspective, something that the art world desperately needs.

DEALERS AS BUSINESSPEOPLE

Finding gallery representation is a task that requires patience. In New York, for example, many artists allow themselves to be strung along by art dealers for several years without any guarantee that eventually they will receive gallery representation. After several rounds of annual studio visits and more rounds of appointment changes or no-shows, a commitment is finally made—an actual exhibition date is scheduled. But the exaltation of gallery status can quickly dissipate when one discovers exactly what being a gallery artist entails.

Nina Pratt, who is mentioned earlier in this chapter (see page 169), for many years served as a New York-based art-marketing advisor to gallery dealers and art consultants, observes:

> If those considering opening a gallery or entering a related pro-
> fession were presented with a checklist of qualities and skills nec-
> essary for a successful career, the majority of people would have
> second thoughts about entering the field![16]

Pratt is knowledgeable about the inner workings of gallery operations, and she sheds light on why so many dealers sink or barely keep
their galleries afloat, and live up to neither their own nor artists'
expectations. If many of the reasons she addresses sound very familiar, it is because they are the very same reasons that prevent artists
from achieving their goals, with or without gallery representation.

As previously mentioned, Pratt believes the root of the problem is
that many dealers believe the myth that art and business do not mix.
She also points out that many people who open galleries naively
assume that an arts-related profession will automatically make them
successful.[17] Parallels can be drawn between these dealers and the
artists who believe that talent is the only skill necessary to guarantee
a constant stream of dealers, curators, and collectors knocking at
the door.

Pratt also points out that since a dealer's selling style usually
matches his or her personal buying style, he or she frequently hires
a staff with a similar selling style. This lack of flexibility can severely
cripple sales. "Collectors come with a variety of backgrounds,
tastes, and buying power," Pratt says. "They also come with a variety of ways they behave as consumers. A gallery must be able to
adapt to the range and differences in consumer habits."[18]

During personal encounters with the public, dealers tend to go to
extremes by either not talking at all or taking too much. The cool,
nonverbal approach can be perceived as intimidating; overly talka-
tive dealers might not hear what the client is saying. "Important
data can be gleaned from listening, including aesthetic learnings, price
range, style of buying, and sincerity of interest," Pratt observes.[19]

Citing greed as one of the most self-defeating business practices,
and noting dealers' unwillingness to split commissions with other
dealers and art consultants, Pratt adds that "dealers should be willing to pass up commissions in order to show clients that they can get
them what they want. This can most definitely strengthen a working
relationship with collectors, stimulate trust, and encourage future

sales. A cooperative spirit between dealers, and between dealers and art consultants, is at an all-time low."[20]

Pratt also faults dealers for their approach to advertising, which is discussed in chapter 6 (see page 117).

"The Attitude"

The late New York dealer André Emmerich once said that "good dealers don't sell art; they allow people to acquire it."[21] Another New York dealer boasts in the *New York Times* that he does not contact museums or collectors on behalf of the artists that he represents; they come to him! This arrogant admission was made in conjunction with an article about why artists change galleries.[22] With this type of self-important and myopic attitude, is it any wonder that an artist would want to defect? Such statements set the tone for the way art is often marketed (or not marketed), an attitude conveyed not only in a gallery's selling style, but by its staff.

For many collectors and potential collectors, the Internet has become a welcome retreat from the abusiveness they have experienced in the art world. As journalist Missy Sullivan points out, "On the Web you don't get that in-your-face snootiness that turns off so many would-be buyers at elite galleries."[23]

In a *New York Times* article the art critic Grace Glueck described some common grievances voiced by the public about galleries.[24] Complaints spanned a range of issues, including the absence of basic civil courtesies and being patronized or treated rudely when purchasing work in the lower end of a gallery's price spectrum.

Dealers, for their part, complained that the public is not knowledgeable about art; they ask too many questions. Dealers further suggested that members of the public do their homework *before* entering a gallery.

The article painted a disheartening picture of the gallery world, primarily in New York City, but the picture is even more disheartening when one realizes how pervasive "the attitude" really is.

Although most dealers are not perceived as used-car salesmen, they often overreact to their fear of being perceived this way by cultivating snobbish airs. However, a haughty attitude coupled with a lack of business acumen often results in a loss of clients and potential clients, and eventually in the loss of their galleries!

Unethical Business Practices

If a dealer is engaged in unethical business practices or emotional abuse, it is not always apparent until an artist is already involved in a formal relationship with the dealer. Some of the ploys used by abusive dealers include playing "mind games," making outrageous demands on artists, and dispensing bad advice. Often, artists are willing to accept a dealer's tyrannical or manipulative behavior as long as they don't feel that the dealer is cheating them financially.

THE MARTYR SYNDROME

Frequently, dealers see themselves as martyrs who are taking a big risk simply by selling art for a living. But many of the dealers who had made their way into the art world in recent years require artists to share the financial risks of running a gallery—without sharing the profits. Because they see themselves as martyrs, dealers also rationalize that it is fair and just to use an *artist's share* of a sale to offset gallery cash-flow problems. Artists are paid when it is convenient— or in some cases they are never paid!

In the second edition of this book, published in 1988, I wrote:

> In the area of finance, there are certain disreputable dealers who are easy to identify, for they blatantly nickel-and-dime artists for every expense that is directly or indirectly related to an exhibition. Up until the time work is placed in a gallery, an artist is financially responsible for the costs of preparing the work for exhibition and transporting the work to a gallery. But once the work is in the gallery, an artist should not have to pay for any costs other than a dealer's commission, and then only if the work is sold!

Tragically, there would be slim pickings if artists limited themselves only to galleries that pay for all exhibition costs. Data compiled in the book *Artists' Gallery Guide to Chicago and the Surrounding Area,* published in 2005 by the Chicago Artists' Coalition, showed that 42 percent of the for-profit galleries polled in Chicago, *who were willing to provide information on who pays for what,* required artists to share some expenses, including promotion materials, installation fees, receptions, and postage. Thirty-four percent of the galleries polled did not provide information about who pays for what. Given the high percentage of galleries unwilling to reveal their policies on who pays for what, it could be ascertained that the galleries that require artists to share some expenses are in the majority. These statistics are indicative of a *trend outside of New York City* to make artists more responsible for gallery costs. In New York City, the practice of requiring artists to share exhibition expenses is not a trend. It is *a fait accompli*!

GALLERY HANKY-PANKY

Sometimes dealers deduct exhibition expenses and/or client discounts from an artist's share of a sale without forewarning the artist of this policy. Sometimes a client discount was not really awarded. And sometimes when work is sold, artists are paid based on a price they previously set, when in reality the work sold for a higher amount. In the fifth edition of this book, I addressed the subject of discount hanky-panky and wrote that the situation can be prevented if an artist requires a copy of a bill of sale or invoice. A reader took issue with the suggested remedy. He sent me an email saying that requiring a copy of a bill of sale doesn't work because art dealers are unwilling to provide them. He mentioned that he had sold approximately forty-five paintings in several galleries and in two transactions at two galleries his paintings had sold for a higher retail price than what had been agreed to in a contract; the dealers pocketed the difference. "That's a fraud rate of 4.4 percent," he wrote, "and I suspect that the actual figure was much higher." Although he sued one of the dealers and won the case, he was looking for a foolproof method of protection.

There really isn't a foolproof way of shielding yourself from art dealer fraud. But one sure way to begin to protect yourself is to *make the decision not to work with art dealers that do not provide a bill of sale*. Keep in mind that even if you are given a bill of sale, the gallery might maintain two sets of records: one for the customer that states the *actual* purchase price and one for the artist with different sales price information.

The artist who sent me the email did not mention how he learned that the two galleries had committed fraud. The good news is that very few individuals who are involved in any type of fraudulent behavior are wise enough to devise foolproof schemes of how not to get caught!

One artist suspected something fishy after his numerous requests to his dealer for copies of sales invoices pertaining to his work went unheeded. He concocted a brilliant scheme to determine whether his suspicions were justified. Knowing that his dealer was out of town, he telephoned the gallery assistant to share a secret: he confided his plans to give the dealer a collage to commemorate his first year as a gallery artist. The collage would incorporate copies of sales receipts pertaining to his work, symbolic of hopes for a continuing prosperous relationship. The artist asked the assistant to cooperate by allowing him to photocopy the receipts. The assistant eagerly complied.

The receipts showed that the artist's suspicions were indeed justified. In one instance, a painting for which he had been compensated based on a selling price of $5,000, had actually been sold for $10,000! The case was settled out of court, and the artist received all of the monies due.

Although the artist was financially compensated for sticking up for his rights, he suffered an emotional blow when he told other gallery artists that he had been cheated and that he planned to take legal recourse. He was chided by some of the artists for "hanging the gallery's dirty laundry in public"; others preferred to look the other way and pretend nothing had happened.

In New York, price manipulation of artwork in galleries was so endemic that in 1988 the city's Department of Consumer Affairs ruled that the prices of artwork in New York galleries must be "conspicuously displayed" for all visitors. Galleries complied, but not without a big fuss. Critic Hilton Kramer wrote a scathing article in the *New York Times* to protest the ruling. His basic point was that galleries are not retail stores and should not be required to display price tags.[25] However, *Times* readers disagreed, and in the following weeks numerous letters to the editor were published contesting Kramer's point of view. One art collector wrote:

> Art galleries are stores. Their proprietors, the art dealers, are merchants. Their primary purpose is to sell art in order to make a profit. They are not houses of worship. They are not museums.

They are not schools. They are not eleemosynary institutions. The dealer is not an altruist dedicated to educate and elevate the public. He is a pragmatic businessman. . . . There is no valid reason why this rule should not apply to galleries so that the collector will get the same information as other consumers.[26]

And an artist wrote:

Mr. Kramer endorses . . . both the "old boy" approach and the "if you must ask the price . . ." snob approach: salesmanship by intimacy and intimidation, respectively, which is exactly what the New York City Department of Consumer Affairs is trying to end. . . . As consumers, we are assured that the amount on whatever price tag is meant for everyone. How strange it is that the art gallery racket is the singular exception to this forthright concept, and how stranger that art dealers should be allowed to hide behind that protective screen of esthetics, of all things.[27]

HOW DEALERS FIND ARTISTS

One of the most annoying and irrational explanations of why the work of more artists is not exhibited in galleries is the cliché that "there are too many artists" or "there are not enough galleries for the number of artists." Such notions reinforce the myth of scarcity that is discussed in chapter 1.

The real reason that the work of more artists is not receiving gallery exposure is that there are too many dealers who are unwilling to take a risk on representing artists who do not have an exhibition track record. There are also too many dealers who know very little about how to sell art or develop an expanding and broad base of collectors, and there are too many dealers who do not know how to tap into new markets and audiences.

On the other hand, many artists without exhibition experience feel trapped by the popular belief that one must have a track record to be considered for gallery representation. Although many galleries are only interested in showing the work of artists with exhibition experience, if an artist has a track record it logically implies that other galleries were willing to exhibit the artist's work without a track record!

The book *The Complete Guide to New York Art Galleries*[28] includes information about the selection process of galleries. Out of 510 galleries in the five boroughs of New York City that show the work of contemporary artists (excluding membership galleries, rental galleries, print publishers, and vanity galleries), 152 galleries stated that they find artists through unsolicited presentation packages; 185 galleries provided no information on their selection process; 85 galleries stated that they select artists through referrals or a combination of referrals, unsolicited presentation packages, publications, and exhibitions; 15 galleries listed a portfolio review as a means of selecting artists; and 73 galleries stated that their galleries are closed to new artists.

It is interesting to compare these findings to a study done in the late 1970s when *Artworkers News* published the first and only comprehensive survey at that time of New York City galleries that showed contemporary art.[29] The study was based on a questionnaire completed by ninety-nine galleries. Although the main purpose of the study was to investigate the extent to which galleries were excluding artists on sexual or racial grounds,[30] it unearthed some insights into the gallery system of the 1970s. The study indicated that the main way galleries got new artists was through artist referrals *and* referrals from other "art-world figures." The study indicated, however, that artist referrals were the *primary* source.[31]

Referral Systems

Understanding how referral systems operate can sometimes be hazy and difficult to decipher. But a clear example of how the artist referral system works is depicted in the following chain of events. One of my clients, a painter, approached a well-known New York gallery dealer. He set up an appointment, showed his slides, and the dealer responded with the "Come back in two years" routine. Several weeks later, while the painter was working as a waiter, he noticed that a famous artist was sitting at one of the tables. He introduced himself to the celebrity and asked whether the celebrity would come to his studio to see his work. The painter and celebrity exchanged telephone numbers, and within the next few weeks the celebrity paid the artist a visit. The celebrity was impressed with the painter's work, so impressed that he bought a painting and insisted that the painter show his work to a specific gallery dealer, coincidentally the same dealer who had rejected him a few weeks before. The celebrity called the gallery dealer, raved about the artist, and shortly afterward my client returned to the gallery. This time he was greeted with another routine, but one more pleasing to his ear: "Where have you been all my life?"

Unfortunately, artists who are willing to refer other artists to galleries are in the minority, and for reasons that reflect on the emotional neediness of many of those who have acquired gallery representation (see chapter 11, "Rationalization, Paranoia, Competition, Rejection, and the Overwhelm Factor").

On the other hand, although artist referrals do exist, referrals from other art-world figures offer more mileage.

For example: Curator tells dealer that critic wrote an excellent review about artist. Dealer checks out artist and invites artist into gallery. Dealer tells curator that artist is now part of gallery. Curator tells museum colleagues that artist is part of gallery and has backing of critic. Curator invites artist to exhibit at museum. Curator asks critic to write introduction to exhibition catalog in which artist is included. Dealer tells clients that artist has been well reviewed and is exhibiting at museums. Clients buy.

There are other variations on the same theme, including curator/dealer/critic conspiracies, which involve each buying the work of an unknown artist for very little money. Press coverage and exhibition exposure begin, and within a short period of time the dealer, curator, and critic have substantially increased their investment. As discussed in chapter 6, for the very purpose of circumventing this type of conflict of interest or the appearance of impropriety, the *New York Times* issued a code of ethics with a provision that the newspaper's art critics, art journalists, and their editors are prohibited from recommending artists to galleries and serving on advisory boards, juries, committees, or panels organized by people they write about. In addition, the code states that if arts writers and arts editors own art, qualified as "exhibition quality," they are required to annually provide an associate managing editor with a list of acquisitions and sales.[32]

Throughout the book *The Art Biz: The Covert World of Collectors, Dealers, Auction Houses, Museums and Critics,* Alice Goldfarb

Marquis describes the many entangled, self-serving relationships among art-world figures, pointing out that the "art marketplace tolerates—indeed fosters—a sleazy, robber-baron style of
capitalism."[33]

New York art dealer Richard Lerner acknowledged the importance of the art-world-figure referral system when he discussed his
criteria for inviting new artists into his gallery. He described his
selection process, which sounds more like a shampoo-judging contest, in this way:

> For the benefit of the people that are already in the gallery, it's
> imperative, if I add names, I add names that already have some
> luster . . . I mean peer approval . . . who are recognized curatori-
> ally, critically as having importance in the mainstream of Ameri-
> can art.[34]

One can ponder at great length over the reasons why a dealer initiates a business relationship with an artist. But there could be as
many reasons as there are dealers, and in the end it is a pointless
task.

Artists who want to gain broad exposure and/or derive a healthy
part-time or full-time income from gallery sales *must be represented
by many dealers*. Relying on one dealer for your livelihood is not
practical for many reasons. For example, your dealer might die, go
into bankruptcy, or go out of business for other reasons. And unless
a dealer understands the importance of expanding his or her client
base and, most important, *is willing to engage in an expansion,* the
gallery's narrowly focused market will soon become saturated, and
sales activity will come to a screeching halt.

Over the years many of my clients in high-end galleries have
expressed bewilderment about why their first two years with a
gallery were a financial success and then everything went downhill.
This can happen when an artist gains entry into a gallery and gallery
patrons purchase a "token" piece of the artist's work, just as they
have done for each artist who is represented by the gallery. If an art
dealer does not have in place an ongoing marketing outreach to
attract new clients, within the context of the gallery, artists will
quickly saturate their market.

INSUFFICIENT TRAINING OF DEALERS

The section "Insufficient Training of Fine Artists" in chapter 1 (see page 5) discusses the problem of art schools not preparing students for real life. The same problem of unpreparedness holds true for dealers, most of whom jump into the field without a clue of how to run a gallery, how to sell art, and how to work with artists in order to achieve a mutually satisfying relationship.

Being an art dealer requires no particular qualifications. *Anyone* can become a dealer, and it seems apparent that *anyone* and *everyone* have become art dealers as witnessed by a general lack of good business and marketing skills, good business standards, and good business attitudes in the dealer's community at large. Also prevalent are a general lack of sensitivity toward artists and a lack of basic knowledge about art.

One of the biggest attractions for becoming an art dealer is that the *immediate* payback is formidable. The *instant* respect, awe, and power gained by dealers are probably unparalleled in any other occupation. On the other hand, obtaining a reputation as a dealer who *actually sells* art is a completely separate matter.

However, positive changes are being made to prepare future art dealers for the gallery world. Degrees in arts administration are now being offered at colleges and universities throughout the United States and abroad, and many of the programs are specifically structured for people who want to become art dealers.

The goals expressed by Columbia College Chicago regarding its graduate program, The Arts, Entertainment and Media Management, are certainly refreshing compared to the reality of how galleries are currently being run:

> Successful arts management is critical to the continued vitality of modern cultural institutions, creative enterprises, and arts organizations. If the public is to benefit, skilled arts managers must facilitate the work of artists. To achieve this end, capable managers combine aesthetic sensibilities and business acumen. Their financial, legal and organizational decisions help make it possible for artists to realize their vision and to share it with the

public. In short, talented arts managers are partners in a collaborative process.[35]

Although the membership list of the Association of Arts Administration Educators is not inclusive of all of the graduate and undergraduate arts administration programs, it includes 44 graduate programs and 14 undergraduate programs in the United States and abroad.[36]

Additional information about colleges and universities that offer degrees in arts administration is listed on the Web site of the Association of Arts Administration Educators and in the *Guide to Arts Administration Training and Research* (see appendix section "Employment Opportunities").

Perhaps in the near future the *majority* of individuals joining the ranks of art dealers will possess the necessary skills and knowledge that can lead to successful careers and make the gallery experience and the experience of working with art consultants much more pleasurable and professional for artists, the public, and other members of the art world.

SELECTING GALLERIES

The most common advice given to artists about selecting galleries is to start small and avoid big cities. The advice is not based on any great truism or profound knowledge; it is simply the way things have been done. However, there is no guarantee that if you start with a small, obscure gallery you will end up in a large, high-profile gallery, just as there is no certainty that if you start big you will automatically be turned away. Since neither of the formulas is guaranteed to work, *approach all galleries that meet your criteria.* Keep all of your options open and do not let supposedly pragmatic advice narrow the possibilities.

Criteria for Selecting Galleries

Deciding whether the gallery is right means paying attention to big and little details. Obviously, respecting the work of gallery artists is an important consideration, but do not limit your selection to those galleries featuring work that is similar to your own. Although it seems like a logical criterion by which to select a gallery, logic does not often prevail in the art world, and a dealer might respond by saying, "We have someone doing that already!" Select galleries that show artists with whom you *share an affinity*.

If you are visiting a gallery in person, the physical properties of a space, including size, ceiling height, and light quality, are another important consideration. Envision your work in the gallery space. Would it be exhibited to its best advantage? Does the gallery have a cluttered or a spacious feeling?

If you are visiting a gallery through the Internet, in some instances gallery Web sites feature installation photographs of exhibitions, and although it is impossible to ascertain all of the physical characteristics of the space, you will be able to glean some information. Another important factor to consider is a gallery's price range. A gallery should offer you pricing *breadth*. Even though your work might currently be priced in a lower range, you want to be able to gradually increase your prices. Therefore, you need a gallery that sells work in a flexible price range. Many galleries have a price ceiling based on what they think their constituency will spend on art.

Let Your Fingers Do the Walking, and Wear a Disguise

Venue Viewer, an online database developed by the Visual Artist Management Project (VAM-P), is an excellent tool for locating nearly 8,200 national and international galleries with Web sites. The *Art in America Annual Guide to Galleries, Museums, Artists* can be a helpful tool for locating galleries throughout the United States. Other publications offer more detailed information on a regional basis, including *Artists' Gallery Guide to Chicago and the Surrounding Area* and *The Complete Guide to New York Art Galleries*. The *Ontario Association of Art Galleries Directory* includes contact information for 457 key individuals in 183 art galleries and organization throughout Ontario, and *The Ontario Gallery Guide* includes commercial galleries, nonprofit galleries, and artist-run galleries and cooperative galleries in Ontario. The names and addresses of the publishers of these resource guides are listed in the appendix section "Exhibition and Performance Places and Spaces."

For galleries in your area follow up by visiting each gallery to ascertain whether it is right for you. Consider this to be an "exploratory" visit—not the time to approach a dealer about your work. On the contrary, *disguise yourself as a collector.* You can glean much more valuable information about the gallery if the dealer thinks you are there to buy! By asking the right questions, you can learn quite a lot about the gallery's profile, including its price range, the career level of artists represented, and whether the dealer and/or his sales force is effective.

On the basis of your experiences during personal gallery visits, eliminate from your list the galleries that are no longer of interest and concentrate on approaching those that have made an impression.

Guidelines for contacting out-of-town galleries are described in "Making National Connections" (see page 156) and "Making International Connections" (see page 158).

What a Gallery Can Do

A gallery has the *potential* to provide artists with many important amenities that are valuable in the present as well as the future. The optimum services to artists can include selling work through single and group exhibitions and on consignment; generating publicity; establishing new contacts and providing entrée into various network systems; developing and expanding markets in all parts of the world; arranging to have work placed in collections; arranging exhibitions in museums and other galleries; and providing financial security in the form of cash advances and/or retainers.

The minimum gallery services can include selling work on consignment (without an exhibition), providing general gallery experience, and adding résumé credits.

Naively, artists either (1) believe that once they are accepted into a gallery, the optimum services will automatically be provided, or (2) enter a gallery relationship without any expectations, thus missing the amenities that a gallery could provide. Keep in mind that dealers in big galleries do not provide any more or fewer amenities than dealers in small galleries. *It really depends on the dealer.*

There are various reasons why some dealers are more supportive than others. In some instances, it is because a dealer is so busy promoting one particular artist that other gallery artists are treated like second-class citizens. Often it is a case of downright laziness. For example, an artist was told by his dealer that he had been nominated for *Who's Who in American Art,* but the dealer had let the deadline pass for providing the required biographical data. In addition, for more than two months she had been "sitting on" sixty-five written inquiries that had resulted from the artist's work being published in a magazine.

Since there are no guidebooks available that evaluate dealers by strengths or weaknesses, the best way to track down this information is to talk to artists who are with a gallery or artists who have left one.

FEAR OF LEAVING A GALLERY

Artists have many excuses for staying with galleries even though the relationship with a dealer might be unproductive or even painful. Many artists believe that it is better to have a gallery with a poor performance record than no gallery at all.

Feelings of financial and/or emotional dependency on a dealer are prevalent among artists who have a difficult time terminating a relationship with a gallery, regardless of whether it is a well-established gallery or it is much less prestigious. The fear of leaving a gallery can be even more intense if an artist has a relationship *only* with *one* gallery.

Regardless of how lazy, contentious, unfair, or ethically dubious a dealer might be, many artists will stay with the dealer through hell and high water because of an underlying fear of *never again* being able to find another gallery. Irrational as the fear might be, it prevents artists from establishing better relationships with other dealers.

Some artists who have achieved success in the art world want to believe that once you are on top you are entitled to stay on top, as if to expect a cosmic IOU slip that is valid for the rest of your life. And even though a dealer's interest in an artist has waned to a point where an artist is treated with disdain, the artist will remain with the gallery because of false pride. Some artists who have experienced success early in their careers have a particularly difficult time at a midlife junction, because they contend that they have passed the point where they should have to initiate new contacts; they see it as degrading or they fear that other people will perceive it as degrading. They are either unaware or refuse to acknowledge the fact that maintaining career recognition and success is a maintenance job, sometimes for the rest of their working lives. Very few successful artists are given the good fortune of being able to coast.

Don't be afraid to leave a gallery if you find that it is no longer serving your best interests. Give a dealer a chance to respond to your needs or requirements, but if he or she is unresponsive, leave.

PRESENTING YOURSELF AND YOUR WORK

> Dealers are so whimsical: I mean, who knows who is going to like what? I just tell people that I know it's a humiliating, horrible process. I don't approve of it at all, the way artists have to trundle around with their wares. I hate being in a gallery when an artist is in there showing slides. It makes me sick to my stomach— I mean, whoever the artist is. But the fact remains, that's how it works and I'm not going to be able to change it singlehandedly. If artists get upset about it, maybe they will do something about it.[37]

Most artists can probably identify with the circumstances and feelings described here by author and critic Lucy Lippard. But showing your work to a dealer doesn't have to be a painful, gut-wrenching experience. Doing everything possible to put yourself on the offensive will make the process easier. In an article in the *Coagula Art Journal*, the artist John Baldessari mentioned that one of his friends pointed out that gallery dealers should really be called merchants, which makes the relationship clear.[38]

The first step is to understand that many dealers play games. *Just realizing that games are being played will give you an edge,* making it less likely that the games will be played at your expense. Having an edge can give you the self-confidence and perception necessary to respond with precision, candor, wit, or whatever the circumstances call for. Compare this power with the many times you have walked out of a gallery thinking of all the brilliant retorts you wished you had said while you were there. Keep in mind that one reason why dealers appear to be in control, even when they are hostile, is that they have a lot of experience talking to artists. Dealers have much more contact with artists than artists have with dealers. The more face-to-face encounters you have with dealers, the more quickly you will be able to psych them out, and the more rapidly your tongue will untwist. Practice makes perfect!

How you contact a gallery can also put you on the offensive. You can walk in cold, lukewarm, warm, or hot. Walking in cold means that you are literally coming off the streets without setting up an appointment or bothering to inquire whether the dealer has regular viewing hours. Chances are you will be interrupting one of the numerous tasks and appointments that consume a dealer's day. Walking in cold leaves you vulnerable to many uncertainties, except the fact that you will receive a cold reception.

Walking in lukewarm means that you have set up an appointment in advance because you have received a positive response to your initial presentation package (see chapter 3), and the dealer has asked to see the work in person.

But before making travel plans or committing to a consignment and/or exhibition arrangement, certain issues need to be addressed. For example, you need to know the gallery's sales commission policy. An artist from New Jersey drove one thousand miles to Chicago at the request of a gallery that had expressed interest in her work. Although the artist had double-checked to make sure that this new contact was not a vanity gallery (see page 135), she had failed to ask about the sales commission, only to learn that the gallery charged 75 percent!

You also need to know whether the gallery uses contracts. Negotiating with out-of-town dealers can be as simple as sending a contract (see pages 32 and 199) that outlines your requirements and, if necessary, being willing to compromise over certain issues. However, it can also be as complicated as persuading a dealer to use a contract!

If you are unfamiliar with a gallery's business reputation, request the names and phone numbers of a few artists who are represented by the gallery. Or if you prefer to contact the artists directly, many of the names of artists represented by a particular gallery are listed in the *Arts in America Annual* and on gallery Web sites.

Walking in warm means that you have been personally referred by an artist or art-world figure. In other words, someone is allowing you to use his or her name. You still might have a hard time getting an appointment, but be persistent. Persistence is not making one telephone call and giving up.

Walking in hot means that a person who is well respected by a dealer has taken the initiative to personally contact the dealer on your behalf.

Don't Show Your Work to Subordinates

Do not show your work to a gallery subordinate (e.g., receptionist, secretary, gallery assistant, assistant manager) for the purpose of eliciting an opinion regarding whether your work is suitable or appropriate for the gallery. Although there are exceptions, subordinates rarely have any power to influence a dealer's decision, and you should not put them in a position to interpret their boss's tastes. Too many artists make the mistake of allowing their work to be judged by gallery underlings. Subordinates are capable of giving compliments, but your ego is in sad shape if you need to hang on to the opinion of each and every staff member who happens to be hanging out at the gallery. Always get the final word straight from the horse's mouth—the gallery owner or director.

Additionally, do not let subordinates discourage you from contacting a dealer. It can be one of the many tactics used by people who feel powerless to usurp what they don't have. In some cases, subordinates want to see your work so *they* can reject it. In other cases, subordinates derive pleasure simply from informing an artist that a dealer is unavailable. Of course, not all subordinates are involved in these power games, and there are those who are sincerely interested in seeing your work. But keep in mind that subordinates are not in a position to make the decision as to whether your work will be accepted by the gallery. Their enthusiasm or discouragement is opinion, not gospel.

There are ways to penetrate the protective shields that surround a dealer. Name-dropping can work. Demonstrating a good sense of humor can also be effective. And then there is basic honesty, letting the person know that *you know* that he or she is playing a power game and why. Honesty is an effective tool in disarming someone.

Agents

The use of agents is an accepted practice and has sometimes proved to be effective for marketing and selling art that is *commercially used*. For example, photographers, illustrators, and fashion and graphic designers use agents ("reps") to establish contacts, obtain commissions, and sell their products.

In such cases, the artist pays a commission to a rep, but not to anyone else. For an agent to make a decent living, he or she must represent several artists simultaneously. The nature of the commercial art business makes this feasible. A rep may work with many publishers, whose business requires and needs many artists, with different styles and different areas of expertise. Thus, a rep can handle many artists without anyone being neglected (although I am sure some commercial artists would argue with me on this point).

However, in the field of fine arts the use of agents is complicated. Dealers do not like to split commissions, and usually if an agent is involved it means the dealer will receive less money on a sale. And if a commission is paid to an agent from an artist's share of a sale, ultimately the artist pays more money in commissions than he or she receives for the sale of the work. For example, if a dealer's commission is 50 percent, and an agent's commission is 20 percent of the artist's share, for a painting priced at $5,000 the dealer receives $2,500, the agent receives $500, and the artist receives $2,000!

Separate from the issue of paying double commissions, the most practical reason why a business relationship between agents and fine artists rarely succeeds is the amount of time required to nurture and develop *one* artist's career, let alone several artists' simultaneously. Any artist who is actively and persistently engaged in marketing and career development understands how time-consuming these endeavors are.

Some artist representatives require fees or a monthly stipend in addition to sales commissions. Although they might try to justify the additional fees or stipends, because they offer other services, such as making telephone calls and writing letters, this is *what they should be doing* to earn a sales commission! Whether or not such services are actually provided can be difficult to determine, and it can take several months or even years and several hundreds of dollars to realize that a lot of time and money were wasted. If an agent is being paid a fee or stipend in addition to a sales commission, the enticement to sell your art work is not as strong.

A few years ago, on the East End of Long Island, New York, where I lived, an agent suddenly vanished with large amounts of money representing unfulfilled promises to more than fifty artists and the proceeds from art sales that belonged to artists and a collector. Each artist had paid her a $2,000 retainer for the promise of exhibitions, sales, publicity, catalogs, and international contacts.

In hundreds of other regions, artists continue to advance money to agents who make promises they do not keep. Some agents are ineffective because they are inexperienced in sales and do not understand the inner workings of the art world. But there are other agents, such as the one on Long Island, with less than honorable intentions, who take advantage of artists who share a particular mind-set that often leads to their victimization. Contributing factors to this mind-set include neediness, gullibility, and the *illusion* that there are actually people in the art world who can look after your best interests better than you.

In 2000, Benny Shaboy, the editor of the former publication *studioNOTES: The Journal for Working Artists* (who is now the editor of *Art Opportunities Monthly*), interviewed gallery dealers and sent questionnaires to 110 top galleries across the country. "We learned that most dealers don't want to work with agents,"[39] he reported.

> On the questionnaire, we listed about 10 ways that galleries might find new art: slide packages from artists, recommendations from collectors or artists already in the "stable," agents, etc. Each dealer was asked to indicate the approximate percentage of new artists he or she took on through each method. The rating for "agent" was zero. A few dealers wrote in "never," and one wrote in "bad idea. . . . "[40]

The article goes on to say that

> galleries want to work directly with the artists because they want
> to have a sense of who the artist is. In addition, a dealer who can
> say "the artist told me that ..." is more likely to impress a poten-
> tial collector than the one who says "I've never met the artist."
> Furthermore, there is a belief that the type of art that agents rep-
> resent is usually the "churn-em-out-sell-em-to-hotels" sort rather
> than the more personal one-of-a kind things that contemporary
> galleries look for. Finally, dealers don't like to share their com-
> missions with agents.[41]

And in my opinion, the fact that galleries do not like to split commissions is the real bottom line!

Over the last several years in the fine arts a new type of agent has
emerged. Known as art consultants (also see page 146), they bypass
galleries and sell work *directly* to businesses, corporations, and individuals. For the most part, since galleries are not involved, an artist
is not faced with the dilemma of having to pay double commissions
totaling more than 50 percent. Even when consultants split commissions with galleries or other consultants, an artist's share of the proceeds of a sale is not larger than 50 percent. Although there are a lot
of misconceptions about the type of work art consultants sell, while
some consultants specialize in mass-produced prints, many other
consultants have a sophisticated and eclectic palate.

When working with art consultants, have realistic expectations.
Art consultants do not nurture artists' careers; they sell artwork.
You might be one of several hundred artists an art consultant represents, and there is a good chance that he or she won't remember
your name unless you are in touch on an ongoing basis.

In addition to art consultants, there are private dealers who are
former gallery owners who found that it was more cost-effective to
represent artists without high gallery overhead costs, and to use
their contacts and networks in a new way. Essentially, an agent who
works this way goes directly to the client, and two commissions are
not involved. Unlike an art consultant, this type of agent represents
a limited number of artists, and is likely to be interested only in
artists with proven track records.

Some artists are using managers. Although a manager functions as an agent, he or she works with only one artist, and is paid a salary or fee in lieu of commission.

In chapter 11 (see page 240), I describe an artist's fantasy of finding the perfect agent. It is important to learn to *manage your own career* because the odds are too low that you will find the fantasy agent, or even one who works well with dealers and splits commissions with them; who takes on emerging artists; who is an effective businessperson; and who works with a small number of artists, giving each of them tender loving care and individual attention.

Studio Visits

Believe it or not, dealers dread studio visits as much as artists dread having them visit. Both parties are nervous and uncomfortable. Dealers are uneasy because they do not like to be put on the spot on an artist's turf. They feel more comfortable rejecting an artist or being vague in their own territory. Dealers also feel anxious about the reception they will receive. They fear that an artist will use the studio visit to give the dealer a taste of the same medicine the artist received in the gallery!

Artists are nervous about the judgment that a studio visit implies. They are anxious about being rejected, or they feel hostile, thus validating a dealer's worst fears that the studio visit will be used as an opportunity to "get even."

One dealer told me that she had to prepare herself mentally weeks in advance of a studio visit. "They are always a nightmare. Artists are so arrogant and hostile." I asked her how she coped with such situations. "I am indecisive and unresponsive. This drives them crazy!"

You have the power to set things up so that the studio visit accomplishes something positive. In some instances, you also must take some of the responsibility if the visit turns out to be unsatisfactory. A successful studio visit should not depend on whether the dealer offers you an exhibition. Many of my clients have been able to score excellent referrals through studio visits. Although the dealers didn't believe that the work was right for their galleries, they were impressed enough to contact other dealers or curators on the artists' behalf, or offered to let artists use their names to set up appointments (enabling them to "walk in warm").

When you host a studio visit, be yourself and don't turn your life upside down. A curator who had spent a concentrated month visiting artists' studios observed that artists who lived and worked in the same space often made a conscious effort to create an atmosphere that suggested their lives were devoid of other living entities. Although the curator saw relics and signs that indicated that the premises were inhabited by dogs, cats, babies, children, and other adults, the studios were conspicuously cleared of all of these other forms of life. She felt very uneasy, as if the artists had a special lifestyle reserved for curators. She sensed that the artists viewed her as subhuman. The strange atmosphere actually diverted her attention away from the art. She couldn't give the artists or their work her undivided concentration.

Even though you might not yet have had a gracious or civilized gallery experience, treat a dealer the way you would want to be treated when you enter his or her domain.

As soon as the studio visit begins, *take control* by defusing tension. Tell the dealer that you understand this is only a preliminary visit and you do not expect a commitment.

Sometimes circumstances are beyond your control. The worst studio visit I ever had involved a well-known art critic who came to look at my work for the purpose of writing an article in a national news magazine. The meeting was going well, but just as he began to select photographs to accompany the article, our meeting was interrupted by an emotionally unstable artist acquaintance who had decided to pay me a visit. Before I had a chance to make introductions, the artist lashed into a series of incoherent insults, *impersonally* directed at anyone who had happened to be in the room.

While the art critic quickly packed up his gear, I tried to make apologies. The critic was unresponsive. He had assumed that the artist's insults were directed at him because he was a critic. He departed and I never heard from him again, although I wrote a letter of apology. I was guilty by association.

At first my anger was directed at the artist, but the more I thought about it, the more I realized that the critic and artist had much in common: they were both devoid of clarity and powers of reason.

I lost the article, but I also lost my awe of the critic. This was an important gain.

ARTIST-GALLERY AGREEMENTS

Including the city of Chicago, the *Artists' Gallery Guide to Chicago and the Surrounding Area* profiled 274 galleries in North Central, Southern and Central Illinois, Indiana, Iowa, Michigan, Wisconsin, and St. Louis, Missouri. Forty-nine percent of the galleries stated that they use contracts; 4 percent stated that they do not use contracts, and 47 percent of the galleries did not provide contract use information.[42]

Beware of dealers who won't use contracts. Requesting someone to enter into a formal agreement does not imply that you are distrustful. It merely attests to the fact that being human lends itself to being misunderstood and misinterpreted. Contracts can help compensate for human frailties. Another important reason for using contracts is that it will save you a lot of time and energy in having to reinvent the wheel each time a situation arises that needs some sort of clarification.

Also beware of contracts prepared by dealers. Just because a contract is *ready,* don't assume that its contents are necessarily in your best interests. This brings to mind a contract recently proposed by a New York gallery to an artist living in the Midwest. The contract tied up the artist for three years, requiring him to pay the dealer a 50 percent commission on work sold through the gallery and a 30 percent commission on all work sold *through other galleries*. The contract did not state whether the 30 percent commission should come from the artist's proceeds of a sale or a third party, but either arrangement would have a devastating impact. It would either paralyze the artist from working with other dealers, or it would leave the artist with only 20 percent of the retail price of artwork sold.

Prior to the artist's establishing a relationship with the New York gallery, his work had been exhibited at museums and prestigious institutions throughout the United States and abroad. He was a National Endowment for the Arts fellowship recipient, and a university professor. But his perception of the importance of having a New York gallery threw his reasoning abilities out of whack, and he signed the contract!

Over the years, most of the dealer-originated contracts that I have screened have not been at all in the best interests of the artists. For the most part they have been narrow in scope and have not taken into account the very realistic scenarios that can develop in an artist/gallery relationship. A contract is a *symbol* that a transaction is being handled in a "professional" manner. What the contract contains is the heart of the matter.

All negotiated points (as well as unnegotiated points) *must* be put into writing. The section "Law: Contracts and Business Forms" in the appendix lists resources for obtaining legal advice and *sample* contracts for various situations that involve artists and dealers. I emphasize *sample* because the contracts should be used as *guidelines*. No two artists or their situations are 100 percent similar, and contracts should reflect these distinctions accordingly.

Gallery Exclusives

Some galleries request exclusive rights to sell an artist's artwork. The exclusive arrangement might be limited to a small geographic region or it could be as broad as world rights. It could be limited to a specific body or series of work, or encompass all of your artwork. It could be limited to only the work that is created during the duration of an artist/gallery contract.

Think twice about entering into an exclusive relationship. What are the benefits and disadvantages of an exclusive arrangement, as compared to being free to exhibit and sell your work through an unlimited number of venues? Does the agreement provide provisions to receive a *realistic* amount of financial compensation to make it worth your while, such as a monthly stipend as an advance against future sales?

What you want to avoid is being exclusively tied to a gallery that is not working hard on your behalf, such as the following worst-case scenario:

An artist accepted an exclusive arrangement with a New York gallery without consulting an attorney. He signed an eight-show contract, giving the gallery exclusive world rights, for all sales, including those made out of his studio. The contract only specified a total number of exhibitions; it did not include an ending date, and the dealer was free to spread the exhibitions over a period of many years, which she did.

Occasionally she advances the artist money, a mere pittance. Since there is no formal arrangement regarding advances against sales, she has the power to oblige or deny his request for money. Making matters worse, the dealer is lazy and has a very limited knowledge of how to sell art. Her husband is wealthy and she is not under pressure to earn money. She has the personality of a barracuda and alienates everyone who crosses her path. Consequently, she sells very little work.

Consignment and Consignment/Exhibition Agreements

A consignment agreement and a consignment/exhibition agreement are the most common types of contracts between an artist and a dealer. Many artists mistake a consignment *sheet* for a contract. A consignment sheet should be *attached* to a consignment agreement or consignment/exhibition agreement; it provides an inventory of the work in a dealer's possession and states the retail value of each piece. A consignment *agreement* should cover basic issues, includingthe length of time the contract is in effect, whether a dealer is limited to selling your work within a specific geographic region, where in the gallery your work will be displayed, the range of sales commissions to be awarded a dealer under *various circumstances,* transportation and packaging responsibilities of the artist and dealer, financial arrangements for rentals and installment sales, artist payment-due schedules, and gallery discount policies.

In addition, a consignment agreement should protect an artist against the assignment or transfer of the contract, and address the very important issues of moral rights, arbitration, copyright, and insurance.

A consignment/exhibition agreement should cover all of the issues just raised, but it should also outline the exhibition-related responsibilities of an artist and dealer. Does the gallery pay for advertising, catalogs, posters, announcements, postage for announcements, press releases, postage for press releases, special installations, photography sessions, opening parties, and private screenings? Or are all or some of these costs split between the artist and gallery—or fully absorbed by the artist?

Artist Sales Contract

An artist sales contract is an agreement between an artist and a collector. Although dealers do not sign this contract, the fact that an artist requires a sales contract as a condition of sale can be a provision in a consignment agreement, consignment/exhibition agreement, or artist/agent contract.

Some dealers are vehemently opposed to the use of an artist sales contract because they are naive and are unilaterally opposed to all artist-related contracts. Other dealers are opposed to the contract because it states the price actually paid for the work. If a dealer is involved in hanky-panky, the last thing he or she wants an artist to know is the work's real selling price. Probably the most common reason some dealers are opposed to the use of the contract is they fear that if an artist knows the name and address of a collector, the artist will try to sell more work to the collector without the dealer's involvement. You can placate some dealers by assuring them that you would much rather be in your studio creating work than going behind their backs trying to sell work. Making an effort to address a dealer's fear often resolves the situation.

From an artist's point of view, a sales contract or artist transfer sales agreement (see below) is very practical. Not only does it provide you with a record of who owns your work at any given time, but it reminds collectors that they cannot alter or reproduce your work without your permission. The contract also states that the artist must be consulted if restoration becomes necessary. And if the work is transferred to a new owner, the sales contract is also transferred.

ARTIST TRANSFER SALES AGREEMENT

An artist transfer sales agreement includes all of the provisions of an artist sales contract, but it goes one step further: it requires the collector to pay the artist a percentage of the increase in the value of a work *each* time it is transferred. The amount of the percentage can vary.

In California, which is the only state that has enacted a resale royalty act, artists are entitled to a royalty on work sold for a gross price of more than $1,000 or has a fair market value of more than

$1,000. The California Resale Royalty Act applies to paintings, drawings, sculpture, or original works in glass. At the time of the sale, the artist must be an American citizen or a California resident for at least two years. The seller must reside in California or the resale of the work must take place in California. The work must be sold by the seller for more money than he or she paid. Detailed information about the California Resale Royalty Act with recommendations to artists for exercising their rights can be found on a Web page provided by the California Arts Council (see the appendix of resource section "Law: Contracts and Business Forms").

Some artists are using 7 *percent,* which was the amount required in the Resale Royalties Act that was proposed but defeated in New York State. Others are using *15 percent,* an amount suggested in what is known as the Projansky Agreement, drafted several years ago by New York attorney Robert Projansky.

Resale royalty contracts are controversial, particularly when they involve the sale of artwork through a gallery. Many art dealers are opposed to the contract in fear that it might complicate a sale; other dealers who are involved in hanky-panky and are selling artwork at a price higher than what an artist agreed to will not use the contract because they do not want an artist to have any documentation about the *real* price paid for the work. In instances of pending studio sales, some artists are also afraid that requesting a resale royalty agreement would jeopardize the transaction. However, some of my clients have used the contract, and, after educating collectors about the purpose of the contract, have had no difficulty in getting it signed on the dotted line.

The appendix section "Law: Contracts and Business Forms" lists publications, including *Business and Legal Forms for Fine Artists, Business and Legal Forms for Crafts,* and *Business and Legal Forms for Photographers,* that provide sample contracts. Each of these publications, written by Tad Crawford, includes instructions for preparing sales, consignment, and exhibition contracts, as well as contracts for a variety of other situations. The publications also come with CD-ROMs so that the contracts can be easily customized. In addition, *The Artist-Gallery Partnership: A Practical Guide to Consigning Art* by Tad Crawford and Susan Mellon presents a model contract between artists and dealers. It also includes a description of consignment acts state by state.

Checking Up on Dealers

Before committing to a consignment and/or exhibition relationship with a dealer, request a contract. If a dealer is unwilling to use a contract, do not get involved. If a dealer provides you with a contract that he or she has prepared, compare it with one of the sample contracts referred to in the appendix section "Law: Contracts and Business Forms." If necessary, amend the dealer's contract to include any important provisions that are missing.

If you have successfully negotiated a contract but are unfamiliar with a gallery's business reputation, talk to other artists represented by the gallery. If you do not know the names and whereabouts of other gallery artists, ask the dealer, or do an Internet search. *It is about time that artists began requesting references!* It is interesting to note that the very same artists who ask me for client references freeze at the thought of asking an art dealer for artist references! Because I am perceived as a supportive ally, artists feel safe to ask for what they want. But because an art dealer is perceived as a person who wields power and makes aesthetic judgments, many artists are unnerved about requesting references.

If you are still unable to get a clear picture of a gallery's business reputation, do a key word search on the Internet using the gallery's name. Complaints or even praise about the gallery could be posted on chat rooms and blogs. If you are still unable to get a clear picture of a gallery's business reputation, contact a local chapter of the Better Business Bureau. Ask whether complaints have been registered against the gallery. You should inquire about the gallery's reputation from both an artist's and a client's point of view.

DEALING WITH DEALERS: IN SUMMARY

Over the years, I have coached hundreds of artists with various gallery-related challenges, from determining whether a gallery's policies are in the best interest of a client to ironing out problems and misunderstandings that arise once an artist is represented. And over the years I have had at least one client in approximately 90 percent of the galleries in New York City that exhibit contemporary work. These experiences have provided me with an unusually broad perspective on what has gone on behind the scenes at many galleries since the late 1970s and what is going on today. I have been privy to intimate information about how artists are treated and mistreated, who is suing whom and why, the names of the dealers who do not pay artists or do not pay on time, and other maladies.

I still cringe when I hear or learn about some of the unintelligent remarks and value judgments made by dealers, or the outrageous rudeness they display. Those rare occasions when an artist praises a dealer for being fair and wise give me hope that perhaps things are changing for the better.

More often, though, I have trouble responding when I am asked to name dealers I respect *both* as businesspeople and as human beings. The dealers on my list could be counted on one hand!

Although for many reasons I consider the gallery system in New York to be the most decadent, New York is certainly not the only place that attracts art dealers with questionable moral and business ethics. Many artists around the country have trying and cumbersome relationships with dealers.

If artists do not learn to *cultivate their own market* and become less dependent on galleries for sales and exposure, they will find themselves paying commissions in the neighborhood of 75 percent and up, just to support dealers in the style to which they are accustomed!

In the last edition of this book I mentioned that some galleries in New York have initiated the policy to charge artists a fee for reviewing unsolicited presentation packages. This trend has now spread to other cities.

It is important that artists develop an autonomous posture and make their own career decisions rather than wasting time waiting for something to happen. The chances are remote that you will find the perfect agent or be introduced to galleries through an art-world-figure referral system, and the so-called artist referral system is virtually nonexistent, because most artists are too paranoid and competitive to refer each other.

You *can* find a gallery without being referred. But do not rely on representation by *one* gallery to provide the exposure or livelihood you are seeking. Build a network of many galleries located throughout the United States and the world. Building such a network requires time and patience. But it can be done.

The Mysterious World
of Grants: Fact and Fiction

Who gets grants and why? The *real* answers to these questions can be provided by jurors who select grant recipients. All other answers are speculative and have more to do with hearsay than reality. When I asked members of various grants panels about their selection criteria, their answers were simple and direct: they liked the artist's work or they liked the project under consideration and thought that the artist was capable of undertaking the work. When I probed further, the answers were predictably numerous, varied, and subjective, and boiled down to "taste buds."

Artists who are apprehensive and skeptical about applying for grants have many misconceptions about who receives them. Skeptical artists deem themselves ineligible for various reasons, such as being too old or young, lacking sufficient or impressive exhibition or performance credits, or lacking the right academic background. They believe that the kind of work they are doing isn't considered "in" or that they lack the right connections, which implies that juries are rigged!

It is perfectly conceivable and probable that some artists have been denied grants by some foundations because of some or all of the above-mentioned factors. However, on the basis of my own experiences as a grant recipient and juror, as well as the experiences of my clients (the majority of whom would not measure up to the tough stereotype that many artists have of "the perfect grant-winning specimen"), I am convinced that, for the most part, grant selection is a democratic process—meaning that everyone has a *real* chance. Many artists believe that because they have applied for the same grant year after year without success, it is a waste to continue to apply. Images are conjured up of a jury sitting around a table moaning, "Oh, no, not him again!" Or conversely, there are artists who believe that one must apply for the same grant at least three or four times before it will be awarded: "It's her fourth application, let's give her a break!" But contrary to the notion that jurists remember who applied for a grant each year, most panels have new members each time they convene. Each time you apply you have a fresh chance.

Since grant selection in the arts is based on taste, and like taste buds, the grants world is mysterious, whimsical, and fickle, you should not depend on or view grants as the only means of providing the opportunity to do what you really want. Grants should be looked upon as "cream" to help alleviate financial pressures, provide time and new opportunities to develop your career, and add another entry to your list of endorsements.

Projects and ideas should not be tossed aside if funding agencies or foundations reject your application(s). Remember, the selection criteria are subjective and *ultimately you must be the judge* of whether your work and ideas have merit. A grant is not the deciding factor.

Also remember that juries are composed of human beings, and humans are not always right. In fact, we have quite a track record of not recognizing talent (until someone dies) and of putting some questionably talented people on a pedestal.

The grants world might seem mysterious, but hundreds of artists each year who take time and energy to investigate grant possibilities and complete well-thought-out applications are reaping the benefits.

BIG GRANTS AND LITTLE GRANTS

Grants come in many different shapes, sizes, and forms. There are grants for visual and performing artists with broad-based purposes and specific project grants for well-defined purposes. For example, there are grants for artists who are women, artists who are grand-mothers, artists with a particular ethnic or religious background; grants for artists born in certain regions, states, and cities; grants for artists involved with conceptual art or traditional art; grants for travel; grants for formal study; grants for independent study; grants for apprenticeship; and grants for teaching.

From year to year grant agencies and foundations open and fold, cut budgets, increase budgets, change their funding interests and pri-orities, emphasize one arts discipline over another or one socioeco-nomic group over another. It is important to keep abreast of these changes. A grant that is not applicable to your current situation and interests could be suitable in the future.

Even when budgets are being cut, don't hesitate to submit grant applications. A case in point: During a time when federal arts bud-gets were being slashed, I received a large matching grant from the National Endowment for the Arts. I was not optimistic that I would receive a grant when I submitted the application. Not only was I sur-prised that I received the grant, I was also surprised that I was awarded every penny that I requested. However, it was pointed out to me by a person familiar with the inner workings of the NEA that when government arts funding is cut, people are reluctant to submit grant applications. Thus, the competition is reduced. In many instances, people have a better chance of receiving a grant when the financial climate is restrained.

Although the National Endowment for the Arts no longer directly awards grants or fellowships to visual artists, many state and regional arts councils award grants and fellowships to visual artists, as well as to performing artists and writers. In addition, sev-eral private foundations give grants to artists, but because they are less well known, fewer people apply for them.

Good sources of information on grants that are specifically geared to artists include the online database NYFA Source spon-sored by the New York Foundation for the Arts. It lists more than 2,900 award programs throughout the United States, and new resources are added on an ongoing basis. *Art Opportunities Monthly,* which is distributed by email, includes grants and fellow-ships for artists. The Web site of the National Assembly of State Arts Agencies includes a state arts agency directory, a helpful source for researching grants and fellowships sponsored by individual state arts agencies. The Web site of the Canada Council on the Arts includes a listing of grants for Canadian artists and provides application information. *Artist Grants Master List* by Bari Caton is an ebook with links to numerous online resources that describe grant opportunities for individual artists. *Guide to Canadian Arts Grants* lists 1,000 art-granting programs and awards throughout Canada for artists in all disciplines. *Guide to Getting Arts Grants* by Ellen Liberatori provides artists and arts organizations with information on facts and skills needed for grant applications in the arts, including insights into understanding the selection and review process. The book provides guidelines on how to formulate budgets, and master the intricacies of the application process. Grant opportunities and online resources are also included.

The Creative Capital Foundation takes a unique approach to grant giving. This national not-for-profit organization supports artists pursuing innovative approaches to form and content in the performing, visual, literary, media, and emerging art fields. In addition to financial support, the foundation provides grant recipients with advisory services and professional development assistance. In return, artists share a portion of any proceeds generated by their projects with Creative Capital to replenish the grantmaking fund so that other artists will benefit in the future. Additional resources for information on grants are listed in the appendix sections "Art Colonies and Artist-in-Residence Programs" and "Grants and Funding Resources."

Art Colonies and
Artist-in-Residence Programs

Acceptance in an art colony, also known as a retreat or artist-in-residence program, is a form of a grant, since the sponsoring organization subsidizes the artists it selects.

Such retreats are scattered throughout the United States and the world. They offer an artist the opportunity to work on a project for a specific amount of time, free from life's daily burdens, responsibilities, and distractions.

Subsidization can be as comprehensive as payment of transportation expenses, room and board, and a monthly stipend. Or it can be limited to partial payment of room and board, with the artist required to pay a small fee.

Some programs, such as the American Academy in Rome and the Bellagio Center Creative Arts Fellowship Program in Italy, sponsored by the Rockefeller Foundation, offer luxurious creature comforts. Other colonies offer a summer-camp ambience and are based on a communal structure.

There are colonies that specialize in one particular arts discipline as well as those that include visual and performing artists and writers.

There are residencies located in parks. For example, the National Park Service sponsors residencies in twenty-nine parks throughout the United States. The Artists in Residence in Everglades (AIRIE) program is open to writers and visual artists, including painters, sculptors, photographers, video artists, and mixed media artists. The Art and Community Landscapes Program, sponsored by the New England Foundation for the Arts in conjunction with the National Endowment for the Arts and the National Park Service, hosts artists' residencies. There are also residencies associated with hospitals, health-care facilities, and schools (described on page 226 in chapter 10).

The Alliance of Artists' Communities is an excellent resource for locating art colonies and artist-in-residence programs. The alliance is a national service organization that supports the field of artists' communities and residency programs. Its Web site provides links to various art colonies and artist-in-residence programs. It also sponsors the publication *Artists Communities,* which is a complete guide to residence opportunities in the United States for visual and performing artists and writers. It includes information on facilities, admission deadlines, eligibility requirements, and the selection process. In Europe, the organization Trans Artists provides artists in all disciplines with information about international artist-in-residence programs and other opportunities.

Additional resource lists and information about art colonies, artist-in-residence programs, and exchange programs are in the appendix sections "Art Colonies and Artist-in-Residence Programs" and "International Connections."

Nonprofit and Umbrella Organizations

There are more grants available to nonprofit art organizations than to individual artists, and the dollar value of the grants available is substantially higher. For this reason, when I was working as an artist I turned myself into a nonprofit, tax-exempt organization. The tax-exempt status also allowed individuals to receive tax breaks on any contributions and donations they made to my projects.

Although there were many advantages to being a nonprofit, tax-exempt organization, there were also disadvantages. For example, while my organization was in operation, I found myself spending a disproportionate amount of time completing the various forms and reports that were required by federal and state agencies. Another drawback was having to contend with a board of directors, which diminished, to a certain extent, the autonomy that I had enjoyed while working on my own. I also spent a lot of time meeting with board members and sustaining their enthusiasm for fund-raising.

Carefully evaluate your situation before taking steps to form a nonprofit organization. For further information about forming a nonprofit organization and working with a board of directors, see the appendix section "Law: Forming a Not-for-Profit Organization."

If you personally do not wish to go nonprofit, there is an option available that allows you to bypass the tax-exemption route: use the services of an *umbrella organization*. Umbrella organizations are nonprofit, tax-exempt groups that let you apply for a grant under their auspices. If a grant is awarded, the umbrella organization receives the award and in turn pays you.

Umbrella services can vary from a minimum of signing a grant application to bookkeeping; managerial advice; preparation of annual, federal, and state reports; assistance with publicity and promotion; and fund-raising. In return for these services, a percentage of any grant that is awarded to an artist or a group of artists goes to the umbrella organization. For example, Fractured Atlas is a national nonprofit arts organization that offers fiscal sponsorship to its members throughout the United States. When a grant is awarded to a member, Fractured Atlas receives an administration fee of 6 percent of the total grant proceeds. Contact information about Fractured Atlas is provided in the appendix section "Grants and Funding Resources."

Umbrella organizations do not take all artists under their wings.

They consider the nature of an artist's project and the impact it will have on the community. Umbrella groups rely on grants to pay their overhead and salaries, and their ability to receive grants depends largely on the success of the projects they sponsor.

The best way to learn about umbrella organizations in your area is to contact your local state arts council.

INCREASING YOUR CHANCES OF BEING FUNDED

Preapplication Research

Before completing a grant application, learn as much as possible about the funding organization. Your homework should include learning about eligibility requirements, funding priorities, the long-term goals of the organization, and the maximum and minimum amount of the grant. Jane C. Hartwig, former deputy director of the Alicia Patterson Foundation, emphasizes the importance of homework: "The fact that you have done your homework, even at the earliest stage, is impressive, and appreciated by the foundation. It will also save you time, money, and possibly grief."[1]

When you receive your application instructions and the background information about the agency or foundation, the kind of language used will give you a strong indication of the types of art and arts projects that are funded. For example, if you are told that the grant is for artists whose work is devoted to the classical or conservative tradition of Western culture, it is very clear what the foundation giving the grant is looking for. If your work or project involves anything other than "the classical or conservative tradition of Western culture," it is a waste of time to apply to this foundation.

Submitting Visual Materials

Grant applications in the visual arts usually require that visual presentations of the artist's work accompany a written application. Although some funding agencies request to see the actual work once an artist passes a semifinal stage, most organizations make their final selections on the basis of slides or a CD-ROM.

Too often artists place great importance on a written application and give too little attention to the photographic material. Both are important for completely different reasons. Here are some guidelines to follow in submitting visual materials. In addition, review the section "Visual Presentations" in chapter 3, page 56.

(1) All photographic material should be of *top quality*: clear and crisp, with good lighting and tone.

(2) Submit photographs of your most *recent* work. Most funding agencies do not want to see a retrospective of your last ten years. They want a strong, clear indication of your current interests and directions.

(3) Select photographs that represent the *best* of your recent work. *You decide what is best*. If you are indecisive about what to submit, consult with someone whose taste you respect.

(4) Even if the funding agency does not require photographic materials to be labeled, *label* each and every slide or photograph with your name and the title, medium, date, and dimensions of the work. Also include a directional indication showing the top of the work. This information could decide whether your work is rejected or enters the next stage of judging. Photographs or slides should seduce the judges, but if they are confused and can't "read" what is going on, they will not take the time to look up your application in hopes of clarification.

A final pointer about slide presentations: since most funding agencies actually project slides on a screen, it is very *important* to project your slides on a large screen *before* you submit a grant application. If your slides are being projected for the first time, you might be shocked to discover the results. Recently, I borrowed slides from various artists for a lecture that I was giving at a museum. I selected the slides from slide sheets and then reviewed them with a hand viewer. However, I made the mistake of not projecting the slides on a screen before the presentation. When projected, half of the slides were so dark that I had the entire audience squinting.

Completing Applications

When you first encounter a grant application, it can seem like Egyptian hieroglyphics. Mastering grant applications *is* like learning a new language, and the more experience you have, the easier it becomes.

In addition to carefully following instructions, the best posture to take when filling out an application is to *put yourself in the shoes of a jurist*. In other words, you want to read applications that are legible and clear and that come quickly to the point. You do not want to have to reread an application in order to understand it clearly. Applications should hold the judge's attention.

I am often called upon to review *unsuccessful* grant applications. These applications tend to have in common one or all of the following mistakes:

(1) They reflect a negative tone, implying that the artist has a chip on his or her shoulder (e.g., "The world owes me a grant").
(2) The description of the grant purpose and/or project talks over the heads of the readers, rambles on with artsy language, and goes off on irrelevant tangents.
(3) Funds are requested for inappropriate or "off-the-wall" purposes, basically insulting the intelligence of the judges.

I was one of eight jury members who met to select a public art project. The proposal I liked best was very imaginative and had a wonderful sense of scale. It would have been relatively easy to install, maintenance free, and able to withstand inclement weather. It was also the least costly of all of the proposals submitted.

However, the project did not win because the artist antagonized the jury! Leaving most of the application questions unanswered, except for a project description, the artist wrote (in barely legible longhand) one arrogant sentence implying that the drawings that accompanied the application would make the sculpture's design and meaning clear to all but the dumbest of viewers.

Although most jurors agreed that this project was the most appealing, they also concurred, based on the attitude expressed in the application, that the artist would probably be difficult to work with during the planning and installation stages. Whether or not that would have been true is open to speculation, but the fact of the matter is that the way in which the artist completed the application prevented her from receiving the commission.

Proposals and Budgets

If you are applying for grants that require a written proposal and a budget, I recommend the book *Guide to Getting Arts Grants* by Ellen Liberatori. The author is a writer and poet who has worked in the nonprofit grant-making sectors of philanthropy for nearly thirty years. The author covers the topics of proposal writing and budget preparation in a very clear and thorough manner. There is also an in-depth discussion about submitting a grant application using a fiscal agent. Throughout the book Liberatori lists "pet peeves" of grant-making decision makers. Another resource is the GYST Software for Artists, which guides users through the process of writing grant proposals or other proposals with detailed instructions.

JUDGING PROCEDURES

Most funding agencies use the first round of judging to sort through applications to make sure that artists have complied with all of the instructions, rules, and regulations. Consider this the "negative" stage of judging, as the agency is on the lookout for applicants who do not follow instructions. This hunt has no deeper purpose than to make the judges' work easier by reducing the number of applications to be considered.

Each funding agency has its own procedures for reviewing grant applications. After eliminating the applications that do not qualify, some agencies then review the artists' creative achievements by such steps as looking at slides and videotapes, listening to audiotapes, and reading manuscripts. After the judges have narrowed down the selection of artists for the final stages of judging, they review written applications. Other agencies that require written proposals and budgets review the application and support material simultaneously.

"Say the Secret Word and Win One Hundred Dollars"

Probably as a result of the many tests one is subjected to in school, artists approach a grant application as an aptitude or IQ test. It is felt that ultimately the application is trying to trick you with double meanings. The fact is that there are definitely "wrong" answers, such as those I have described from the unsuccessful grant applications, but there is no one "right" answer.

For example, many grant applications request information on *educational background* and *salary*. Those artists who believe their formal education is inadequate, in terms of the "right" academic credentials, erroneously believe that they will have virtually no chance of being funded. Artists also worry that if their salaries are above poverty level they will be ineligible for a grant. Although there are grants available that are specifically designed to assist impoverished or low-income artists, if this criterion is not stated in a foundation's application guidelines, one can safely assume that the grant is awarded on the basis of merit or merit combined with moderate financial needs. Such situations might include, for example, artists who are on a tight budget and lack the funds to be able to take a leave of absence from a job or reduce the number of hours of employment to devote time to their artwork.

Another part of the "secret word" syndrome is how much money to ask for. Arriving at a funding-request figure is not like competing in a jelly-bean-counting contest—you don't have to guess down to the exact penny how much you think the foundation will give you.

Some foundations give a set amount of money (e.g., twenty grants of $5,000 each). Other foundations state a maximum amount but say that smaller grants—the amount of which will be left to the discretion of the jury—will also be given. In recent years, the discretion of the jury resulted in awarding one of my clients *almost double* the amount of the grant that she requested!

Letters of Recommendation

When foundations request that an applicant include a letter or letters of recommendation, it means that they are asking for testimony from other people that your work is good and/or that your project has merits and is relevant and important. I often encounter blank expressions when I ask applicants whom they are going to use as a reference. They believe there is not one person available to help. Of course, it is impressive if you are recommended by an art-world superstar. However, if such a person is not part of your network, do not let this become a stumbling block. Jane C. Hartwig puts it this way:

You certainly shouldn't shy away from using someone well known in your field if that person happens to know you and your work and has indicated a willingness to write a letter in your behalf. Just don't think that you haven't a chance if you don't know any luminaries. Happily, it really doesn't matter.[2]

In summary, if you were on a grant panel, what would impress you more? An insipid but well-meaning letter of recommendation from a celebrity or a perceptive and analytical letter from someone you have never heard of?

There is a range of possibilities of obtaining letters of recommendation: for example, the curator or director of a museum or nonprofit gallery, a critic, a member of the academic art community, an art historian, another artist, or the director of a nonprofit arts organization.

Less effective sources of letters of recommendation are from those people in positions that could be interpreted as a conflict of interest. For example, gallery directors and collectors have a vested interest in awards that artists receive. Such recognition can contribute to a rise in the monetary value of artwork and heighten an artist's standing in the art world. Since gallery dealers and collectors can directly and indirectly benefit from an artist's achievements, letters of recommendation pumping up an artist's virtues from either source are much less impressive than those letters written by people in much more objective positions.

Remember, the worst thing that can happen is that the person you ask to write the recommendation will say no. Although this happens, it doesn't happen that often, because almost everyone has been in the position of asking for help.

AN UNTRADITIONAL GRANTSMANSHIP ROUTE

The traditional way to apply for grants is to rely on a foundation to announce the availability of a grant and submit an application. However, there is an untraditional route, which I have personally used with very successful results.

Corporate Detective Work

I obtained corporate sponsors for many exhibitions and projects by taking the initiative and contacting companies, regardless of whether they were in "the grants business." I first located corporations that either provided services or manufactured goods and materials that had some relationship to my project or exhibition. I began my detective work at the library using *Standard & Poor's Rating Guide,* a massive directory that lists American corporations, cross-referenced according to product and/or service.

In one instance, I was planning an exhibition of sculpture in which aluminum would be used extensively. Through *Standard & Poor's* I came up with a list of major aluminum companies, their addresses, and the names of key officers and public- or corporate-relations directors.

I sent a letter to each public- or corporate-relations director, with a copy to each key officer; I indicated on each original letter that company officers were also receiving the letter.

The letter detailed the purpose of the exhibition, told where it was being held, and included a description and a budget. I also included a sentence or two about what the company would receive in turn for its sponsorship, namely, public-relations benefits. *Within six weeks* I landed a sponsor.

Value of Sending Copies

Sending copies of the sponsorship request to key corporate officers is very important. It increases the chances that the letter will really be given careful consideration and it decreases the chances that a sponsorship decision will be blocked by one person. For example, if only the public-relations director receives a letter and that person, for one reason or another, is unmoved, the request dies a quick death. By submitting the request to many officers, you increase the chances that you will find an ally with clout!

YES, YOU CAN FIGHT CITY HALL

For four consecutive years I applied for a grant from a state arts council for three different projects. Each year I was rejected. After the fourth rejection, I launched my own investigation and learned that one staff member was blocking my application, but for reasons that were so petty I could attribute them only to a "personality conflict." Venting my frustration, I wrote to the director of the arts council, detailing the four-year history of grant applications, documenting all the hours spent on applications, answering questions, meetings, appointments, interviews, letters of recommendation, and more letters of recommendation. But most important, I reiterated the merits of the project that I wanted funded. I also named the staff member who had been giving me such a hard time and sent a copy of my diatribe to that person. About three weeks later I received a letter from the arts council stating that it had reversed its decision—the project would be funded.

Generating Income:
Alternatives to Driving a Cab

In 2008 the National Endowment for the Arts (NEA) published the study *Artists in the Workforce: 1990–2005*,[1] which was the first nationwide look at artists' demographic and employment patterns in the Twenty-first century. It revealed interesting tidbits of information including the fact that "artists are one of the largest classes of workers in the nation, only slightly smaller than the U.S. military's active-duty and reserve personnel (2.2 million)."[2] The study also revealed that "artists generally earn less than workers with similar education levels. The median income from all sources in 2005 was $34,800 for artists, higher than the $30,100 median for the total labor force, and lower than the $43,200 for all professionals."[3] The results of the study showed that "more than one in three artists is self-employed compared with less than 10 percent of the labor force."[4] Although the gist of the study results was optimistic in looking at the status of "artists" as a whole, the downfall of the study is that it lumped together fine artists who do *self-generated work* with artists who receive compensation for doing art-related assignments. The fine-artist category included art directors and animators, but excluded photographers, who were placed in a separate category that included scientific photographers, aerial photographers, and photojournalists. Other categories included actors, announcers, architects, dancers and choreographers, designers, entertainers and performers, musicians, producers and directors, and writers and authors. Hopefully, the next time the NEA conducts a similar study, artists who do only self-generated work will be singled out.

Being able to support yourself as an artist, and maintain a high-quality life through finances generated from your work, can and does happen all the time. But rarely does it happen overnight, and realistically, until your career gets rolling, it is necessary to earn a living through other means. This chapter covers the assets and drawbacks of conventional jobs, and it discusses some job opportunities and ways of generating income within the fine-arts field. It also provides ideas for minimizing business expenses and saving money.

ASSETS AND DRAWBACKS
OF CONVENTIONAL JOBS

To solve the problem of supporting yourself as an artist you must take into account your financial and emotional needs and your physical capabilities. Whether the options suggested in this chapter are appealing or you prefer traditional forms of employment that offer more financial security depends on your personality, temperament, and energy level. What works for one artist doesn't necessarily work for another. But the *common goal* is to generate income that simultaneously allows you to maintain a good standard of creature comforts, a good state of mind and health, energy for your own projects, and energy to develop your career. Each of these criteria is equally important.

However, in the name of art and the "myth of the artist," compromises and sacrifices are constantly made. Contrary to the teachings of the myth, you are entitled to what you want, and there are ways to get it.

Before jumping into employment, assess carefully and *honestly* what you are looking for and why. Does the job provide a *real means to an end,* or is the job likely to annihilate your end? For example, two of my clients took jobs with arts service organizations. Both jobs provided the artists with sufficient income as well as opportunities to meet people related to their profession and expand contacts and networks. One job involved low-pressure, routine duties. Although the artist was not mentally stimulated, she had energy to sculpt and develop her career because her responsibilities were minimal. The other job was full of responsibilities. It was demanding and stimulating. Although the artist found the work fulfilling, at the end of the day she was drained and did not have the energy for her artwork.

If you want to work within the arts, there are some good resources available. *Artjobonline,* sponsored by the Western States Art Federation (WESTAF), is a biweekly, online newsletter that lists employment opportunities in the visual and performing arts, literature, education, and arts administration. Other Web sites that include arts-related employment opportunities include ArtCareer Network, Art & Design Career Employment, Arts Opportunities, Chronicle Careers, and Hire Culture. Teaching Artist Source sponsored by the New York Foundation for the Arts is an online, telephone, and email information service for artists to learn about teaching opportunities on a local, regional, state, and national level. *ArtSearch,* published by the Theatre Communications Group, is a national employment bulletin for the performing arts. It includes art and art-related positions in education, production, and management. *Career Solutions for Creative People: How to Balance Artistic Goals with Career Security* by Dr. Ronda Ormont focuses on how to find the time and freedom to pursue art while making a stable living. *Careers in Art* by Blythe Camenson provides a breakdown of educational requirements and additional training for specific jobs, and surveys salaries and job opportunities. Information about the above-mentioned resources can be found in the appendix section "Employment Opportunities."

USING YOUR TALENTS
TO GENERATE INCOME

Teaching: A Boon or a Trojan Horse?

Teaching is attractive to artists for several reasons: it offers financial security as well as the fringe benefits of health insurance, life insurance, sick leave, vacation pay, and long vacations. In addition, it is a highly respected occupation.

Because of these attractions, the competition to teach is horrendous—so horrendous that, unless one is a superstar, getting a job usually necessitates returning to school for more degrees. On the other hand, even if your qualifications are superlative, there is no job guarantee. There are more qualified artists than teaching positions available in colleges and universities and within school systems.

The scarcity of jobs is not the only drawback. When you are an artist and a teacher, you wear two hats. If teaching consisted only of lecturing, critiquing, and advising students, it would be relatively simple. However, teaching means a lot more. It means extracurricular involvement with faculty politics and yielding to the special demands and priorities of academia. Theoretically, these roles should be compatible and supportive, but often they are not.

Artists who teach *and* want to develop their careers must contend simultaneously with the occupational hazards of both professions. The situation is particularly complex because many of the demands and priorities of the art world and academic world are in conflict. Often, artists involved in the academic world face peer pressure based on how much they know about the past rather than what they are doing in the present. Sometimes artists are forced to change their methods of teaching and/or style of work to conform to current academic trends and ideology. Getting tenure often becomes the most important goal in life. Academia also puts demands on teachers to exhibit their artwork and publish articles, essays, and books about art history and art criticism. An artist may have little time for his or her personal work.

Nevertheless, teaching can be an important and vital adjunct to an artist's work. A case in point, after reading the fifth edition of my book, Zacher Vaks, a painter based in New York, sent me the following email:

> Along with being a visual artist I teach an art and activism course at the Community School for Justice in the South Bronx. Before taking the job I was afraid that teaching would take me away from my artwork. I was reminded of this anxiety after I read the section of your book "Teaching: A Boon or a Trojan Horse?" I must say that working with these kids, although exhausting, has begun seeping into my paintings and drawings.

There are teaching opportunities available within and outside academic compounds that allow artists autonomy and flexibility. Some of these opportunities are described on the following pages.

Apprenticeships

Serving as an apprentice to another artist is a viable means of earning a living for a certain period of time. But keep in mind that contrary to the myth, working for a *famous* artist is not a prerequisite to achieving success in the art world. However, serving as an apprentice to an experienced artist can be helpful to less-experienced artists. It can provide an opportunity to learn more about the business of art and see firsthand what being an artist is all about.

An apprenticeship experience can be particularly advantageous if the apprenticeship is with an artist who is surefooted and emotionally secure. Insecure artists might not be generous in sharing career information or their contacts. Insecure people also tend to have difficult personalities. Before accepting an apprenticeship position, ask your potential employer for the names and phone numbers of previous apprentices. You have every right to request references.

Whether you are seeking an apprenticeship position or are seeking an apprentice, additional information about apprenticeships is listed in the appendix section "Apprenticeships and Internships" and on page 42 of chapter 2.

Internships

Many not-for-profit organizations, for-profit companies, museums, galleries, and art consultants offer internships to artists. These entry-level positions can lead to interesting job opportunities to supplement your fine-art income or lead to transitional positions until you are a self-supporting artist. Some of the publications that offer information about internships and internship sponsors include *Gardner's Guide to Internships at Multimedia and Animation Studios* by Garth Gardner, which profiles hundreds of computer graphics, animation, and multimedia companies in the United States and Canada that offer internships; *Gardner's Guide to Internships in New Media: Computer Graphics, Animation and Multimedia*, which profiles hundreds of companies in the visual-effects industry that offer internships; and *The National Directory of Art Internships*.

For additional information about internships, see the appendix sections "Apprenticeships and Internships" and "Employment Opportunities" and page 42 of chapter 2.

Artist-in-Residence Programs

There are various forms of artist-in-residence programs. Some have the fundamental purpose of providing artists with opportunities to live in an environment in which they may work unimpeded by life's daily worries (see page 210). Other artist-in-residence programs pay artists to teach on a temporary, part-time, or full-time basis in school systems and communities throughout the United States. For example, the Studio in a School Program places professional artists in public schools in New York City. An artist can participate in several ways: by establishing a studio in a specific school building; by performing hands-on visual-arts workshops at various locations; or by serving as a mentor to teachers, helping to create lesson plans for art projects, conducting art lessons, and using art in the classroom.

There are numerous artist-in-schools and artist-in-education programs throughout the United States, and many of the sponsors have compiled directories that list artists available for residencies. For example, the online *Directory of Performing Artists* and *Directory of Teaching Artists*, sponsored by the Connecticut Commission on Culture and Tourism, lists Connecticut-based artists who specialize in public performances and those who participate in classroom residencies and other types of residencies. Other online resources include the *Directory of Artists in Schools* that lists artists who participate in arts-in-education programs; the *Directory of Teaching Artists*, a list of artists who participate in artist-in-residence programs in schools in Idaho.

There are also many residency programs affiliated with social service and health-care facilities. For example, Hospital Audiences, Inc., brings visual and performing art programs to New Yorkers confined in hospitals and health-care facilities, shelters, et cetera. The National Training Program for Hospital Artists-In-Residence is a program that provides professional training to artists to work with cancer patients in their hometown, medical centers, clinics, and hospitals. The Children's National Medical Center in Washington, D.C., sponsors the New Horizons program, which provides residecies for artists, writers, and musicians. In addition, the Web site SchoolShows contains a national directory of performers who present assemblies, workshops, and residencies in schools.

For information about artist-in-schools and artist-in-education programs, contact local, state, and regional arts councils and agencies. Information about organizations and resources on artist-in-residency programs can be found in the appendix sections "Art Colonies and Artist-in-Residence Programs," "Employment Opportunities," and "Art and Healing."

Lectures and Workshops

Lectures, slide presentations, demonstrations, and workshops are excellent means of generating income. They also offer exposure and serve as good public-relations vehicles.

Colleges; universities; social-service agencies; civic, cultural, and educational organizations; and cruise ships often hire artists for "guest appearances."

You can base presentations on your own work alone or also discuss the work of other contemporary artists, art history, and art criticism. Subjects and themes of arts-related presentations are unlimited.

The financial rewards of public appearances can be considerable if you repeat your performance several times. For example, when I receive an out-of-town invitation to conduct career workshops for artists, I use the opportunity to create more opportunities by contacting other educational or cultural institutions in the same region. What starts out as a one-shot engagement ends up as a lecture tour. This generates more revenue and exposure, and since the institutions involved split my travel expenses (apart from the fees I am paid), they all save money.

SETTING UP ARTIST-IN-RESIDENCE POSITIONS, LECTURES, AND WORKSHOPS

The best way to approach an organization or institution about sponsoring an artist-in-residence position, public appearance, or workshop is to provide a concrete proposal that describes the purpose of your idea or program, why it is relevant, and what the audience will gain. A proposal for a lecture workshop should not be limited to a title. It should elaborate on the contents of your presentation, including the purpose, relevance, and benefit to the audience.

The value of preparing a proposal in advance is that you avoid having to rely on the institution or organization to figure out a way to use your talents. This could take months.

The other value of preparing a proposal is that it can be used to generate residencies, public appearances, and workshops independent of organizations and institutions that sponsor such programs. In other words, you can initiate contacts yourself.

Send proposals to schools, colleges, universities, social-service agencies, and educational and cultural organizations. Corporations are also receptive to sponsoring lectures and workshops, and many organize educational and cultural programs specifically for their employees.

How to Make Money Performing in Schools: The Definitive Guide to Developing, Marketing, and Presenting School Assembly Programs by David Heflick provides information on creating a show that utilizes your talents and meets the educational needs of the school. It also gives tips on organizing a successful tour. Advice and information about organizing and publicizing public appearances can be found in the books *How to Run Seminars & Workshops: Presentation Skills for Consultants, Trainers, and Teachers* by Robert L. Jolles and *How to Develop & Promote Successful Seminars & Workshops: The Definitive Guide to Creating and Marketing Seminars, Workshops, Classes, and Conferences* by Howard L. Shenson (see the appendix section "Employment Opportunities").

Generating Income through the Printed Image

Mail art, book art, rubber-stamp art, photocopy art, postcard art, and digital art are art forms created by artists exploring new communication tools and resources of mass communication and the electronic age. Not only do some of these art forms respond to the aesthetic sensibilities of mass communication, they are mass communication and are mass-produced. Thus, they are art forms with nonexclusive price tags and have the potential to broaden the art-buying market.

A market and marketing vehicles for these art forms have developed over the last twenty-three years. This can be attributed to the efforts of Printed Matter, which was founded in New York City in 1976. This retail store and gallery also offers a mail-order service. It exhibits and sells a vast range of artists' books and other types of artist-created printed materials. Although Printed Matter is considered the largest distributor of artists' books worldwide, artists' books are also sold through retail stores, galleries, and distribution outlets throughout the United States. Their names and addresses are listed on the Web site *Book Arts Directory*. The *Directory* also includes information for papermakers, calligraphers, paper decorators, printmakers, book designers, fine printers and publishers, traditional bookbinders, and makers of artist books.

The addresses of Printed Matter, *Book Arts Directory*, and other artists' book resources are listed in the appendix section "Artists' Books."

PRINTMAKING

In recent years the integration of digital technology into the art-making process happened at a breathtaking pace and created an explosion in the multiples market. For the most part, hand-pulled prints, the traditional method of printmaking, have been replaced with a digital process known as giclée printing. Giclée printing offers the money-saving advantage of creating a print on demand without the necessity of printing a complete edition at one time. In addition, it eliminates use of toxic materials associated with some forms of traditional printmaking.

Painters who would have never before considered creating hand-pulled prints have gained access to the printmaking field by using digital technology to convert their artwork into multiples, resulting in a marketplace flooded with giclées.

With the explosion of this new form of technology an ongoing battle has developed, led by hand-pulled printmakers and traditionalists, who make a case that a giclée is really a *reproduction* and should not be considered a print.

Regardless of the controversy, giclée printing has become an accepted form of "printmaking" and in many instances demand prices that do not discern between labor-intensive hand-pulled prints and those works created by digital technology.

Although I have accepted *giclées on paper* as a new form of printmaking and have somewhat adjusted to the prices being charged, artists who are focused on selling work within the fine-art market should stay clear of printing *giclées on canvas,* a gimmicky product that was invented to make a print "look like a painting." It is my hope that the *giclées on canvas* phenomena will quickly run its course and end up in the same graveyard as all of the paintings-by-number.

PLANNING A GICLÉE PROJECT
To counteract the overabundance of the giclée market, some gallery owners and art consultants require artists to limit giclées editions to 25 prints. On the other hand, when art consultants commission artists to do special print projects for the hospitality and health-care industries, they might require larger editions. Other types of distribution outlets, such as online galleries, work with giclée editions of 200 to 300 prints, and there are some online galleries that only sell open editions.

If you are considering a giclée project, it is important to arrive at a price structure that reflects the number of prints in an edition. In other words, the fewer number of prints available, the higher the price of the giclée. For example, a giclée monoprint should be priced higher than an edition of 5 prints, an edition of 5 prints should be priced higher than an edition of 20 prints, and an edition of 20 prints should be priced higher than an edition of 200 prints.

If you are having a giclée edition produced by a top-quality printing studio, overhead expenses per print can be high. These expenses should be incorporated into the retail price of each print and should also be reflected in a special format retail price list to ensure that you are not paying sales commissions on your overhead. This issue is addressed in chapter 5, "Pricing Your Work: How Much Is It Worth?" (see page 96).

Giclée projects should incorporate many of the guidelines used in traditional printmaking, including the use of archival paper and archival inks. The number of prints in an edition need to be declared *in advance,* and each print should be signed and numbered. Additional information about giclées and traditional printmaking can be found in the book *How to Profit from the Art Print Market* by Barney Davey, which was written to help artists understand the world of prints. It covers a wide range of issues, including the economics of self-publishing, examples of successful self-published artists, finding and working with a publisher, marketing and selling self-published prints, and more. Another book of interest, *Mastering Digital Printing: The Photographer's and Artist's Guide to High-Quality Digital Output* by Harald Johnson, was written for photographers and artists working in digital technology and traditional materials. It includes instructions in the latest digital printing techniques. The Web site Giclée Information is devoted to information about giclées, including marketing and criteria for selecting a printer. Additional information about these and other resources can be found in the appendix section "Prints and Printmaking."

LICENSING ART

Although not all artwork is appropriate for licensing, many artists license the right to use their visual images on various products in return for financial compensation. Products include prints, posters, textiles, towels, sheets, duvet covers, wearing apparel, greetings and note cards, napkins, gift bags, wall coverings, giftwrap and other paper goods, household accessories, wallpaper, and many other types of products.

Many artists use licensing agents to find potential clients. Michael Woodward, author of *Licensing Art 101: Publishing and Licensing Your Artwork for Profit,* began licensing photography in London in 1974, and in 1979 he formed an art licensing company in Europe. He is credited as the first art licensing agent in Europe and possibly in the United States. He actually coined the term *art licensing agent.*

Woodward observed that "in the last few years there has been a huge shift in how products are bought, in that buyers now have shopping lists of what they actually want in terms of subject matter, color and even style of art. If you intend to license your work in this market, you need to have the right information."[5]

He works with a very select group of artists through his agency Out of the Blue, although his passion now is focused on teaching artists what he has learned about the art licensing industry in the last thirty years. Through the company Art Licensing International, Inc., he offers consultations, workshops, seminars, and *The Licensing Course,* a 264-page how-to manual for artists, illustrators, and photographers who are entering the field of licensing for the first time and for those who are interested in taking their licensing careers to the next level. The package also includes the DVD *Art and Design Licensing,* and *Licensing Art 101: Publishing and Licensing Your Artwork for Profit.*

Woodward has also produced a series of video seminars that are available online. They include various art-licensing subjects, such as trends, self-publishing, working with agents, attending trade shows, and exhibiting at trade shows.

"Artists always ask how much money they will make from licensing and I always reply that 'It's impossible to estimate in this business climate.' It usually takes two to three years to see income of any significance. I only work with artists who are looking to use art licensing as an adjunct to their income and not as the primary source of income."[6]

Compensation for awarding a license is usually in the form of a royalty based on the retail or wholesale price of the product. Some licensing agreements require the licensee to pay an artist a nonrefundable advance against royalties.

Many artists use licensing agents to find potential clients. "An agent's reputation and credentials should be scrutinized carefully,"[7] warns Caryn R. Leland, attorney and author of the very helpful book *Licensing Art and Design: A Professional's Guide to Licensing and Royalty Agreements.*

> This can be done rather simply. Ask the prospective agent for references and for the names of some past and present clients; then speak to them. Find out about the agent's reputation; ask about his or her success rate with negotiating lucrative or high-profile licenses. Do not be shy or hesitant in asking about the agent's fee or negative points or problems that may have arisen during the course of prior representations.[8]

The names of licensing agents can be found in *Licensing Art 101: Publishing and Licensing Your Artwork for Profit* and the *Licensing Letter Sourcebook.* In addition, the International Licensing Industry

Merchandiser's Association, with offices in New York, London, and Munich, offers members access to many services, including an online licensing database, and a 1,600-page *Worldwide Licensing Resource Directory*. The association also sponsors an annual International Licensing Exposition and Conference. Additional information about licensing resources can be found in the appendix section "Licensing Art."

Other Ways of Generating Income from Fine-Art Skills

Using talents and skills acquired in the fine arts, some artists generate income by working in applied-arts fields, such as graphic design, fashion illustration, book and book cover design, scenic design, and fabric design.

One very imaginative way of generating income using fine-art skills was achieved by the East Hampton, New York, artist Eleanor Allen Leaver. Leaver has established a network of real estate companies that commission her to create pen-and-ink drawings of homes that have been purchased and sold by their clients. Once a sales transaction has been completed, the artist's drawing is presented as a gift to the real estate agent's clients. It is interesting to note that the artist began this particular freelance business in 1996 when she was seventy-six years old. As of this writing, Leaver is now eighty-eight years old, and she and her business are still going strong.

I have sold numerous prints through my studio, just on the basis of distributing a press release. In one instance I was involved with a silk-screen series consisting of five prints based on one theme. Press releases announcing the series and availability details were sent to arts-related publications and museum shops. Except for the prints that I retained for myself, the entire series sold. Marketing involved neither paid advertising nor a middleperson.

There are many potential markets for artists' work. If you limit yourself to one-of-a-kind objects, your market is one-of-a-kind buyers, those who consider exclusivity and scarcity important and are willing and able to pay for it. However, there are many others who appreciate and want to buy art and are not concerned with these issues.

USING YOUR "OTHER" CAREER TO GENERATE INCOME

Wearing two hats can be used to an artist's advantage if one utilizes and transfers the resources and contacts of a second career into the fine arts. Such was the opportunity created by Molly Heron, a New York artist, who parlayed a series of timely events and a freelance position into a one-person exhibition located in prime space on the ground floor of a choice midtown Manhattan office building.

Heron was hired as a freelance book designer at HarperCollins, which, coincidentally, was the publisher of *The Writing Life* by Annie Dillard, a book that she had recently read, savored, and reread.

Six months after she obtained the freelance position, Heron attended an exhibition at the HarperCollins Gallery, located in an open and attractive bilevel space. Impressed with the physical attributes of the gallery and its opportune location, she made inquiries regarding how the space could be acquired for an exhibition. She learned through the gallery curator that all exhibitions in the space *had to be related to a HarperCollins book.*

Eureka! Before the lightbulbs in Heron's head had a chance to dim, she developed an exhibition proposal. Within four weeks she submitted the proposal and a set of slides to the HarperCollins curator, and soon afterward she received an invitation to install a solo exhibition in the gallery later in the year.

Heron's proposal was based on the inspiration she had received from *The Writing Life*. The book had infused her with a new energy force, and she felt compelled to interpret Dillard's metaphors and observations visually. In the proposal she wrote:

> Annie Dillard's *The Writing Life* describes the elusive process of creation in a way that is a strong invitation to try to feel the edge and see if it's possible to have the sun hit you. With her metaphors conjuring up strong visual images, this book inspires me to take color to hand and dance around the mystery with marks on paper. To wonder, to wonder if the dance will take me to the dawn. Will it take me to the abyss?[9]

Heron selected twenty of Dillard's phrases to interpret. Using the medium of collage, she incorporated candy wrappers, paper cups, handmade paper, paper doilies, lace, and other fabrics in combination with a variety of paint, crayons, pencils, and ink. "Combining these materials and building the picture in layers reflected the creative process of making a whole piece out of parts while working in stages," said Heron.[10]

> A phrase like, "The life of the spirit requires less and less"[11] is so provocative that I made several pieces based on Ms. Dillard's insight. At times it was a completely new and mysterious idea and then it would remind me of something that I have known all my life.
>
> Perhaps the most central of Dillard's metaphors are about climbing. Working in the dark, going to the dangerous edge, searching for the opening into the mystery, finding the moment when everything is in place and you are overwhelmed by clarity. I found myself responding with central images of portals as passageways to that mystery and circles as symbols of continuity and connection. The circle allows you to go out into the bright light and also to return. Then you begin the journey again.[12]

Entitled *Impressions on Annie Dillard's* The Writing Life: *Works on Paper by Molly Heron,* the exhibition was organized with the discerning eye and grace of a major museum event. Each collage was displayed with the respective Dillard text that had been the source of Heron's inspiration, and the title of each collage was found within the accompanying prose.

Exhibition visitors were given a nine-page package of information, including a press release, artist's statement, excerpts from the Dillard book, and Molly Heron's and Annie Dillard's biographies.

Molly Heron sold five pieces of work while the exhibition was installed. And as soon as the show closed, she handled the ending as a new beginning and wasted no time in taking the next step. She revised the original proposal and, along with a one-page cover letter, a set of slides, and promotion materials from her HarperCollins show, she began making contacts.

Her new initiatives resulted in exhibition invitations from a university museum, a nonprofit gallery, and a commercial gallery. She also received requests to present lectures and workshops.

In addition, a curator of a branch gallery of the Whitney Museum of American Art informed Heron that, due to the branch museum's policy of only sponsoring group shows, she was unable to offer her a solo exhibition, but that she was so impressed with Heron's work, she had contacted another cultural institution on the artist's behalf.

In part, Molly Heron's adventures and her success can be attributed to the cosmic phenomenon of being at the right place at the right time. But most of the credit belongs to the artist, who through very earthly pursuits took the initiative to utilize in her fine-arts career the resources and contacts of the publishing world.

Rationalization, Paranoia, Competition, Rejection, and the Overwhelm Factor

RATIONALIZATION

A fifty-two-year-old painter wrote me a very long letter to tell me that although she had read my book and combed through the appendix of resources and various Web sites on the Artist Help Network "nothing seems to apply to this single, aging female artist that no one knows, who has no budget for self promotion or advertising, let alone groceries or rent. Who do *we* turn to, to get help as we try to reestablish our careers?" She went on to say that her local arts council and contemporary arts center are inept at answering this question because "they mainly deal with artists who have résumés and social connections." She told me that she couldn't afford to make slides of her artwork, go to the dentist, or have a breast examination. "All my earnings go into art supplies, rent and dog food. I live on lettuce and coffee." Although she acknowledged that grants are available, "the first thing they want is your most recent tax return. . . . I stopped paying taxes when my income dipped so low it seemed silly to file." She also stated that in the region where she was living "all tax accountants seemed to be facing criminal charges" and that she didn't trust anyone. I responded with a brief email saying that it seemed that her life was a series of catch-22 situations and advised her to do whatever it took to gain financial stability and take control of her life. A simplistic answer for what appeared to be a great mass of complications, but the complications seemed to be self-inflicted, beginning with the way she described her self-image and how she held on ever so tightly to owning a belief system that was designed to create failure.

I have also received correspondence from artists with manipulative undertones and overtones. Some artists have told me point blank that I *was their only hope,* to which I responded, "Actually you are your only hope." I have also received a few complaints from artists who blamed me for a lackluster response to their brochures. It was much more comfortable to transfer the responsibility onto me than to accept the reality that at a particular time of life their artwork did not resonate with members of the art world.

If you want to avoid fulfilling your potential as an artist, there are many ways of going about it. Excuses are easy to find. It is also easy to blame others for disappointments and place the onus of rejection on other people's shoulders. It is also easy to become paralyzed by insecurities and fears—a fear of the marketplace—a fear of rejection—a fear of not measuring up to the talents of other artists. The fear list can go on and on.

When excuses linger unresolved too long they become rationalizations. Webster defines the word *rationalize* as "to attribute [one's actions] to rational and creditable motives without analysis of true and especially unconscious motives," and "to provide plausible but untrue reasons for conduct."

Rationalization in one form or another is common to the human species, and sometimes it can be used constructively. However, when rationalization is used to evade fulfilling one's potential, it is being used to disguise a lack of self-confidence and/or fear of rejection.

The most common kinds of rationalizations practiced by artists are rationalizations to *avoid the work process* and rationalizations to *avoid getting work out of the studio and into the public domain,* the marketplace.

Avoiding Work

"I'll get going once I find a work space" and "I'll get going when I have the right working environment" are some of the rationalizations

I hear most often from artists who want to postpone or avoid knuckling down. Artists who engage in this form of rationalization do little or nothing, financially or motivationally, in order to attain their goal of finding a suitable work space.

There are many variations on the theme: One artist tells me he can't begin work until he can afford stationery embossed with his studio address. He believes that no one will take him seriously until he has a business letterhead. Another artist, who has spent the last four years traveling, tells me she needs more life experience in order to paint. Another artist tells me that he is waiting for technology to invent the right material that he needs for sculpture. Chances are that when the letterhead, life experience, and new technology are attained, the artists will quickly find another excuse to avoid confronting their work.

For the artist who chronically finds an excuse to avoid work, the consequences of rationalization are not limited to getting nothing accomplished. Guilt sets in because you are not doing what you think you want to be doing and because you are practicing self-deceit. Animosities and tensions develop internally and toward others, whom you blame for your circumstances. Jealousy and contempt rear their miserable heads, directed toward any artists (and nonartists as well) who have managed to put their lives together in such a way that they are accomplishing, or are really trying to accomplish, their goals.

With so much negativity festering, no wonder work is impossible. The distance between what you want to achieve and what you are actually achieving grows wider. And if you try to work you find each product of self-expression tainted and influenced by your anger and hostility. Creativity is used to vent frustration and addresses nothing else.

Avoiding Public Exposure

Some artists have no problem working but begin the rationalization process when it comes time for their work to leave the studio and enter the marketplace. To insure yourself against experiencing any form of rejection, you begin to rationalize: your work isn't ready, you don't have enough work to show, you don't fit into the latest trend, you're working for your own pleasure and do not want to derive money from art, and no one will understand your work anyway—it's too deep!

Gail McMeekin, author of *The Twelve Secrets of Highly Creative Women* and a career coach and psychotherapist, points out that "putting yourself out there and sharing your work qualifies as an act of courage and tests your fortitude."[1] Unfortunately, many artists do not see the relationship between fortitude, courage, and career development. Other artists limit their courage and fortitude to the art-making process.

The Search for the Perfect Agent

One of the more popular rationalizations is the *perpetual search for the perfect agent*. Once this person is found, he or she will take your work to the marketplace. This person, you tell yourself, will shield you from criticism and rejection; schlepp your presentation materials from gallery to museum; bargain, negotiate, and establish your market value; arrange exhibitions; write letters; attend cocktail parties; and make important connections. In addition, the agent will have excellent press contacts and your work will be regularly featured in leading publications, with critics fighting among themselves for the opportunity to review your shows. And, of course, this agent will fill out grant applications on your behalf and will be very successful in convincing foundations to subsidize your career. And when cash flow is a problem, the agent will tide you over with generous advances. When your ego needs stroking, the agent will always be on call. All you have to do is stay in your ivory tower and work.

I estimate that the majority of artists who contact me for assistance have the notion in the backs of their minds that I will fulfill this fantasy and provide the buffer zone they are seeking. Apart from my belief that within the visual-arts field this fairy godperson is practically nonexistent, I strongly believe that artists are their own best representatives.

Meanwhile, the search for the perfect agent, the supposed saint of all saints, continues while the artist's work accumulates in the studio, to be seen only by four walls.

Rationalization can become a style of life—an art unto itself.

Artists who use rationalization as a style of living tend to associate with other artists who are skilled at the same game, supporting and reinforcing each other, pontificating in unison that "life is hell," and that it's everyone else's fault. It's less lonely going nowhere fast in a group than by yourself.

PARANOIA

Rationalization has a twin: paranoia. Webster defines *paranoia* as a "tendency on the part of an individual or group toward excessive or irrational suspiciousness and distrustfulness of others."

Sometimes the twins are inseparable and it is difficult to know where rationalization ends and paranoia begins. Sometimes rationalization is the aggressor and paranoia takes over, and other times paranoia prevails on its own. But the twins always meet again at the same junction, called *insecurity*.

For example, a painter tells me she dislikes showing her work to dealers because when she invites them to her studio she believes that her invitation is interpreted as a sexual proposition. I asked whether she had encountered this kind of experience. "No," she replied, "but I know what they are all thinking." Consequently, dealers are not invited for studio visits. Thus, she eliminates any possibility of being rejected or hearing that her work isn't good enough. Another artist, who was part of a group that I was assisting with public relations for an upcoming exhibition, told me that he did not want press coverage in certain newspapers and on television out of fear that the "wrong kind of people" would come to the show. I could never figure out who the "wrong kind of people" might be—street gangs, muggers? Nor could the artist shed light on the subject when I asked for an explanation. But in his mind there was a special group of people who were not meant to view or buy art.

The belief that there *is* a special group of people who are not meant to view or buy art is common among artists. It translates into the "creating art for friends" syndrome, a principle that, on the surface, sounds very virtuous, but all too often means that anyone who likes your work is worth knowing, and anyone who doesn't isn't. It is a tidy black-and-white package: a handpicked audience that you create for the purpose of lessening the possibility that you will be rejected and increasing your sense of security and self-esteem.

I don't mean to understate or underrate the importance of support and compliments, but there are many dangers in being paranoid about new audiences. In addition to propagating elitist notions about art, it also creates incestuous attitudes and incestuous results. To continually create only what you know will please your peanut gallery impedes your creative growth and limits your creativity. The fear of new audiences also applies to artists who are afraid to leave their galleries or expand into new local, regional, national, and international territories.

One area where paranoia runs rampant is within the so-called community of artists. Artists are often fearful of ideas being stolen, competition, and losing the status quo. By this reasoning every artist is a potential enemy.

An artist who served as an apprentice for two years to a well-known sculptor was preparing a grant application and needed three letters of recommendation. He felt comfortable asking his former employer for a letter because on numerous occasions the sculptor had praised his talents. Yet the sculptor turned him down, saying that on principle he does not give artists letters of recommendation.

Reading between the lines, it is likely that the younger artist posed a threat to the sculptor's status. The sculptor felt that there was no more room at the top, and just to ensure that no one else would inch his or her way up, he thwarted every opportunity that might give someone else upward mobility.

A painter who had recently moved to New York and was eager to begin making gallery contacts told me that she had a good friend who was with an established New York gallery where she would like to exhibit. I suggested that she ask her friend for a personal introduction. "I already did," she glumly replied. "But she said that *she* would be heartbroken if the dealer didn't like my work."

In this example, the artist tried to disguise her own insecurities with a protective gesture. She would not allow herself to be put in a position where her "taste" would be questioned, and/or she saw her friend as a potential threat to her status in the gallery—a realistic enough threat to warrant cutting her friend out of a network.

I once asked a sculptor who was sharing a studio with other

artists whether her colleagues were supportive and helped each other with contacts. "Oh, no," she replied, "just the opposite. Whenever one of the artists has a dealer or curator over for a studio visit, the day before the appointment she asks us to cover up our work with sheets." Then she added, "I don't blame her. If I were in her position I would do the same."

In this example there is little room to read between the lines. It is a blatant example of paranoid behavior. Oddly enough, her studio mates complied with the outrageous request because they deeply identified with and understood the artist's fear.

Paranoia also manifests itself in the hoarding and concealment of information. I have seen artists smother in their bosoms any tidbit of information or leads that they believed would be a *weapon in the hands of other artists*. A dancer told me that she holds back information from colleagues about scheduled auditions. A sculptor complained that his best friend entered a competition whose theme was very relevant to his own work; when he learned of the opportunity only after the deadline closed, his friend nonchalantly said, "Oh, I thought I mentioned it to you." A photographer suspiciously asked me how many other photographers I had advised to approach a certain gallery.

OVERREACTING TO COMPETITION

Some of the examples cited above might sound familiar—so familiar and ordinary that you most likely never thought to consider them examples of rationalization and paranoid behavior. This is part of the problem. In the art world, illogical and unsubstantiated fears and scapegoating have become the norm.

One of the basic reasons why rationalization and paranoia are condoned in the art world is overreaction to competition. Everyone tells us how competitive the art world is, how competitive being an artist is. We hear it from critics, curators, dealers, educators, our parents, and other artists. We enter contests and juried shows; vie for the interest of dealers, collectors, patrons, and critics; fight for grants, teaching jobs, and commissions. We write manifestos to be more profound than others.

Competition is an occupational hazard in every profession; it is not exclusive to the art world. But all too often in the art world we have let rivalry assume the predominant role in how we relate to one another. Although for some artists the mere thought of being judged is so overwhelming that they won't even allow themselves to compete, others plunge into the match but let a dog-eat-dog mentality pilot their trip. These are artists who backstab, hoard information, and exercise selective memories.

Some artists try to deal with competition by establishing elitist values, adamantly contending that only a select few were meant to understand their work. Trying to win the interest of a select audience makes competition seem less threatening. Other artists have concocted a myth that dealers, curators, and collectors are incapable of simultaneous appreciation of or interest in more than a few artists. Such artists cultivate a brutal "It's me or you" attitude.

The main reason competition has become so fierce is that many artists really believe only a limited number of artists *can* achieve success. Although it might be true that only a limited number of artists do achieve success, the *potential number* of artists who can succeed *is not limited*. Achieving success has nothing to do with "beating out the competition" through deception, lies, manipulation, and viciousness. Artists who succeed have beaten out the competition through exercising powers of perseverance and discipline, and by cultivating good marketing skills.

Until competition in the art world is recognized for what it really is, rationalization and paranoia will continue to be used by many artists as tools of the trade. They are odious, unproductive, and self-defeating props that are dangerous to your health, career, and the present and future of the art world.

There is no need to expound on why it is unhealthy to live a life predicated on fear, lies, and excuses and what it can do to us physically and mentally. Some artists are at least consistent, allowing self-destruction and self-deceit to govern all facets of their existence. But other artists have a double standard: honesty, intellect, courage, discipline, and integrity are their ruling principles, except when it comes to their art and careers!

Those who let rationalization and paranoia rule their careers in order to avoid rejection, assuage insecurity, and fend off competition must face the fact that their careers can come to a screeching halt, limp along in agonizing frustration, or be limited in every possible sense. Their work suffers (reflecting lies, excuses, and fears) and their network of friends and contacts degenerates to the lowest common denominator, as they stop at nothing to eliminate what is perceived as a possible threat.

On a more positive note, in New York City there is a group of visual artists who, since 1996, meet regularly for two hours once a month for the purpose of exchanging art business information, including grant and exhibition opportunities; leads on curators and galleries; tips and advice on new materials, crating and shipping of artwork, documentation and promotion; classes and workshops; and other arts-related and career-related concerns.

"This easy sharing of information is in contrast to the isolation of individual artists in what is usually seen as the extremely competitive environment of the New York art world,"[2] said the group's president. "The sharing of information has led to many successes for our members."[3] From time to time representatives from New York's arts and arts service organizations, as well as critics, art dealers, and curators, have served as guest speakers.

By 2008 the membership grew to more than 350 artists. In an email interview, the organization's president requested that I not include the actual name of the organization and contact information in this book. "It is because of the great success of our meetings and membership that we have recently become a closed group. We made this decision in order to meet the needs of our current artist-members. The success of our meetings isn't solely based on the sheer number of artists but in the relationships they create among themselves and with the larger group. These relationships provide a sense of trust in order to share vital information about the art world."[4]

Because I believe in the importance of the group's mission and goals, I consented to the president's request. It is my hope as well as the hope of the group's president that in writing about the organization, it will inspire other artists to form similar groups in other parts of the country. I also hope that splinter groups will form in New York City so that it will return to an "open" membership policy.

At each meeting the group maintains a three-part structure: The first section is an information session where members recommend exhibitions in New York and share information about upcoming lectures by artists, art historians, and critics. Members might also offer information about a gallery that is open to receiving presentation packages, discussing their experiences, and providing submission details. During the second section artists are given the opportunity to ask for information that they need. For example, an artist may request information on where to find a good postcard printer, a Web site designer, a studio assistant, reasonably priced health insurance, and where to purchase materials in bulk. In the last fifteen minutes of the meeting, artists share information about their own upcoming exhibitions.

The group has a Listserv membership of 500 artists. The Listserv covers the same types of information that is discussed at the membership meeting. It is used as a way for members to stay in touch between meetings and ensures that members who are unable to attend meetings on a regular basis are included in the loop. There is a Listserv moderator who organizes some of the content.

THE OVERWHELM FACTOR

For many years I made the mistake of taking for granted an ability to work simultaneously on creative projects and administrative tasks and do a comprehensive marketing and public relations outreach without feeling stressed. I naively assumed that everyone performed at the same level.

Some artists are able to multitask with ease and spend part of the day or week in their studio creating and another part of the day or week on their computer or on the phone handling arts administration and career development chores. Other artists immediately jump ship once they begin to understand all of the tasks necessary to attain career goals. Other artists put their toes in the water for a year or so, do a bit of marketing, and then give up.

Although today's artists are more business savvy than thirty years ago (when I first began career coaching), and a large percentage of artists can persevere in *creating art* on an ongoing basis, a much smaller percentage of artists are able to maintain momentum on an ongoing basis when it comes to the implementation of career development strategies.

There are many reasons why some artists lack the stamina to maintain momentum. Chapter 1, "Launching or Relaunching Your Career: Overcoming Career Blocks" covers some of the obstacles that artists face. Combating overwhelming feelings is another formidable challenge. When overwhelming feelings occur, everything can come to a screeching halt and nothing gets accomplished. The overwhelm factor can negatively impact creativity, motivation, patience, perseverance, and stamina.

Overwhelming feelings can be created by stress, fear, and anxiety. When tasks, chores, and responsibilities are not compartmentalized or prioritized, it is easy to form a mental picture of everything in life running together in one huge indecipherable heap. Some artists feel overwhelmed as a result of being devoted perfectionists and have completely unrealistic expectations of how life should be. Other artists experience overwhelming feelings because they have not established boundaries in their personal or professional lives. Overwhelming feelings can create physical sensations and make you feel that you are being overpowered and are out of control.

Dyslexia, Attention-Deficit Disorders, and Other Learning Disorders

During an initial career consultation, I always ask a new client whether she or he has read my book. I started to realize that my question was rattling the nerves of a lot of people who had not read the book. Some artists displayed embarrassment; others were defensive and volunteered that they did not enjoy reading. I started wondering if there was a correlation between reading problems and the various negative generalizations associated with artists, such as artists are bad business people, artists are flaky and scattered, and artists are obsessively focused.

I have clients who can glide through the business aspects of their career and admit that they actually like this type of work. I also have clients who are not only able to simultaneously perform business and administrative tasks and create artwork, they can do these activities while coping with physical challenges, a health crisis, a family crisis, or a family health crisis. I also have clients who have difficulties completing one administrative task, such as compiling a résumé or a price list.

I turned to the Internet to research whether any thought has been given to the relationship between creatively gifted people and those people who have dyslexia or attention-deficit disorders. I discovered there are reams of information as it pertains to artists. Knowing that many creative individuals *unknowingly* suffer from these challenges has provided insights into a better understanding of why some artists can breeze through career-related business tasks and other artists are thrown into an overwhelmed state when attempting to do more than creating artwork.

The appendix section "Creative Challenges, Career Blocks, and the Psyche" lists a few of the Web sites that are devoted to the subject of creativity as it relates to dyslexia and attention-deficit disorders.

In the introduction to this book, I wrote that it took me *several years to build a career* as an artist. It also took a lot of time to learn, master, and apply the skills that are described herein. It is important to mention this again to help readers counteract sensations of being overwhelmed by all of the suggestions and information that are provided. My career did not develop overnight; it was a slow but constant buildup. I absorbed information that I needed to know at the time when I needed to know it. When I listened to my inner voice, I moved forward; when I didn't, I stumbled.

DEALING WITH REJECTION

Eden Maxwell, an artist and author of *An Artist Empowered: Define and Establish Your Value as an Artist—Now,* wrote that "While having the dream to be an artist is admirable, persevering against the collective drag of disappointment, doubt, and adversity demands more: artists must fortify—not coddle—themselves with strength of character if they are to fulfill their mission. The artist must not only be self-reliant, he must also remain vigilant of those who would co-opt his fire from heaven to roast marshmallows."[5]

An artist described her experience with rejection in this way: "I, like most young artists, romanticized the idea of 'being an artist' and in so doing anticipated a degree of rejection, but had I known the degree of rejection that would be in store . . . I might have chosen to become a doctor instead. Frankly, I don't get it."[6]

I have a client who is both a psychotherapist and a visual artist. He has a few gallery owners as patients (who do not know that he is an artist). He told me how "crazy and insecure" the art dealers are—and although rationally he knows this, he has a hard time keeping this in mind and making the connection that "crazy and insecure" people could very well be judging his artwork!

There are many reasons why an artist's work is rejected. Artists are constantly turned down from galleries, museums, alternative spaces, juried shows, and teaching jobs. A bad review is a form of rejection; so is not being reviewed.

Some artists are rejected for reasons for which they are *ultimately responsible,* and for these artists rejection can be an asset. It might be the only indication an artist has that his or her career is being mismanaged.

Artists who are responsible for rejection include those who make no effort to improve their chances by taking the initiative or creating career opportunities. Examples of such artists have been described throughout this book: those who haphazardly enter the marketplace, those who prepare poor presentations, and those who can't abandon "the myth of the artist."

Some artists rely on moods to enter the marketplace. A burst of energy tells them it is time to make contacts and take action, and for a week or two, or perhaps a month, they are sincerely dedicated to showing their work around. But the goal is instant gratification, and if expectations are not rewarded, they retreat. Depending on the artist, it can take months—sometimes years—for anything constructive to happen.

Artists who are controlled by moods further encourage self-defeat by drawing the conclusion that rejection is an absolute: once they are rejected, a museum's or gallery's doors are always closed. Consequently, these artists will not return with a new body of work.

But there are many instances in which artists are not responsible for rejection. These instances are caused by subjective forces, including "taste buds," trends, norms, and other people's priorities. These forces can be illogical and arbitrary, and are, by nature, unfair.

I once had a grant application rejected. The grant's panel had confused me with another artist whose name was similar. That artist had previously received a grant from the same foundation, but had misused the funds. It was only by accident, and many months later, that I learned what had happened.

This was luxurious rejection: I could not take it personally or hold myself responsible, and I was able to learn the *real* reason. It is rare, though, that artists know the real reasons why they are rejected. Consequently, they think they are untalented and that their ideas are without merit.

The side effects of rejection are more horrendous than the actual rejection. For this reason, once you have ascertained that you are no longer responsible for the situation, it is important to build up an immunity against being affected by rejection.

The painter Delia Brown developed a very proactive and humorous stance to rejection. When she learned that she was not included in the 2004 Whitney Biennial, she persuaded the three curators who rejected her to pose for a group portrait. The painting was then sold to an art collector.

The artist Billy Curmano described his immunity system in *Artworkers News:* "One day, while reflecting on . . . accumulated rejections, I composed an equally impersonal rejection rejection and have begun systematically sending it to everyone in my file. . . . Striking back immediately becomes a ritual to look forward to."[7] Here is the letter Mr. Curmano composed:

> Hello:
>   IT HAS COME TO OUR ATTENTION that you sent a letter of rejection concerning BILLY CURMANO (hereinafter the "Artist") or his work dated ____ to the Artist.
>   BE IT KNOWN TO ALL, that the said MR. CURMANO no longer accepts rejection in any form.
>   KNOW YE THAT, this document, as of the day and year first written, shall serve as an official rejection rejection.
>   IN WITNESS WHEREOF, Artist and Counsel have set their hands and seals as of the date above first written.[8]

Mr. Curmano provided space for his signature as well as his counsel's and ended his rejection rejection notice with: "We are sorry for the use of a form letter, but the volume of rejections received makes a personal response impossible."[9]

One starting point for developing an immunity to rejection is to look at rejection in terms of its counterpart—acceptance, or what is commonly referred to as *success*. Rejection and success are analogous for various reasons. What artists define as rejection and success are usually borrowed from other people's opinions, values, and priorities. Artists who measure success and rejection in terms of what society thinks have the most difficult time coping with both phenomena.

Both success and rejection are capable of producing an identity crisis. Some artists who attain success find themselves stripped of goals, direction, and a sense of purpose. The same holds true for artists who are rejected.

Stagnation is a by-product of success and rejection. Artists who are rejected can be diverted and blocked in their creativity. Artists who attain success can lose momentum and vision.

It *is* possible for artists to be unscathed by rejection or success, and continue with new goals, directions, and explorations, irrespective of other people's aesthetic judgments.

The sooner you lose an obsession with rejection, the sooner your real potential develops, and the better equipped you will be to handle success.

If you accept the premise that the reasons for rejection are not truths or axioms, analyze rejection under a microscope. Reduce it to its lowest common denominator. Who is rejecting you? What does the person or entity mean relative to your existence? Is this entity blocking your energy, self-confidence, and achievements? Are you so vulnerably perched that other people's opinions can topple you?

When you can have a good laugh over the significance you had once placed on the answers to these questions, you will be able to respond to rejection the same way you respond to any other form of junk mail.

Building Immunities to Rejection

Keep in mind that generally it takes fifty presentation packages of the same body of work to generate one positive response (see page 58). A number less than fifty does not even begin to approach an effective market penetration level that justifies any sense of defeat or rejection.

Each time you receive a letter of rejection, initiate a new contact, send out another presentation package, or pick up the phone. Replace feelings of rejection with a sense of anticipation. This process increases the odds of acceptance and keeps your psyche in good shape.

Stop putting all of your eggs in one basket. Submitting one grant application a year or submitting work to one gallery every six months is only a gesture; strong, affirmative results do not come from gestures. Create opportunities for things to happen. Think big and broad. Make inroads in many directions. *What you want are lots of baskets filled with lots of eggs.*

Appendix of Resources

The following listing includes contact information for the organizations, agencies, publications, Web sites, and other resources cited in this book and other resources of interest. This listing is a beginning and by no means covers all of the career information available to artists. But it is a good starting point from which to develop a library of materials and contacts to launch (or relaunch) and sustain your career.

Web site addresses are provided for appendix entries, *with the exception of books and periodicals that are available through online bookstores*. A table of contents of the appendix of resources is located on pages viii–ix at the beginning of the book.

An adjunct to the appendix of resources is a new Web site that I have created, the Artist Help Network (www.artisthelpnetwork.com), a free information service devoted to resources that will help *artists take control of their careers*. The Web site contains most of the contacts listed in the sixth edition's appendix of resources. Readers can use the Web site to receive updated contact information and listings of new resources that have come to my attention. The Artist Help Network is a work in progress, with new information added on an ongoing basis.

ACCOUNTING, BOOKKEEPING, AND INCOME TAX
Publications

Accountants and Bookkeepers. Chicago Artists' Coalition, 70 E. Lake, Suite 230, Chicago, IL 60601. A resource list is available online to Chicago Artists' Coalition Members. www.caconline.org

The Artist in Business: Basic Business Practices by Craig Dreesen. Arts Extension Service, Division of Outreach, 100 Venture Way, Suite 201, Hadley, MA 01035-9430, revised 1996. Includes information on record keeping and taxes. www.umass.edu/aes

Artists' Bookkeeping Book. Chicago Artists' Coalition, 70 E. Lake, Suite 230, Chicago, IL 60601, revised 2008. Explains legal tax deductions for artists and record-keeping procedures. www.caconline.org

Artists' Taxes: The Hands-On Guide: An Alternative to "Hobby" Taxes by Jo Hanson. San Francisco: Vortex Press, 1987. Includes comprehensive information on how to prepare and manage a tax audit; tips for avoiding an audit; and a discussion of an artist's right to deduct art expenses.

Business Entities for Artists by Mark Quail. CARFAC Ontario, 401 Richmond Street West, Suite 440, Toronto, Ontario M5V 3A8, revised 1996. Summarizes information on sole proprietorships and corporations, including tax perspectives, registration procedures, and legal liability. Available online to CARFAC Ontario members. www.carfacontario.ca

The Business of Art, edited by Lee Caplin. Englewood Cliffs, N.J.: Prentice-Hall Direct, revised 2000. See "Understanding Everyday Finances" by Robert T. Higashi.

Legal Guide for the Visual Artist by Tad Crawford. New York: Allworth Press, revised 1999. See four chapters on taxes.

New Tax Guide for Artists of Every Persuasion by Peter Jason Riley. New York: Limelight Editions, revised 2004. Provides an overall understanding of the unique aspects of taxation for people in the arts. Includes checklists to help artists do a better job of collecting data and be better prepared to present tax information. Includes real-life examples of what artists might encounter.

Quick Fix Tax Kits for Artists by Barbara A. Sloan. AKAS II, P.O. Box 123, Hot Springs, AR 71902-0123, updated on a yearly basis. Presented in two parts: "The General Tax Guide" enumerates the various types of taxes affecting artists who sell their artwork; "Schedule C Kit" is for visual artists who are sole proprietors of their art business. www.akasii.com

Recordkeeping Kit for Visual Art Professionals and Hobbyists by Barbara A. Sloan. AKAS II, P.O. Box 123, Hot Springs, AR 71902-0123, revised annually. Includes bookkeeping basics for artists' business and personal records, with suggested alternatives to formal bookkeeping and accounting, and completed sample record-keeping forms. www.akasii.com

Taxation of the Visual and Performing Artist: An Insight into Federal Income Tax. Texas Accountants and Lawyers for the Arts, 1540 Sul Ross, Houston, TX 77006, revised annually. A step-by-step guide to assist artists in completing income tax returns. Answers frequently asked questions and provides examples of completed returns. www.talarts.org

Software

QuickBooks. Recommended software program for accounting and bookkeeping. www.quickbooks.intuit.com

Quicken. Recommended software program for accounting and bookkeeping. www.quicken.com

Web Sites

Artist Help Network (www.artisthelpnetwork.com). Founded by Caroll Michels, career coach and artist-advocate, this site is devoted to all aspects of career development. See heading "Money" and subheadings "Accounting and Bookkeeping" and "Business Volunteers for the Arts."

Resource Handbook for Minnesota Artists (www.springboardforthearts.org/ Resources/Resources.asp). Sponsored by Springboard for the Arts. An online listing of resources and services, including those related to financial management and accounting, for Minnesota artists.

Organizations by State

CALIFORNIA

Center for Cultural Innovation, 244 S. San Pedro Street, Suite 401, Los Angeles, CA 90012 and 651 Brannon Street, Suite 410, San Francisco, CA 94107. Promotes knowledge, sharing, networking, and financial independence for individual artists and creative entrepreneurs in California. Provides financial services. http://cciarts.org

ILLINOIS

St. Louis Volunteer Lawyers and Accountants for the Arts, 6128 Delmar, St. Louis, MO 63112. Serves artists in Southwest Illinois and Missouri. www.vlaa.org

INDIANA

Creative Arts Legal League (CALL), Volunteer Lawyers for the Arts, 20 N. Meridian Street, Suite 500, Indianapolis, IN 46204. Provides accounting services to income-eligible artists. www.indycall.org

MISSOURI

St. Louis Volunteer Lawyers and Accountants for the Arts, 6128 Delmar, St. Louis, MO 63112. Serves artists in Missouri and Southwest Illinois. www.vlaa.org

RHODE ISLAND

Business Volunteers for the Arts, Arts and Business Council of Rhode Island, Inc., 10 Dorrance Street, Suite 102, Providence, RI 02903. Provides business advice to artists. www.artsandbusinessri.org/programs/bva.asp

TEXAS

Texas Accountants and Lawyers for the Arts, 1540 Sul Ross, Houston, TX 77006. www.talarts.org

APPRENTICESHIPS AND INTERNSHIPS

Publications

Gardner's Guide to Internships at Multimedia and Animation Studios by Garth Gardner. Annandale, Va.: Garth Gardner Inc., revised 2004. Profiles hundreds of computer graphics, animation, and multimedia companies in the United States and Canada that offer internships.

Gardner's Guide to Internships in New Media: Computer Graphics, Animation and Multimedia by Garth Gardner and Bonney Ford. Annandale, Va.: Garth Gardner Inc., 2002. Profiles hundreds of companies in the visual-effects industry that offer internships.

National Directory of Arts Internships, edited by Warren Christensen and William Barton. Los Angeles: The National Network for Artist Placement, revised 2008. Lists hundreds of internship opportunities in the arts.

Web Sites

Artist Help Network (www.artisthelpnetwork.com). Founded by Caroll Michels, career coach and artist-advocate, this site is devoted to all aspects of career development. See heading "Money" and subheading "Apprenticeships and Internships."

Artjobonline (www.artjob.org). Lists internships in visual and performing arts, literature, education, and arts administration. A service of the Western States Arts Federation (WESTAF).

Arts Opportunities (www.artsopportunities.org). Posts opportunities for artists, including internships. Sponsored by the Southern Arts Federation and the Center for Arts Management & Technology at Carnegie Mellon University.

hireCulture.org (www.hireculture.org/jobbook/index.asp). A listing of creative, administrative, production, volunteer, and internship opportunities in Massachusetts. Sponsored by the Massachusetts Cultural Council.

NYFA Source (www.nyfa.org/source/content/search/search.aspx?SA=1). An extensive database for visual and performing artists, writers, and arts organizations. Includes a section on apprenticeship programs. Sponsored by the New York Foundation for the Arts.

Organizations

The National Network for Artist Placement, 935 West Avenue, Suite 37, Los Angeles, CA 90065. www.artistplacement.com

New York Arts Program, 305 West 29th Street, New York, NY 10001. Provides students with the opportunity to serve as apprentices to established professional artists or arts institutions in New York City for one semester. Sponsored by Ohio Wesleyan University. www.newyorkartsprogram.org

Also see "Employment Opportunities."

ART COLONIES AND
ARTIST-IN-RESIDENCE PROGRAMS

Publications

Art Colonies & Retreats. Chicago Artists' Coalition, 70 E. Lake, Suite 230, Chicago, IL 60601, regularly revised. A list of artist-in-residence programs available online to Chicago Artists' Coalition members. www.caconline.org

Art Opportunities Monthly. P.O. Box 502, Benicia, CA 94510-0502. A listing of opportunities for artists, including residencies. Published monthly and distributed by email. www.artopportunitiesmonthly.com

Artists Communities, edited by Robert MacNeil. New York: Allworth Press, revised 2005. A complete guide to residence opportunities in the United States for visual and performing artists and writers. Includes information on facilities, admission deadlines, eligibility requirements, and the selection process.

The Fine Artist's Guide to Marketing and Self-Promotion by Julius Vitali. New York: Allworth Press, revised 2003. Provides background information about teaching-residency opportunities in the arts. See the chapter "Artists-in-Education."

Web Sites

Artist Help Network (www.artisthelpnetwork.com). Founded by Caroll Michels, career coach and artist-advocate, this site is devoted to all aspects of career development. See heading "Money" and subheadings "Art Colonies and Artist-in-Residence Programs" and "Grants and Funding." Also see heading "Exhibitions, Commissions and Sales" and subheading "International Connections."

Directory of Artists in Schools (www.artsineddirectory.org). A listing of artists who participate in arts-in-education programs and use the New York State Learning Standards for the Arts. Sponsored by the Board of Co-operative Educational Services.

Directory of Performing Artists (www.cultureandtourism.org). A listing of Connecticut-based artists who specialize in public performances. Sponsored by the Connecticut Commission on Culture and Tourism.

Directory of Teaching Artists (www.arts.idaho.gov/ae/roster/directory/index.html). A listing of artists who participate in artist-in-residence programs in Idaho schools. Sponsored by the Idaho Commission on the Arts.

Directory of Teaching Artists (www.cultureandtourism.org). A listing of Connecticut-based artists who participate in classroom residencies and other types of residencies. Sponsored by the Connecticut Commission on Culture and Tourism.

The National Park Service (www.nps.gov/archive/volunteer/air.htm). Offers artist-in-residence opportunities to visual and performing artists and writers in twenty-nine parks throughout the United States.

NYFA Source (www.nyfa.org/source/content/search/search.aspx?SA=1). An extensive database for visual and performing artists, writers, and arts organizations. Includes artists-in-residence programs. Sponsored by the New York Foundation for the Arts.

SchoolShows.com (www.schoolshows.com). Includes a national directory of performers who present assemblies, workshops, and residencies in schools.

Organizations

Alliance of Artists' Communities, 255 South Main Street, Providence, RI 02903. A
national service organization that supports the field of artists' communities and
residency programs. Web site provides link to numerous art colonies and artist-
in-residence programs. www.artistcommunities.org

American Academy in Rome, 7 East 60th Street, New York, NY 10022-1001.
Offers residencies to artists. www.aarome.org/prize.htm

Art and Community Landscapes Program, New England Foundation for the Arts,
145 Tremont Street, Boston, MA 02111. Awards grants to artists and hosts
artists' residencies. Administered in conjunction with the National Endowment
for the Arts, the New England Foundation for the Arts, and the National Park
Service. www.nefa.org/grantprog/acl/index.html

Artists in Residence in Everglades (AIRIE), AIRIE Everglades National Park, 40001
State Road 9336, Homestead, FL 33034. Open to writers and visual artists,
including painters, sculptors, photographers, video artists, and mixed-media
artists. www.everglades.national-park.com/cal.htm

Bellagio Center Creative Arts Fellowship Program, Rockefeller Foundation, 420
Fifth Avenue, New York, NY 10018. Offers residencies to artists, composers,
and writers. www.rockfound.org/bellagio/bellagio.shtml

Hospital Audiences, Inc., 548 Broadway, 3rd Floor, New York, NY 10012-3950.
Brings visual- and performing-art programs to New Yorkers who are confined
to hospitals and health-care facilities, shelters, etc. www.hospitalaudiences.org

Lower Manhattan Cultural Council, Workspace Residencies, 125 Maiden Lane,
2nd Floor, New York, NY 10038. Sponsors various workspace residency programs in Lower Manhattan and on Governors Island. Also sponsors a residency
program in Paris. www.lmcc.net

National Training Program for Hospital Artists-In-Residence, The Creative Center,
273 Bowery, New York, NY 10002. Provides professional training to artists to
work with cancer patients in their hometown, medical centers, clinics, and hospitals. http://thecreativecenter.org/National_Programs

Studio in a School, 410 West 59th Street, New York, NY 10019. Places professional
visual artists in New York City's public schools. www.studioinaschool.org

Young Audiences, Inc., 115 East 92nd Street, New York, NY 10128-1688.
National organization that offers opportunities for artists in all disciplines to
work in school systems throughout the United States. www.youngaudiences.org

Also see "Art and Healing," "Grants and Funding Resources," and "International
Connections."

ART AND HEALING

Publications

Artists-In-Residence: The Creative Center's Approach to Arts in Healthcare by
Geraldine Herbert, Jane Waggoner Deschner, and Robin Glazer, 2006. The Creative Center, 273 Bowery, New York, NY 10002. Offers artists and health-care
professionals a unique look at artmaking with patients and caregivers in health-
care settings. http://thecreativecenter.org

The Arts in Health Care: A Palette of Possibilities, edited by Charles Kaye and Tony
   Blee, 1996. Jessica Kingsley Publishers, c/o Taylor & Francis, Inc., 325 Chestnut
   Street, Philadelphia, PA 19106. Chronicles the expanding use of the arts in the
   United Kingdom's National Health Service and at selected medical centers in the
   United States. Discusses the therapeutic value of using the arts in health and
   health care. www.jkp.com

Web Sites

Art as a Healing Force (www.artashealing.org). Provides links to hospitals that are
   involved with art and healing programs.
Artist Help Network (www.artisthelpnetwork.com). Founded by Caroll Michels,
   career coach and artist-advocate, this site is devoted to all aspects of career
   development. See heading "Career" and subheading "Career Challenges and the
   Psyche," and heading "Other Resources" and subheading "Art and Healing."
Artslynx (www.artslynx.org/heal/index.htm). Provides information on programs
   around the world dedicated to healing individuals and communities through the
   arts.
Healthcare Fine Art (www.healthcarefineart.com). Blog of photographer Henry
   Domke, who sells his work within the heath-care field. Site contains information, tips, and examples of artists' work in health-care facilities.
Jariscope (www.jariscope.com). Provides caregivers and people in helping
   professions—including mental health professionals, parents, teachers, ministers,
   authors, and artists—with the tools to quickly and reliably recharge themselves
   holistically and relieve stress. Produced by Jari Chevalier.
North Carolina Arts for Health Network (www.ncartsforhealth.org). An organization formed to promote, sustain, encourage, improve, and expand the incorporation of the arts in healing and well-being in North Carolina.

Organizations

Aesthetics, Inc., 301 Spruce Street, San Diego, CA 92103. Incorporates art into
   heath care, validating the relationship between the community and the hospital.
   Health-care designers, art directors, and artists collaborate on projects, including the design of healing centers and the design of interior and architectural elements. www.aesthetics.net
Art for Healing, Inc., NYC, 2350 Broadway, Suite 618, New York, NY 10024-
   3200. A nonprofit organization devoted to educating the public about the healing power of the arts. Donates work to children's hospitals, nursing homes, and
   other institutions that have limited funding for the arts. Sponsors an art gallery.
   www.artforhealingnyc.org
Art Without Boundaries Foundation, 7591 Northtree Club Drive, Suite 16, Lake
   Worth, FL 33467. Awards matching grants to train visual artists to become certified Mnemetecnic therapists, a multidiscipline therapy for Alzheimer's patients.
   www.artwithoutboundaries.org
Arts and Healing Network, Box 276, Stinson Beach, CA 94970. Sponsors a Web
   site devoted to information on arts and healing, including recommended books,
   conferences, and opportunities for artists. www.artheals.org
Children's National Medical Center, 111 Michigan Avenue NW, Washington, DC

20010-2970. Sponsors the New Horizons program that hosts exhibitions, performances, and an artists, writers, and musicians residency program. www.dcchildrens.com/dcchildrens/forparents/arts.aspx

The Creative Center, 273 Bowery, New York, NY 10002. A community of artists and cancer patients and survivors. Offers workshops and a "bedside" art program in hospitals and hospices throughout New York City. Sponsors exhibitions and an artist-in-residence program. http://thecreativecenter.org

Duke University Medical Center, Cultural Services Program, P.O. Box 3071, Durham, NC 27710. Sponsors professional arts programming in health care for the benefit of medical and support staff, patients and their families, including art in patients' rooms and display cases. www.dukehealth.org/PatientsAndVisitors/VolunteerServices/Program/eyecenterartgallery?search_highlight=art%20gallery

The Foundation for Hospital Art, 120 Stonemist Court, Roswell, GA 30076. Provides original artwork to hospitals and nursing homes for the purpose of supplementing the healing work of hospital staffs. www.hospitalart.com

Gifts of Art, NI-5C06, NIB, 300 North Ingalls, Ann Arbor, MI 48109-5470. A program of the University of Michigan hospitals. Open to Michigan artists. Sponsors exhibitions in nine hospital galleries. www.med.umich.edu/goa

Healing Arts Initiative, Massachusetts Cultural Council, 10 St. James Avenue, 3rd Floor, Boston, MA 02116-3803. A program active in Massachusetts, Vermont, and New Hampshire that uses the arts as an innovative new treatment method for patients living with chronic disabling diseases. www.massculturalcouncil.org/services/healingarts.html

Hospital Audiences, Inc., 548 Broadway, 3rd Floor, New York, NY 10012-3950. Brings visual and performing art programs to New Yorkers who are confined in hospitals and health-care facilities, shelters, etc. www.hospitalaudiences.org

RX Art, Inc., 208 Forsyth Street, New York, NY 10002. A nonprofit organization that selects and installs original works of art in patient rooms, treatment rooms, and public areas of health-care facilities. www.rxart.net

Shands Arts in Medicine, P.O. Box 100326, Gainesville, FL 32610. A program of the College of Medicine, University of Florida. Combines standard medical practices with innovative healing methods that include a program involving artists, patients, and their families. Sponsors an artist-in-residence program. www.shands.org/aim

Smith Farm Center for the Healing Arts, 1632 U Street NW, Washington, DC 20009. Sponsors various creative arts projects for cancer patients that involve artists, writers, and health-care professionals. www.smithfarm.com

Society for the Arts in Healthcare, 2437 15th Street NW, Washington DC 20009. A national membership organization dedicated to promoting the incorporation of the arts as an integral component of health care. Conducts conferences and publishes a newsletter and membership directory. www.thesah.org

The Survivors Art Foundation, P.O. Box 383, Westhampton, NY 11977. Committed to empowering trauma survivors with expressive outlets, including national exhibitions, an online gallery, publications, and career development services. www.survivorsartfoundation.org

ART SALES AND COMMISSIONS
Publications

The Art of Buying Art: An Insider's Guide to Collecting Contemporary Art by Paige West. HarperCollins, 2007. Although the book is written for the novice art collector, it gives artists a good reality check regarding advice that collectors are given on a wide range of subjects—from discounts and prices for artwork—to artist/gallery relations and studio visits.

The Art of Creating Collectors by Zella Jackson. Rhinebeck, N.Y.: The Consultant Press, revised 1994. Although written for art dealers, the book contains information of use to artists for obtaining private and corporate collectors.

The Art of Selling Art by Zella Jackson. Rhinebeck, N.Y.: The Consultant Press, revised 1998. Contains tips on how to sell art and build collections.

The Art of Selling Art: Between Production and Livelihood by Bill H. Ritchie. Ritchie's Perfect Press, 500 Aloha #105, Seattle, WA 98109, revised 1991.

The Art of Selling to the Affluent by Matt Oechsli. Hoboken, N.J. John Wiley & Sons, 2004. Shows how to meet the needs of affluent clients based on extensive research of the buying patterns and expectations of the wealthy. Provides a step-by-step sales guide that reveals the secrets of attracting and keeping wealthy clients for life, boosting sales, and getting repeat business.

The Artist's Guide to New Markets: Opportunities to Show and Sell Art Beyond Galleries by Peggy Hadden. New York: Allworth Press, 1998. Provides advice on selling art to markets and clients that many artists would never consider approaching.

Cultivating Collectors by Alyson N. Stanfield. Stanfield Art Associates, P.O. Box 988, Goldon, CO 80402. Provides tips on developing mailing lists, contacting people by phone and email, and developing newsletters. Available as an ebook or as a printout. www.artbizcoach.com

A Gallery without Walls: Selling Art in Alternative Venues by Margaret Danielak. Nevada City, Calif.: ArtNetwork, 2005. Discusses innovative ways to market and sell art without a gallery. Includes information on effective sales strategies, locating alternative venues, and dealing effectively with the press.

How to Get Started Selling Your Art by Carole Katchen. North Light Books, 1998. Presents various venues for selling artwork.

How to Start a Faux Painting or Mural Business: A Guide to Making Money in the Decorative Arts by Rebecca Pittman. New York: Allworth Press, 2003. Culled from the author's many years in the business, provides information on a variety of subjects, including securing work through referrals, building contacts, project planning, portfolio development, contracts and forms, startup supplies, and the growing pains of a successful business.

Marketing to the Affluent by Thomas J. Stanley. New York: McGraw-Hill, revised 1997. Provides information on the buying and patronage habits of the wealthy, and marketing tips.

Publishing Your Art as Cards, Posters & Calendars by Harold Davis. Rhinebeck, N.Y.: The Consultant Press, revised 1996. A guide to creating, designing, and marketing cards, posters, and calendars.

Selling Art 101: The Art of Creative Selling by Robert Regis Dvorak. Nevada City, Calif.: Artnetwork Press, revised 2007. Provides information and advice on selling artwork.

Selling Art Without Galleries: Toward Making a Living from Your Art by Daniel Grant. New York: Allworth Press, 2006. Topics include creative ways to find prospective collectors; ideas to break into specialized markets; how to arrange and curate exhibitions; rewards and risks of selling art on the Internet: and more.

Selling Your Crafts by Susan Joy Sager. New York: Allworth Press, revised 2003. Provides tips and tactics for promoting and marketing crafts, and the necessary forms to start a business.

Organizations

ArtNetwork, P.O. Box 1360, Nevada City, CA 95959. Rents arts-related mailing lists including museum store buyers. www.artmarketing.com

Museum Store Association, 4100 East Mississippi Avenue, Suite 800, Denver, CO 80246. Provides members with a mailing list of museum shops nationwide and in other parts of the world. Affiliate memberships are available to artists who are already selling work to a museum shop at wholesale prices. www.museumdistrict.com

ARTISTS' BOOKS

Publications

Art on Paper. 150 W. 28th Street #504, New York, NY 10001. Covers information on a range of paper-based media, including limited edition prints, independently published artist's books, photography, drawings, and specialized museum and dealer catalogs. Published semimonthly.

Artist Book News. Mystical Places Press, 1400 Central Avenue, Suite 107, Wenatchee, WA 98801-1499. Published online biannually. Promotes book works by professional book artists. www.mysticalplaces.com/abnews.html

Hand Papermaking. Hand Papermaking, Inc., P.O. Box 1070, Beltsville, MD 20704-1070. Repository of information on the art and craft of hand papermaking. Published semiannually. www.handpapermaking.org

Hand Papermaking Newsletter. Hand Papermaking, Inc., P.O. Box 77027, Washington, DC 20013-7027. Includes information and listings for national and international exhibitions, lectures, workshops and other events. Published quarterly. www.handpapermaking.org

Umbrella. Umbrella Associates, P.O. Box 3640, Santa Monica, CA 90408. Digest of current trends in artists' books, artists' publications, and mail art. Also available online. Published three to four times a year. www.colophon.com/umbrella

Web Sites

Artist Help Network (www.artisthelpnetwork.com). Founded by Caroll Michels, career coach and artist-advocate, this site is devoted to all aspects of career development. See heading "Other Resources" and subheading "Artists' Books."

Book Arts Classified (www.bookarts.com). Lists opportunities and information of interest to book artists.

Book Arts Directory (www.bookarts.com). A resource for artists working in the book-arts field. Also includes information for papermakers, calligraphers, paper decorators, printmakers, book designers, fine-art printers, publishers, traditional bookbinders, and artist bookmakers.

Fine Press and Artists' Books (www.califiabooks.com/finepress/index.html). Links to artist book presses and book artists in the United States and abroad. Provided by Vamp & Tramp Booksellers, LLC.

Otis Artists' Books Collection (httpl/content.library.otis.edu/collections/artistsbooks .htm). An online public database of more than 8,000 images of 2,000 artists' books. Sponsored by the Otis College of Art and Design.

Organizations

Art Metropole, 788 King Street West, Toronto, 2nd Floor, Ontario M5V 1N6, Canada. An artist-run center that operates a shop that specializes in artists' products, including bookworks. www.artmetropole.org

Artists' Books Johan Deumens, Dr. N.G. Piersonstraat 1, NL-2104 VG, Heemstede, The Netherlands. Sells artists' books. www.artistsbook.com

Bookartbookshop, 17 Pitfield Street, London N1 6HB, United Kingdom. Sells artists' books and small-press publications. www.bookartbookshop.com

Carnegie Mellon University, Fine Arts and Special Collections Department, Hunt Library, 4909 Frew Street, Pittsburgh, PA 15213. Collects and exhibits artists' books of individual international artists and established-artist book distributors and publishers. www.library.cmu.edu/Research/Arts/Art/artistsbooks.html

Center for Book & Paper Arts, Columbia College, 1104 South Wabash, 2nd Floor, Chicago, IL 60605. Sponsors exhibitions and workshops. Offers a master's program in book and paper arts. www.colum.edu/centers/bpa/

Center for Book Arts, 28 West 27th Street, 3rd Floor, New York, New York 10001. Nonprofit educational and exhibition facility. Offers classes and production facilities for artists' books. www.centerforbookarts.org

Dieu Donné Papermill, 315 West 36th Street, New York, NY 10018. A nonprofit hand-papermaking studio. Sponsors exhibitions, workshops, residencies, and other programs. www.dieudonne.org

871 Fine Arts, 49 Geary Street, Suite 513, San Francisco, CA 94108. Features exhibitions of artists' books. www.abebooks.com/home/fineart

Granary Books, 168 Mercer Street, 2nd Floor, New York, NY 10012. Publisher of artists' books. www.granarybooks.com

Hand Papermaking, Inc., P.O. Box 1070, Beltsville, MD 20704-1070. A nonprofit organization dedicated to advancing traditional and contemporary ideas in the art of hand papermaking. Sponsors a slide registry and publishes *Hand Papermaking* and a newsletter. www.handpapermaking.org

Joshua Heller Rare Books, P.O. Box 39114, Washington, DC 20016-9114. Sells artists' books. www.joshuahellerrarebooks.com

Florence Loewy, Books by Artists, 9/11 rue de Thorigny, 75003, Paris, France. Sells artists' books. www.florenceloewy.com

Minnesota Center for Book Arts, 1011 Washington Avenue South, Minneapolis, MN 55415. Offers studio space, workshops, and classes in papermaking, bookbinding, and letterpress. www.mnbookarts.org

Printed Matter, 195 Tenth Avenue, New York, NY 10011. Nonprofit distributor and retailer of artists' books. Also sponsors exhibitions. www.printedmatter.org

Vamp and Tramp, Booksellers, LLC, South Hall Building, 1951 Hoover Court, Suite 105, Birmingham, AL 35226-3606. Sells artists' books. www.vampandtramp .com

Visual Studies Workshop, 31 Prince Street, Rochester, NY 14607. Publishes artists' books and offers residencies and internships related to book arts. www.vsw.org

Zybooks, 6 Grenville Road, London N19 4EH, United Kingdom. Features artists' books created mainly by British artists. www.zyarts.com/zybooks

ARTISTS' HOUSING AND STUDIO/PERFORMANCE SPACE

Publications

The Art Studio-Loft Manual: For Ambitious Artists and Creators by Eric Rudd. North Adams, Mass.: CIRE Corporation, 2001. Provides practical solutions to help creative people find, secure, renovate, and finance studio space.

Artist's Assets. Artist Trust, 1835 12th Avenue, Seattle, WA 98122, revised 2005. A resource guide for artists in Washington State. Includes information about work/live space opportunities. Available online and as a printout. www.artisttrust .org/services/aa

The 100 Best Small Art Towns in America: Where to Discover Creative Communities, Fresh Air, and Affordable Housing by John Villani. Woodstock, Vt.: Countryman Press, revised 2005. An annotated list of communities that are particularly artist-friendly.

Web Sites

ArtHome (www.arthomeonline.org). Helps artists build assets and equity through financial literacy and home-ownership.

Artist Help Network (www.artisthelpnetwork.com). Founded by Caroll Michels, career coach and artist-advocate, this site is devoted to all aspects of career development. See heading "Creature Comforts" and subheadings "Health Hazards in Your Workspace," "Housing & Studio Space," and "Studio Insurance."

Artspacefinder (www.artistlink.org/?q=artspacefinder). Lists artists' spaces available for rent or purchase in Massachusetts and the Boston Metro area. Sponsored by Artistlink in collaboration with The Artists Foundation.

Guide to Leasing Studio Space (www.vlaa.org/publications.asp). Sponsored by the St. Louis Volunteer Lawyers and Accountants for the Arts. Prepared by Sue Greenberg and updated by Céline Bondard, revised 2004.

Live/Work Institute (www.live-work.com/lwi). A nonprofit organization that advocates and assists in the development of live/work housing and communities.

Web site provides information about live/work planning and building codes and examples of live/work projects.

Resource Handbook for Minnesota Artists (www.springboardforthearts.org/ Resources/Resources.asp). Sponsored by Springboard for the Arts. An online listing of resources for Minnesota artists, including housing and studio space.

Square Feet: The Artist's Guide to Renting & Buying Work Space (www .torontoartscape.on.ca/squarefeet). By Jennifer Ginder with Carol-Ann Ryan. Answers many questions about locating, renting, and buying space relevant to Canadian artists. Sponsored by Toronto Artscape.

Square Feet Chicago: An Artist's Guide to Buying and Renting Space (www.chicago artistsresource.org/?q=node/591). An online manual published by the Chicago Department of Cultural Affairs.

Warehouse Studio Health & Safety (www.carfacontario.ca/resources). Addresses health and safety risks of artists living and/or working in warehouses and suggests workable solutions. Sponsored by CARFAC Ontario.

Organizations

Art Space Clearinghouse, Volunteer Lawyers for the Arts, 6128 Delmar, St. Louis, MO 63112. Supports and facilitates the development of affordable work and living spaces for artists. Provides an online St. Louis Art Space Data Bank that lists studio and workspace. www.vlaa.org/artsspace.asp

ArtHouse, 1360 Mission Street, Suite 200, San Francisco, CA 94103. Nonprofit organization created to serve as a clearinghouse for information about artists' studio and live/work space and cultural facilities. Provides a hotline listing of available space. www.arthouseca.org

Artist Relocation Program, City Hall, P.O. Box 2267, Paducah, KY 42002-2267. Provides economic and business incentives to artists who wish to relocate to Paducah, Kentucky. www.pacucaharts.com

Artspace, 230 S. 500 West, Suite 235, Salt Lake City, UT 84101. A nonprofit arts organization that creates affordable housing and workspace for artists. www.artspaceutah.org

Artspace Projects, Inc., 250 Third Avenue North, Suite 500, Minneapolis, MN 55401. Assists artists in finding or developing affordable studio and performance space in vacant and underutilized buildings. www.artspaceusa.org

City of Seattle Office of Housing, P.O. Box 94725, Seattle, WA 98124-4725. Sponsors artist live/work space projects. www.ci.seattle.wa.us/housing

Contemporary Art Institute of Detroit, 5141 Rosa Parks Boulevard, Detroit, MI 48208. Administrates the Whitdell Apartment project, the first affordable housing development in Detroit specifically designed for artists. www.thecaid.org

Elizabeth Foundation for the Arts Studio Center, P.O. Box 2670, New York, NY 10108. Provides 120 reasonably priced workspaces for visual artists in Manhattan. www.efa1.org

Fort Point Arts Community, Inc., 300 Summer Street, Boston, MA 02210. An advocacy organization that helps Boston area artists obtain studio space. www .fortpointarts.org

Marie Walsh Sharpe Art Foundation, 830 North Tejon Street #120, Colorado Springs, CO 80903. Provides free studio space in New York City to visual artists. Artists living throughout the United States are eligible to apply for work spaces. www.sharpeartfdn.org

PS1 Art Center Studio Program, 22-25 Jackson Avenue, Long Island City, NY 11101. An international studio program, sponsored by P.S. 1, the Institute for Contemporary Art, which provides visual artists with free, nonliving studio space for one year at the P.S. 1 Museum in Long Island City and the Clocktower Gallery in Manhattan. www.ps1.org

Toronto Artscape, 171 East Liberty Street, Suite 224, Toronto, Ontario, Canada M6K 3P6. A nonprofit organization that devises practical solutions for securing and maintaining artist live/work space in Toronto. www.torontoartscape.on.ca

ARTISTS' REGISTRIES

Organizations

Arkansas Arts Council, 1500 Tower Building, 323 Center Street, Little Rock, AR 72201. Sponsors the Arkansas Artist Registry, an online registry of Arkansas artists. www.arkansasarts.com/programs/registry

Artist Help Network (www.artisthelpnetwork.com). Founded by Caroll Michels, career coach and artist-advocate, this site is devoted to all aspects of career development. See heading "Exhibitions, Commissions and Sales" and subheading "Public Art" and "Slide Registries."

Artists Space, 38 Greene Street, 3rd Floor, New York, NY 10013. The Irving Sandler Artists File is one of the largest registries in the country. A digitized image database and artist registry. www.artistsspace.org

The Arts Council in Buffalo and Erie County, 700 Main Street, Buffalo, NY 14202. Sponsors the Buffalo Artist Registry, an online registry for arts council members. www.artscouncilbuffalo.org/registry

Brooklyn Arts Council, 55 Washington Street, Suite 218, Brooklyn, NY 11201. Sponsors an online registry for Brooklyn artists. www.brooklynartscouncil.org

City of Las Vegas Arts Commission Artist Registry, 300 E. Charleston Boulevard, Suite 109, Las Vegas, NV 89109. An artist registry that is open to local artists and artists nationwide. www.lasvegasnevada.gov/files/Artist_Registry_Application _Form.pdf

Connecticut Commission on Culture and Tourism, One Constitution Plaza, 2nd Floor, Hartford, CT 06103. Sponsors the Connecticut Visual Arts Slide Bank, a collection of slides of the work of contemporary visual artists, including crafts artists, residing in Connecticut. www.cultureandtourism.org

The Drawing Center, 35 Wooster Street, New York, NY 10013. Sponsors the Viewing Program Artist Registry, a curated registry that features the work of artists nationwide. Artists who are not attending school and do not have New York gallery representation are eligible to submit a portfolio for consideration. International artists living in the United States are also eligible to apply. Twice a year the Drawing Center presents "Selections," a group exhibition of artists curated from the Viewing Program. www.drawingcenter.org/viewingprogram/index.cfm

Hand Papermaking, Inc., P.O. Box 1070, Beltsville, MD 20704-1070. A not-for-profit organization dedicated to advancing traditional and contemporary ideas in the art of hand papermaking. Sponsors an artist registry housed in the Robert C. Williams Paper Museum in Atlanta, Georgia. www.handpapermaking.org

International Sculpture Center, 1900 Fairgrounds Road, Suite B, Hamilton, NJ 08619. Sponsors Portfolio, an online registry for International Sculpture Center members. www.sculpture.org/redesign/port.shtml

Maryland State Arts Council Visual Artists' Registry, c/o Maryland Art Place, 8 Market Place, Suite 100, Baltimore, MD 21201. An online registry of more than 2,300 regional artists. www.mdartplace.org

Metro Nashville Arts Commission, P.O. Box 196300, Nashville, TN 37219-6300. Sponsors an online registry of Nashville-area artists. www.artsnashville.org/registry

New Jersey State Council on the Arts, P.O. Box 306, Trenton, NJ 08625. Sponsors the Visual Arts Registry, a slide registry that features the work of New Jersey artists. www.njartscouncil.org/vas_registry.cfm

NURTUREart, 910 Grand Street, Brooklyn, NY 11211. A not-for-profit organization dedicated to helping promising visual artists. Organizes group exhibitions. Sponsors an artist registry. www.nurtureart.org

Ohio Arts Council, 727 East Main Street, Columbus, OH 43205-1796. Sponsors the Ohio Online Visual Artist Registry, which features the work of regional and national artists. www.ohioonlinearts.org

Pittsburgh Artist Registry, Office of Public Art, c/o Greater Pittsburgh Arts Council, 707 Penn Avenue, 2nd Floor, Pittsburgh, PA 15222. An online artist database of artists living in southeastern Pennsylvania. www.pittsburghartistregistry.org

Southern Arts Federation, 1800 Peachtree Street NW, Suite 808, Atlanta, GA 30309-7603. SouthernArtistry is an online registry designed to showcase the South's artistic diversity by spotlighting artists of all disciplines who live and work in the region. Sponsored by the Southern Arts Federation and the Center for Arts Management and Technology at Carnegie Mellon. www.southernartistry.org/about_us.cfm

VSA arts Artists Registry, 818 Connecticut Avenue, Suite 600, Washington, DC 20006. An online registry open to artists with disabilities. www.vsarts.org/prebuilt/artists/registry/artistlisting.cfm

Western States Arts Federation (WESTAF), 1743 Wazee Street, Suite 300, Denver, CO 80202. Sponsors ArtistRegister, a juried online registry of regional and national artists. http://artistsregister.com

White Columns, 320 W. 13th Street, New York, NY 10014. An alternative space that sponsors the Curated Artist Registry. It is open to artists worldwide. http://registry.whitecolumns.org

Women and Their Work, 1710 Lavaca Street, Austin, TX 78701. Sponsors an online registry open to organization members. www.womenandtheirwork.org

Women's Art Registry of Minnesota (WARM), 550 Rice Street, St. Paul, MN 55103. An online registry of WARM members. www.thewarm.org

Also see "Online Galleries" and "Public Art Programs."

ARTISTS' SOURCEBOOKS
Publications

American Art Collector. Alcove Books, 930 Dwight Way #7, Berkeley, CA 94710. A juried sourcebook that does not charge jurying fees. The sourcebook is mailed to galleries, art consultants and designers throughout the United States. www.alcovebooks.com

New American Paintings. The Open Studio Press, 450 Harrison Avenue, #47, Boston, MA 02118. A series of artists' sourcebooks published several times a year. A registration fee is required. Artists are selected by a juried procedure. www.newamericanpaintings.com

The Sourcebook of Architectural & Interior Art. The Guild, 931 East Main Street, Suite 9, Madison, WI 53703. A fee-based resource directory that contains contact information and photographs of the work of American fine arts and crafts artists, as well as biographical information. Distributed free of charge to more than 10,000 architects, interior designers, public art specialists, landscape architects, liturgical consultants, art consultants, and other professions. Published annually. www.guild.com

The Sourcebook of Residential Art. The Guild, 931 East Main Street, Suite 9, Madison, WI 53703. A fee-based resource directory that contains contact information and photographs of the work of American fine arts and crafts artists, as well as biographical information. Distributed free of charge to more than 7,000 art consultants, high-end consumers, residential design firms, architectural firms, and galleries. Published annually. www.guild.com

Web Sites

Artist Help Network (www.artisthelpnetwork.com). Founded by Caroll Michels, career coach and artist-advocate, this site is devoted to all aspects of career development. See heading "Exhibitions, Commissions and Sales" and subheading "Artist Sourcebooks."

ARTISTS WITH DISABILITIES
Publications

Kaleidoscope: International Magazine of Literature, Fine Arts, and Disability. United Disability Services, 701 South Main Street, Akron, OH 44311. Published twice a year. Examines the experiences of disability through the fine arts and literature. Voice mail: 330-762-9755. TTY: 330-379-3349. Web site: www.udsakron.org/kaleidoscope.htm

Putting Creativity to Work: Careers in the Arts for People with Disabilities, edited by Paul Scribner. Very Special Arts, 818 Connecticut Avenue NW, Suite 600, Washington DC 20006, 2000. Provides visual and performing artists and writers who have disabilities with information to pursue careers that are creative and challenging. Describes more than 110 arts-related careers and includes the biographies of 25 artists with disabilities and the personal strategies used to succeed in pursing their dreams. PDF format. http://www.vsarts.org/x630.xml

Web Sites

Artist Help Network (www.artisthelpnetwork.com). Founded by Caroll Michels, career coach and artist-advocate, this site is devoted to all aspects of career development. See heading "Other Resources" and subheading "Artists with Disabilities."

Organizations

Coalition for Disabled Musicians, Inc., P.O. Box 1002M, Bay Shore, NY 11706-0533. Volunteer, self-help organization for individuals with disabilities that provides assistance in the pursuit of musical aspirations. www.disabled-musicians.org

Disabled Artists' Network, 2701 California Avenue SW, Suite 263, Seattle, WA 98116. Support group for disabled professional visual artists. www .disabledartistsnetwork.net

The London Disability Arts Forum, 20-22 Waterson Street, London E2 8HE, United Kingdom. Strengthens and develops the image of disability in arts and culture. Publishes *Disability Arts in London* and sponsors events and programs. www.ldaf.org

Mouth and Foot Painting Artists, FL- 9494, Im Riette 25, Furstentum, Liechtenstein. An international information clearinghouse for artists who paint with their mouth or foot. Conducts workshops and organizes exhibitions. www .amfpa.com

Mouth and Foot Painting Artists, Inc., Attn: James March, 2070 Peachtree Court, Suite 101, Atlanta, GA 30341. Sponsors a gallery featuring exhibitions of artists who paint with their mouth or foot. Also sponsors a Web site with a selection of greeting cards, calendars, and other items designed by mouth and foot artists. www.mfpausa.com

National Arts and Disability Center, Tarjan Center, University of California Los Angeles, 300 UCLA Medical Plaza, Room 3310, Los Angeles, CA 90095-6967. A resource, information, and training center that provides information on the arts and disabilities. http://nadc.ucla.edu

National Endowment for the Arts, Office for AccessAbility, 1100 Pennsylvania Avenue NW, Washington, DC 20506. An advocate-technical assistance arm of the NEA for people with disabilities, as well as for older adults, veterans, and people living in institutions. www.nea.gov/resources/Accessibility/index.html

National Exhibits by Blind Artists, Inc., 919 Walnut Street, Philadelphia, PA 19107. Sponsors exhibitions and awards. http://nebaart.org

National Institute of Art and Disabilities, 551 23rd Street, Richmond, CA 94804. Provides studios to artists with developmental disabilities. Sponsors a gallery. www.niadart.org

VSA arts, 818 Connecticut Avenue NW, Suite 600, Washington, DC 20006. Sponsors several programs for challenged artists, including an online gallery. www .vsarts.org

ARTS SERVICE ORGANIZATIONS
Publications

Directory of Minority Arts Organizations, edited by Carol Ann Huston. Office of Civil Rights, National Endowment for the Arts, 1100 Pennsylvania Avenue NW, Washington, DC 20506. Regularly updated. Lists art centers, galleries, performing groups, presenting groups, and local and national arts service organizations with leadership and constituencies that are predominantly Asian-American, African-American, Hispanic, Native American, or multiracial. www.arts.endow .gov/learn/civil.html

Directory of the Arts, Canadian Conference of the Arts, 804-130 Albert Street, Ottawa, Ontario K1P 5G4, Canada, revised 2004. A complete listing of Canadian cultural departments and agencies, national arts associations, arts councils, and cultural agencies. www.ccarts.ca.

Web Sites

API News (www.communityarts.net/apinews/index.php). Sponsored by Art in the Public Interest. Reports items of interest regarding community-based arts organizations. Available online and through a free e-mail subscription.

Artist Help Network (www.artisthelpnetwork.com). Founded by Caroll Michels, career coach and artist-advocate, this site is devoted to all aspects of career development. See heading "Other Resources" and subheadings "Art Service Organizations Abroad," "National Art Service Organizations," and "Regional Art Service Organizations."

Arts Over America (www.nasaa-arts.org/aoa/aoa_contents.shtml). Provides links to state arts agencies. Sponsored by the National Assembly of State Arts Agencies.

ArtWomen.org (www.artwomen.org). A site devoted to the exchange of information pertaining to visual art and feminist cultural production across and between disciplines and geographical boundaries. Provides news, art reviews, book reviews, exhibition opportunities, and other career-related opportunities for women artists.

Resources for Immigrant Artists (www.nyfa.org). Lists art service organizations and other resources for immigrants and refugees. Sponsored by the New York Foundation for the Arts.

National Organizations

American Association of Museums, 1575 Eye Street NW, Suite 400, Washington, DC 20005. Membership organization open to professional and volunteer museum staff, independent curators, and consultants. www.aam-us.org

American Craft Council, 72 Spring Street, 6th Floor, New York, NY 10012. National organization that sponsors exhibitions, seminars, workshops, and an international exchange program. Publishes *American Craft.* www.craftcouncil.org

American Print Alliance, 302 Larkspur Turn, Peachtree City, GA 30269-2210. A nonprofit consortium of printmakers' councils. Publishes the journal *Contemporary Impressions.* www.printalliance.org

American Society of Portrait Artists, P.O. Box 230216, Montgomery, AL 36106.

Publishes a quarterly journal. Sponsors a Web site for members and offers other services. www.asopa.com.

Americans for the Arts, 1000 Vermont Avenue NW, 6th Floor, Washington, DC 20005, and 1 East 53rd Street, New York, NY 10022. National organization for groups and individuals dedicated to advancing the arts and culture in communities throughout the United States. Sponsors a Job Bank and a publications program and distributes career-related books for visual and performing artists. www.artsusa.org

Aperture Foundation, 547 W. 27th Street, 4th Floor, New York, NY 10001. A nonprofit organization devoted to photography and related visual arts. Sponsors exhibitions, publications, research, and the Paul Strand Archive. www .aperture.org

Art & Science Collaborations, Inc., 130 East End Avenue, #1A, New York, NY 10028. An organization formed to raise public awareness about artists and scientists who use science and technology to explore new forms of creative expression and to increase communication and collaboration between these fields. www.asci.org

Artists Network of Refuse and Resist, 305 Madison Avenue, #1166, New York, NY 10165. An organization consisting of artists and arts presenters who create and promote art that contributes to a culture of resistance. Sponsors events and projects. Also has an office in Los Angeles: 2658 Griffith Park Boulevard, #353, Los Angeles, CA 90039-2520. www.artistsnetwork.org

Arts Extension Service, Division of Outreach, 100 Venture Way, Suite 201, Hadley, MA 01035-9430. Serves as a catalyst for better management of the arts in communities through continuing education for artists and arts organizations. Sponsors programs in arts management, business development, fund-raising, advocacy leadership, and marketing. Publishes and distributes books, guides, and pamphlets. www.umass.edu/aes

Arts and Healing Network, P.O. Box 276, Stinson Beach, CA 94970. Sponsors a Web site that serves as an international resource and exchange for those interested in the healing potential of art, including environmentalists, social activists, artists, health-care practitioners, and those challenged by illness. The site features a list of various events and resources and a registry of visual artists. www.artheals.org

Asian American Arts Alliance, Inc., 155 Avenue of the Americas, 6th Floor, New York, NY 10013. Sponsors exhibitions, publications, and programs for Asian-American artists. www.aaartsalliance.org

Asian American Women Artists Alliance, 136 15th Street, Basement, Brooklyn, NY 11215. Supports and promotes Asian-American women artists in the visual, literary, and performing arts. Sponsors exhibitions, performances, readings, and career development workshops and seminars. www.aawaa.org

Association of Hispanic Arts, Inc., P.O. Box 1169, El Barrio, NY 10029. Offers a variety of services geared toward professional Hispanic artists and arts organizations. www.latinoarts.org

Blue Earth Alliance, P.O. Box 94388, Seattle, WA 98124-6688. A membership organization devoted to exhibitions and photographic projects that educate the public about endangered cultures, threatened environments, and social concerns. www.blueearth.org

Colored Pencil Society of America. Sponsors an annual exhibition, publishes a newsletter, and provides information on product research. Regional chapters throughout the United States. www.cpsa.org

Community Arts Network (CAN), Art in the Public Interest, P.O. Box 68, Saxaphaw, NC 27340. Promotes information exchange, research, and a critical dialogue within the field of community-based arts. Provides various services online, including the newsletter *API News*. www.communityarts.net

En Foco, 1738 Hone Avenue, Bronx, NY 10461. National organization that supports contemporary fine art and documentary photographers of diverse cultures, primarily U.S. residents of Latino, African, and Asian heritage, and Native Peoples of the Americas and the Pacific. Sponsors traveling exhibitions, an image library, and publishes the photographic journal *Nueva Luz*. www.enfoco.org

Fractured Atlas, 248 W. 35th Street, Suite 1202, New York, NY 10001. Nonprofit organization that offers many support services to artist-members throughout the United States, including health insurance, event liability insurance, fiscal sponsorship, legal services, grants, and career development information. www.fracturedatlas.org

Friends of Fiber Art International, P.O. Box 468, Western Springs, IL 60558. Sponsors programs and publishes a quarterly newsletter. www.friendsoffiberart.org

The Glass Art Society, 3131 Western Avenue, Suite 414, Seattle, WA 98121. An international nonprofit organization that promotes the appreciation and development of glass arts. Publishes the *Glass Art Society Journal* and a bimonthly newsletter, and sponsors a conference. www.glassart.org

Graphic Artists Guild, 32 Broadway, Suite 1114, New York, NY 10004. National membership organization with local chapters throughout the United States. Advances the rights and interests of graphic artists through legislative reform and organizes networking activities, including job-referral services. Offers group health insurance to members. Publishes the newsletter *Guild News*. www.gag.org

Guerrilla Girls. A group of women artists, writers, performers, filmmakers, and arts professionals dedicated to fighting sexual discrimination. www.guerrillagirls.com

Hand Papermaking, Inc., P.O. Box 1070, Beltsville, MD 20704-1070. A nonprofit organization dedicated to advancing traditional and contemporary ideas in the art of hand papermaking. Sponsors a registry and publishes *Hand Papermaking* and *Hand Papermaking Newsletter*. www.handpapermaking.org

Handweavers Guild of America, Inc., 1255 Buford Highway, Suite 211, Suwanee, GA 30024. Provides forums for the education of hand weavers, hand spinners, basket makers, and fiber artists in related disciplines. www.weavespindye.org

International Sculpture Center, 14 Fairgrounds Road, Suite B, Hamilton, NJ 08619-3447. A member-supported nonprofit organization for sculptors, collectors, architects, curators, and others. Publishes *Sculpture* and sponsors an online registry. www.sculpture.org

Intuit: The Center for Intuitive and Outsider Art, 756 N. Milwaukee Avenue, Chicago, IL 60622. Established to recognize the work of artists who demonstrate little influence from the mainstream art world and who are motivated by a unique personal vision. Sponsors exhibitions, lectures, and public programs. Publishes *In'Tuit,* a quarterly newsletter. http://www.art.org

The Leslie/Lohman Gay Art Foundation, 26 Wooster Street, New York, NY 10013. A nonprofit organization committed to providing a forum to further the awareness, appreciation, and preservation of lesbian, gay, bisexual, transgender, and queer art. Sponsors a gallery, a newsletter, and other programs. www.leslielohman.org

The National Association of Independent Artists, 1426 Hazen Street SE, Grand Rapids, MI 49507-3713. An advocacy organization dedicated to the professional and economic success of its members. http://naia-artists.org

National Association of Women Artists, 80 Fifth Avenue, Suite 1405, New York, NY 10011. The oldest professional women's fine-arts group in the United States. Encourages the growth and development of women artists, and provides cultural and educational programs. www.nawanet.org

National Endowment for the Arts, 1100 Pennsylvania Avenue NW, Washington, DC 20506. A federal agency that aims to support America's cultural heritage and nurture and support the arts. Sponsors grants and various programs. www.arts.endow.gov

National Sculpture Society, 237 Park Avenue, New York, NY 10017. Publishes *Sculpture Review* and a bimonthly newsletter. Also provides members with information on grants, awards, and competitions. www.nationalsculpture.org

National Women's Caucus for Art, P.O. Box 1498, New York, NY 10013. National organization with regional chapters throughout the United States. Represents the professional and economic concerns of women artists, art historians, educators, writers, and museum professionals. Sponsors conferences and exhibitions and publishes a newsletter. Provides members with access to heath insurance. www.nationalwca.com

National Wood Carvers Association, P.O. Box 43218, Cincinnati, OH 45243. Publishes *Chip Chats* six times a year with how-to information and feature articles about wood carvers. www.chipchats.org

Photographic Resource Center at Boston University, 832 Commonwealth Avenue, Boston, MA 02215. A membership organization that provides a range of programs and services for photographers, journalists, critics, curators, students, and other individuals and organizations interested in photography. www.bu.edu/prc

The Santa Fe Center for Photography, P.O. Box 2483, Santa Fe, NM 87504. (Formerly The Center for Photographic Projects.) A nonprofit organization that honors and supports gifted and committed photographers, and provides various career opportunities. www.sfcp.org

Society for Photographic Education, 2530 Superior Avenue #403, Cleveland, OH 44114. Nonprofit membership organization that provides a forum for the discussion of photography and related media as a means of creative expression and cultural insight. Sponsors publications, services, and interdisciplinary programs. www.spenational.org.

Society for the Arts in Healthcare, 2437 15th Street NW, Washington, DC 20009. A national membership organization that is dedicated to the incorporation of the arts as an appropriate and integral component of health care. Members include physicians, nurses, medical students, arts administrators, architects, designers, and artists in all disciplines. Publishes a newsletter and membership directory and sponsors an annual conference. www.thesah.org

Surface Design Association, P.O. Box 360, Sebastopol, CA 95473-0360. A national membership organization for artists involved in surface design, textiles, weavings, quilts, and other forms of fiber art. Publishes *Surface Design*. www .surfacedesign.org

UrbanGlass, 647 Fulton Street, Brooklyn, NY 11217-1112. Dedicated to promoting the use of glass as a medium for creative endeavors in art, craft, and design. www.urbanglass.org

YLEM: Artists Using Science and Technology, P.O. Box 31923, San Francisco, CA 94131-0923. A membership organization of artists working in various technology-based media or integrating the subject of science in any media. Sponsors a newsletter and exhibitions. www.ylem.org

Regional Organizations

ALABAMA

Alabama State Council on the Arts, 201 Monroe Street, Montgomery, AL 36130. Sponsors fellowships and provides individual artist grants and technical assistance grants. www.arts.state.al.us

ALASKA

Alaska State Council for the Arts, 411 West 4th Avenue, STE 1E, Anchorage, AK 99501-2343. Awards grants and sponsors a newsletter. www.eed.state.ak.us/aksca

ARKANSAS

Arkansas Art Council, 1500 Tower Building, 323 Center Street, Little Rock, AR 72201. Sponsors grants, an artists' registry, and exhibitions. www.arkansasarts .com

CALIFORNIA

Alliance of California Artists, P.O. Box 821, Clovis, CA 93612. A membership organization that sponsors exhibitions and workshops. www.allianceof californiaartists.com

Artists Network of Refuse and Resist, 2658 Griffith Park Boulevard, Los Angeles, CA 90039-2520. Regional office of a national organization of artists and arts presenters who create and promote art that contributes to a culture of resistance. Sponsors events and projects. www.artistsnetwork.org

The Asian American Women Artists Association, 1890 Bryant Street, #302, San Francisco, CA 94110. A San Francisco Bay Area organization that supports and promotes Asian-American women artists in the visual, literary, and performing arts. www.aawaaart.com

The Center for Cultural Innovation, 244 S. San Pedro Street, Suite 401, Los Angeles, CA 90012 and 651 Brannon Street, Suite 410, San Francisco, CA 94107. Promotes knowledge, sharing, networking, and financial independence for individual artists and creative entrepreneurs in California by providing business training, grants and loans, workshops, and the incubation of innovative projects. http://cciarts.org

Northern California Women's Caucus for Art, Box 11512, Oakland, CA 94611-0512. Provides resources and services to members, including an online gallery, a quarterly newsletter, and shopping discounts. www.ncwca.org

Pro Arts, 550 Second Street, Oakland, CA 94607. Nonprofit membership organization serving artists of all disciplines in the Bay Area. Offers technical assistance, consultations, seminars, workshops, artist-in-residence programs, and exhibitions. www.proartsgallery.org

San Francisco Camerawork, 657 Mission Street, 2nd Floor, San Francisco, CA 94105-4104. A nonprofit artists' organization dedicated to contemporary photography and related media. Sponsors exhibitions, publications, lectures, and an educational program. www.sfcamerawork.org

Southern Exposure, 417 14th Street, San Francisco, CA 94103. An artist-run organization. Sponsors exhibitions, panels, symposia, and educational programs. www.soex.org

Visual Aid, 116 New Montgomery Street, Suite 640, San Francisco, CA 94105. Assists artists who have life-threatening illnesses. Provides services, including art material vouchers, a free materials art bank, and more. Serves nine counties in the Bay Area. www.visualaid.org

COLORADO

Chicano Humanities and Arts Council, Inc., 772 Santa Fe Drive, Denver, CO 80204. Sponsors exhibitions and publishes a newsletter. www.chacweb.org

Colorado Council on the Arts, 1625 Broadway, Suite 2700, Denver, CO 80202. Awards grants and fellowships, provides technical assistance, and sponsors a public arts program. www.coloarts.state.co.us

Western States Arts Federation (WESTAF), 1743 Wazee Street, Suite 300, Denver, CO 80202. Serves artists and arts organizations in Alaska, Arizona, California, Colorado, Hawaii, Idaho, Montana, Nevada, New Mexico, Oregon, Utah, Washington, and Wyoming. Sponsors exhibitions, performances, publications, and provides other services. www.westaf.org

CONNECTICUT

Connecticut Commission on Culture and Tourism (formerly the Connecticut Commission on the Arts), One Constitution Plaza, 2nd Floor, Hartford, CT 06103. Sponsors many programs for artists, including fellowships, a registry, a public-art program, and Volunteer Lawyers for the Arts. www.cultureandtourism.org

Real Art Ways (RAW), 56 Arbor Street, Hartford, CT 06106. Sponsors exhibitions, performances, publications, educational programs, residencies, grants, and provides other services. www.realartways.org

DELAWARE

The Delaware Center for the Contemporary Arts, 200 South Madison Street, Wilmington, DE 19801. Sponsors exhibitions, publications, workshops, educational programs, residencies, and studio space. www.thedcca.org

Delaware Division of the Arts, 820 North French Street, Wilmington, DE 19801. Also has an office at Division of Libraries Building, Edgehill Shopping Center, Route 13, Dover, DE 19901. Sponsors grants and artist-in-residence programs. www.artsdel.org

DISTRICT OF COLUMBIA

Cultural Alliance of Greater Washington, 1436 U Street NW, Suite 103, Washington DC 20009-3997. Membership organization that sponsors workshops and seminars. Publishes *Arts Washington*. www.cultural-alliance.org

Washington Project for the Arts (WPA), 2023 Massachusetts Avenue NW, Washington, DC 20036-1011. Sponsors exhibitions, performances, publications, residencies, and ArtFile Online, a registry of the work of WPA members. www.wpadc.org

FLORIDA

ArtServe, Inc., 1350 East Sunrise Boulevard, Fort Lauderdale, FL 33304. An arts service organization assisting Florida artists and cultural not-for-profit organizations. Sponsors exhibitions and career development workshops. www.artserve.org

Atlantic Center for the Arts, 1414 Art Center Avenue, New Smyrna Beach, FL 32168. Sponsors an artist-in-residence program. Sponsors an artist-in-residence program, exhibitions, and workshops. www.atlanticcenterforthearts.org

Cultural Development Group, P.O. Box 140099, Coral Gables, FL 33114. Offers artists in south Florida consultations on various career-related subjects including grant writing, printing, and graphic design. Also has a fund to assist artists through bartering arrangements, payment advances, and delayed payment plans. www.cdgfl.org

Florida Division of Cultural Affairs, R. A. Gray Building, 3rd Floor, 500 S. Bronough Street, Tallahassee, FL 32399-0250. Sponsors an artist fellowship program, public-art programs, and artist residencies. Publishes an email newsletter. www.florida-arts.org

GEORGIA

The Atlanta Contemporary Art Center, 535 Means Street NW, Atlanta, GA 30318. (Formerly Nexus Contemporary Art Center.) Sponsors exhibitions, performances, publications, workshops, residencies, educational programs, grants, and studios. www.thecontemporary.org

Georgia Council on the Arts, 260 14th Street, Suite 401, Atlanta, GA 30318. Sponsors grants and an artist-in-residence program. www.gaarts.org

Southern Arts Federation, 1800 Peachtree Street NW, Suite 808, Atlanta, GA 30309-7603. Serves artists and arts organizations in Alabama, Florida, Georgia, Kentucky, Louisiana, Mississippi, North Carolina, South Carolina, and Tennessee. Sponsors networking programs and an online registry. Also provides information online regarding various career opportunities. Publishes a newsletter. www.southarts.org

HAWAII

Pastel Artists of Hawaii, P.O. Box 240207, Honolulu, HI 96824-0207. Sponsors exhibitions, workshops, and seminars. Membership open to residents of Hawaii. www.pastelartistsofhawaii.org

IDAHO

Idaho Commission on the Arts, P.O. Box 83720, Boise, ID 83720-0008. Sponsors grants and an online artists' directory. http://www.arts.idaho.gov/

ILLINOIS

Chicago Artists' Coalition, 70 E. Lake, Suite 230, Chicago, IL 60601. A service organization for visual artists that offers members an online gallery, a Job Bank, workshops, and more. Publishes *Chicago Artists' News* and various resource lists. www.caconline.org

Chicago Women's Caucus for Art, c/o ARC Gallery, 1801 W. Larchmont Avenue, #410, Chicago, IL 60613-2476. Sponsors exhibitions, a newsletter, and a members' blog. www.chicagowca.com

INDIANA

Indiana Arts Commisson, 150 W. Market Street, Suite 618, Indianapolis, IN 46204. Awards grants to artists and sponsors a technical assistance program, a crafts marketing and development program, and an email newsletter, *ArtsEye*. http://in.gov/arts

IOWA

Iowa Arts Council, 600 E. Locust, Des Moines, IA 50319. Sponsors an arts-in-education program and workshops. www.iowaartscouncil.org

KANSAS

Kansas Watercolor Society, P.O. Box 1796, Hutchinson, KS 67504-15117. Sponsors exhibitions, juried competitions, and workshops. www.kansaswatercolor.com

KENTUCKY

Kentucky Arts Council, Capital Plaza Tower, 21st Floor, 500 Mero Street, Frankfort, KY 40601. Sponsors fellowships, professional development grants, product development grants, and other grants for visual artists. http://artscouncil.ky.gov

LOUISIANA

Contemporary Arts Center, 900 Camp Street, New Orleans, LA 70130. Sponsors exhibitions, performances, publications, workshops, educational programs, grants, and provides other services. www.cacno.org

MAINE

Maine Arts Commision, 193 State Street, Augusta, ME 04333. Sponsors grants and provides various services. http://mainearts.maine.gov

MARYLAND

Maryland Art Place, 8 Market Place, Suite 100, Baltimore, MD 21202. Sponsors exhibitions, performances, publications, workshops, educational programs, an online registry, and residencies. www.mdartplace.org

Mid Atlantic Arts Foundation, 201 N. Charles Street, Suite 401, Baltimore, MD 21201. Serves artists and arts organizations in Delaware, the District of Columbia, Maryland, New Jersey, New York, Pennsylvania, Virginia, and West Virginia. Sponsors performances, fellowships, residencies, and provides other services. www.midatlanticarts.org

MASSACHUSETTS

The Artists Foundation, 516 East Second Street, South Boston, MA 02127. A statewide nonprofit organization devoted to enhancing the careers of individual artists and the position of artists in society. Sponsors exhibitions and performances and provides other services. www.artistsfoundation.org

The Graphic Artists Guild, Boston Chapter, P.O. Box 1806, Brookline, MA 02446. http://boston.gag.org

Massachusetts Cultural Council, 10 St. James Avenue, 3rd Floor, Boston, MA 02116-3803. Sponsors programs and residencies, and awards grants for a wide range of arts-related programs. www.massculturalcouncil.org

New England Foundation for the Arts, 145 Tremont Street, Boston, MA 02111. Serves artists and arts organizations in Connecticut, Maine, Massachusetts, New Hampshire, Rhode Island, and Vermont. Sponsors exhibitions, performances, workshops, residencies, publications, and provides other services. www.nefa.org

MICHIGAN

Detroit Artists Market, 4719 Woodward Avenue, Detroit, MI 48201. Promotes and assists Detroit metropolitan-area artists and Michigan artists. Sponsors exhibitions, publications, and educational programs. www.detroitartistsmarket.org

National Conference on Artists, Michigan Chapter, 18100 Meyers, Suite 395, Detroit, MI 48235. The oldest national organization for African-American artists in the United States. Devoted to the preservation, promotion, and development of the work of African-American artists through its various services, publications, and programs. www.ncamich.org

Urban Institute for Contemporary Arts, 41 Sheldon Boulevard SE, Grand Rapids, MI 49503. Sponsors exhibitions, performances, publications, workshops, educational programs, and residencies. www.uica.org

MINNESOTA

Arts Midwest, 2908 Hennepin Avenue, Suite 200, Minneapolis, MN 55408-1954. Regional arts organization serving Illinois, Indiana, Iowa, Michigan, Minnesota, North Dakota, Ohio, South Dakota, and Wisconsin. Provides services, publications, workshops, exhibitions, and grants. www.artsmidwest.org

Springboard for the Arts, 308 Prince Street, Suite 270, Saint Paul, MN 55101-1437. Provides business-related information, advice, and technical assistance to artists in Minnesota and surrounding states through workshops, consultations, publications, and other support services. www.springboardforthearts.org

Women's Art Registry of Minnesota (WARM), 550 Rice Street, St. Paul, MN 55103. Membership organization serving women visual artists in Minnesota. Maintains an online registry and administers a mentor program that matches emerging women artists with more established women artists for a period of one year. www.thewarm.org

MISSISSIPPI

Mississippi Arts Commission, 501 North West Street, Suite 1101A, Woolfolk Building, Jackson, MS 39201. Sponsors fellowships and professional development grants. www.arts.state.ms.us

MISSOURI

Mid-America Arts Alliance, 2018 Baltimore Avenue, Kansas City, MO 64108. Provides recognition and opportunities for artists and arts institutions in Arkansas, Kansas, Missouri, Nebraska, Oklahoma, and Texas. Sponsors exhibitions, performances, workshops, residencies, grants, and other services. www.maa.org

MONTANA

Montana Arts Council, P.O. Box 202201, Helena, MT 59620-2201. Sponsors grants, artist-in-residence programs, and an online registry. Publishes the newsletter *State of the Arts*. www.art.state.mt.us

NEBRASKA

Nebraska Arts Council, 1004 Farnam Street, Plaza Level, Omaha, NE 68102. Awards grants and fellowships. Sponsors residencies and a mentoring program. www.arts.nebraska.gov

NEVADA

Nevada Arts Council, 716 N. Caarson Street, Suite A, Carson City, NV 89701. Southern Office: 2755 East Desert Inn, Suite 160, Las Vegas, NV 89121. Sponsors grants and an artist-in-residence program. http://dmla.clan.lib.nv.us/docs/arts

NEW HAMPSHIRE

New Hampshire State Council on the Arts, 2 1/2 Beacon Street, 2nd Floor, Concord, NH 03301. Sponsors fellowships and artist entrepreneurial grants. www.nh.gov/nharts

NEW MEXICO

The Center for Contemporary Arts of Santa Fe, 1050 Old Pecos Trail, Santa Fe, NM 87505. Sponsors exhibitions, workshops, internships, and other services. www.ccasantafe.org

NEW YORK CITY

Alliance for the Arts, 330 West 42nd Street, #1701, New York, NY 10036. A nonprofit research center that gathers, analyzes, and publishes information about the arts in New York City. Sponsors the Estate Project for Artists with AIDS, the New York Citywide Cultural Database, and other projects. www.allianceforarts.org

Art in General, 79 Walker Street, New York, NY 10013-3523. A nonprofit membership organization. Sponsors publications, exhibitions, and workshops. www.artingeneral.org

Artists Space, 38 Greene Street, 3rd Floor, New York, NY 10013. One of the first alternative spaces in New York. Encourages experimentation, diversity, and dialogue in contemporary arts practice. Sponsors an exhibition space and the Irving Sandler Artists File Online. www.artistsspace.org

Artists Talk On Art, P.O. Box 1384, Old Chelsea Station, New York, NY 10113. Sponsors lectures and panel discussions on topics of interest to artists. Offers members health insurance. www.atoa.ws

Brooklyn Arts Council, 55 Washington Street, Suite 218, Brooklyn, NY 11201. Provides support services to artists and arts organizations in Brooklyn, including professional development seminars, grants, an arts-in-education program, exhibitions, and an online registry of Brooklyn artists. www.brooklynartscouncil.org

Lower Manhattan Cultural Council, 125 Maiden Lane, 2nd Floor, New York, NY 10038. One of Manhattan's oldest and largest arts councils. Provides services to artists, including grants. Publishes a newsletter. www.lmcc.net

New York Artists Equity Association, Inc., 498 Broome Street, New York, NY 10013. Sponsors the Web site Art Niche New York, devoted to furthering the cause of New York artists and arts-related organizations. www.anny.org

New York Foundation for the Arts, 155 Avenue of the Americas, 6th Floor, New York, NY 10013-1507. Supports the development of individual professional artists, their projects, and their organizations. Provides grants and services, and sponsors the Visual Artist Information Hotline, a toll-free information and referral service for visual artists nationwide: 800-232-2789. www.nyfa.org

Organization of Independent Artists, 45 W. 21st Street, #504, New York, NY 10010. Provides artists with exhibition opportunities in New York City. Sponsors artist-curated shows and publishes *OIA Newsletter*. www.oiaonline.org

NEW YORK STATE

Arts and Cultural Council for Greater Rochester, 277 North Goodman Street, Rochester, NY 14607. A coalition of arts organizations, artists, businesses, and county government. Provides support services to individual artists, including promotion, consultation, management workshops, volunteer legal assistance, group health insurance, and a registry. www.artsrochester.org

Arts Council in Buffalo and Erie County, 700 Main Street, Buffalo, NY 14202. Dedicated to promoting the cultural industry within Buffalo and Erie County. Provides various services to artists and arts organizations. www.artscouncilbuffalo.org

Association of Teaching Artists. Strengthens and serves teaching artists from all disciplines in New York State by empowering the practice of teaching artists as a profession. Provides a network for communication and exchange of resources, advocacy, training, and professional development. www.teachingartists.com

The Center for Photography at Woodstock, 59 Tinker Street, Woodstock, NY 12498. Sponsors exhibitions, fellowships, lecture/workshops, and publications for photographers, video artists, and filmmakers. www.cpw.org

Visual Studies Workshop, 21 Prince Street, Rochester, NY 14607. Provides services, including educational and publishing programs, exhibitions, residencies, and grants for artists working in photography, artists' books, video, and independent film. www.vsw.org

NORTH CAROLINA

North Carolina Arts Council, MSC #4632, Department of Cultural Resources, Raleigh, NC 26799-4632. Sponsors grants and other services. www.ncarts.org

NORTH DAKOTA

North Dakota Council on the Arts, 1600 East Century Avenue, Suite B, Bismarck, ND 58503. Sponsors fellowships, professional development grants, and an artist-in-residence program. www.nd.gov/arts

OKLAHOMA

Individual Artists of Oklahoma, P.O. Box 60824, Oklahoma City, OK 73146. Sponsors exhibitions, performances, publications, and workshops. www.iao gallery.org

Oklahoma Visual Arts Coalition, P.O. Box 1946, Oklahoma City, OK 73101. Supports artists living and working in Oklahoma through grants, juried exhibitions, an online gallery, and professional workshops. www.ovac-ok.org

OREGON

Northwest Print Council, 416 NW 12th Avenue, Portland, OR 97209. Open to printmakers in the Pacific Northwest, including Canada. Sponsors exhibitions and educational programs. www.northwestprintcouncil.org

PENNSYLVANIA

The Center for Emerging Visual Artists (formerly the Creative Artists Network), 237 S. 18th Street, Suite 3A, Philadelphia, PA 19103. A nonprofit organization that provides artists with support services and programs needed to build successful and sustainable careers. Visual artists must live within a 100-mile radius of Philadelphia and not have an affiliation with a commercial gallery. www .cfeva.org

Greater Pittsburgh Arts Council, 707 Penn Avenue, 2nd Floor, Pittsburgh, PA 15222. Serves artists and arts organizations in southwest Pennsylvania. Awards grants, sponsors an artist opportunity database, and offers legal assistance through Volunteer Lawyers for the Arts. www.pittsburghartscouncil.org

Painted Bride Art Center, 230 Vine Street, Philadelphia, PA 19106. Sponsors exhibitions, performances, publications, and workshops. www.paintedbride.org

RHODE ISLAND

Rhode Island State Council on the Arts, One Capitol Hill, 3rd Floor, Providence, RI 02908. Sponsors grants and a blog for artists with career opportunity information. www.arts.ri.gov

SOUTH CAROLINA

South Carolina Arts Commission, 1800 Gervais Street, Columbia, SC 29201. Sponsors fellowships and other grants and services for artists. www.southcarolina arts.com

SOUTH DAKOTA

South Dakota Arts Council, 711 E. Wells Avenue, Pierre, SD 57501-3369. Provides grants to artists and sponsors artists in schools and artists in communities programs. www.artscouncil.sd.gov

TENNESSEE

Delta Axis, P.O. Box 11527, Memphis, TN 38111. Sponsors exhibitions, lectures, and other programs. www.deltaaxis.org

TEXAS

Arthouse, The Jones Center for Contemporary Art, 700 Congress Avenue, Austin, TX 78701. Sponsors exhibitions and provides information and referrals. Offers members a group health insurance plan, emergency assistance grants, and credit union banking. Publishes a newsletter. www.arthouse texas.org

Austin Visual Arts Association, P.O. Box 13313, Austin, TX 78711-3313. Sponsors exhibitions and workshops and provides various services to members. Publishes a newsletter. www.avaaonline.org

DiverseWorks Artspace, Inc., 1117 East Freeway, Houston, TX 77002-1108. Sponsors exhibitions, performances, publications, and workshops. www.diverse works.org

Houston Center for Photography, 1441 West Alabama, Houston, TX 77006. Sponsors exhibitions, educational programs, a fellowship program, and an artist database for members. Publishes a newsletter. www.hcponline.org

Women and Their Work, 1710 Lavaca Street, Austin, TX 78701. Sponsors exhibitions, performances, workshops, educational programs, and an online registry. www.womenandtheirwork.org

UTAH

Utah Arts Council, Glendinning Home, 617 East South Temple, Salt Lake City, UT 84102-1177. Sponsors an Arts and Artists Database, an Artist Resource Center, competitions, commissions, and workshops. Awards grants and fellowships to artists. http://arts.utah.gov/home.html

VERMONT

Vermont Arts Council, 136 State Street, Drawer 33, Montpelier, VT 05633-6001. Sponsors an Art in State Buildings program, creation grants, and artist professional development grants. www.vermontartscouncil.org

VIRGINIA

1708 Gallery, P.O. Box 12520, Richmond, VA 23241. Sponsors exhibitions, performances, publications, and workshops. www.1708gallery.org

WASHINGTON

Allied Arts of Seattle, 216 First Avenue South, Suite 253, Seattle, WA 98104. Serves as a referral and information center for artists and arts organizations. www .alliedarts-seattle.org

Artist Trust, 1835 12th Avenue, Seattle, WA 98122-2437. Provides information services and grants to artists. www.artisttrust.org

Seattle Women's Caucus for Art, 2318 Second Avenue, #344, Seattle, WA 98121. Sponsors exhibitions and publishes a newsletter. www.scn.org/arts/swca/swca.htm

WEST VIRGINIA

West Virginia Commission on the Arts, 1900 Kanawha Boulevard East, Charleston, WV 25305. Sponsors fellowships and other grants. www.wvculture.org/arts/ artsindex.aspx

WISCONSIN

Wisconsin Painters and Sculptors, Inc. Sponsors exhibitions, performances, publications, workshops, and educational programs. Publishes *Art in Wisconsin*. www.artinwisconsin.com

WYOMING

Wyoming Arts Council, 2320 Capitol Avenue, Cheyenne, WY 82002. Awards fellowships and professional development grants. Sponsors an Artist Image Registry. http://wyoarts.state.wy.us

Organizations Outside of the United States

Canadian Crafts Federation, P.O. Box 6000, Fredericton, New Brunswick E3B 5H1, Canada. Provides information and services to artists. http://canadiancrafts federation.ca

CARFAC-BC, P.O. Box 2359, Vancouver, British Columbia V6B 3W5, Canada. A regional branch of a national advocacy organization for Canadian artists. www.carfacbc.org

CARFAC Manitoba, 407-100 Arthur Street, Winnipeg, Manitoba R3B 1H3, Canada. An advocacy organization that provides career-related services and publications for artists. www.carfac.mb.ca

CARFAC Maritimes, 732 Charlotte Street, Fredericton, New Brunswick E3B 1M5, Canada. An advocacy organization for artists in Nova Scotia, New Brunswick, and Prince Edward Island. cf.maritimes@nb.aibn.com

CARFAC National, 2 Daly Avenue, Suite 250, Ottawa, Ontario K1N 6E2, Canada. A national advocacy organization for Canadian artists. www.carfac.ca

CARFAC Ontario, 401 Richmond Street West, Suite 440, Toronto, Ontario M5V 3A8, Canada. A regional branch of an advocacy organization for Canadian artists. www.carfacontario.ca

CARFAC Saskatchewan (Regina), 1734-A Dewdney Avenue, Regina, Saskatchewan SK SR4 1G6, Canada. Provides legal and financial advisory services. Sponsors professional development workshops and publishes a monthly newsletter. www.carfac.sk.ca

CARFAC Saskatchewan (Saskatoon), #412, 220 3rd Avenue South, Saskatoon, Saskatchewan SK S7K 1M1, Canada. Provides many services, including a legal and financial advisory service. Also sponsors professional development workshops and publishes a monthly newsletter. www.carfac.sk.ca

CARFAC-VANL: Visual Arts Newfoundland and Labrador, Devon House, 59 Duckworth Street, St. John's A1C 1E6, Newfoundland, Canada. A regional branch of CARFAC, a national advocacy organization for Canadian artists. vanl-carfac@nf.aibn.com

The Crafts Council, 44a Pentonville Road, Islington, London N1 9BY, United Kingdom. Promotes contemporary crafts in Great Britain. Sponsors exhibitions and provides business advice to craft artists. Publishes *Crafts Magazine.* www .craftscouncil.org.uk

European Council of Artists, Borgergade 111, 1300 Copenhagen K, Denmark. Represents the interests of professional artists in Europe, including visual and performing artists and writers. Serves as a forum between artists and political decision makers in Europe. www.eca.dk/index.html

National Association for the Visual Arts, Ltd., P.O. Box 60, Potts Point, NSW 1335, Australia. Represents the interests of professional visual artists in Australia through advocacy campaigns and services. Provides career advice on various issues. www.visualarts.net.au

Ontario Crafts Council, 990 Queen Street West, Toronto, Ontario M6J 1H1, Canada. Publishes *STUDIO,* a newsletter and resource guide. Sponsors conferences. Members are eligible for group health insurance and liability and business insurance. www.craft.on.ca

The Sculptors Society of Canada, c/o Judi Young, Studio 204, 60 Atlantic Avenue, Toronto, Ontario, Canada M6K 1X9. Dedicated to the education, promotion, and exhibition of contemporary Canadian sculpture. http://cansculpt.org

Visual Arts Ontario, 1153A Queen Street West, Toronto, Ontario M6J 1J4, Canada. Provides a wide range of programs and services that address the professional development needs of the visual-arts community. www.vao.org

World Crafts Council (WCC), International Secretariat, Pontificia Universidad Catolica de Chile, El Comendador 1916, Providencia, Santiago de Chile, Republic of Chile. Promotes strengthening the status of crafts as a vital part of cultural and economic life and fellowship among craftspeople of the world. www.wccwis.gr

Also see "Artists with Disabilities" and "International Connections."

ARTWORK CARE AND MAINTENANCE

Publications

The Care of Bronze Sculpture: Recommended Maintenance Programs for the Collector by Patrick V. Kipper. Seattle: Path Publications, 1996.

Caring for Your Art: A Guide for Artists, Collectors, and Art Institutions by Jill Snyder. New York: Allworth Press, revised 2001. Covers the best methods to store, handle, mount, frame, display, document and inventory, photograph, pack, transport, insure, and secure art. Also discusses proper environmental controls to enhance longevity of work.

Caring for Your Ceramic & Glass Objects by Julie A. Reilley. The American Institute for Conservation of Historic and Artistic Works, 1717 K Street NW #200, Washington, DC 20006, 2001. Covers handling, storage, display, cleaning, repairs and maintenance, and other related topics. A free brochure. http://aic.stanford.edu/pubs/pblist.html

Caring for Your Documents and Art on Paper by Mary Todd Glaser, The American Institute for Conservation of Historic and Artistic Works, 1717 K Street NW, #200, Washington, DC 20006, 2003. Discusses storage, proper care and handling, light exposure, temperature control, and other related topics. A free brochure. http://aic.stanford.edu/pubs/pblist.html

Caring for Your Paintings by Jill Whitten, The American Institute for Conservation of Historic and Artistic Works, 1717 K Street NW, #200, Washington, DC 20006. Covers environmental factors, display, handling, and other related topics. A free brochure. http://aic.stanford.edu/pubs/pblist.html

Caring for Your Photographs by Deborah Derby, The American Institute for Conservation of Historic and Artistic Works, 1717 K Street NW, #200, Washington, DC 20006, 1997. Covers storage, handling, environmental factors, and other related topics. A free brochure. http://aic.stanford.edu/pubs/pblist.html

Curatorial Care of Works of Art on Paper by Anne F. Clapp. New York: The Lyons Press, revised 1991. Includes advice on conservation techniques and describes the effect of light, acid, and temperature on works on paper.

Guide to Maintenance of Outdoor Sculpture by Virginia Naude and Glenn Wharton. American Institute of Conservation, 1717 K Street NW, #200, Washington, DC 20006, 1991. Describes how to care for and maintain outdoor sculpture. http://aic.stanford.edu

Permanence and Care of Color Photographs: Traditional and Digital Color Prints, Color Negatives, Slides and Motion Pictures by Henry Wilhelm and Carol Brower. Grinnell, Iowa: Preservation Publishing, 1993.

Web Sites

Artist Help Network. Founded by Caroll Michels, career coach and artist-advocate, this site is devoted to all aspects of career development. See heading "Other Resources" and subheading "Artwork Care and Maintenance." www.artisthelpnetwork.com.

Also see "Exhibition and Performance Planning."

BARTERING

Publications

BarterNews, P.O. Box 3024, Mission Viego, CA 92690. Published quarterly. Includes information and ideas about bartering with contact information. www.barternews.com

Web Sites

ArtBusiness (www.artbusiness.com/barter.html). "Bartering Art? Don't Forget the Tax Man," by Alan Bamberger.

Artist Help Network (www.artisthelpnetwork.com). Founded by Caroll Michels, career coach and artist-advocate, this site is devoted to all aspects of career development. See heading "Money" and subheading "Bartering Organizations."

Barter.Net (www.barter.net). Provides a listing of bartering networks. Search "Barter and Trade Exchanges" and "Barter Service."

Gigafree (www.gigafree.com/barter.html). Lists barter exchanges on the Internet and in the United States and in Canada.

Krislyn's Strictly Business Sites (www.strictlybusinesssites.com/barter.htm). Provides links to numerous business barter sites.

CAREER MANAGEMENT, BUSINESS, AND MARKETING

Publications

Agenda. Visual Arts Ontario, 1153A Queen Street West, Toronto, Ontario M6J 1J4, Canada. Lists competitions, funding opportunities, workshops, and a free classified section. Published quarterly. www.vao.org

Alaska Native Arts Marketing: A Handbook for Expanding Audiences and Markets for Your Art by Claudia J. Bach. Alaska State Council for the Arts, 411 West 4th Avenue, STE 1E, Anchorage, AK 99501-2343. Information for Native American artists on reaching new audiences and expanding new markets. Topics include portfolio development, pricing, documentation, and other resources. www.eed.state.ak.us

Art and Reality: The New Standard Reference Guide and Business Plan for Actively Developing Your Career as an Artist by Robert J. Abbott. Santa Ana, Calif.: Seven Locks Press, 1997. A guide through the process of executing a fast-track career plan.

Art Business News. 1801 Park 270 Drive, Suite 550, Maryland Heights, MO 63146. Provides information about the art framing industry, business management, new products, and art industry trends. Published monthly.

Art Calendar. 1500 Park Center, Orlando, FL 32835. Contains career-related articles and provides listings of opportunities for artists. Published eleven times a year.

Art Marketing 101: A Handbook for the Fine Artist by Constance Smith. Nevada City, Calif.: Artnetwork Press, revised 2007. Covers various aspects of career development, including publicity, contacting galleries, and preparing a marketing plan.

The Art Opportunities Book: Finding, Entering and Winning by Benny Shaboy. Benicia, Calif.: AO Books, 2004. Art Opportunities Monthly, P.O. Box 502, Benicia, CA 94510-0510. A workbook for artists who want to show and support their work outside the commercial gallery system. Includes tips and advice. www.artopportunitiesbook.com

Art Opportunities Monthly, P.O. Box 502, Benicia, CA 94510-0510. A listing of opportunities for artists. Listings are screened to include those opportunities that are free to entrants or offer good rewards in relation to the fees and increase the exposure of those accepted or are prestigious or special in some way. Also includes an "editor's choice" plus mark for opportunities deemed particularly a good fit. Published monthly. Only available via email. www.artopportunities monthly.com

Art That Pays: The Emerging Artist's Guide to Making a Living by Adele Slaughter and Jeff Kober. Los Angeles: National Network for Artist Placement, 2004. A guidebook for dealing with all of the practical aspects of an artist's life.

The Art World Dream: Alternative Strategies for Working Artists by Eric Rudd. North Adams, Mass.: CIRE Corporation, 2001. Discusses the peaks and challenges of an artist's career and offers practical advice.

The Artist in Business: Basic Business Practices by Craig Dreesen. Arts Extension Service, Division of Outreach, 100 Venture Way, Suite 201, Hadley, MA 01035-9430, revised 1996. Includes information on record keeping, legal issues, grants, commissions, and competitions. www.umass.edu/aes

The Artist's and Graphic Designer's Market, edited by Mary Cox. Cincinnati, Ohio: Writer's Digest Books, revised annually. www.writersdigest.com

An Artist's Guide: Making it in New York by Daniel Grant. New York: Allworth Press, 2001. A guide to getting started in New York for artists who wish to move to the city on a temporary or permanent basis.

The Artist's Marketing and Action Plan Workbook by Jonathan Talbot and Geoffrey Howard. Jonathan Talbot, revised 2005. Guides artists through the process of learning how to sell artwork and develop a personalized, step-by-step marketing action plan.

The Artist's Resource Handbook by Daniel Grant. New York: Allworth Press, revised 1997. Guide to career assistance for artists on a wide range of topics.

The Artist's Survival Manual: A Complete Guide to Marketing Your Work by Toby Judith Klayman with Cobbett Steinberg. Originally published by Charles Scribner's Sons, the book is now being published by Toby Judith Klayman and Joseph Branchcomb, revised in 1996. Full of sensible, good-natured practical advice.

Arts Management Bibliography and Publishers, compiled by Dyan Wiley and edited by Sarah Elliott. Arts Extension Service, Division of Outreach, 100 Venture Way, Suite 201, Hadley, MA 01035-9430, 1995. Topics include artist self-management and career development. www.umass.edu/aes

ASMP Professional Business Practices in Photography, edited by the American Society of Media Photographers. New York: Allworth Press, revised 2001. Covers information on standard practices in stock and assignment photography. Includes business and legal forms.

Becoming a Successful Artist by Lewis Barrett Lehrman. North Light Books, 1996. Twenty-one painters share their stories, inspiration, and advice.

Breaking Through the Clutter: Business Solutions for Women, Artists and Entrepreneurs by Judith Luther Wilder. The National Network for Artist Placement, 935 West Avenue, Los Angeles, CA 90065, 1999. Includes business advice and tips for artists.

Business Entities for Artists by Mark Quail. CARFAC Ontario, 401 Richmond Street West, Suite 440, Toronto, Ontario M5V 3A8, Canada, revised 1996. Summarizes information on sole proprietorships and corporations, with information on tax perspectives, registration, and legal liability. Available online to CARFAC Ontario members. www.carfacontario.ca

Business Information Folder. Ontario Crafts Council, 990 Queen Street West, Toronto, Ontario M6J 1H1, Canada. Revised annually. A compilation of business information sheets for craft artists, including a bibliography, grant information, business registration and incorporation, marketing, and copyright. www.craft.on.ca

The Business of Art, edited by Lee Caplin. Paramus, N.J.: Prentice Hall Press, revised 2000. Includes information on working with galleries and museums, financial planning, and more.

The Business of Being an Artist by Daniel Grant. New York: Allworth Press, revised 2000. Covers a range of career-related topics.

Career Solutions for Creative People: How to Balance Artistic Goals with Career Security by Dr. Ronda Ormont. New York: Allworth Press, 2001. Focuses on how to find the time and freedom to pursue art while making a stable living.

Ceramic Review, 25 Foubert's Place London W1F 7QF, United Kingdom. Includes information on equipment, materials, and techniques. Published bimonthly.

Chicago Artists' News. Chicago Artists' Coalition, 70 E. Lake, Suite 230, Chicago, IL 60601. Includes information on local exhibition opportunities and national art issues. Published monthly. www.caconline.org

Craft & Design (formerly *Craftsman Magazine*). P.O. Box 5, Driffield YO25 8JD, United Kingdom. Bimonthly magazine that features craft artists and provides business advice and practical information. www.craftsman-magazine.co.uk

The Crafts Business Answer Book: Starting, Managing and Marketing a Home-based Arts, Crafts or Design Business by Barbara Brabec. New York: M. Evans & Company, Inc., revised 2006. Includes startup, marketing, and management tips for artists who are starting a craft business.

Crafts News, The Craft Center, 8601 Georgia Avenue, Suite 800, Silver Spring, MD 20910. Features updates on market trends and trade regulations, sources of assistance, successful artisan projects, and crafts-related publications and events. Published quarterly.

The Crafts Report: The Business Journal for the Crafts Industry. P.O. Box 5000, Iola, WI 54945-5000. Contains articles, departments, and columns about the business of art for craft artists. Published monthly.

Creating a Life Worth Living by Carol Lloyd. New York: Harper Perennial, 1997. A practical course in career design for artists, innovators, and others aspiring to a creative life.

Creating a Successful Career in Photography by Dan Fear. ArtSupport, 1717 150th Avenue SE #16, Bellevue, WA 98007. An ebook that includes artist business forms, computer templates, and advice on using the forms. Also provides art resources for a successful career in the visual arts. www.art-support.com

Creating a Successful Craft Business by Rogene and Robert Robbins. New York: Allworth Press, 2003. Written by an established craft artist and a business manager who have lived through the trials, tribulations, and triumphs of starting a crafts business. Includes advice, tips, and hundreds of Internet resources.

Creating the Work You Love: Courage, Commitment and Career by Rick Jarlow. Rochester, Vt.: Inner Traditions International Limited, 1995. Focuses on the cultural influences on work that affect life choices. Explores the chakra system as a tool for career counseling.

The Fine Artist's Career Guide by Daniel Grant. New York: Allworth Press, revised 2004. Contains practical advice, discussions, interviews, and success stories gleaned from a wide range of professional artists.

The Fine Artist's Guide to Marketing and Self-Promotion by Julius Vitali. New York: Allworth Press, revised 2003. Covers various topics related to marketing and publicity. Includes chapters on other career-related issues.

Hand Papermaking Newsletter. P.O. Box 1070, Beltsville, MD 20704-1070. Lists information and opportunities of interest to hand-papermaking artists, including exhibits, competitions, conferences, and workshops. Published four times a year. www.bookarts.com/handpapermaking

How to Become a Famous Artist and Still Paint Pictures by W. Joe Innis. iUniverse.com, 2000. Advice for career success as an artist.

How to Grow as a Photographer: Reinventing Your Career by Tony Luna. New York: Allworth Press, 2006. The advent of digital photography has meant that many traditional photographers have had to reinvent themselves and their work. This book helps with this sometimes difficult transition with advice on how to get back on the path to creative fulfillment.

How to Grow as an Artist by Daniel Grant. New York: Allworth Press, 2002. A guide to improving your skills as an artist. Topics include finding and selecting appropriate art materials, working safely and effectively from a home art studio, educational and exhibition opportunities, and more.

How to Make Money as an Artist by Sean Moore. Chicago: Chicago Review Press, 2000. Written for artists who want to present themselves and their work in the best possible light to the largest possible audience.

Information for Artists. CARFAC Ontario, 401 Richmond Street West, Suite 440, Toronto, Ontario M5V 3A8, Canada, revised 2005. Covers a variety of subjects relevant to Canadian visual and media artists. www.carfacontario.ca

Most Art Sucks: Five Years of Coagula, edited by Mat Gleason, Walter Robinson, and Tom Patchett. Santa Monica, Calif.: Smart Art Press, 1998. A compilation of the work of many authors who view the art world with humor, insight, and guts.

On the Needs of Visual Artists: A Roundtable 2001. Marie Walsh Sharpe Art Foundation, 830 North Tejon Street, Suite 120, Colorado Springs, CO 80903, 2004. A free publication based on a roundtable discussion involving a group of thirty-three artists from across the country. www.sharpeartfdn.org

187 Tips for Artists: How to Create a Successful Art Career—and Have Fun in the Process! by Kathy Gulrich. Center City Publishing, P.O. Box 1292, New York, NY 10156, 2003. Includes practical tips, ideas, and advice on developing a career as an artist.

Opportunities in Animation and Cartooning Careers by Terence J. Sacks. New York: McGraw-Hill, revised 2007. Describes various career possibilities in the field of animation. Includes contact information for schools and training facilities with step-by-step details on how to submit your work.

Opportunities in Arts and Crafts Careers by Elizabeth B. Gardner. Lincolnwood, Ill.: Contemporary Publishing Group, VGM Career Horizons, revised 2005. Provides tips for obtaining the best education in the field of arts and crafts.

The Photographer's Guide to Marketing and Self-Promotion by Maria Piscopo. New York: Allworth Press, revised 2001. Discusses publicity, networking, researching prospective clients, and developing a personal marketing strategy.

Photographer's Market. Cincinnati, Ohio.: Writer's Digest Books, revised annually. Provides more than 2,000 contacts for selling photographs, finding marketing resources, finding buyers, and more.

Photography: Focus on Profit by Tom Zimberoff. New York: Allworth Press, 2002. Demonstrates hundreds of proven procedures for making a profit in photography. Includes a CD-ROM.

Photography Your Way: A Career Guide to Satisfaction and Success by Chuck DeLaney. New York: Allworth Press, 1999. Outlines career avenues and options and includes grant information, business strategies, and discussions on business and legal and ethical issues.

Poor Dancer's Almanac: Managing Life and Work in the Performing Arts, edited by David R. White, Lise Friedman, and Tia Tibbits Levenson. Durham, N.C.: Duke University Press, revised 1993.

Potter's Professional Handbook by Steve Branfman. Westerville, Ohio: American Ceramic Society, 1998. Information on how to set up a pottery studio, including studio layout. Also covers issues related to marketing and selling work.

The Practical Handbook for the Emerging Artist by Margaret R. Lazzari. Wadsworth Publishing, revised 2001. Designed to help visual-art students make the transition from art school to their own art practice.

Shuttle, Spindle and Dyepot. Handweavers Guild of America, 1255 Buford Highway, Suite 211, Suwanee, GA 30024. International magazine of the Handweavers Guild of America. For weavers, spinners, and dyers. Contains technical and historical articles and marketing and business information. Published quarterly.

Success Now! For Artists: A Motivational Guide for the Artrepreneur by Renée Phillips. New York: Manhattan Arts International, revised 2003. Essays on various career-related topics for artists.

Successful Syndication: A Guide for Writers and Cartoonists by Michael Sedge. New York: Allworth Press, 2000. Systematically details how cartoonists and writers can get their work syndicated. Includes advice on finding a syndication agency and setting up self-syndication. Also includes information on fees and marketing through the Internet and direct mail.

Supporting Yourself as an Artist: A Practical Guide by Deborah A. Hoover. New York: Oxford University Press, revised 1989. Provides advice on how to deal with common problems confronting artists. Emphasis is on obtaining funding and proposal writing.

Taking the Leap: Building a Career as a Visual Artist by Cay Lang. San Francisco: Chronicle Books, revised 2006. Covers a comprehensive range of career-related topics.

The Warhol Economy: How Fashion, Art, and Music Drive New York City by Elizabeth Currid. Princeton, N.J.: Princeton University Press, 2007.

Women Environmental Artists Directory, produced by Jo Hanson and Susan Leibovitz Steinman. Available from Andrée Singer Thompson, 4227 M.L. King Jr. Way, Oakland, CA 94609, revised 2006. Listings in the directory are open to all women arts professionals concerned with environmental issues and environmentally conscious methods and materials. Includes a broad range of media and work. The database is also available online. www.weadartists.org

Audio/Visual Materials

Seven Mistakes Artists Make—and How You can Avoid Them by Kathy Gulrich. New York: Center City Publishing, 2006. CD-ROM by art coach Kathy Gulrich aimed at beginning artists. Includes practical tips and the most common career development mistakes that artists make.

Web Sites

About the Arts (www.aboutthearts.com). An offshoot of the Boston television show *About the Arts*. Features career resources, the work of guest artists, and upcoming events and exhibitions in the Boston area.

ArtDeadline (www.artdeadline.com). Lists juried shows, grants, internships, scholarships, residencies, fellowships, and more. Subscription required.

Artist Help Network (www.artisthelpnetwork.com). Founded by Caroll Michels, career coach and artist-advocate, this site is devoted to all aspects of career development. See heading "Career" and subheading "General Career Information."

Artists* at Work. A Professional Practices Blog (http://gyst-ink.com/blog). An extensive monthly blog produced by GYST Ink. Provides artists with career development advice and information on a multitude of subjects.

ARTnewsletter (http://artnewsletter.artnews.com/index.aspx). Sponsored by *ARTnews*. Available online by subscription.

ArtScope (www.artscope.net). A news and resource site for visual and performing artists primarily in the Chicago area.

ArtStudy.org (www.artstudy.org). Includes information on what to look for in an art school and tips for attending art school. Also includes information on art scholarships, student loans, and financial aid.

ArtUW.com (http://labweb.education.wisc.edu/artcommunity/index.asp). Produced by the University of Wisconsin. Provides resources and offers artists career information on various career-related topics.

CaFÉ™ (www.callforentry.org). A user-friendly online system that provides open call information on public-art commissions, exhibitions, grants, and awards. Users create a profile with contact information and upload digital images of their work, and CaFÉ™ allows you to apply to the respective open-call entries *directly from its Web site*. Sponsored by the Western States Arts Federation (WESTAF).

Chicago Artists Resource (www.chicagoartistsresource.org). Online information that includes career information and opportunities for artists. Sponsored by the Chicago Department of Cultural Affairs.

Fuel4arts (www.fuel4arts.com). An international online community that delivers free marketing tools and ideas to artists and those in art-marketing professions. Sponsored by The Australian Council on the Arts.

The Informed Artist (www.viewit.com/nwarts/arts/informed/informed.htm). Sponsored by the Seattle Public Library. Provides links to various career topics for visual and performing artists, including resources for employment, grants, awards, scholarships, and opportunities for exhibitions, auditions, and competitions.

NYFA Source (www.nyfa.org/nyfa_source.asp?id=47&fid=1). An extensive database for visual and performing artists, writers, and arts organizations. Includes numerous resources on career-related topics. Sponsored by the New York Foundation for the Arts in conjunction with the Urban Institute.

Resource Handbook for Minnesota Artists (www.springboardforthearts.org/Resources/Resources.asp). Sponsored by Springboard for the Arts. An online listing of career resources for Minnesota artists.

Resources for Individual Artists (www.florida-arts.org). Sponsored by the Florida Department of State, Division of Cultural Affairs. Focuses on opportunities for Florida artists and resources for artists nationwide.

Rhizome (www.rhizome.org). A Web site devoted to artists who are using technology.

TextileArts.net (www.textilearts.net). Devoted to career-related information for fiber artists, including materials, publications, marketing, techniques, and contacts in the fiber art world.

WPS1 Art Radio (www.wps1.org). Sponsored by the PS1 Center for Contemporary Art, part of the Museum of Modern Art. Presents interviews with contemporary artists and curators.

Organizations

Art-Support, 1717 150th Avenue SE, #16, Bellevue, WA 98007. Sponsors a Web site that offers various support materials and career advice to photographers on a variety of subjects. Provides links to recommended photography galleries, museums, and other sites of interest. http://art-support.com

Career Transition for Dancers, 165 W. 46th Street, Suite 701, New York, NY 10019-5284. A national career counseling organization for professional dancers. Also has an office in Los Angeles: 5757 Wilshire Boulevard, Suite 902, Los Angeles, CA 90036-3635. Toll free hotline: 800-581-2833. www.careertransition.org

CUE Art Foundation, 511 W. 25th Street, Ground Floor, New York, NY 10001. Helps underrecognized artists throughout the United States with career development through exhibitions, residencies, and other programs. www.cueartfoundation.org

International Studio and Curatorial Program (ISCP), 1040 Metropolitan Avenue, 3rd Floor, Brooklyn, NY 11211. Provides career development opportunities for a select community of international artists. Participating artists are sponsored by governments, corporations, foundations, galleries, and individuals for periods from two months to two years. www.iscp-ny.org

Caroll Michels, career coach and artist-advocate, 1724 Burgos Drive, Sarasota, FL 34238. Author of *How to Survive & Prosper as an Artist*. Assists artists throughout the United States and abroad with career development through phone consultations and in-person consultations. Also publishes various arts-related mailing lists. www.carollmichels.com

The National Network for Artist Placement, 935 West Avenue 37, Los Angeles, CA 90065. Devoted to bringing career counseling and employment and survival skills services to visual and performing artists. www.artistplacement.com

Springboard for the Arts, 308 Prince Street, St. Paul, MN 55101-1437. Provides career management information to independent artists and small to mid-sized cultural organizations. Offers consultations, training, and information. www .springboardforthearts.org

Visual Arts Ontario,1153A Queen Street West, Toronto, Ontario M6J 1J4, Canada. A not-for-profit organization that offers one-on-one consultations and online training programs. Also publishes many artist career-related materials. www .vao.org

Also see "Arts Sales and Commissions," "Creative Challenges, Career Blocks, and the Psyche," "Organizing Paperwork," "Periodicals," "Presentation Tools," and "Press Relations and Publicity."

COMPETITIONS AND JURIED EXHIBITIONS
Publications

Art Calendar, 1500 Park Center, Orlando, FL 32835. Includes a listing of juried exhibitions and competitions. Published eleven times a year.

Art Opportunities: Finding, Entering and Winning by Benny Shaboy with contributions by more than thirty-five professional artists. AO Book, studio-NOTES, P.O. Box 502, Benicia, CA 94510-0502, 2004. Includes information on juried shows, with articles and tips for getting into the minds of jurors. www .artopportunitiesbook.com

Art Opportunities Monthly. P.O. Box 502, Benicia, CA 94510-0502. A listing of opportunities for artists, including juried shows. Listings are screened to include those opportunities that are free to entrants or offer good rewards in relation to the fees and increase the exposure of those accepted or are prestigious or special in some way. Also includes an "editor's choice" code for opportunities deemed particularly a good fit. Published monthly. Only available via email. www.art opportunitiesmonthly.com

The Business of Being an Artist by Daniel Grant. New York: Allworth Press, revised 2000. See book's index entry "Jurying Art Shows."

Guidelines for Professional Standards in the Organization of Juried Exhibitions. CARO/CARFAC, revised 1988. Available from CARFAC Ontario, 400 Richmond Street West, Suite 440, Toronto, Ontario, M5V 3A8, Canada. www.carfac ontario.ca

Juried Art Exhibitions: Ethical Guidelines and Practical Applications. Chicago Artists' Coalition, 70 E. Lake, Suite 230, Chicago, IL 60601, revised 1997. Discusses ethical standards to be used by individuals or groups that are organizing a juried exhibition. Also provides a step-by-step guide on how to organize juried shows. www.caconline.org

Web Sites

ArtDeadline (www.artdeadline.com). Lists juried shows, art festivals, grants, internships, scholarships, residencies, fellowships, and writing competitions. Available by subscription.

Artist Help Network. Founded by Caroll Michels, career coach and artist-advocate, this site is devoted to all aspects of career development. See heading "Exhibitions, Commissions and Sales" and subheadings "Competitions and Juried Shows" and "Public Art." www.artisthelpnetwork.com

Artsopportunities.com (www.artsopportunities.com). A database of opportunities for artists on a state and national level, including competitions and juried shows. Sponsored by the Southern Arts Federation.

Suggested Guidelines for Art Competitions and Contests. Sponsored by the Graphic Artists Guild. www.gag.org/resources/compet_rules.php

Also see "Public Art."

CORPORATE ART MARKET

Publications

Art Business News. 1801 Park 270 Drive, Suite 550, Maryland Heights, MO 63146. Lists the names of corporations that have purchased art and commissioned art projects. Each listing also includes the name of the artist, a short project description, and, if applicable, the name of the art consultant or advisor involved. Published monthly. www.artbusinessnews.com

Art Consultants List, compiled by Caroll Michels. Available from Caroll Michels, career coach and artist-advocate, 1724 Burgos Drive, Sarasota, FL 34238. Updated several times a year. An annotated list of art consultants and art advisors that sell work to corporate markets. Includes names, addresses, telephone and fax numbers, email addresses, Web sites, and information about art disciplines and markets of interest. Also available on CD-ROM. www.caroll michels.com

Art in America Annual Guide to Galleries, Museums, Artists. Published annually. See "Corporate Consultants" in index.

Artists Representatives and Consultants. Chicago Artists' Coalition, 70 E. Lake, Suite 230, Chicago, IL 60601. An online resource list available to Chicago Artists' Coalition members. www.caconline.org

The Business of Art, edited by Lee Caplin. Paramus, N.J.: Prentice Hall Press, revised 2000. See "Art Advisory Services: The Age of the Art Advisor" and "Art Collections in Corporations."

Corporate Art Consulting by Susan Abbott. New York: Allworth Press, revised 1999. Although written for those who want to enter or expand their art consulting business, it provides advice and tips for artists interested in corporate sales.

Dodge Reports. McGraw-Hill, 1221 Avenue of the Americas, New York, NY 10020, revised on a regular basis. Computerized printouts of construction projects nationwide, including the name of the design firm in charge and whether a budget has been allocated for the purchase or commissioning of artwork. Individual state reports are also available. www.fwdodge.com/reports

Interior Design & Architecture Press Contacts, compiled by Caroll Michels, Career Coach and Artist-Advocate, 1724 Burgos Drive, Sarasota, FL 34238. More than 200 writers, editors, and publications covering interior design, architecture, landscape architecture, and garden design. Updated on an ongoing basis. Printout formatted for reproduction on labels. www.carollmichels.com

International Directory of Corporate Art Collections, edited by S. R. Howarth. International Art Alliance, Inc., P.O. Box 1608, Largo, FL 33779, revised on an ongoing basis. Available as a CD-ROM or printout. www.humanities-exchange .org/corporateart

New York Business Online Directory. Crain's New York Business, 711 Third Avenue, New York, NY 10017-4036. Contains hundreds of New York–based companies. Identifies decision makers by occupation. www.newyorkbusinessdirectory.com

Reed Design Registry of Architectural Firms. Reed Construction Data. Available from First Source, 30 Technology Parkway South, Suite 100, Norcross, GA 30092. A database of architecture firms nationwide. www.reedfirstsource.com /profile/index.asp

The Sourcebook of Architectural & Interior Art. The Guild, 931 East Main Street, Suite 9, Madison, WI 53703. A fee-based resource directory that contains the names, addresses, telephone numbers, and photographs of the work of American fine artists and craft artists, as well as biographical information. Distributed free of charge to more than 10,000 architects, interior designers, public art specialists, landscape architects, liturgical consultants, art consultants, and other professions. Published annually. www.guild.com

The Sourcebook of Residential Art. The Guild, 931 East Main Street, Suite 9, Madison, WI 53703. A fee-based resource directory that contains the names, addresses, telephone numbers, and photographs of the work of American fine artists and craft artists, as well as biographical information. Distributed free of charge to more than 7,000 art consultants, high-end consumers, residential design firms, architectural firms, and galleries. Published annually. www.guild.com

Web Sites

Architect Finder (http://architectfinder.aia.org). A database for locating architects by building type and services they provide. Sponsored by the American Institute of Architects.

Artist Help Network (www.artisthelpnetwork.com). Founded by Caroll Michels, career coach and artist-advocate, this site is devoted to all aspects of career development. See heading "Exhibitions, Commissions and Sales" and subheading "Corporate Art Market."

Corporate Art Brief (http://home.earthlink.net/~corporate.directory). A newsletter published by the International Art Alliance with information and news about the corporate art market. Includes news on collections, books about corporate art collections, and corporate collection links. Also profiles a corporate collection each month.

Hospitality Index (www.hospitality-index.com). A list of companies that supply art to the hotel industry. See "art" under the heading "furnishings and finishings."

Organizations

American Institute of Architects, 1735 New York Avenue NW, Washington, DC 20006. www.aiaonline.com

American Society of Interior Designers, 608 Massachusetts Avenue NE, Washington, DC 20002-6006. www.asid.org

International Association for Professional Art Advisors, 433 Third Street, Suite 3, Brooklyn, NY 11215. Provides guidelines and standards for professional art advisors and a network for communication among art advisors, curators, and art service professionals. A membership list is published online. www.iapaa.org

International Facility Management Association, 1 East Greenway Plaza, Suite 1100, Houston, TX 77046-0194. A not-for-profit organization dedicated to serving facility management professionals, many of whom are decision makers for purchasing art for corporate facilities. www.ifma.org

Set Decorators Society of America, 1646 N. Cherokee Avenue, Hollywood, CA 90028. Maintains a list of art consultants and prop houses involved in art placement for use in film, television commercials, and other media. www.set decorators.org

Also see "Interior Design and Architecture."

CREATIVE CHALLENGES, CAREER BLOCKS, AND THE PSYCHE

Publications

Affirmations for Artists by Eric Maisel. New York: Putnam Publishing Group, 1996. Deals with issues of introspection, self-examination, and a willingness to take risks.

Art and Fear by David Bayles and Ted Orland. Santa Barbara, Calif.: Capra Press, 1994. Explores the way art gets made and the nature of the difficulties that cause so many artists to give up along the way.

An Artist Empowered: Define and Establish Your Value as an Artist—Now Triumph Over Rejection by Eden Maxwell (Lulu.com: 2007). A primer for understanding the truths and myths about rejection.

The Artist Inside: A Spiritual Guide to Cultivating Your Creative Self by Tom Crockett. New York: Bantam Doubleday Dell, 2000. Discusses how to tap into creativity using the images and artifacts in dreams.

The Artist's Quest for Inspiration by Peggy Hadden. New York: Allworth Press, revised 2004. Instructs artists how to work their way out of a creative slump. Offers practical tips about using color, form, light, and other technical elements.

The Artist's Way: A Spiritual Path to Higher Creativity by Julia Cameron. New York: J. P. Tarcher, revised 2002. A twelve-week program to recover your creativity from a variety of blocks, including limiting beliefs, fear, self-sabotage, jealousy, guilt, addictions, and other inhibiting forces.

The Blank Canvas: Inviting the Muse by Anna Held Audette. Boston: Shambhala Publications, 1993. Includes strategies for getting unstuck. Offers advice to artists who are struggling with creative blocks or personal expression.

The Career Guide for Creative and Unconventional People by Carol Eikleberry and

Richard Nelson Bolles. Berkeley, Calif.: Ten Speed Press, revised 2007. Offers advice and support for creative people who are uncertain about their future and finding a place in the world.

Career Management for the Creative Person by Lee Silber. New York: Harmony Books, Three Rivers Press, 1999. Covers various aspects of professional life— from freelancing to working as a full-time employee to changing careers midstream. Offers coping strategies and tips and warns the right-brainer of common self-sabotaging behavior with advice on how to spot it and stop it early.

Career Solutions for Creative People: How to Balance Artistic Goals with Career Security by Dr. Ronda Ormont. New York: Allworth Press, 2001. Focuses on how to find the time and freedom to pursue art while making a stable living.

Coaching the Artist Within by Eric Maisel. Novato, Calif.: New World Library, 2005. Discusses how to defuse your own excuses and break through the dreaded "artist's block" with provocative questions, stimulating challenges, common sense, and real-life success stories.

The Creative Habit: Learn It and Use It for Life by Twyla Tharp. New York: Simon & Schuster, 2005. Delves into the nature of creativity, exploring themes of process versus product and the influences of inspiration and rigorous study. In this part memoir, the author shares the lessons she has learned in her thirty-five-year career as a choreographer. Also includes various exercises to ease the fears of facing a blank beginning and open the mind to new possibilities, regardless of the creative impulses and disciplines you follow.

Creatively Self-employed: How Writers and Artists Deal with Career Ups and Downs by Kristen Fischer. Iuniverse, Inc., 2007. Covers how to build confidence and self-esteem in your work, cope with rejection, handle creative voids and time issues, combat loneliness and isolation, and deal with anxiety, depression, and stress.

Creativity: How to Catch Lightning in a Bottle by George Gamez and Jack Segal. Los Angeles: Peak Publications, 1996. A practical program for artists, performers, and others who want to unleash their creative power.

The Energy of Money: A Spiritual Guide to Financial and Personal Fulfillment by Maria Nemeth. New York: Balantine Publishing Company, revised 2000. Provides spiritual and practical techniques to create a unique program for achieving personal life goals and financial wealth.

Fearless Creating by Eric Maisel. New York: Putnam Publishing Group, 1995. Includes exercises designed to help you blast through inertia and fear.

Leonardo's Ink Bottle: The Artist's Way of Seeing by Roberta Weir. Berkeley, Calif.: Ten Speed Press/Celestial Arts, 1998. Guides readers through the rediscovery of instinct and intuition and the quicksilver nature of inspiration in creating art.

Making Room for Making Art: A Thoughtful and Practical Guide to Bringing the Pleasure of Artistic Expression Back into Your Life by Sally Warner. Chicago Review Press, 1994. Offers advice for artists who are becoming discouraged or feel stalled and want to rekindle their passion for making art.

Marry Your Muse: Making a Lasting Commitment to Your Creativity by Jan Phillips. Wheaton, Ill.: Theosophical Publishing House, 1997. A course in creative expression.

The Money Mirror: How Money Reflects Women's Dreams, Fears, and Desires by Annette Lieberman and Vicki Lindner. New York: Allworth Press, 1996. Helps women understand and overcome cultural and personal barriers to intelligent money management.

The 9 Steps to Financial Freedom: Practical & Spiritual Steps So You Can Stop Worrying by Suze Orman. New York: Crown Books, revised 2006. Explores the psychological and spiritual power money has in our lives, emphasizing that before we can get control of our finances, we must get control of our attitudes about money.

Pencil Dancing: New Ways to Free Your Creative Spirit by Mari Messer. San Francisco: Walking Stick Press, 2001. Focuses on developing creative confidence, overcoming blocks, and taming your inner critics.

The Power of Positive Choices: Adding and Subtracting Your Way to a Great Life by Gail McMeekin. Berkeley, Calif.: Conari Press, 2001. Making the right choices can be as easy as adding and subtracting. A step-by-step process of throwing out the bad to accommodate the good by identifying deterrents, such as bad habits and people who cause drama in our lives—and adding goals, priorities, and people to support your journey.

Pushcart's Complete Rotten Reviews & Rejections, edited by Bill Henderson and André Bernard. Wainscott, N.Y.: Pushcart Press, 1998. A compilation of nasty reviews and ridiculous rejections of great authors and classical books.

The Secret Life of Money: How Money Can Be Food for the Soul by Tad Crawford. New York: Allworth Press, revised 1996. Reveals positive and negative ways in which money impacts our lives, using examples from ancient myths to contemporary times.

Thank You for Being Such a Pain: Spiritual Guidance for Dealing with Difficult People by Mark I. Rosen. New York: Three Rivers Press, 1998. Provides insights, anecdotes, and guidelines to help overcome the distractions and energy drain of dealing with difficult people.

Trust the Process: An Artist's Guide to Letting Go by Shaun McNiff. Boston: Shambhala Publishing, 1998. Expands the reader's view of what it means to live in tune with the labyrinthine ways of the creative spirit.

The 12 Secrets of Highly Creative Women: A Portable Mentor by Gail McMeekin. Berkeley, Calif.: Conari Press, 2000. An empowering book for those ready to confront self-defeating patterns related to creativity.

The War of Art: Break Through the Blocks and Win Your Inner Creative Battles by Steven Pressfield. Warner Books, revised 2003. Diagnoses the malaise that keeps creators from creating and shows how to defeat the naysayer within.

Why Art Cannot Be Taught: A Handbook for Art Students by James Elkins. Urbana and Chicago: University of Illinois Press, 2001. A critical portrait of what really goes on in art schools. Addresses the brutality of art critiques and suggests ways to make them more helpful. A survival guide for students and teachers.

Work With Passion: How to Do What You Love for a Living by Nancy Anderson. Novato, Calif.: New World Library, revised 2004. Packed with inspiration for taking chances, making choices, and recognizing opportunities.

Web Sites

About.com (http://painting.about.com/od/rightleftbrain/a/ArtistDyslexia.htm). A discussion about "The Artist and Dyslexia" by Marion Boddy-Evans.

Adholes (http://adholes.com/postings/aba31012ffa40ed975c7cde0a5a41051). "Dyslexia is a Source of Artistic Talent," a blog by Michael Iva.

Artist Help Network (www.artisthelpnetwork.com). Founded by Caroll Michels, career coach and artist-advocate, this site is devoted to all aspects of career development. See heading "Career" and subheadings "Creative Challenges, Career Blocks, and the Psyche." Also see heading "Other Resources" and subheading "Art and Healing."

Born to Explore (http://borntoexplore.org/adhd.htm). "The Coincidence of Attention Deficit Hyperactivity Disorder and Creativity," by Bonnie Cramond.

Rejection Collection (www.rejectioncollection.com). Share your rejection stories and letters with the arts community.

EMPLOYMENT OPPORTUNITIES

Publications

Artist's Assets: A Guide to Artist Resources. Artist Trust, 1835 12th Avenue, Seattle, WA 98122, revised 2006. A resource guide for artists in Washington State. Includes employment information. www.artisttrust.org

ArtSearch. Theatre Communications Group, 520 8th Avenue, 24th Floor, New York, NY 10018. Published biweekly, this is a national employment-service bulletin for jobs in the performing arts and arts administration. Available in print format or online. www.tcg.org/artsearch

Career Opportunities in Art: A Comprehensive Guide to the Exciting Careers Open to You in Art by Susan H. Haubenstock and David Joselit. New York: Facts on File Publications, revised 2001. Provides information on eighty-three specific jobs for people with art experience, art education, or ambition to work in the arts.

Career Solutions for Creative People: How to Balance Artistic Goals with Career Security by Dr. Ronda Ormont. New York: Allworth Press, 2001. Focuses on how to find the time and freedom to pursue art while making a stable living.

Careers by Design: A Business Guide for Graphic Design by Roz Goldfarb. New York: Allworth Press and the American Council for the Arts, revised 2002. Discusses jobs, hiring practices, sales, portfolios, résumés, networking, headhunters, freelancing, and more.

Careers for Nonconformists: A Practical Guide to Finding and Developing a Career Outside the Mainstream by Sandra Gurvis. New York: Marlowe & Company, 1999. Covers a multitude of careers in which people can shine and be authentic.

Careers in Art by Blythe Camenson. New York: McGraw-Hill, revised 2006. Lists educational requirements and additional training necessary for specific jobs in the arts, and surveys salaries and job opportunities.

Careers in Art: An Illustrated Guide by Gerald F. Brommer and Joseph A. Gatto. Worcester, Mass.: Davis Publications, 1999. Covers hundreds of visual arts professions and gives practical advice on the necessary steps required to be successful in those careers.

Current Jobs in Art. Foster Opportunities, Inc., P.O. Box 3494, Falls Church, VA 22043. A national listing of employment opportunities for new and early career art graduates. Available monthly by subscription. www.graduatejobs.com

The Fine Artist's Guide to Marketing and Self-Promotion by Julius Vitali. New York: Allworth Press, revised 2003. Provides background information about teaching-residency opportunities in the arts. See the chapter "Artists-in-Education."

Gardner's Guide to Internships at Multimedia and Animation Studios by Garth Gardner. Annandale, Va.: Garth Gardner, Inc., 2001. Profiles hundreds of computer graphics, animation, and multimedia companies in the United States and Canada that offer internships.

Gardner's Guide to Internships in New Media: Computer Graphics, Animation and Multimedia by Garth Gardner and Bonney Ford. Annandale, Va.: GGC, Inc., revised 2004. Profiles hundreds of companies in the visual-effects industry who offer internships.

Heart & Soul Resumes by Chuck Cochran and Donna Peerce. Palo Alto, Calif.: Davies-Black Publishing, 1998. Advice on how to prepare creative résumés for job searching. Includes twenty real-life résumé makeovers.

How to Develop and Promote Successful Seminars and Workshops: The Definitive Guide to Creating and Marketing Seminars, Workshops, Classes, and Conferences by Howard L. Shenson. New York: John Wiley, 1990.

How to Make Money Performing in Schools: The Definitive Guide to Developing, Marketing, and Presenting School Assembly Programs by David Heflick. Orient, Wash.: Silcox Production, 1997. Includes marketing secrets, program ideas, and information on what administrators look for in programs and factors in determining who gets booked.

How to Run Seminars & Workshops: Presentation Skills for Consultants, Trainers and Teachers by Robert L. Jolles. New York: John Wiley, 2005. Provides effective techniques for winning over an audience, holding their interest, and conveying important information. A step-by-step self-teaching guide that provides the confidence and the techniques speakers need to survive and thrive in front of an audience.

More Than Once in a Blue Moon: Multiple Jobholdings by American Artists by Neil O. Alper and Gregory H. Wassall, Santa Ana, Calif.: Seven Locks Press, 2000. Published in conjunction with the National Endowment for the Arts, Research Division Report #40. Results of the first systematic study about artists and "moonlighting."

Opportunities in Visual Arts Careers by Mark Salmon and Bill Barrett. New York: McGraw-Hill/Contemporary Books, 2001. Offers information on a variety of careers in the field of visual arts, including training and educational requirements, salary statistics, and professional and Internet resources.

The Photographer's Assistant by John Kieffer. New York: Allworth Press, revised 2001. Provides information on how to become a photographer's assistant, what skills and personal attributes professionals seek, and how they hire assistants. Also includes technical tips on lighting, camera equipment, and more.

Teaching Artist Journal, edited by Nick Jaffe, Center for Arts Policy. Published by Lawrence Erlbaum Associates, 10 Industrial Avenue, Mahway, NJ 07430-2262. Published quarterly. A professional development resource for teaching artists. www.leaonline.com

What Color Is Your Parachute? A Practical Manual for Job Hunters and Career Changers by Richard Nelson Bolles. Berkeley, Calif.: Ten Speed Press, revised regularly.

The Work We Were Born to Do: Find the Work You Love, Love the Work You Do by Nick Williams and Robert Holden. London: HarperCollins, 1999. Offers insights to explore the infinite possibilities inherent in every human being.

Work with Passion: How To Do What You Love for a Living by Nancy Anderson. Novato: Calif.: New World Library, revised 2004.

Web Sites

Art & Design Career Employment (http://art.nmu.edu/department/AD_Career .html). Sponsored by the Department of Art & Design, Northern Michigan University. Includes contacts lists in the fields of new media, graphics, photography, film, video, museums, architecture, and teaching.

ArtCareer Network (www.artcareer.net). Lists opportunities in the visual arts, including employment. Available by subscription.

Artist Help Network (www.artisthelpnetwork.com). Founded by Caroll Michels, career coach and artist-advocate, this site is devoted to all aspects of career development. See heading "Money" and subheadings "Apprenticeships and Internships," "Art Colonies & Artist-in-Residence Programs," and "Employment."

Artjobonline (www.artjob.org). Biweekly online listing of positions in visual and performing arts, literature, education, and arts administration. Résumés can be posted on the site. Sponsored by the Western States Arts Federation.

Arts Job Bank (www.artpridenj.com/jobbank/joblist.php). Sponsored by Art-PRIDE. Lists opportunities for arts professionals and students seeking jobs and internships with arts organizations in New Jersey.

Arts Opportunities (www.artsopportunities.org). Posts opportunities for artists, including employment. Sponsored by the Southern Arts Federation and the Center for Arts Management & Technology at Carnegie Mellon University.

Association of Arts Administration Educators (www.artsadministration.org/find). Provides links to arts administration undergraduate and graduate programs at colleges and universities.

Chronicle Careers (http://chronicle.com/jobs). Lists employment information for faculty, administrators, and executives in art, art history, communication, and the performing arts from more than 1,200 institutions. Sponsored by the *Chronicle of Higher Education.*

eLance (www.eLance.com). A fee-based site for freelancers to list their skills and search for work. Includes graphic design, illustration, and animation.

HigherEdJobs.com (www.higheredjobs.com). Lists faculty positions and part-time adjunct positions at colleges, including those in the art field.

hireCulture.org (www.hireculture.org/jobbook/index.asp). A listing of creative, administrative, production, volunteer, and internship opportunities in Massachusetts. Sponsored by the Massachusetts Cultural Council.

Job Bank (http://www.americansforthearts.org). A searchable database of nonprofit and for-profit arts management positions. Sponsored by Americans for the Arts.

The Job Bank (www.cultural-alliance.org/programs/jobank.html). Lists of opportunities in arts and arts administration in the greater Washington, D.C., area. Sponsored by the Cultural Alliance of Greater Washington.

MatchBook.org (www.matchbook.org.). A cultural marketplace designed to bring together New England's performing and teaching artists and sponsors. A program of the New England Foundation for the Arts and the Massachusetts Cultural Council, in partnership with state arts agencies of Connecticut, Maine, New Hampshire, Rhode Island, and Vermont.

NYFA Source (www.nyfa.org/nyfa_source.asp?id=47&fid=1). An extensive database for visual and performing artists, writers, and arts organizations. Includes employment opportunities. Sponsored by the New York Foundation for the Arts in conjunction with the Urban Institute.

NYFA Teaching Artist Source (www.nyfa.org/teachingartistsource). An online, telephone, and email information service for teaching artists to learn about teaching opportunities, grants, services, and publications specifically for teaching artists on the local, regional, state, and national level.

Online Job Bank (www.caconline.org). An online listing of employment opportunities for artists in the Chicago area. Available to members of the Chicago Artists' Coalition.

Telecommuting Jobs (www.tjobs.com/index.shtml). Fee-based listing of jobs for artists in the telecommunications field, including graphic designers, user-interface specialists, fontographers, Internet producers, virtual professionals, and Web site designers.

Organizations

Association of Arts Administrators Educators, c/o Andrew Taylor, Bolz Center for Arts Administration, 975 University Avenue, Madison, WI 53706. A nonprofit organization created to advocate formal training and high standards of education for arts administrators. Web site provides links to graduate and undergraduate programs in arts administration and other resources. www.artsadministration.org

Hospital Audiences, Inc., 548 Broadway, 3rd Floor, New York, NY 10012-3950. Brings visual and performing art programs to New Yorkers who are confined in hospitals, health-care facilities, shelters, and other social service agencies. www.hospitalaudiences.org

The National Network for Artist Placement, 935 West Avenue 37, Los Angeles, CA 90065. Offers career counseling, employment services, and career resources to visual and performing artists. www.artistplacement.com

National Training Program for Hospital Artists-In-Residence, The Creative Center, 273 Bowery, New York, NY 10002. Provides professional training to artists to work with cancer patients in their hometown, medical centers, clinics, and hospitals. http://thecreativecenter.org/national_programs

Prison Arts Project, William James Association, P.O. Box 1632, Santa Cruz, CA 95061. Open to visual and performing artists interested in conducting workshops in California correctional facilities. www.williamjamesassociation.org

Professionals for NonProfits, 515 Madison Avenue, Suite 900, New York, NY 10022 and 1629 K Street NW, Suite 501, Washington, DC 20006. An employment agency that offers part-time and full-time temporary and permanent positions to people interested in working for arts-related organizations. www.pnp-inc.com

Also see "Apprenticeships and Internships" and "Art Colonies and Artist-in-Residence Programs."

EXHIBITION AND PERFORMANCE PLACES AND SPACES
Publications

Annual Crafts Shows Book. Ontario Crafts Council, 990 Queen Street, West Toronto, Ontario M6J 1H1, Canada. Published annually. A comprehensive directory of hundreds of annual craft shows listing dates, contact information, application details, and jurying information. www.craft.on.ca/publication-acsbPage.php

Art Guide Texas: Museums, Art Centers, Alternative Spaces, and Nonprofit Galleries by Rebecca S. Cohen. Austin: University of Texas Press, 2004. Entries include contact information, Web sites, and a description of collections and past exhibitions. Organized regionally.

Art in America Annual Guide to Galleries, Museums, Artists. Art in America, 575 Broadway, New York, NY 10012. Alphabetical listing of American museums, galleries, private dealers, and alternative spaces arranged by state and city. Each entry includes the address, phone number, Web site, and email address, names of key staff members, a short description of type of art shown, and artists represented.

Art on Campus: The College Art Association's Official Guide to American College and University Art Museums and Exhibition Galleries, edited by John J. Russell and Thomas S. Spencer. Friar's Lantern, 2000. An alphabetical listing of institutions by city and state with descriptive information for each entry.

Art Opportunities: Finding, Entering and Winning by Benny Shaboy with contributions by more than thirty-five professional artists. AO Book, P.O. Box 502, Benicia, CA 94510-0502, 2004. Includes advice about entering juried shows and applying for public art commissions and residencies. Also includes articles and tips on writing public art proposals. www.artopportunitiesbook.com

Art Opportunities Monthly. P.O. Box 502, Benicia, CA 94510-0502. Published monthly. A listing of opportunities for artists, including exhibitions. Only available via email. www.artopportunitiesmonthly.com

The Artist-Museum Relationship Package by Alyson B. Stanfield. Stanfield Art Associates, P.O. Box 988, Golden, CO 80402. An ebook that deals with various aspects of cultivating museum relationships. www.artbizcoach.com

The Artist's and Graphic Designer's Market. Cincinnati: Writer's Digest Books, revised annually. Describes a selection of galleries throughout the United States. www.writersdigest.com

Artists' Gallery Guide for Chicago and Surrounding Areas. Chicago Artists' Coalition, 70 E. Lake, Suite 230, Chicago, IL 60601, revised 2005. A comprehensive and well-organized guide to commercial and alternative spaces, museums, and arts organizations in Chicago, North Central Illinois, Iowa, Southern and Central Illinois, Indiana, Michigan, St. Louis, and Wisconsin. www.caconline.org

Booking and Tour Management for the Performing Arts by Rena Shagan. New York: Allworth Press, revised 2001. Provides information on how to book performances, organize tours, and succeed on the road as a performing artist.

The Complete Guide to New York Art Galleries by Renée Phillips. Manhattan Arts International, 200 East 72nd Street, Suite 26L, New York, NY 10021, revised 2007. Profiles more than 1,000 galleries, private dealers, alternative spaces, nonprofit organizations, corporate art consultants, and museums in New York City.

Getting Exposure: The Artist's Guide to Exhibiting the Work, edited by Carolyn Blakeslee, Drew Steis, and Barb Dougherty. Art Calendar, 1500 Park Center, Orlando, FL 32835, 1995. Compiled by the editors of *Art Calendar,* this guide includes information on juried shows, cooperative galleries, commercial galleries, college and university galleries, and more.

Little Museums by Lynne Arany and Archie Hobson. New York: Owl Books, Henry Holt and Company, 1998. Describes more than 1,000 little museums throughout the United States, including those that specialize in themes.

Museum and Independent Curators List, compiled by Caroll Michels, career coach and artist-advocate, 1724 Burgos Drive, Sarasota, FL 34238. Contains the names of more than 500 museum and independent curators nationwide. Updated on an ongoing basis. www.carollmichels.com

Official Museum Directory. New Providence, N.J.: R. R. Bowker, in cooperation with the American Association of Museums, regularly revised. Profiles more than 8,150 museums and institutions.

On Your Own: Alternative Exhibition Strategies. Visual Arts Ontario, 1153A Queen Street West, Toronto, Ontario M6J 1J4, Canada. A step-by-step analysis of how to mount your own exhibition. www.vao.org

Ontario Association of Art Galleries Directory, 2005. The Ontario Association of Art Galleries, 111 Peter Street, Suite 617, Toronto, Ontario M5V 2H1, Canada, 2005. Includes contact information for 457 key individuals in 183 art galleries and organization throughout Ontario. www.oaag.org

The Ontario Gallery Guide. Visual Arts Ontario, 1153A Queen Street West, Toronto, Ontario M6J 1J4, Canada. A comprehensive guide to galleries in Ontario, Canada, including commercial venues, public, artist-run, and cooperatives. www.vao.org

Photograph. 64 West 89th Street, New York, NY 10024. A bimonthly guide to photography galleries throughout the United States. www.photography-guide.com

Photographer's Market. Cincinnati: Writer's Digest Books, revised annually. Lists photography galleries.

Resource Bulletin. Maryland Art Place, 8 Market Place, Suite 100, Baltimore, MD 21202. Lists hundreds of exhibition opportunities. Published quarterly. www .mdartplace.org/artists/opportunities.html

University Galleries in Illinois. Chicago Artists' Coalition, 70 E. Lake, Suite 230, Chicago, IL 60601. A list of university galleries in the Chicago area available to members of the Chicago Artists' Coalition. www.caconline.org

Web Sites

Art in Context (www.artincontext.com). An extensive database that includes contact information on galleries, including Web site links that can be searched by discipline, geography, and other criteria. Also provides a geographic listing of museums with Web site links. Developed by the Center for Arts Management, Carnegie Mellon University.

Art in Embassies Program, U.S. Department of State (http://aiep.state.gov). Loans artwork to American embassies throughout the world for up to three years. Accepts applications from individual artists only online.

ArtDeadline (www.artdeadline.com). A monthly digest of career-related information, including exhibition opportunities. Available by subscription.

Artist Help Network (www.artisthelpnetwork.com). Founded by Caroll Michels, career coach and artist-advocate, this site is devoted to all aspects of career development. See heading "Exhibitions, Commissions and Sales" and subheading "Exhibition Places & Spaces," and "Exhibition Planning."

Arts Opportunities (www.artsopportunities.org). Posts opportunities for artists, including exhibitions. Sponsored by the Southern Arts Federation and the Center for Arts Management & Technology at Carnegie Mellon University.

International Directory of Sculpture Parks (www.artnut.com/intl.html). An annotated list of sculpture parks throughout the world, with addresses, descriptions, and links. Compiled by sculptor Benbow Bullock, who has visited or worked in many of the parks.

Musée (www.musee-online.org). Provides links to museum shops.

Museum Stuff (www.museumstuff.com). Provides links to various museum shops, including those that specialize in art and design.

MuseumsUSA (www.museumsusa.org). A searchable directory of more than 15,000 museums throughout the United States.

Visual Artist Management Project (VAM-P) (http://vam-p.net/vam_p.html). Offers a very reasonably priced database called "Venue Viewer", compiled by artist Brian David Dennis, of nearly 8,200 national and international galleries with Web sites, and when possible, it includes a contact person's name.

World Wide Art Resources. Provides links to galleries in the United States and abroad. www.wwar.com

Organizations

The Art Connection, 539 Tremont Street, Boston, MA 02116. An art donation and placement program for artists and collectors who want to donate artwork to public and nonprofit organizations. Serves as an art clearinghouse, simplifying the donation process and offering a wide range of original works for selection by qualifying nonprofit agencies. There are similar organizations in Baltimore, San Francisco, and Washington, D.C. www.theartconnection.org

ArtNetwork, P.O. Box 1360, Nevada City, CA 95959. Rents arts-related mailing lists that include the addresses of curators, art galleries, university galleries, and museum art buyers. www.artmarketing.com

Art-Support, 1717 150th Avenue SE, #16, Bellvue, WA 98007. Offers various mailing lists related to photography, including galleries. www.art-support.com

Dorsky Gallery Curatorial Programs, 11-03 45th Avenue, Long Island City, New York 11101. A nonprofit organization that presents independently curated exhibitions of contemporary art. Explores timely themes that are relevant to understanding visual arts today. www.dorsky.org

ExhibitsUSA, MidAmerica Arts Alliance, 2018 Baltimore Avenue, Kansas City, MO 64108. Organizes exhibits that travel to small and mid-sized museums, university galleries, and community art centers throughout the United States.

Also provides various exhibition-related services. www.maaa.org/exhi_usa/index.php3

Independent Curators International, 799 Broadway, Suite 205, New York, NY 10003. Develops, organizes, and circulates exhibitions focusing on recent trends and aesthetic concerns. Also underwrites exhibition booking fees. www.ici-exhibitions.org

Museum Store Association, 4100 East Mississippi Avenue, Suite 800, Denver, CO 80246. Provides members with a mailing list of museum shops nationwide, as well as in other parts of the world. Affiliate memberships are available to artists who are already selling work to a museum shop at wholesale prices. www.museumdistrict.com

Smith Kramer, Inc., 1622 Westport Road, Kansas City, MO 64111. Organizes traveling exhibitions that encompass a variety of themes, including those related to paintings, ceramics, photography, graphics, and textiles. www.smithkramer.com

Also see "Art Sales and Commissions," "International Connections," and "Online Galleries."

EXHIBITION AND PERFORMANCE PLANNING

Publications

The Art of Displaying Art by Lawrence B. Smith. Rhinebeck, N.Y.: The Consultant Press, 1998. Provides advice and tips on displaying art, including oils, graphics, drawings, and photographs.

The Art of Showing Art by James K. Reeve. Tulsa, Okla.: Council Oak Books, revised 1995. Includes guidelines for protecting and displaying paintings, sculpture, and photographs, and information on display concepts, storage, records, and appraisals.

The Crate Itself: Proven Design Techniques and Alternative Ideas. American Association of Museums, Washington, D.C., 1996. Covers the packing case from the conservator's perspective, the slat crate, the standard wood crate, and an alternative to wood. Filled with dozens of illustrations. Available through the Packing, Art Handling & Crating Information Network. www.pacin.org

Good Show! A Practical Guide for Temporary Exhibitions by Lothar P. Witteborg. Smithsonian Institution Traveling Exhibition Service, Washington, D.C., revised 1991. A how-to manual for developing temporary exhibitions.

On the Road Again: Developing and Managing Traveling Exhibitions by Rebecca A. Buck and Jean Allman Gilmore. American Association of Museums, Washington, D.C.: 2003. Provides pointers for developing traveling exhibitions, including the development of an exhibition concept and budget, crating and shipping, and dealing with foreign custom officials. Also includes contracts and loan agreements.

On Your Own: Alternative Exhibition Strategies. Visual Arts Ontario, 1153A Queen Street West, Toronto, Ontario M6J 1J4, Canada, 1995. A step-by-step analysis of how to mount your own exhibition. Includes sample budgets, timelines, sample press releases, and other information. www.vao.org

Presenting Performances by Thomas Wolf. Association of Performing Arts Presenters, Washington, D.C., revised 2000. Covers the topics of acquiring space, handling promotion, dealing with unions, and dependable technical assistance.

Soft Packing: Methods and Methodology for the Packing and Transport of Art and Artifacts. American Association of Museums, Washington, D.C., 1994. Addresses the methods, principles, and decisions involved in safely transporting soft-packed art and artifacts. Available through the Packing, Art Handling & Crating Information Network. www.pacin.org

Technical Drawing Handbook of Packing and Crating Methods. The Packing, Art Handling & Crating Information Network, 1993. Crating styles and designs for packing two-dimensional and three-dimensional objects. Available through the Packing, Art Handling & Crating Information Network. www.pacin.org

Web Sites

Artist Help Network (www.artisthelpnetwork.com). Founded by Caroll Michels, career coach and artist-advocate, this site is devoted to all aspects of career development. See heading "Exhibitions, Commissions and Sales" and subheading "Exhibition Places & Spaces, and Exhibition Planning." Also see heading "Other Resources" and subheading "Artwork Care and Maintenance."

CARFAC Fee Schedule Introduction and Guidelines (www.carcc.ca/fee_schedule _2008_0_introduction.html). A bilingual official exhibition fee schedule outlining the amounts of money that visual artists in Canada receive for exhibiting in nonprofit galleries.

Craters and Freighters (www.cratersandfreighters.com). An online service that provides quotes for shipping artwork. Also provides the names of art transport companies on a state-by-state basis.

The Packing, Art Handling & Crating Information Network (www.pacin.org). Dedicated to expanding the network of information and resources available to museum and art handling communities.

Also see "Artwork Care and Maintenance."

GALLERY RELATIONS
Publications

The Art Biz: The Covert World of Collectors, Dealers, Auction Houses, Museums, and Critics by Alice Goldfarb Marquis. Chicago: Contemporary Books, 1991. Reveals the hype, hypocrisy, greed, manipulation, and secrecy that takes place in the contemporary art world.

The Artists' Survival Manual: A Complete Guide to Marketing Your Work by Toby Judith Klayman with Cobbett Steinberg. San Francisco: Klaman and Branchcomb, revised 1996. Desktop edition. See "Preparing to Negotiate with Dealers" and "Questions to Ask Your Gallery."

Framed: Hollywood's Dealer to the Stars Tells All by Tod Volpe. Toronto: ECW Press, 2003. A blow-by-blow chronicle of the rise and fall of international art dealer Tod Volpe, who, at the height of his success, had a star-studded Hollywood clientele. A detailed probe into the shadowy world of art dealing exposes how high culture and civility conceal boardroom swindling, illegal price fixing, and money laundering.

High Art Down Home: An Economic Ethnography of a Local Art Market by Stuart Plattner. Chicago: University of Chicago Press, 1997. Examines the social and economic factors that govern art markets outside of New York and explains the conundrums and paradoxes of the art world.

Taking the Leap: Building a Career as a Visual Artist by Cay Lang. San Francisco: Chronicle Books, revised 2006. See "When Things Begin to Happen."

Web Sites

Artist Help Network (www.artisthelpnetwork.com). Founded by Caroll Michels, career coach and artist-advocate, this site is devoted to all aspects of career development. See heading "Exhibitions, Commissions and Sales" and subheading "Gallery Relations." See heading "Legal" and subheading "Law: Contracts."

How's My Dealing (http://howsmydealing.blogspot.com). Provides a well-organized venting and feedback service that invites artists to share their positive and negative direct dealings with galleries, curators, and critics. The blog also invites current and former gallery employees to contribute comments that will be useful to artists. In addition, galleries are invited to comment on various arts-related topics.

Also see "Law: Contracts and Business Forms."

GENERAL ARTS REFERENCES

Publications

American Art Directory. New Providence, N.J.: National Register Publishing, revised triennially. A directory of arts organizations, art schools, museums, periodicals, scholarships, and fellowships.

International Directory of the Arts. Munich: K. G. Saur Verlag, revised biennially. Two-volume guide to museums, universities, associations, dealers, galleries, publishers, and others involved in the arts in Europe, the United States, Canada, South America, Asia, and Australia.

The Official Museum Directory. New Providence, N.J.: National Register Publishing, revised biennially. Describes hundreds of museums throughout the United States. Provides contact information and the names of key personnel.

Web Sites

Absolutearts (www.absolutearts.com). A daily news update featuring articles about the arts, including international, national, and regional coverage.

Artist Help Network (www.artisthelpnetwork.com). Founded by Caroll Michels, career coach and artist-advocate, this site is devoted to all aspects of career development. See heading "Other Resources" and subheading "General Arts References."

Artlex (www.artlex.com). An online dictionary of more than 3,200 terms used in visual culture, along with thousands of pronunciation notes, quotations, and cross-references. Prepared by Michael Delahunt.

Arts Journal (www.artsjournal.com). A daily digest of arts and cultural journalism from around the world.

Ask Art. The Artists Bluebook (www.askart.com). Lists information on more than 30,000 American artists.

World Wide Arts Resources (www.wwar.com). Links to numerous art resources throughout the world.

GRANTS AND FUNDING RESOURCES

Publications

Art Opportunities: Finding, Entering and Winning by Benny Shaboy with contributions by more than thirty-five professional artists. AO Book, studioNOTES, P.O. Box 502, Benicia, CA 94510-0502, 2004. Includes information on grants, fellowships, and residencies. www.artopportunitiesbook.com

Art Opportunities Monthly, P.O. Box 502, Benicia, CA 94510-0502. A listing of opportunities for artists, including grants. Published monthly. Available only via email. www.artopportunitiesmonthly.com

Artist Grants Master List by Bari Caton. An ebook with links to numerous online resources that describe grant opportunities for individual artists. www.artgrants.com

Artist's Assets: A Guide to Artist Resources. Artist Trust, 1835 12th Avenue, Seattle, WA 98122, revised 2006. A resource guide for artists in Washington State. Includes information about funding opportunities. www.artisttrust.org

Breaking Through the Clutter: Business Solutions for Women, Artists and Entrepreneurs by Judith Luther Wilder. Los Angeles: The National Network for Artist Placement, 1999. Includes information on writing successful grant proposals and on grant resources for individual artists.

Directory of Financial Aids for Women by Gail Schlachter and R. David Weber. San Carlos, Calif.: Reference Service Press, updated regularly. Identifies fellowships, grants, awards, loans, and internships, designed primarily or exclusively for women.

The Fine Artist's Guide to Marketing and Self-Promotion by Julius Vitali. New York: Allworth Press, revised 2003. Includes information on how to find corporate support, grants, and other funding.

The Foundation Center's Guide to Grantseeking on the Web, edited by Kief Schladweiler. New York: The Foundation Center, revised 2003. Discusses how to maximize the use of the Web for funding research.

Foundation Grants to Individuals by Phyllis Edelson. New York: The Foundation Center, revised 2007. Contains hundreds of entries. Lists scholarships, educational loans, fellowships, residencies, internships, awards, and prizes available to individuals from private foundations. Also includes information on how to approach foundations. www.fdncenter.org

Getting Funded: A Complete Guide to Proposal Writing by Mary Stewart Hall and Susan Howeltt. Portland, Ore.: Continuing Education Press, revised 2003. An overview of all aspects of grant writing.

Grants for Arts, Culture & the Humanities, New York: The Foundation Center, revised 2007. Lists grants to nonprofit arts and cultural organizations in the United States and abroad.

Grants Primer, Visual Arts Ontario. 1153A Queen Street West, Toronto, Ontario M6J 1J4, Canada. Advice on how to apply for a grant for individuals and the relative importance of visual support materials, artist statements, and proposals. www.vao.org

Guide to Canadian Arts Grants. Canada Grants Service, 100–2 Bloor Street West, Toronto, Ontario M4W 3E2, Canada, revised 2007. Lists 1,000 art-granting programs and awards throughout Canada for artists in all disciplines. Also available on CD-ROM. http://pages.interlog.com/~cgs/prod03.htm

Guide to Getting Arts Grants by Ellen Liberatori. New York: Allworth Press, 2006. Provides artists and arts organizations with information on facts and skills needed for grants applications in the arts, including formulating budgets, mastering the intricacies of the application process, online resources and application opportunities, insights into understanding the selection and review process, and more.

The National Guide to Funding in Arts and Culture, edited by Jose Santiago. The Foundation Center, 79 Fifth Avenue, New York, NY 10003, revised 2004. Lists thousands of grants for arts and cultural programs from independent, corporate, and community foundations. www.fdncenter.org

The Only Grant-Writing Book You'll Ever Need: Top Grant Writers and Grant Givers Share Their Secrets by Ellen Karsh and Arlen Sue Fox. New York: Carroll and Graft, revised 2006. Interviews experts in the grants field who provide advice and tips to improve your chances to win a grant.

Shaking the Money Tree: How to Get Grants and Donations for Film and Video by Morrie Warshawski. Studio City, Calif.: Michael Wiese Productions, revised 2003. Provides advice on how to get grants and donations for film and video projects from individuals, foundations, government agencies, and corporations in the twenty-first century.

Supporting Yourself as an Artist by Deborah A. Hoover. New York: Oxford University Press, revised 1989. Demonstrates how any artist can develop a network of individuals, organizations, and information resources in his or her own community and beyond. Outlines a clear, step-by-step approach that enables artists to identify sources of support and obtain assistance.

Software Programs

GYST Software for Artists, 4223 Russell Avenue, Los Angeles, CA 90027-4511. Available for MAC, PC, and Vista. Guides users through the process of writing grant proposals or other proposals with detailed instructions. Also includes many business-related functions. www.gyst-ink.com

Web Sites

ArtDeadline (www.artdeadline.com). A monthly digest of career-related information, including grants and artist-in-residence programs. Available by subscription.

Artist Help Network (www.artisthelpnetwork.com). Founded by Caroll Michels, career coach and artist-advocate, this site is devoted to all aspects of career development. See heading "Money" and subheadings "Art Colonies and Artist-in Residence Programs" and "Grants and Funding."

The Canada Council on the Arts (www.canadacouncil.ca/visualarts). Includes a listing of grants for Canadian artists and application information.

Cultural Funding. Federal Opportunities (www.arts.gov/federal.html). Sponsored by the National Endowment for the Arts. Includes government-sponsored funding programs for artists and organizations.

Funding for Individual Artists (www.caconline.org). Available to members of the Chicago Artists' Coalition members.

Grants and Awards Online Database (www.pen.org). A listing of 2,000 domestic and foreign grants, literary awards, fellowships, and residencies. Available by subscription. Sponsored by the PEN American Center.

National Assembly of State Arts Agencies (www.nasaa-arts.org). Provides links to state arts agencies. A good resource for researching state-supported grants and fellowships for artists.

NYFA Source (www.nyfa.org/nyfa_source.asp?id=47&fid=1). An extensive database for visual and performing artists, writers, and arts organizations. Includes sections on grants, awards, emergency grants, honorary prizes, students scholarships, artists-in-residence programs, live/work space awards, and equipment access awards. Sponsored by the New York Foundation for the Arts.

Philanthropy News Digest (http://foundationcenter.org/pnd). A free weekly news service of the Foundation Center, this is a compendium, in digest form, of philanthropy-related articles and features culled from print and electronic media outlets nationwide.

Resource Handbook for Minnesota Artists (www.springboardforthearts.org/Resources/Resources.asp). A listing of resources for Minnesota artists, including grants and funding opportunities. Sponsored by Springboard for the Arts.

Organizations

The Canada Council for the Arts, P.O. Box 1047, Ottawa, Ontario K1P 5V8, Canada. Offers grants to individual Canadian artists and arts organizations. www.canadacouncil.ca

Center for Cultural Innovation, 244 S. San Pedro Street, Suite 401, Los Angeles, CA 90012 and 651 Brannon Street, Suite 410, San Francisco, CA 94107. Promotes knowledge, sharing, networking, and financial independence for individual artists and creative entrepreneurs in California. Provides grants and loans. http://cciarts.org

Creative Capital Foundation, 65 Bleecker Street, 7th Floor, New York, NY 10012. A national not-for-profit organization that supports artists pursuing innovative approaches to form and content in the performing, visual, literary, and media arts, and in emerging art fields. In addition to financial support, the foundation provides grant recipients with advisory services and professional development assistance. www.creative-capital.org

The Foundation Center, 79 Fifth Avenue, New York, NY 10003-3076. A national service organization that provides information on foundation funding. Services include disseminating information on foundations and publishing reference books on foundations and foundation grants. www.fdncenter.org/newyork

The Foundation Center, 1422 Euclid Avenue, Suite 1600, Cleveland, OH 44115-2001. www.fdncenter.org/cleveland

The Foundation Center, 312 Sutter Street, Suite 606, San Francisco, CA 94108. www.fdncenter.org/sanfrancisco

The Foundation Center, 50 Hurt Plaza, Suite 150, Atlanta, GA 30303-2914. www.fdncenter.org/atlanta

The Foundation Center, 1627 K Street NW, 3rd Floor, Washington, DC 20016-1708. www.fdncenter.org/washington

Fractured Atlas, 248 W. 35th Street, Suite 1202, New York, NY 10001. Nonprofit organization that offers many support services to artist-members throughout the United States, including fiscal sponsorship. www.fracturedatlas.org

The Fund for Women Artists, 3789 Balboa Street, PMB 181, San Francisco, CA 94121. Offers fiscal and administrative umbrella services to women artists who need a short-term affiliation with a nonprofit organization to raise funds. Focus is on theater artists and film and video artists. Also provides information on funding resources. Publishes a bimonthly newsletter. www.womenarts.org

Max's Kansas City Project, P.O. Box 53, Woodstock, NY 12498. An international nonprofit organization that provides funding and resources for emergency situations, including medical aid, health care, legal aid, housing, food, and grants to individuals in the arts. www.maxskansascity.org

National Endowment for the Arts, The Nancy Hanks Center, 1100 Pennsylvania Avenue NW, Washington DC 20256. Awards grants to organizations to support projects in the visual arts. www.arts.endow.gov

Also see "Art Colonies and Artist-in-Residence Programs."

HEALTH HAZARDS

Publications

ACTS FACTS. 181 Thompson Street, #23, New York, NY 10012-2586. A monthly newsletter that focuses on health hazards for artists, published by the organization Arts, Crafts and Theater Safety. www.artscraftstheatersafety.org

Artist Beware: The Hazards in Working with All Art and Craft Materials and the Precautions Every Artist and Craftsperson Should Take by Michael McCann. New York: The Lyons Press, revised 2005. A comprehensive overview on preventing and correcting health hazards of art and craft materials. Analyzes materials and the harm they can cause.

The Artist's Complete Health and Safety Guide by Monona Rossol. New York: Allworth Press, revised 2001. A guide to using potentially toxic materials safely and ethically. Designed to help artists and teachers comply with applicable health and safety laws, including the American and Canadian right-to-know laws and the U.S. Art Materials Labeling Act.

The Artist's Resource Handbook by Daniel Grant. New York: Allworth Press, revised 1997. See chapter "Health and Safety in the Arts."

Health Hazards for Photographers by Siegfried and Wolfgang Rempel. New York: The Lyons Press, 1992. A reference guide to the safe use of all chemicals used in black-and-white and color photography.

Health Hazards Manual for Artists by Michael McCann. New York: The Lyons Press, revised 2003. Details harmful effects caused by art materials and outlines procedures that can make working with these materials safer.

Making Art Safely: Alternative Methods and Materials in Drawing, Painting, Printmaking, Graphic Design, and Photography by Merle Spandorfer, Deborah Curtiss, and Jack Snyder. New York: John Wiley, 1995. Identifies hazardous materials and techniques that are commonly used in art. Demonstrates safe alternatives through text and step-by-step illustrations.

Overexposure: Health Hazards in Photography by Susan D. Shaw and Monona Rossol. New York: Allworth Press, revised 1991. Covers all facets of the risks faced by photographers, lab personnel, and others involved with photographic chemicals. Includes pointers for setting up a safe workplace.

Web Sites

Artist Help Network (www.artisthelpnetwork.com). Founded by Caroll Michels, career coach and artist-advocate, this site is devoted to all aspects of career development. See heading "Creature Comforts" and subheading "Health Hazards in Your Workspace."

Health and Health Hazards Information Resources (www.caconline.org). Available to members of the Chicago Artists' Coalition. www.caconline.org

Health Hazards for the Artist (www.cia.edu/academicResources/library_content/specialized_guides/hazards.pdf). Sponsored by the Gund Library of the Cleveland Institute of Art.

Health Hazards in the Arts. Information for Artists, Craftspeople and Photographers (http://wally.rit.edu/pubs/guides/healthhaz.html). Sponsored by the Rochester Institute of Technology.

Health in the Arts Articles (www.chicagoartistsresource.org/?q=node/6056). Hundreds of articles on health and safety issues for artists, originally published as part of *Art Hazard News*. Sponsored by Chicago Artists Resource in conjunction with the Health in the Arts Program, University of Illinois at Chicago.

Organizations

Art and Creative Materials Institute, Inc., P.O. Box 479, Hanson, Boston, MA 02341. Provides the public with art and creative materials for children and artists that are nontoxic. All products in the program undergo extensive toxicological evaluation and testing before they are granted the right to bear the ACMI certification seal. www.acminet.org

Arts, Crafts and Theater Safety (ACTS), 181 Thompson Street, #23, New York, NY 10012-2586. A not-for-profit organization that provides health, safety, and industrial hygiene, technical services, and safety publications to the arts, crafts, museums, and theater communities. Provides copies of educational and technical materials and refers callers to doctors, health services, and other resources. Publishes the newsletter *ACTS FACTS* and various data sheets. www.artscraftstheatersafety.org

HEALTH INSURANCE AND MEDICAL PLANS
Publications

Artist's Assets. Artist Trust, 1835 12th Avenue, Seattle, WA 98122, revised 2006. A resource guide for artists in Washington State. Includes information about health insurance resources. www.artisttrust.org

Web Sites

Artist Access Program (www.nyfa.org/level3.asp?id=377&fid=6&sid=17). A new program sponsored by the Woodhull Medical and Mental Health Center. Allows artists in New York City to exchange their art for health-care credits, through performances or interactive programs for patients. Credits accrued in the artist's personal account can be used in lieu of dollars to cover sliding scale fees in Woodhull's HHC Options program.

Artist Help Network (www.artisthelpnetwork.com). Founded by Caroll Michels, career coach and artist-advocate, this site is devoted to all aspects of career development. See heading "Creature Comforts" and subheading "Health Insurance."

ArtistHealthSource.Org (www.artishealthsource.org). An organization that offers affordable, comprehensive health-care benefits designed for the artistic community.

Artists United for Healthcare (www.artistsunitedforhealthcare.org). Provides information on health-care options for artists in California.

Insurance Resources for Craftspeople (www.craftsreport.com/resources/insurance .htm). Lists guilds and arts associations that provide insurance for artists and other related information.

Organizations

The Al and Malka Green Artists' Health Centre, Toronto Western Hospital, 399 Bathurst Street, Toronto, Ontario, M5T 2S8 Canada. Promotes the well-being of professional artists with a facility that offers alternative, complementary, and traditional direct health care. www.ahcf.ca/centre.shtml

American Institute of Graphic Arts, 164 Fifth Avenue, New York, NY 10010. Offers members group health insurance. www.aiga.org

Arthouse, The Jones Center for Contemporary Art, 700 Congress Avenue, Austin, TX 78701. A membership organization for Texas artists. Offers members a group health insurance plan. www.arthousetexas.org

Artists' Access to Health Care (AAH), Springboard for the Arts, 308 Prince Street, Suite 270, St. Paul, MN 55101. Offers a low-cost medical-care plan to help uninsured and underinsured artists in the St. Paul, Minnesota, metropolitan area. www.springboardforthearts.org/services/aah.asp

Artists' Health Insurance Resource Center, The Actors' Fund, 729 Seventh Avenue, 10th Floor, New York, NY 10019. Provides the arts community information necessary to make informed choices about individual and small-business group health insurance options in all fifty states. Sponsors a toll-free telephone number (800-798-8447). www.actorsfund.org/ahirc

Artists Talk On Art, P.O. Box 1384, Old Chelsea Station, New York, NY 10113. Offers health insurance to members. www.artiststalkonart.org

Arts & Cultural Council for Greater Rochester, 277 North Goodman Street, Rochester, NY 14607. Offers group health insurance to artist-members who reside in the New York counties of Monroe, Livingston, Yates, Ontario, Seneca, and Wayne. www.artsrochester.org/artscouncil/health.htm

Arts Council in Buffalo and Erie County, 700 Main Street, Buffalo, NY 14202. Offers group health insurance to members who reside in the New York State counties of Allegany, Cattaraugus, Chautauqua, Erie, Genesee, Niagara, Orleans, and Wyoming. www.artscouncilbuffalo.org/artist_resources/insurance.asp

Arts Healthcare Coalition, Massachusetts Cultural Council, 10 St. James Avenue, 3rd Floor, Boston, MA 02116. Provides information about the statewide program that requires all Massachusetts residents over eighteen years of age to have health insurance. www.massculturalcouncil.org/healthcare/healthcare.htm

Center for Cultural Innovation, 244 S. San Pedro Street, Suite 401, Los Angeles, CA 90012 and 651 Brannon Street, Suite 410, San Francisco, CA 94107. Promotes knowledge, sharing, networking, and financial independence for individual artists and creative entrepreneurs in California. Offers group health insurance and dental insurance plans. http://cciarts.org

Chicago Artists' Coalition,70 E. Lake, Suite 230, Chicago, IL 60601. Offers group medical insurance to members. www.caconline.com

College Art Association of America, 275 Seventh Avenue, New York, NY 10001. Offers members group health insurance and life insurance. www.collegeart.org

Cultural Alliance of Greater Washington, 1436 U Street NW, Suite 103, Washington, DC 20009. Offers members health and dental insurance. www.cultural-alliance.org

Fractured Atlas, 248 W. 35th Street, Suite 1202, New York, NY 10001. A nonprofit organization that offers many support services to artist-members throughout the United States, including health insurance. www.fracturedatlas.org

Freelancers Union (formerly Working Today), 45 Main Street, Suite 710, Brooklyn, NY 11201. A national not-for-profit membership organization that promotes the interests of America's independent workforce, including freelancers and the self-employed. Eligible members have access to health insurance products. www.freelancersunion.org

Graphic Artists Guild, 32 Broadway, Suite 1114, New York, NY 10004. Offers members health insurance and dental insurance. www.gag.org

Healthcare for Artists, Artists Foundation, 516 East Second Street, #49, Boston, MA 02127. Assists Massachusetts artists in all disciplines in finding healthcare providers, health-care resources and information, and health-care advocacy organizations. Offers three programs for artists who are uninsured Massachusetts residents in conjunction with the South Boston Community Health Center. www.artistsfoundation.org/art_pages/resources/resources_healthcare_sbchc.htm

National Association for the Self-Employed, P.O. Box 612067, DFW Airport, TX 75261-2067. Offers health insurance to members. Membership is open to all self-employed persons. www.nase.org

National Women's Caucus for Art, P.O. Box 1498, Canal Street Station, New York, NY 10013. Membership organization open to women and men who are artists and others involved in the visual-arts field. Offers health insurance to members through Fractured Atlas. www.nationalwca.com

Ontario Crafts Council, 990 Queen Street West, Toronto, Ontario M6J 1H1, Canada. Members are eligible for group health insurance. www.craft.on.ca

PEN American Center, 588 Broadway, Suite 303, New York, NY 10012. Offers medical insurance at group rates to members. www.pen.org

Physician Volunteers for the Arts, 475 West 57th Street, 2nd Floor, New York, NY 10019. A free medical clinic in New York City for entertainment-industry professionals sponsored by the Actor's Fund of America and Broadway Cares/Equity Fights AIDS. (212-489-2020, ext. 140)

INTERIOR DESIGN AND ARCHITECTURE
Publications

AmericanStyle. 3000 Chestnut Avenue, Suite 504, Baltimore, MD 21211. Published bimonthly. Focuses on handmade objects, and covers decorating, interior design, lighting, designer jewelry, art glass, art furniture, and sculptural ceramics.

The Architect's Newspaper. 21 Murray Street, 5th Floor, New York, NY 10007. Published monthly. Covers projects and commissions and cultural developments related to architecture, with an emphasis on New York's tristate region. www.archpaper.com

Architectural Digest. 6300 Wilshire Boulevard, Suite 1100, Los Angeles, CA 90048-5204. Published monthly.

Architectural Record. 2 Penn Plaza, New York, NY 10121-0101. Published monthly.

Canadian Architect. 12 Concorde Place, Suite 800, Toronto, Ontario M3C 4J2, Canada. Published monthly. www.cdnarchitect.com

Contract. 770 Broadway, New York, NY 10003. Published monthly. Covers interior design, architecture, and furniture design.

Dwell. 40 Gold, San Francisco, CA 94133. Publishes ten issues per year. Focuses on the aesthetic in home design that is modern, idea-driven, and sensitive to social and physical surroundings.

Elle Decor. 1633 Broadway, New York, NY 10019-6708. Published ten times a year.

Harvard Design Magazine. 48 Quincy Street, Cambridge, MA 02138. Published biannually. Provides a forum on architecture, landscape architecture, and urban design and planning. Essays, book reviews, and features on recent projects.

House Beautiful. 300 W. 57th Street, New York, NY 10019. Published monthly.

Interior Design. 360 Park Avenue South, New York, NY 10010. Published monthly.

Interior Design, Landscape Design, and Architecture Press Contacts. Caroll Michels, career coach and artist-advocate, 1724 Burgos Drive, Sarasota, FL 34238. More than 180 writers, editors, and publications covering interior design, architecture, landscape architecture, and gardening. Updated on an ongoing basis. Available as a printout formatted for reproduction on labels. www.carollmichels.com

Interiors and Sources. P.O. Box 1888, Cedar Rapids, IA 52406-1888. Published nine times a year.

Landscape Architecture. 636 Eye Street NW, Washington, DC 20001-3736. Published monthly.

Metropolis. 61 West 23rd Street, New York, NY 10010. Published eleven times a year.

Metropolitan Home. 1633 Broadway, New York, NY 10019-6714. Published bimonthly.

Natural Home. 1503 SW 42nd Street, Topeka, KS 66609. Published bimonthly.

The Sourcebook of Architectural & Interior Art. The Guild, 931 East Main Street, Suite 9, Madison, WI 53703. A fee-based resource directory that contains the names, addresses, telephone numbers, and photographs of the work of American fine arts and craft artists, as well as biographical information. Distributed free of charge to more than 10,000 architects, interior designers, public art specialists, landscape architects, liturgical consultants, art consultants, and other professions. Published annually. www.guild.com

The Sourcebook of Residential Art. The Guild, 931 East Main Street, Suite 9, Madison, WI 53703. A fee-based resource directory that contains the names, addresses, telephone numbers, and photographs of the work of American fine arts and craft artists, as well as biographical information. Distributed free of charge to more than 7,000 art consultants, high-end consumers, residential design firms, architectural firms, and galleries. Published annually. www.guild.com

Southern Accents. 2100 Lakeshore Drive, Birmingham, AL 35209-6721. Published six times a year. www.southernaccents.com

Web Sites

Apartment Therapy (www.apartmenttherapy.com). Features design projects, furniture, and related items.

Archinect (www.archinect.com). A blog that includes news and feature items about the built environment.

Architect Finder (http://architectfinder.aia.org). A database for locating architects by building type and services they provide. Sponsored by the American Institute of Architects.

Architecture Ink (www.architectureink.com). A monthly journal of ideas and observations about the human environment.

Artist Help Network (www.artisthelpnetwork.com. Founded by Caroll Michels, career coach and artist-advocate, this site is devoted to all aspects of career development. See heading "Other Resources" and subheading "Design and Architecture Publications."

Bldg Blog (http://bldgblog.blogspot.com). Publishes projects related to architecture, the urban environment, and landscape design.

CasaSugar (http://casasugar.com). A home decorating and design blog.

Design Sponge (www.designsponge.blogspot.com). Features design projects, furniture, and related items.

Designboom (www.designboom.com). Publishes projects related to furniture, interiors, lighting design, etc.

Land & Living: Modern Lifestyle + Design (www.landliving.com). Features architecture, interior design, and landscape design projects, art, and more.

MocoLoco (www.mocoloco.com). Features projects related to contemporary architecture, design, and art, with news and views.

Reluct (www.reluct.com). Features design and architecture projects.

Sensory Impact (www.sensoryimpact.com). Features design and architecture-related projects.

Organizations

American Institute of Architects, 1735 New York Avenue NW, Washington, DC 20006. www.aia.org

American Society of Interior Designers, 608 Massachusetts Avenue NE, Washington, DC 20002-6006. www.asid.org

American Society of Landscape Architects, 636 Eye Street NW, Washington, DC 20001. www.asla.org

Also see "Corporate Art Market."

INTERNATIONAL CONNECTIONS

Publications

A-N Magazine. The Artists Information Company, 7–15 Pink Lane, Newcastle Upon Tyne NE1 5DW, United Kingdom. A monthly publication with a comprehensive listing of opportunities for artists primarily in the United Kingdom. www.a-n.co.uk

Angola Arts Directory. London: Visiting Arts, 1999. Available from Cornerhouse Publications, 70 Oxford Street, Manchester M1 5NH, United Kingdom. Includes general background information, and lists cultural agencies, arts venues, and resource centers. www.cornerhouse.org

Art Diary International. Giancarlo Politi Editore, P.O. Box 95, 06032 Borgo Trevei (PG) Italy. Published annually. Lists artists, galleries, museums, critics, organizations, agencies, and magazines.

The Art Newspaper. 78 South Lambeth Road, London SW8 1R2, United Kingdom. Also has an office in New York: 594 Broadway, Suite 406, New York, NY 10012. Contains a comprehensive account of international art news. Published eleven times a year.

Artists Communities by the Alliance of Artists Communities, edited by Robert MacNeil. New York: Allworth Press, revised 2005. A complete guide to artists-in-residence opportunities in the United States for visual and performing artists and writers. Features a special section that lists artists' communities, art agencies, and key contacts that support international artist exchanges.

Export Development of Artisanal Products by Caroline Ramsey Merriam and Malcolm Benjamin. The Crafts Center and the International Trade Center UNC-TAD/WTO. The Crafts Center at CHF International, 8601 Georgia Avenue, Suite 800, Silver Spring, MD 20910, 1998. A study that reviews the various steps and approaches for marketing handcrafts in international markets. www.craftscenter.org

Financial Aid for Research and Creative Activities Abroad by Gail A. Schachter and R. David Weber. San Carlos, Calif.: Reference Service Press, updated regularly.

Financial Aid for Study and Training Abroad by Gail A. Schachter and R. David Weber. San Carlos, Calif.: Reference Service Press, updated regularly.

Guide to Funding for International and Foreign Programs by Sara Wyszomierski. New York: The Foundation Center, revised 2006. Designed to help those seeking grants from U.S. corporations and foundations for international and foreign projects.

Hungary Arts Directory. London: Visiting Arts, 1999. Available from Cornerhouse Publications, 70 Oxford Street, Manchester M1 5NH, United Kingdom. Includes contacts across the cultural sectors, programs, technical and policy information, an overview of the country's arts scene, funding contacts, and practical guidelines on cultural exchange. www.cornerhouse.org

International Directory of the Arts. Munich: K. G. Saur Verlag, revised biennially. Three-volume guide to museums, universities, associations, dealers, galleries, publishers, and others involved in the arts in Europe, the United States, Canada, South America, Asia, and Australia.

Israel Arts Directory. London: Visiting Arts, 1999. Available from Cornerhouse Publications, 70 Oxford Street, Manchester M1 5NH, United Kingdom. Includes contacts across the cultural sectors, programs, technical and policy information, an overview of the country's arts scene, funding contacts, and practical guidelines on cultural exchange. www.cornershouse.org

London Art and Artists Guide by Heather Waddell. London Art and Artists Guide, 27 Holland Park Avenue, London W11 3RW, United Kingdom, revised 2005. Provides details of contemporary galleries, including the types of work shown and contact information, studio information, press contacts, and more.

Norway Arts Directory. London: Visiting Arts, 1999. Available from Cornerhouse Publications, 70 Oxford Street, Manchester M1 5NH, United Kingdom. Includes contacts across the cultural sectors, programs, technical and policy information, an overview of the country's arts scene, funding contacts and practical guidelines on cultural exchange. www.cornerhouse.org

On the Road Again: Developing and Managing Traveling Exhibitions by Rebecca A. Buck and Jean Allman Gilmore. Washington, D.C.: American Association of Museums, 2003. Covers dealing with foreign custom officials when shipping work abroad.

Performing Arts Yearbook for Europe, edited by Wiebke Morgan. Alain Charles Publishing Ltd., revised 2006. Lists more than 14,000 organizations in fifty countries, including ministries of culture, funding agencies, national organizations, networks, resource centers, arts centers, promoters, agents, festivals, and publications.

Quebec Arts Directory. London: Visiting Arts, 2000. Available from Cornerhouse Publications, 70 Oxford Street, Manchester M1 5NH, United Kingdom. Includes contacts across the cultural sectors, programs, technical and policy information, an overview of the country's arts scene, funding contacts, and practical guidelines on cultural exchange. www.cornerhouse.org

South Africa Arts Directory. London: Visiting Arts, 1999. Available from Cornerhouse Publications, 70 Oxford Street, Manchester M1 5NH, United Kingdom. Includes contacts across the cultural sectors, programs, technical and policy information, an overview of the arts scene, funding contacts, and practical guidelines on cultural exchange. www.cornerhouse.org

Zero Gravity: Diary of a Travelling Artist by Elizabeth Bram, 1995. Available from Elizabeth Bram, 4 Prospect Street, Baldwin, NY 11510. A detailed account of the adventures and impressions of an American artist who took the initiative to explore exhibition opportunities abroad and in the United States and in Canada.

Web Sites

Art Beyond Borders (www.artbeyondborders.org). An international project of artists who use the Web to exchange ideas and information and to organize exhibitions in members' respective countries. Open to artists worldwide.

Art Education Australia (www.arteducation.com.au). Links to Australian art schools.

Art Forum (www.artforum.com.au). A chat room devoted to all aspects of Australian art, including career opportunities for artists.

Art World City (www.artworldcity.com). Includes an Artworld Directory with information on Canadian art associations, art schools, galleries, and more.

Artist Help Network (www.artisthelpnetwork.com). Founded by Caroll Michels, career coach and artist-advocate, this site is devoted to all aspects of career development. See heading "Exhibitions, Commissions and Sales" and subheading "International Connections."

Fuel4artists (www.fuel4artists.com). International art marketing and career development resources.

German Galleries (www.germangalleries.com). A site that features German galleries.

Visual Artist Management Project: (VAM-P) (http://vam-p.net/vam_p.html). Offers a very reasonably priced database called "Venue Viewer" compiled by artist Brian David Dennis of nearly 8,200 national and international galleries with Web sites and, when possible, it includes a contact person's name.

World Wide Arts Resources (www.wwar.com). Links to international galleries and resources.

Organizations

American Academy in Rome, 7 East 60th Street, New York, NY 10021. An American study and advanced research center in the fine arts and humanities. Sponsors the Rome Prize Fellowship and other residency programs. www.aarome.org

American Council on Germany, 14 East 60th Street, Suite 1000, New York, NY 10022. Awards professional fellowships annually to promising young Germans and Americans in a variety of fields, including the arts. www.acgusa.org

The American Scandinavian Foundation, 58 Park Avenue, New York, NY 10016. Awards fellowships and grants to professionals and scholars, including those in the creative and performing arts, born in the United States or Scandinavian countries. www.amscan.org

A-N. The Artists Information Company, 7–15 Pink Lane, Newcastle Upon Tyne NE1 5DW, United Kingdom. Sponsors publications, programs, and projects that widen artists' access to professional-development information. www.a-n.co.uk

Bellagio Center Creative Arts Fellowship Program, Rockefeller Foundation, 420 Fifth Avenue, New York, NY 10018. Offers residencies in Como, Italy, to artists, composers, and writers. www.rockfound.org/bellagio/bellagio.shtml

CECArtsLink, Inc., 435 Hudson Street, 8th Floor, New York, NY 10014. Sponsors exchanges between American artists and artists from Central Europe, Russia, and Eurasia. www.cecartslink.org

Res Artis, The International Association of Residential Art Centres and Networks, Arie Biemondstraat 105, 1054 PD, Amsterdam, The Netherlands. An organization composed of arts centers and artists' organizations that encourage the development of contemporary art and artists through residential exchange programs. www.resartis.org

Trans Artists, Arie Biemondstraat 105, 1054 PD, Amsterdam, The Netherlands. A foundation that provides artists working in all disciplines with information about international artist-in-residence programs and other opportunities. www.transartists.nl

U.S./Japan Creative Artists' Program, Japan/U.S. Friendship Commission, 1201 15th Street NW, Suite 330, Washington, DC 20005. Provides six-month residences in Japan for individual artists in all disciplines. Artists work on individual projects, which may include the creation of new work or other pursuits related to their artistic goals. www.jusfc.gov/creativeartists.asp

Visiting Arts, 4.01 & 4.02 Enterprise House, 1–2 Hatfields, London SE1 9PG, United Kingdom. Promotes and facilitates the inward flow of international arts into England, Scotland, Wales, and Northern Ireland in the context of contributions they can make to cultural relations, cultural awareness, and fostering mutually beneficial international arts contacts and activities at national, regional, local, and institutional levels. www.visitingarts.org.uk

INTERNET ART MARKETING

Publications

Aiming at Amazon: The New Business of Self-Publishing, or How to Publish Books for Profit with Print on Demand by Lightning Source and Book Marketing on Amazon.com by Aaron Shepard. Shepard Publications, 2007.

Best in Self-Publishing & Print on Demand by David Rising. Pt. Reyes Station, Calif.: Reality Publishing Ink, revised 2006. Provides marketing and promotion strategies for self-published books.

Complete Guide to Internet Publicity by Steve O'Keefe. New York: John Wiley, 2002. Provides information on vehicles for obtaining Internet publicity, including search engine optimization, newsletters, email merge programs, syndication, and more.

Internet 101 for Artists by Constance Smith with Susan Greaves. Nevada City, Calif.: Artnetwork Press, revised 2007. For Internet beginners as well as those who are more advanced. Topics include acquiring a URL; designing your Web site; meta tags; promotional techniques to attract clients to your site; pay-per-click advertising; guerrilla marketing tactics; search engines; tracking visitors to your site; and selling art through eBay, Internet lingo; doing business via email; email communication shortcuts; and creative tricks for research on the Web.

Marketing and Buying Fine Art Online: A Guide for Artists and Collectors by Marques Vickers. Allworth Press, 2005. Walks artists through the process of establishing an effective Web site geared to attract viewers and promote sales. Filled with more than 1,200 Internet resources.

The New Rules of Marketing and PR: How to Use News Releases, Blogs, Podcasting, Viral Marketing and Online Media to Reach Buyers Directly by David

Meerman Scott. Hoboken, N.J.: John Wiley, 2007. Provides the technical novice with an accessible guide to cutting-edge media arenas and formats.

101 Ways to Promote Your Web Site by Susan Sweeney. Gulf Breeze, Fla.: Maximum Press, revised 2008. Filled with proven Internet marketing tips, tools, techniques, and resources to increase Web site traffic.

Online Art Marketing by Steven Marwick. An ebook written by the founder of an online marketing agency. www.onlineartmarketing.com

Poor Richard's Web Site Marketing Makover: Improve Your Message and Turn Visitors into Buyers by Marcia Yudkin. Denver, Colo.: Top Floor Publishing, 2001. Delves into the details that make or break a Web site. It shows how to transform a site to generate more interest. Topics covered include gathering leads, marketing copy, content as bait, and graphics and layout. Also included are complete sample makeovers and commentary on ten different kinds of sites, including multiproduct sales.

Print on Demand Book Publishing: A New Approach to Printing and Marketing Books for Publishers and Self-Publishing Authors by Morris Rosenthal. Foner Books, 2004.

Web Sites

Artist Help Network (www.artisthelpnetwork.com). Founded by Caroll Michels, career coach and artist-advocate, this site is devoted to all aspects of career development. See heading "Presentation Tools" and subheading "Web Site Design" and heading "Exhibitions, Commissions and Sales" and subheading "Online Galleries."

Artists Web Wiki (www.theartistsweb.net/wiki/Main_Page). See articles "How to Get an Artists Website," "Preparing Images for the Web," "How to Get Your Artists Site In Search Engines," "and 'Building a Website for Selling Art Online."

Blogging News (www.blogging-news.info/self-hosted-blog-options). "Self Hosted Blog Options."

Blurb.com (www.blurb.com). Print-on-demand publishing service.

Constant Content (www.constantcontact.com). An email marketing service. Offers mailing list management. Provides templates for producing newsletters, invitations, and cards.

eHow (www.ehow.com/how_2289008_networking-sites-help-business-grow.html). Adrianne Fritze, "How to Use Social Networking Sites to Help Your Business Grow."

Empty Easel (http://emptyeasel.com/selling-art-online). Selling Art Online. Information on Where (and How) to Sell Art on the Internet. Posts information and advice about selling art online.

EzineArticles.com (http://ezinearticles.com/?Remote-Blog-or-Self-Hosted-Blog?&id=1101009). "Remote Blog or Self Hosted Blog?" by Chris Haycock.

Google Analytics (www.google.com/analytics). A free service that generates detailed statistics about Web site and blog visitors.

Lulu.com (www.lulu.com). Print-on-demand publishing service.

Ready Set Connect Insider Blog (http://blog.readysetconnect.com/2008/05/advantages-of-self-hosted-blogs). Discusses the advantages of hosting your own blog.

Web Pages That Suck (www.webpagesthatsuck.com). If you are contemplating
   designing a Web site or are having one designed, this Web site presents information on the do's and don'ts of Web site design.
Also see "Press Relations and Publicity."

LAW: CONTRACTS AND BUSINESS FORMS
Publications

Artist Business Forms: Creating a Successful Career in Photography by Dan Fear.
   Art-Support, 1717 150th Avenue SE, #16, Bellevue, WA 98007. An ebook with
   thirty-five business forms and contracts for exhibiting and selling artwork.
   www.art-support.com
Artist/Dealer Checklist: What Should You Include in an Agreement with a Dealer?
   CARFAC Ontario, 401 Richmond Street West, Suite 440, Toronto, Ontario
   M5V 3A8, Canada. For Canadian artists. Available online to CARFAC Ontario
   members. www.carfacontario.ca
*Artist/Exhibition Checklist: What Should You Include in an Agreement with a
   Dealer?* CARFAC Ontario, 401 Richmond Street West, Suite 440, Toronto,
   Ontario M5V 3A8, Canada. For Canadian artists. Available online to CARFAC
   Ontario members. www.carfacontario.ca
The Artist-Gallery Partnership: A Practical Guide to Consigning Art by Tad Craw-
   ford and Susan Mellon. New York: Allworth Press, revised 2008. Offers a clear
   explanation of consignment contracts. Provides information on consignment
   laws on a state-by-state basis.
Artists Contracts: Agreements for Visual and Media Artists by Paul Sanderson and
   Ron H. Heir. CARFAC Ontario, 401 Richmond Street West, Suite 440,
   Toronto, Ontario M5V 3A8, Canada, 2006. Includes model contracts pertinent
   to visual and media artists in Canada. www.carfacontario.ca
The Artists' Survival Manual: A Complete Guide to Marketing Your Work by Toby
   Judith Klayman with Cobbett Steinberg. Originally published by Charles Scribner's Sons, the book is now being published by Toby Judith Klayman and Joseph
   Branchcomb, revised in 1996. See sample contracts in appendix section.
Business and Legal Forms for Crafts by Tad Crawford. New York: Allworth Press,
   revised 2005. Contains thirty ready-to-use forms with detailed instructions
   and negotiation checklists. Includes forms for sales, commissions, limited editions, exhibition loans, gallery agreements, consignments, licensing contracts,
   and permission forms. A CD-ROM with electronic versions of each form is also
   provided.
Business and Legal Forms for Fine Artists by Tad Crawford. New York: Allworth
   Press, revised 2005. Contains twenty-six ready-to-use contracts and forms
   detailed for a variety of situations, including artist-gallery agreements, licensing
   agreements, contracts for sales, commissions, and limited editions. A CD-ROM
   with electronic versions of each form is also provided.
Business and Legal Forms for Illustrators by Tad Crawford. New York: Allworth
   Press, revised 1998. It includes twenty-one forms accompanied by instructions,
   advice, and negotiation checklists. Forms include licensing of electronic rights,

contracts for the sale of artwork, and agreements with agents, collaborators, book publishers, galleries, and licensing. A CD-ROM with electronic versions of each form is also provided.

Business and Legal Forms for Photographers by Tad Crawford. New York: Allworth Press, revised 2002. Includes negotiation tactics and twenty-eight forms, including electronic rights and sample contracts and instructions for a variety of situations. A CD-ROM with electronic versions of each form is also provided.

An Introduction to Artists' Legal Agreements. CARFAC Ontario, 401 Richmond Street West, Suite 440, Toronto, Ontario M5V 3A8, Canada. For Canadian artists. Available online to CARFAC Ontario members. www.carfacontario.ca

The Rights of Authors, Artists, and Other Creative People. Carbondale, Ill.: Southern Illinois University Press in cooperation with the American Civil Liberties Union, revised 1992. Explains how authors and visual artists can protect themselves and their work under the present law. Discusses contracts between writers and artists and their agents, collaborators, publishers, and galleries.

Web Sites

Artist Help Network (www.artisthelpnetwork.com). Founded by Caroll Michels, career coach and artist-advocate, this site is devoted to all aspects of career development. See heading "Legal" and subheading "Contracts & Forms."

California Resale Royalty Act (www.cac.ca.gov/resaleroyaltyact/resaleroyaltyact .php). Includes detailed information about the California Resale Royalty Act with recommendations to artists about exercising their rights. Provided by the California Arts Council.

St. Louis Volunteer Lawyers and Accountants for the Arts (www.vlaa.org/ publications.asp). Provides downloadable publications, including *Guide to Artist-Gallery Contracts* and *Anatomy of a Contract.*

LAW: COPYRIGHTS, PATENTS, AND TRADEMARKS
Publications

Canadian Copyright Law by Lesley Ellen Harris. Toronto: McGraw-Hill Ryerson Limited, revised 2001. Written for visual and performing artists and writers. Includes information on current copyright laws in Canada.

Copyright for Performing, Literary and Visual Artists. Texas Accountants and Lawyers for the Arts, 1540 Sul Ross, Houston, TX 77006. Explains copyright as it applies to musical, literary, and visual works of art. www.talarts.org

The Copyright Guide: A Friendly Guide to Protecting and Profiting from Copyright by Lee Wilson. New York: Allworth Press, revised 2004. Reflects recent changes in the U.S. copyright law. Includes information for artists and those interested in understanding and benefiting from copyrights in the Information Age.

Electronic Highway Robbery: An Artist's Guide to Copyrights in the Digital Era by Mary E. Carter. Berkeley, Calif.: Peachpit Press, 1996. A guide to copyright law as it applies to the digital-arts market.

The Patent Guide: A Friendly Guide to Protecting and Profiting from Patents by Carl W. Battle. New York: Allworth Press, 1997. A step-by-step guide to apply for a patent. Follows an application through the Patent Office, shows how to select legal representation if needed, and concludes with information on infringement procedures, foreign protection options, and licensing and marketing.

The Trademark Guide: A Friendly Guide for Protecting and Profiting from Trademarks by Lee Wilson. New York: Allworth Press, revised 2004. An introduction to trademark protection with tips for creating trademarks and pitfalls to watch out for when using or licensing a trademark.

Web Sites

Artist Help Network (www.artisthelpnetwork.com). Founded by Caroll Michels, career coach and artist-advocate, this site is devoted to all aspects of career development. See heading "Legal" and subheading "Copyrights, Trademarks & Patents."

Copyright and Art Issues (http://darkwing.uoregon.edu/~csundt/copyweb). Provides numerous resources that address various arts-related copyright issues. Compiled by Christine Sundt.

Copyright Basics (www.vlaa.org/publications.asp). Written by Sue Greenberg with Terry Mahoney. Sponsored by the St. Louis Volunteer Lawyers and Accountants for the Arts. Revised 2004.

Copyright Registration for Works of the Visual Arts, Circular 40 (www.copyright .gov/circs/circ40.html#effective). Copyright Office, Library of Congress. Provides good background information about obtaining a copyright for visual art.

Demystifying Copyright (www.carfacontario.ca/resources/demystifying_copyright). A downloadable publication by Kellie Cullihall and Brian Perry, sponsored by CARFAC Ontario. Includes general information about copyright and specific information for visual artists.

Organizations

Artists Rights Society, 536 Broadway, 5th Floor, New York, NY 10012. Protects the rights and permissions interests of artists within the United States. Monitors the reproduction, publication, merchandising, advertising, or public display of artworks by member artists. www.arsny.com

Canadian Artists Representation Copyright Collective (CARCC), 109A 4th Avenue, Ottawa, Ontario K1S 2L3, Canada. Creates opportunities for increased income for visual and media artists. Provides services to artists affiliated with the collective, including negotiating the terms for copyright use and issuing an appropriate license to the user. www.carcc.ca

Copyright Office, Library of Congress, 101 Independence Avenue SE, Washington, DC 20559-6000. Copyright application forms can be obtained from this address. www.loc.gov/copyright

Design and Artists Copyright Society, 33 Great Sutton Street, London EC1V 0DX, United Kingdom. Rachel Duffield and Mimmi Pinnington. Represents visual artists and protects members' copyright interests. Gives advice, checks on infringements, and collects reproduction fees. Also publishes fact sheets on copyright clearance and other matters. www.dacs.co.uk

United States Patent and Trademark Office, Commissioner for Patents, P.O. Box 1450, Alexandria, VA 22313-1450 and Commissioner for Trademarks, P.O. Box 1451, Alexandria, VA 22313-1451. www.uspto.gov

LAW: ESTATE PLANNING
Publications

Artists' Estates: Reputations in Trust edited by Magda Salvesen and Diane Cousineau. New Brunswick, N.J.: Rutgers University Press, 2005. Surveys the lives of important twentieth-century American artists and the management of their accumulated works. Opens a window into the problems of taxes, wills, and trusts, the inheritors' role in conservation, succession, and interpretation, and the responsibility for our visual heritage.

The Business of Art, edited by Lee Caplin. Upper Saddle River, N.J.: Prentice Hall Press, revised 2000. See "Estate and Gift Tax Planning."

Estate Planning and Administration: How to Maximize Assets, Minimize Taxes, and Protect Loved Ones by Edmund T. Fleming. New York: Allworth Press, revised 2005. Covers wills, trusts, powers of attorney, health-care directives, probate, and settling an estate.

A Legal Guide for Lesbian and Gay Couples by Hayden Curry, Frederick Hertzl, and Emily Doskow. Berkeley, Calif.: Nolo Press, revised 2007. A detailed legal survey of the laws affecting gay and lesbian couples, including estate planning.

Legal Guide for the Visual Artist by Tad Crawford. New York: Allworth Press, revised 1999. See chapter "The Artist's Estate."

Plan Your Estate by Denis Clifford and Cora Jordan. Berkeley, Calif.: Nolo Press, revised 2000. Explains the use of wills, trusts, and other planning devices, and suggests ways to minimize estate taxes and maneuver through probate. Sample estate plans are included. www.nolo.com

A Visual Artist's Guide to Estate Planning. Marie Walsh Sharpe Art Foundation, 711 North Tejon, Suite B, Colorado Springs, CO 80903, revised 2007. Introduces general estate-planning concepts and offers practical advice and a discussion of legal issues. Also includes an in-depth discussion of policy and law on selected issues of estate planning and administration for visual artists. Only available online. www.sharpeartfdn.org/supplement/supplement08.htm

A Visual Artist's Guide to Estate Planning, 2008 Supplement Update. Marie Walsh Sharpe Art Foundation, 711 North Tejon, Suite B, Colorado Springs, CO 80903, updated 2008. Updates information regarding changes in tax and copyright laws pertaining to artists' estates and other pertinent information. Only available online. www.sharpeartfdn.org/supplement/supplement08.htm

Your Living Trust and Estate Plan: How to Maximize Your Family's Assets and Protect Your Loved Ones by Harvey J. Platt. New York: Allworth Press, revised 2002. A guide to using a living trust to create a flexible estate plan. Covers estate planning for small business owners and others with special needs.

Web Sites

Artist Help Network (www.artisthelpnetwork.com). Founded by Caroll Michels, career coach and artist-advocate, this site is devoted to all aspects of career development. See heading "Legal" and subheading "Estate Planning."

Estate Planning for Artists (www.seniorartistsinitiative.org/01_about_sai/guidelines_louis.html). Provides basic information for artists regarding estate planning. Written by Robert H. Louis, Esq.

Future Safe: A Guide to Planning for the Future of Your Art in All Disciplines (www.artistswithaids.org/planning/index.html). Sponsored by the Estate Project for Artists with AIDS, Alliance for the Arts. A guide with information on estate planning for artists.

A Life in Dance: A Guide to Dance Preservation and Estate Planning for Dance Artists (www.artistswithaids.org/planning/index.html). Sponsored by the Estate Project for Artists with AIDS, Alliance for the Arts. A guide with information on estate planning for dancers.

Organizations

The Art Connection, 539 Tremont Street, Boston, MA 02116. An art donation and placement program for artists and collectors who want to donate artwork to public and nonprofit organizations. Serves as an art clearinghouse, simplifying the donation process and offering a wide range of original works for selection by qualifying nonprofit agencies. There are similar organizations in Baltimore, San Francisco, and Washington, DC. www.theartconnection.org

Art for Healing, Inc., 230 Scott Street, San Francisco, CA 94117. Accepts donations of art for free loans to health-care facilities, including Ronald McDonald House, cancer projects, AIDS hospices, general hospitals, and homes for the aged. www.artforhealing.org

Estate Project for Artists with AIDS, Alliance for the Arts, 330 West 42nd Street, Suite 1701, New York, NY 10036. Provides practical estate-planning advice to all artists, especially those living with HIV/AIDS. www.artistswithaids.org

Volunteers Lawyers for the Arts, Artist Legacy Project, 1 East 53rd Street, New York, NY 10022. Provides free and specialized estate planning and related legal services to artists. www.vlany.org/legalservices/legacy.php

LAW: FORMING A NOT-FOR-PROFIT ORGANIZATION

Publications

The Art of Creating Nonprofit Organizations by Peter Wolk. Washington Area Lawyers for the Arts and Volunteer Lawyers for the Arts, New York. Available from Volunteer Lawyers for the Arts, 1 East 53rd Street, 6th Floor, New York, NY 10022-4201. A booklet that explains the pros and cons of corporate status, legal responsibilities and requirements, and alternatives to incorporation. www.vlany.org

Getting Organized: A Not-for-Profit Manual. New York: Lawyers Alliance of New York, 1994. Available from Volunteer Lawyers for the Arts, 1 East 53rd Street, 6th Floor, New York, NY 10022-4201. A comprehensive handbook on forming a not-for-profit organization. Includes a detailed discussion of New York State not-for-profit law. www.vlany.org

How to Form a Non-Profit Corporation by Anthony Mancuso. Berkeley, Calif.: Nolo Press, revised 2005. Explains the legal formalities involved in forming and operating a tax-exempt, nonprofit corporation.

LAW: GENERAL RESOURCES

Publications

Art, Artifact & Architecture Law by Jessica L. Darraby. St. Paul, Minn.: Clark Boardman Callaghan, West Group, revised 2003. Discusses policies and laws concerning the creation, display, production, distribution, and preservation of visual art. Web site: www.cbclegal.com

Art Law: The Guide for Collectors, Investors, Dealers and Artists by Ralph E. Lerner and Judith Bresler. New York: Practicing Law Institute, revised 2005.

Art Law Handbook, edited by Roy S. Kaufman. New York: Aspen Law & Business, revised 2004. Covers legal aspects relating to new media, copyright, intellectual property protection, international art transactions, taxes, trusts, and estate planning for artists, gallery-artist relationships, business structures for artists, and more. Includes a CD-ROM of forms and contracts.

An Artist's Guide to Small Claims Court. Volunteer Lawyers for the Arts, 1 East 53rd Street, 6th Floor, New York, NY 10022-4201, revised 1994. A step-by-step guide for preparing a case in New York City's small-claims court. www.vlany.org/forms/PublicationCatalog.pdf

Business Entities for Artists by Mark Quail. CARFAC Ontario, 401 Richmond Street West, Suite 440, Toronto, Ontario M5V 3A8, Canada, revised 1996. Summarizes information on sole proprietorships and corporations for Canadian artists, with tax perspectives, registration, and legal liability. Available online to CARFAC Ontario members. www.carfacontario.ca

Columbia Journal of Law and the Arts. Columbia University Law School, 435 West 116th Street, New York, NY 10027. Published quarterly. A student-edited publication dedicated to up-to-date and in-depth coverage of various legal issues related to art. www.lawandarts.org

Ethics in the Visual Arts, edited by Elaine A. King and Gail Levin. New York: Allworth Press, 2006. An anthology of essays by nineteen artists and art world figures covering a broad range of urgent topics related to the "dark side" of the arts, including preservation of Iraqi heritage in the aftermath of the U.S. invasion; the role of new media; art and censorship; the impact of 9/11 on artists; authenticity and forgeries; cultural globalization; fair use; how tax laws encourage donations of art to museums; how art critics function and their differing ethical codes; and much more.

Journal of Art and Entertainment Law. DePaul University College of Law, 25 E. Jackson Boulevard, Room 712, Chicago, IL 60604. Published twice a year by the students of the DePaul University College of Law in cooperation with Chicago Lawyers for the Creative Arts. Up-to-date analysis of contemporary legal issues affecting the art and entertainment communities. http://condor .depaul.edu/~journae/entmain.html

The Law (in Plain English) for Crafts by Leonard Duboff. New York: Allworth Press, revised 2005. Helps crafts artists understand the law and tackle the business and legal issues they face each day.

The Law (in Plain English) for Galleries by Leonard D. Duboff. New York: Allworth Press, revised 1999. Covers all legal aspects of gallery business—from trademarks and copyright to contracts, consignments, taxes, product liability, advertising, catalog sales, and customer relations. The author also advises on how to find a good lawyer.

The Law (in Plain English) for Photographers by Leonard D. DuBoff. New York: Allworth Press, revised 2002. Drawing from examples of real cases, this book discusses everyday legal and business issues affecting professional photography. Topics include copyright, defamation and libel, censorship and obscenity, business organization and taxes, working and living space, contracts and remedies, agents, estate planning, and digitalization.

Legal Guide for the Visual Artist by Tad Crawford. New York: Allworth Press, revised 1999. Provides updated legal information and vital data on new media and electronic rights. Covers copyright and moral rights; sale of art by artist, gallery, or agent; sale of reproduction rights, including assignment confirmations, licensing, and book contracts; taxation, hobby-loss challenges, and the IRS; studios and leases; and estate planning. Model contracts are also included.

Visual Artist's Business and Legal Guide, edited by Gregory T. Victoroff. Englewood Cliffs, N.J.: Prentice-Hall, 1995. Offers business and legal information about such matters as selling, promotion, copyrights, licenses, privacy, art destruction, fraud, fund-raising, and grants. Also includes artists' contracts with comments by lawyers on negotiable clauses.

Your Crafts Business: A Legal Guide by Richard Stim. Berkeley, Calif.: Nolo Press, 2003. Covers a wide range of issues, including contracts, copyrights, preventing infringement, getting your crafts business on the Internet, and more.

Web Sites

Art Law (www.tfaoi.com/articles/andres/aa1.htm). Attorney Ann Avery Andres gives legal advice to artists.

Artist Help Network (www.artisthelpnetwork.com). Founded by Caroll Michels, career coach and artist-advocate, this site is devoted to all aspects of career development. See heading "Legal" and subheading "Art Law Resources."

Guide to Small Claims Court (www.vlaa.org/publications.asp). Sponsored by the St. Louis Volunteer Lawyers and Accountants for the Arts. Prepared by Sue Greenberg and revised by Kathryn Lamont.

Resource Handbook for Minnesota Artists (www.springboardforthearts.org/Resources/Resources.asp). Sponsored by Springboard for the Arts. A listing of resources for Minnesota artists, including business and legal services.

Starving Artists Law (www.starvingartistslaw.com). Provides resources to artists and writers who are looking for self-help legal information.

LAW: LEGISLATION AND ARTS ADVOCACY
Publications

Censorship and the Arts: Law, Controversy, Debate, Facts by Brenda Cossman. The Ontario Association of Art Galleries, 111 Peter Street, Suite 617, Toronto, Ontario M5V 2H1, Canada, 1995. An overview of art censorship in Canada. www.oaag.org

The Cultural Battlefield: Art Censorship & Public Funding. Edited by Jennifer A. Peter and Louis M. Crosier. Gilsom, Mass.: Avocus Publishing, 1997. Offers perspectives on the validity of public funding, the meaning of obscenity, and targets of censorship. It also explores why and how the government has tried to stifle artistic expression that challenges the status quo.

Understanding, Preparing, and Responding to Challenges to Your Freedom of Artistic Expression by David Greene. Published by the National Campaign for Freedom of Expression. Available from Volunteer Lawyers for the Arts, 1 East 53rd Street, 6th Floor, New York, NY 10022-4201. Provides an overview of legal concepts, tips for organizing and empowering local arts communities, summaries of past incidents, examples of censored work, and a resource directory. www.vlany.org

Web Sites

Artist Help Network. (www.artisthelpnetwork.com) Founded by Caroll Michels, career coach and artist-advocate, this site is devoted to all aspects of career development. See heading "Legal" and subheading "Arts Legislation and Advocacy."

Organizations

Americans for the Arts, 1000 Vermont Avenue NW, 6th Floor, Washington, DC 20005. New York office: 1 East 53rd Street, 2nd Floor, New York, NY 10022. National organization that provides information on legislative issues and government policies affecting the arts. Also promotes the development of the arts by strengthening the role of local arts agencies. www.artsusa.org

Arts Advocacy Project, National Coalition Against Censorship, 275 Seventh Avenue, New York, NY 10001. Devoted to the protection of artists' rights to participate in the democratic dialogue by defending public access to their work and supporting their ability to freely express views that might be unpopular or controversial. www.ncac.org/advocacy_projects/Arts_Advocacy.cfm

CARFAC-BC, P.O. Box 2359, Vancouver, British Columbia V6B 3W5, Canada. A regional branch of a national advocacy organization for Canadian artists. www.carfacbc.org

CARFAC Manitoba, 407-100 Arthur Street, Winnipeg, Manitoba MB R3B 1H3, Canada. An advocacy organization that provides career-related services and publications for artists. www.carfac.mb.ca

CARFAC Maritimes, 732 Charlotte Street, Fredericton, New Brunswick. E3B 1M5, Canada. An advocacy organization for artists in Nova Scotia, New Brunswick, and Prince Edward Island. cf.maritimes@nb.aibn.com

CARFAC National, 2 Daly Avenue, Suite 250, Ottawa, Ontario K1N 6E2, Canada. A national advocacy organization for Canadian artists. www.carfac.ca

CARFAC Ontario, 401 Richmond Street West, Suite 440, Toronto, Ontario M5V 3A8, Canada. A regional branch of an advocacy organization for Canadian artists. www.carfacontario.ca

CARFAC Saskatchewan (Regina), 1734-A-Dewdney Avenue, Regina, Saskatchewan SR4 1G6, Canada. A regional branch of a national advocacy organization for Canadian artists. www.carfac.sk.ca

CARFAC Saskatchewan (Saskatoon), #412, 220 3rd Avenue South, Saskatoon, Saskatchewan S7K 1M1, Canada. A regional branch of a national advocacy organization for Canadian artists. www.carfac.sk.ca

CARFAC-VANL: Visual Arts Newfoundland and Labrador, Devon House, 59 Duckworth Street, St. John's A1C 1E6, Newfoundland, Canada. A regional branch of CARFAC, a national advocacy organization for Canadian artists. vanl-carfac@nf.aibn.com

Graphic Artists Guild, 32 Broadway, Suite 1114, New York, NY 10004. National membership organization with local chapters throughout the United States. Advances the rights and interests of graphic artists through legislative reform. www.gag.org

The National Association of Independent Artists, 1426 Hazen SE, Grand Rapids, MI 49507-3713. Dedicated to the professional and economic success of its membership. Serves as a vocal advocate for improvement in the artist profession. http://naia-artists.org

Visual Arts Newfoundland and Labrador (VANL), Devon House, 59 Duckworth Street, St. John's A1C 1E6, Newfoundland. A regional branch of CARFAC, a national advocacy organization for Canadian artists. vanl@thezone.net

LAW: ORGANIZATIONS

Publications

VLA Listing of NYC Attorneys. Volunteer Lawyers for the Arts, 1 East 53rd Street, New York, NY 10022-4201. A comprehensive list of lawyers in the New York area that are interested in representing artists and arts organizations. www.vlany.org/forms/PublicationCatalog.pdf

Web Sites

Artist Help Network (www.artisthelpnetwork.com). Founded by Caroll Michels, career coach and artist-advocate, this site is devoted to all aspects of career development. See heading "Legal" and subheadings "Art Law Organizations" and "Art Law Organizations Abroad."

VLA National Directory (www.vlany.org/legalservices/vladirectory.php). A directory of various Volunteer Lawyers for the Arts programs and art-law organizations throughout the United States and Canada and Australia Volunteer Lawyers for the Arts.

Organizations

CALIFORNIA

Barristers Committee for the Arts, Beverly Hills Bar Association, P.O. Box 7277, Beverly Hills, CA 90212. Serves artists in Los Angeles County. www.bhba.org

California Lawyers for the Arts, 1127 11th Street, Suite 214, Sacramento, CA 95814. Serves artists in California. Also handles requests from artists outside of the state. www.calawyersforthearts.org

California Lawyers for the Arts, C-255, Fort Mason Center, San Francisco, CA 94123. Serves artists in California. Also handles requests from artists outside of the state. www.calawyersforthearts.org

California Lawyers for the Arts, 1641 18th Street, Santa Monica, CA 90404. Serves artists in California. Also handles requests from artists outside of the state. www.calawyersforthearts.org

Center for Cultural Innovation, 244 S. San Pedro Street, Suite 401, Los Angeles, CA 90012 and 651 Brannon Street, Suite 410, San Francisco, CA 94107. Provides legal services to artists. http://cciarts.org

Lawyers for the Arts, San Diego Performing Arts League, 111 W. C Street, Suite 1414, San Diego, CA 92101. Serves artists in San Diego county. www.sandiego performs.com/volunteer/lawyer_arts.html

COLORADO

Colorado Lawyers for the Arts, P.O. Box 48148, Denver, CO 80204. Serves artists in Colorado. www.coloradoartslawyers.org

CONNECTICUT

Connecticut Volunteer Lawyers for the Arts, Connecticut Commission on Culture and Tourism, One Constitution Plaza, 2nd Floor, Hartford, CT 06103. Serves artists in Connecticut. www.cultureandtourism.org

DISTRICT OF COLUMBIA

Washington Area Lawyers for the Arts, 901 New York Avenue NW, Suite P1, Washington, DC 20001-4413. Serves artists in Washington, D.C., Northern Virginia, Delaware, and parts of Maryland. www.thewala.org

FLORIDA

Volunteer Lawyers for the Arts, Arts & Business Council of Miami, Inc., 111 SW Fifth Avenue, Suite 201, Miami, FL 33130. A joint program with the Dade County Bar Association. Provides pro-bono legal services to qualified artists. www.http://www.artsbizmiami.org

GEORGIA

Georgia Lawyers for the Arts, 887 W. Marietta Street NW, Suite J-101, Atlanta, GA 30318. Serves artists in Georgia. www.glarts.org

ILLINOIS

Lawyers for the Creative Arts, 213 West Institute Place, Suite 411, Chicago, IL 60610-3125. Serves artists in Illinois. www.law-arts.org

INDIANA

Creative Arts Legal League (CALL), Volunteer Lawyers for the Arts, 20 N. Meridian Street, Suite 500, Indianapolis, IN 46204. Provides legal services to income-eligible artists. www.indycall.org

KANSAS

Mid-America Arts Resources, c/o Susan J. Whitfield-Lungren, P.O. Box 363, Linds-
    borg, KS 67456. Provides legal services to artists living in Kansas and informa-
    tion services to artists living in Nebraska and Oklahoma.

LOUISIANA

Louisiana Volunteer Lawyers for the Arts, Arts Council of New Orleans, 818
    Howard Avenue, Suite 300, New Orleans, LA 70113. Serves artists in Louisiana.
    www.artscouncilofneworleans.org

MAINE

Maine Lawyer Referral & Information Service, Maine Bar Association, P.O. Box
    788, Augusta, ME 04332-0788. www.mainebar.org/lawyer_need.asp
Maine Volunteer Lawyers Project, P.O. Box 547, Portland, ME 04112. Serves
    artists in Maine. www.vlp.org

MARYLAND

Maryland Lawyers for the Arts, 113 West North Avenue, Baltimore, MD 21201.
    Serves artists in Maryland. www.mdartslaw.org

MASSACHUSETTS

Volunteer Lawyers for the Arts of Massachusetts, 249 A Street, Studio 14, Boston,
    MA 02210. Serves artists in Massachusetts. www.vlama.org

MICHIGAN

Volunteer Lawyers for Arts and Culture, ArtServe Michigan, 17515 West Nine Mile
    Road, Suite 1025, Southfield, MI 48075. Provides pro-bono legal assistance to
    income-eligible artists. www.artservemichigan.org/service/index.asp
Volunteer Lawyers for Arts and Culture, ArtServe Michigan (Lansing Office), 1310
    Turnere Street, Suite C, Lansing, MI 48906. Provides pro-bono legal assistance
    to income-eligible artists. www.artservemichigan.org/service/index.asp

MINNESOTA

Springboard for the Arts, 308 Prince Street, Suite 270, St. Paul, MN 55101. Pro-
    vides contracts and legal templates and attorney referrals in Minnesota and out-
    side of the state. www.springboardforthearts.org/services/services.asp

MISSOURI

Kansas City Volunteer Lawyers and Accountants for the Arts, 118 W. 18th Street,
    Kansas City, MO 64108. www.kcvlaa.org
St. Louis Volunteer Lawyers and Accountants for the Arts, 6128 Delmar, St. Louis,
    MO 63112. Serves artists in Missouri and southwestern Illinois. www.vlaa.org

NEW HAMPSHIRE

Lawyers for the Arts/New Hampshire, One Granite Place, Concord, NH 03301.
    Serves artists in New Hampshire. www.nhbca.com/lawyersforarts.php

NEW JERSEY

New Jersey Volunteer Lawyers for the Arts, P.O. Box 1520, Laurel Springs, NJ 08021. www.njvla.org

NEW YORK

Buffalo Area Lawyers Supporting the Arts, Arts Council in Buffalo and Erie County, 700 Main Street, Buffalo, NY 14202. Provides artists and arts organizations in the Buffalo area assistance with legal issues through workshops and referrals. www.artscouncilbuffalo.org/artist_resources/legal.asp

Fractured Atlas, 248 W. 35th Street, Suite 1202, New York, NY 10001. A nonprofit organization that offers many support services to artist-members throughout the United States, including legal services at reduced prices. www.fracturedatlas.org

Volunteer Lawyers for the Arts, 1 East 53rd Street, New York, NY 10022-4201. Sponsors a legal hotline; legal clinics for VLA members, in-house appointments with staff attorneys, and pro-bono placements for low-income artists and non-profit arts organizations. www.vlany.org

NORTH CAROLINA

North Carolina Volunteer Lawyers for the Arts, Inc., P.O. Box 26513, Raleigh, NC 27611-6513. Serves artists in North Carolina. www.ncvla.org

OHIO

Toledo Volunteer Lawyers for the Arts, c/o Arnold Gottlieb, Esq., 608 Madison Avenue, Suite 1523, Toledo, OH 43604. Serves artists in northwest Ohio.

PENNSYLVANIA

Philadelphia Volunteer Lawyers for the Arts, 1616 Walnut Avenue, Suite 1800, Philadelphia, PA 19103. Serves artists in Pennsylvania, Delaware, and New Jersey. www.libertynet.org/pvla

Pittsburgh Volunteer Lawyers for the Arts, c/o Greater Pittsburgh Arts Council, 707 Penn Avenue, 2nd Floor, Pittsburgh, PA 15222. Provides legal assistance to low-income artists and small arts organizations. www.pittsburghartscouncil.org/vla.htm

RHODE ISLAND

Ocean State Lawyers for the Arts, P.O. Box 19, Saunderstown, RI 02874. Serves artists in Rhode Island and southeastern New England. www.artslaw.org

TEXAS

Texas Accountants and Lawyers for the Arts, 1540 Sul Ross, Houston, TX 77006. www.talarts.org

UTAH

Utah Lawyers for the Arts, P.O. Box 652, Salt Lake City, UT 84110-0652. Serves artists in Utah. Contact Andrew Deiss. adeiss@joneswaldo.com

WASHINGTON

Washington Lawyers for the Arts, 6512 23rd Avenue NW, #320, Seattle, WA 98117. Sponsors an Arts Legal Clinic for artists twice a month and offers private consultations on various art law–related topics. www.wa-artlaw.org

AUSTRALIA

Arts Law Centre of Australia, The Gunnery, 43–51 Cowper Wharf Road, Woolloomooloo, Sydney NSW 2011, Australia. Provides legal and business advice and referral services for artists and arts organizations. www.artslaw.com.au

CANADA

Artists' Legal Advice Service (ALAS). An organization of volunteer lawyers and law students who assist artists in Ontario, Canada. (416-367-ALAS) http://artists law.org/index.htm

Canadian Artists Representation Copyright Collective (CARCC), 109A 4th Avenue, Ottawa, Ontario K1S 2L3, Canada. Creates opportunities for increased income for visual and media artists. Provides services to artists affiliated with the collective, including negotiating the terms for copyright use and issuing an appropriate license to the user. www.carcc.ca

Le Regroupement des artistes en arts visuels du Québec (RAAV), 460 Ste-Catherine Ouest, #913, Montréal, Quebec H3B 1A7, Canada. Regulates the collective representation of artists and contracts for any form of artwork use. www .raav.org

LICENSING ART

Publications

The Fine Artist's Career Guide by Daniel Grant. New York: Allworth Press, revised 2004. See section on "Licensing."

Licensing Art and Design by Caryn R. Leland. New York: Allworth Press, revised 1995. A comprehensive and helpful guide to the mechanics of licensing images for use on apparel, ceramics, posters, stationery, and many other products.

Licensing Art 101: Publishing and Licensing Your Artwork for Profit by Michael Woodward. Nevada City, Calif.: ArtNetwork, revised 2007. Includes very useful information and advice about conducting business with the publishing and licensing industries. Provides contact information of licensing agents, greeting card publishers, fine-art publishers, stationery publishers, and more.

The Licensing Course by Michael Woodward. Art Licensing International, Inc., 711 South Osprey Avenue, Suite 1, Sarasota, FL 34236. A 264-page manual for artists, illustrators, and photographers who are entering the field of licensing for the first time, and for those who want to take their licensing careers to the next level. The package also includes the DVD *Art and Design Licensing* and the book *Licensing Art 101: Publishing and Licensing Your Artwork for Profit.* www.licensingcourse.com

The Licensing Letter. EPM Communications, Inc., 160 Mercer Street, 3rd Floor, New York, NY 10012. A guide to licensing contacts, trends, and deals. Published twenty-two times a year. www.epmcom.com

Licensing Letter Sourcebook. EPM Communications, Inc., 160 Mercer Street, 3rd Floor, New York, NY 10012. Revised annually. Includes the names of licensing agents with contact information and a list of properties they represent. www.epmcom.com

Licensing Photography by Richard Weisgrau and Victor S. Perlman. New York: Allworth Press, 2006. Written by a photographer and intellectual-property attorney. Provides advice on writing licensing agreements, how to successfully negotiate fees, and the price value of licenses.

Web Sites

Artist Help Network (www.artisthelpnetwork.com). Founded by Caroll Michels, career coach and artist-advocate, this site is devoted to all aspects of career development. See heading "Legal" and subheading "Licensing Art & Design."

Organizations

Art Licensing International, Inc., 711 South Osprey Avenue, Suite 1, Sarasota, FL 34236. Licensing agent Michael Woodward offers artists consultations to determine whether their work is suitable for the licensing industry. Also sponsors seminars and workshops and other licensing resources. www.licensingcourse.com

International Licensing Industry Merchandiser's Association, 350 Fifth Avenue, Suite 1408, New York, NY 10118. Offers members access to an online licensing database, and a *Worldwide Licensing Resource Directory*. Also sponsors an annual International Licensing Exposition and Conference. www.licensing.org

MAILING LISTS

Publications

New York Business Online Directory. 711 Third Avenue, New York, NY 10017. Contains hundreds of New York-based companies, identifying decision makers by occupation, taken from the publication *Crain's New York Business*. Available as a printout or online. www.crainsny.com

Web Sites

Art California (www.artcalifornia.com). Lists curators, critics, galleries, and museums in California.

Artist Help Network (www.artisthelpnetwork.com). Founded by Caroll Michels, career coach and artist-advocate, this site is devoted to all aspects of career development. See heading "Career" and subheadings "Art World Mailing Lists" and "Press and Public Relations."

Organizations

ArtNetwork, P.O. Box 1360, Nevada City, CA 95959. Rents arts-related mailing lists in several categories. www.artmarketing.com

Art-Support, 1717 150th Avenue SE, #16, Bellevue, WA 98007. Offers various mailing lists related to photography, including galleries, private dealers, and nonprofit photography organizations. www.art-support.com

Best Mailing Lists, 7505 East Tanque Verde Road, Tucson, AZ 85711. Sells the names and addresses of America's most wealthy people in hundreds of categories, including medical doctors (by speciality) and lawyers. www.bestmailing.com

Mailing List Labels Packages, P.O. Box 1233, Weston, CT 06883-0233. Publishes the Mailing List Labels Package for percent-for-art and art in public places programs. The package includes a directory of percent-for-art and art in public places programs in the United States, and related mailing labels, postcards, and forms that can be used to make cost-effective and systematic contact with the programs. Available in diskette, CD-ROM, and DVD formats, and via email transmission. http://home.att.net/~mllpackage/package_information.htm

Caroll Michels, career coach and artist-advocate, 1724 Burgos Drive, Sarasota, FL 34238. Offers various arts-related mailing lists, including the names and addresses of art consultants, museum and independent curators, art critics, international, national and regional arts press, New York City arts press, and interior design and architecture press. Some lists available as a CD-ROM. Updated on an ongoing basis. www.carollmichels.com

Visual Arts Ontario, 1153A Queen Street West, Toronto, Ontario M6J 1J4, Canada. Offers a media list that contains 140 listings of major art world press outlets, critics, periodicals, radio, television, and Internet contacts in Ontario. Available to Visual Arts Ontario members. www.vao.org

Also see "Press and Public Relations."

MATERIALS FOR THE ARTS PROGRAMS

Publications

The Artist's Resource Handbook by Daniel Grant. New York: Allworth Press, revised 1997. See sections "Materials for the Arts" and "Obtaining In-Kind Contributions."

Web Sites

Artist Help Network (www.artisthelpnetwork.com). Founded by Caroll Michels, career coach and artist-advocate, this site is devoted to all aspects of career development. See heading "Money" and subheading "Materials for the Arts."

L.A. SHARES (www.lashares.org). A nonprofit materials reuse program that redistributes reusable goods and materials, both new and used, free of charge to schools and nonprofit organizations throughout Los Angeles County.

Organizations

Materials for the Arts, Department of Cultural Affairs, 33-00 Northern Boulevard, 3rd Floor, Long Island City, NY 11101. Provides individual artists—who work with a registered New York City cultural organization—office equipment and supplies, furnishings, art materials, and other items free of charge. www.mfta.org

Materials for the Arts, Monroe County Solid Waste Management District, 3400 South Walnut, Bloomington, IN 47401. Sponsors a recyling program for artists and educators. http://mcswmd.org/index.php

New York Wa$teMatch, c/o New York City Materials Exchange Development Program, City College of New York, Steinman Hall, Room 102, 140th Street and Convent Avenue, New York, NY 10031. Provides information on the availability of raw materials, such as marble scraps, fabrics and textiles, mahogany, plastics, and materials that are being discarded. The price of materials is much less expensive than on the open market, and in most cases, users can negotiate prices directly with companies that have materials. www.wastematch.org

ONLINE GALLERIES
Web Sites

Abstract Earth Gallery (www.abstractearth.com). A juried and commission-based online gallery that specializes in abstract art.

American Print Alliance (www.printalliance.org). A nonprofit consortium of printmakers' councils. Sponsors an online gallery open to members and subscribers of *Contemporary Impressions*.

Artist Help Network (www.artisthelpnetwork.com). Founded by Caroll Michels, career coach and artist-advocate, this site is devoted to all aspects of career development. See heading "Exhibitions, Commissions and Sales" and subheadings "Online Galleries" and "Slide Registries."

Artists Space (www.artistsspace.org). Sponsors the Irving Sandler Artists File Online.

Brooklyn Arts Council (www.brooklynartscouncil.org). Sponsors an online registry of Brooklyn, New York, artists.

Craft Site Directory (www.craftsitedirectory.com). Devoted to crafts with links to Web sites of craft artists working in various fields.

The Guild (www.guild.com). Juried, commission-based online gallery.

Portfolio (www.sculpture.org/redesign/port.shtml). An online gallery for members of the International Sculpture Center.

Stroke of Genius (www.portraitartist.com). A fee-based site for portrait painters and those who want to commission a portrait.

The Varo Registry (www.varoregistry.com). A membership online gallery for women artists.

Also see "Artists' Registries."

ORGANIZING PAPERWORK
Publications

Artist Business Forms: Creating a Successful Career in Photography by Dan Fear. Art-Support, 1717 150th Avenue SE, #16, Bellevue, WA 98007. An ebook with thirty-five business forms and contracts for artists pertaining to exhibiting and selling artwork. www.art-support.com

Conquering the Paper Pile-Up: Moving Those Mountains of Paper Out of Your Life by Stephanie Culp. Cincinnati, Ohio: Writer's Digest Books, 1990. Advice on how to organize, file, and store every piece of paper in your office or home, with tips on how to categorize and create files.

The Organization Map by Pam McClellan. Cincinnati, Ohio: Betterway Books, 1993. See chapter "The Office."

Organizing for the Creative Person by Dorothy Lehmkuhl with Dolores Cotter Lamping. New York: Crown Publishing, 1994. Helps right-brain people with conquering clutter, mastering time, and reaching goals. Includes practical solutions in harmony with the way creative people think and act.

Organizing from the Right Side of the Brain: A Creative Approach to Getting Organized by Lee Silber. New York: St. Martin's Griffin, 2004. Specifically written for people who are creative and spontaneous rather than logical and detail-oriented. Offers unique solutions that complement the unorthodox lifestyle of the creative "right-brainer."

A Question of Balance: Artists and Writers on Motherhood by Judith Pierce Rosenberg. Milford, Conn.: Papier-Mache Press, 1995. Interviews with women artists and writers who share how they organize their lives to nurture both their children and their craft.

Time Management for the Creative Person by Lee T. Silber. New York: Three Rivers Press, 1998. Helps right-brain people learn to focus on more than one thing at a time, including hundreds of time-saving tips and how to improve memory.

Software Programs

ArcherArtist Business Software, Masterpiece Solutions, Inc., 1220 Hawthorne Road, Golden, CO 80401. Helps artists keep track of information on sales, sales tax, shipping details, consignments, inventory, and more. www.masterpiecemanager.com/artistfnb.html

GYST Software for Artists, 4223 Russell Avenue, Los Angeles, CA 90027-4511. Available for MAC, PC, and Vista. Tracks artwork, prices, sales, and provides sales invoices. Includes a database for a mailing list. Provides an artwork checklist for exhibitions and many other business-related functions. Guides users through the process of writing grant proposals and other proposals with detailed instructions, and more. www.gyst-ink.com

WorkingArtist. The Artist's Business Tool for Windows. Software for Artists, 7700 Earling Street NE, Olympia, WA 98506. Helps artists track artwork including multiple editions, view provenance and display images, create slide labels, track patrons and patron activities, create standard and custom price lists, and create consignment forms and invoices. www.workingartist.com

Web Sites

Artist Help Network (www.artisthelpnetwork.com). Founded by Caroll Michels, career coach and artist-advocate, this site is devoted to all aspects of career development. See heading "Career" and subheading "Getting Organized" and heading "Legal" and subheading "Contracts & Forms."

PENSION PLANS AND SAVINGS AND LOAN PROGRAMS
Web Sites

Artist Help Network (www.artisthelpnetwork.com). Founded by Caroll Michels, career coach and artist-advocate, this site is devoted to all aspects of career development. See heading "Creature Comforts" and subheading "Pension Plans, Savings & Loan Programs."

Retirement Plans for Small Business (www.irs.gov/pub/irs-pdf/p560.pdf). Internal Revenue Service, Publication 560. Describes retirement plans for small businesses.

Small Business Administration (www.sbaonline.sba.gov). Provides loans and loan guarantees to independently owned and operated profit-making small businesses, including culture-related businesses (teaching studios; performing-arts schools; retail music or art-and-crafts shops). Describes the various loan programs and eligibility requirements and contact information for SBA offices state-by-state.

Organizations

Arthouse, The Jones Center for Contemporary Art, 700 Congress Avenue, Austin, TX 78701. Serves Texas artists. Sponsors a credit union. www.arthousetexas.org

Artist Loan Fund, Springboard for the Arts, 308 Prince Street, Suite 270, St. Paul, MN 55101. Makes low-interest loans from $1,000 to $5,000 to Twin Cities area artists to cover a broad range of artists' needs. www.springboardforthearts.org

Artist Pension Trust, 298 Fifth Avenue, 4th Floor, New York, NY 10001. A for-profit company and the first investment program dedicated to the needs of beginning and mid-career artists. Provides long-term financial planning services. The collateralization of artworks is the basis for a range of financing products. Application forms are provided online. www.aptglobal.com

The Artists Community Federal Credit Union, 351A W. 54th Street, New York, NY 10019. A federally insured credit union for artists and arts organizations. Offers savings accounts, loans, CDs, IRAs, and a money market fund. Assists artists in establishing a credit rating. www.artistscommunityfcu.org

Craft Emergency Relief Fund, P.O. Box 838, Montpelier, VT 05601-0838. Provides craft artists with interest-free loans and a flexible payment schedule. www.craftemergency.org

PERIODICALS

(Web site addresses are provided only for those periodicals that cannot be ordered through online bookstores.)

American and Canadian Periodicals

Afterimage. Visual Studies Workshop, 31 Prince Street, Rochester, NY 14607. For photographers, independent filmmakers, and video artists. Published bimonthly.

American Art Collector. P.O. Box 8629, Scottsdale, AZ 85252-8629. Previews artists' upcoming shows at galleries coast-to-coast, and includes columns by art appraisers, gallery owners, museum curators, and art consultants. Published monthly.

American Artist. 770 Broadway, New York, NY 10003. Published monthly. www.myamericanartist.com

American Ceramics. 207 E. 32nd Street, New York, NY 10016. Published quarterly. www.amceram.org/contact.html

American Craft. American Craft Council, 72 Spring Street, New York, NY 10012-4090. Articles on all aspects of crafts and information on grants, marketing, and exhibitions. Published bimonthly.

American Photo Magazine. 1633 Broadway, 43rd Floor, New York, NY 10019-6708. Published bimonthly.

AmericanStyle. 3000 Chestnut Avenue, Suite 304, Baltimore, MD 21211. Focuses on contemporary American crafts with feature articles about artists and their work. Published quarterly.

Aperture. 547 W. 27th Street, New York, NY 10001. Quarterly journal of contemporary photography.

Art and Antiques. 1177 Avenue of the Americas, 10th Floor, New York, NY 10036. Published eleven times a year.

Art and Auction. ArtPress International, 111 8th Avenue #302, New York, NY 10011-5204. Published monthly.

Art in America. 575 Broadway, New York, NY 10012-3230. Articles and reviews, with primary focus on New York. Published monthly.

Art New England: A Resource for Visual Artists. 425 Washington Street, Brighton, MA 02135. Focuses on artists and exhibitions in New England. Published bimonthly.

Art on Paper. 150 W. 28th Street #504, New York, NY 10001. Covers information on a range of paper-based media, including limited edition prints, independently published artist's books, photography, drawings, and specialized museum and dealer catalogs. Six issues per year.

Art Papers. P.O. Box 5748, Atlanta, GA 31107-5748. Articles on contemporary art, architecture, photography, and video. Published bimonthly.

Art Times. P.O. Box 730, Mount Marion, NY 12456-0730. A literary journal that publishes essays on music, dance, theater, visual arts, film, art book reviews, short stories, and poetry. Also a resource for the Arts in the Hudson Valley Region of New York State. Eleven issues per year.

Artforum International. 350 7th Avenue, 19th Floor, New York, NY 10001-5013. Published ten times a year.

The Artist's Magazine. 4700 Galbraith Road, Cincinnati, OH 45236. Published ten times a year.

ARTnews. 48 West 38th Street, 9th Floor, New York, NY 10018-6238. News and reviews with primary focus on New York. Eleven issues a year.

Arts Across Kentucky. 387 Codell Drive, Lexington, KY 40509. Published quarterly. Profiles artists and covers exhibitions, events, and activities sponsored by arts and cultural organizations.

Arts Washington. Cultural Alliance of Greater Washington, 1436 U Street NW, Suite 103, Washington, DC 20009-3997. Published monthly. www.cultural-alliance.org

Artscene Iowa. 8657 Douglas Avenue, #36, Urbandale, IA 50322. Includes art-related news and reviews. Published monthly. www.artsceneiowa.com

Artweek. P.O. Box 52100, Palo Alto, CA 94303-0751. Covers contemporary art on the West Coast, including Washington, Oregon, and Nevada. Published ten times a year. July/August and December/January issues are combined.

Backflash. P.O. Box 7381 Station Main, Saskatoon, Saskatchewan S7K 4J3, Canada. Contemporary photography. Published quarterly.

C: International Contemporary Art. P.O. Box 5, Station B, Toronto, Ontario M5T 2T2, Canada. Covers Canadian and international contemporary art. Published quarterly. www.cmagazine.com

Camerawork: A Journal of Photographic Arts. 657 Mission Street, 2nd Floor, San Francisco, CA 94105. Published biannually. Devoted to presenting quality reproductions and writing on contemporary issues in the photographic arts. www.sfcamerawork.org

Ceramics Monthly. American Ceramics Society, 735 Ceramic Place, Suite 100, Westerville, OH 43081. Ten issues per year.

Clay Times: The Journal of Ceramics, Trends & Techniques. P.O. Box 365, Waterford, VA 20197. Published bimonthly. www.claytimes.com

Coagula Art Journal: The Low Down on High Art. 2100 N. Main Street #A-8, Lincoln Heights, CA 90031. Contains articles and interviews and insider information on the art world. Six issues per year.

Contemporary Impressions. The American Print Alliance, 302 Larkspur Turn, Peachtree City, GA 30269-2210. Includes articles, reviews, and interviews related to printmaking. Published semiannually. www.printalliance.org

Crafts News. The Crafts Center, 8601 Georgia Avenue, Suite 800, Silver Spring, MD 20910. Features updates on market trends and trade regulations, sources of assistance, successful artisan projects, and crafts-related publications and events. Published quarterly. www.craftscenter.org

Decor. 1801 Park 270 Drive, Maryland Heights, MO 63146. Focuses on art and framing retailers, distributors, and wholesalers. Published monthly.

Fiberarts. 201 E. Fourth Street, Loveland, CO 80537. Includes, news, reviews, artists' profiles, and international opportunities. Five issues per year.

Fuse Magazine. 401 Richmond Street West #454, Toronto, Ontario M5V 3A8, Canada. Contemporary arts and culture. Published quarterly.

Glass: The Urbanglass Art Quarterly. Urban Glass, 647 Fulton Street, Brooklyn, NY 11217. Provides a critical voice for glass art within the contemporary art world. Includes essays, reviews, artist profiles, news, and more. Published quarterly. www.urbanglass.org

Hand Papermaking. Hand Papermaking, Inc., P.O. Box 1070, Beltsville, MD 20704-1070. Published twice a year. Repository of information on the art and craft of hand papermaking. www.handpapermaking.org

Handwoven. Interweave Press, Inc., 201 East Fourth Street, Loveland, CO 80537-5655. Devoted to handweavers. Includes articles, profiles of weavers, tips and techniques, product information, and book reviews. Published five times a year.

Leonardo: Journal of the International Society for the Arts, Sciences and Technology. Leonardo/SAST, 211 Sutter Street, Suite 501, San Francisco, CA 94108. Covers contemporary visual art, new media art, and new technology. Published bimonthly. www.leonardo.info/isast/contact.html

Modern Painters. LTD Media, 111 8th Avenue, #302, New York, NY 10011. Covers contemporary visual arts, architecture, and aesthetics. Published ten times a year.

Nueva Luz. En Foco, 1738 Hone Avenue, Bronx, NY 10461. Devoted to the work of contemporary fine-art and documentary photographers of diverse cultures, primarily U.S. residents of Latino, African, and Asian heritage, and Native Peoples of the Americas and the Pacific. www.enfoco.org

Parkett. 145 Avenue of the Americas, New York, NY 10013. Contemporary visual arts. Published three times a year.

The Pastel Journal. F&W Publications, 4700 E. Galbraith Road, Cincinnati, OH 45236. Devoted to artists working with pastels. Includes information on techniques, materials, exhibition, career opportunities, and workshops. Also features interviews with pastel artists. Published six times a year.

The Photo Review Journal. The Photo Review, 140 East Richardson Avenue, Suite 301, Langhorne, PA 19047-2824. Contains exhibition reviews, essays, interviews, portfolios, and book reviews. Published quarterly. www.photoreview.org

Photograph. 64 West 89th Street, New York, NY 10024. A comprehensive guide to photography galleries in New York City. Also includes national and international listings. Published bimonthly.

Raw Vision. C/o 163 Amsterdam Avenue, #203, New York, NY 10028-5001 and 1 Watford Road, Radlett, Herts, WD7 8LA, United Kingdom. An international journal of intuitive and visionary art. Published quarterly.

Sculpture. 1633 Connecticut Avenue NW, 4th Floor, Washington DC 20029. Covers international contemporary sculpture. Published monthly.

Sculpture Review. National Sculpture Society, 56 Ludlow Street, 5th Floor, New York, NY 10002. Published quarterly.

Southwest Art. 521 Walnut Street, Suite 250, Boulder, CO 80302. Focuses on artists who are living in the Southwest and Southwest-related work. Published monthly.

Spot. Houston Center for Photography, 1441 West Alabama, Houston, TX 77006. Focuses on news and criticism of photography in the South and Southwest. Published twice a year. www.hcponline.org

Surface Design. Surface Design Association, 83 Ivy Lane, Englewood, NJ 07631. Quarterly publication of a professional organization of artists involved in surface design, textiles, weaving, quilts, and other forms of fiber art. www.art.uidaho.edu/sda

Watercolor. 770 Broadway, New York, NY 10003. Published quarterly. Features articles about contemporary watermedia painters, their methods, and materials.

Wildlife Art: The Art Journal of the Natural World. 947 D Street, Ramona, CA 92065. The largest journal on wildlife art. Published seven times a year, including an annual yearbook.

Women in the Arts. National Museum of Women in the Arts, 1250 New York Avenue NW, Washington, DC 20005. A quarterly publication devoted to promoting the achievements of women in the visual and performing arts and literature.

International Periodicals

Art Monthly. 28 Charing Cross Road, 4th Floor, London WC2H ODB, United Kingdom. Published in the United Kingdom. Features include in-depth exhibition, book, video, film, and performance reviews, artists' books, art notes, and art law. Published ten times a year.

Art Monthly Australia. LPO Box 8321, ANU Acton, ACT 2601, Australia. Focuses on contemporary visual art in Australia, New Zealand, and the Asia/Pacific region. Published ten times a year.

Art New Zealand. P.O. Box 10-249, Dominion Road, Auckland 3, New Zealand. Published quarterly.

The Art Newspaper. 78 South Lambeth Road, London SW8 1R2, United Kingdom. Covers international art-market news. Eleven issues per year.

Art Review. 1 Sekforde Street, London EC1R 0BE, United Kingdom. A monthly guide to exhibitions. Also includes news and reviews. www.art-review.com/index2.htm

Artlink Australia. 363 Esplanade, Henley Beach, South Australia 5022. Contemporary art in Australia. Published quarterly. www.artlink.com.au

Asian Art News. 28 Arbuthnot Road, Central Hong Kong. Covers contemporary Asian art and artists. Published bimonthly.

British Journal of Photography. Haymarket House, 28–29 Haymarket, London Sw1Y 4RX, United Kingdom. Includes photography industry news and exhibition listings. Fifty-one issues per year.

Ceramic Review. Ceramic Review Publishing Ltd., 25 Foubert's Place, London W1F 7QF, United Kingdom. Includes reviews of ceramic exhibitions and news and events. Also includes information on equipment, materials, and techniques. Published bimonthly.

Ceramics, Art and Perception. 120 Glenmore Road, Paddington, Sydney NSW 2021, Australia. International ceramics magazine. Published quarterly.

Circa. 43/44 Temple Bar, Dublin 2, Republic of Ireland. Covers Irish and international contemporary visual culture. Published quarterly. www.recirca.com

Crafts. Crafts Council, 44a Pentonville Road, Islington, London N1 9BY, United Kingdom. Focuses on decorative and applied arts, including news, reviews, and features. Published bimonthly. www.craftscouncil.org.uk

Eyeline. Eyeline Publishing Ltd., c/o Visual Arts QUT, Victoria Park Road, Kelvin Grove, Brisbane QLD, Australia 4059. Australian visual-arts magazine with reviews, news, and artists' pages. Published three times a year.

Flash Art. Via Carlo Farini 68, Milan 20159, Italy. Focuses primarily on European art and artists. Publishes *Flash Art International, Flash Art Italy,* and *Flash Art Czech.* Published bimonthly.

Frieze. 3–4 Hardwick Street, London EC1R 4RB, United Kingdom. Covers international contemporary art and culture. Publishes eight issues a year.

Live Art Magazine. P.O. Box 501, Nottingham NG3 5LT, United Kingdom. A bimonthly publication and online magazine devoted to hybrid art forms. Includes news, reviews, listings, and opportunities. www.liveartmagazine.com

Printmaking Today. Cello Press Ltd., 99–101 Kingsland Road, London E2 8AG, United Kingdom. Devoted to contemporary international printmaking, including reviews, interviews, information, and resources. Published quarterly.

Source. P.O. Box 352, Belfast BT1 2WB, Northern Ireland. Quarterly review of contemporary photography. www.sourcemagazine.demon.co.uk

Studio Pottery. Ceramics Society, 2 Bartholemew Street West, Exeter EX4 3AJ, United Kingdom. Features contemporary ceramics in the United Kingdom, including artists' profiles, news, and exhibition listings. Published quarterly. www.ceramic-society.co.uk

Web Sites, Ezines, and Blogs

Art Access (www.artaccess.com). Reviews and articles about visual art.

Art for Real (www.sitefour.com/artforreal.org). Articles and reviews about art exhibitions and events.

Art Vent (http://artvent.blogspot.com). Carol Diehl, an artist and contributing editor of *Art in America,* writes about the absurdities of art and life, including the language of contemporary art criticism.

Art.blogging.la (http://art.blogging.la). An art-related blog that announces upcoming exhibitions in the Los Angeles area.

Artcritical.com (www.artcritical.com). A magazine of art and ideas, including exhibition reviews.

ArtDaily (www.artdaily.com). Specializes in exhibition news from around the world.

ARTiculations (http://articulations.smithsonianmag.com). A blog sponsored by the Smithsonian Institution. It contains news and information about artists, paintings, sculpture, photography, architecture, and performance art. Penned by Maggie Frank and Sam Hunter.

Artinfo (www.artinfo.com). Provides art news on a daily basis.

Artist Help Network (www.artisthelpnetwork.com). Founded by Caroll Michels, career coach and artist-advocate, this site is devoted to all aspects of career development. See heading "Other Resources" and subheadings "Design and Architecture Publications" and "Periodicals." Also see heading "Career" and subheading "Career Management, Business and Marketing."

ArtKrush. (www.artkrush.com). Daily coverage of international art news, interviews, reviews, and features.

Artopia. (www.artsjournal.com/artopia). John Perreault's art diary. Devoted to news and exhibition reviews.

Artsy Magazine (www.artsymag.com). Unites a variety of perspectives and voices targeting women artists at the start of their struggle to become recognized. A resource for women looking for a community where they can share support, inspiration, and confidence.

Code Z On Line (www.codezonline.com). Links to articles about news and exhibitions related to African American artists throughout the United States and internationally.

Culturegrrl (www.artsjournal.com/culturegrrl). Blog of cultural journalist Lee Rosenbaum, who is a contributing editor of *Art in America.*

Roberta Fallon and Libby Rosof's Artblog (http://fallonandrosof.blogspot.com). Art reviews, deep thoughts, and gossip from Philadelphia and beyond.

Iconoduel (www.iconoduel.org). Blog of Chicago art critic Dan Hopewell.

Modern Art Notes (www.artsjournal.com/man). Blog of art critic Tyler Green, who is based in Washington, D.C., and writes for *Bloomberg News.*

NEWSgrist (http://newsgrist.typepad.com). Dedicated to bridging the gap between digital and nontechnical art and activism.

The Next Few Hours (http://thenextfewhours.com/blog). An art blog that focuses on Miami.

Reality X: Portland Photojournal and Arts Magazine (www.realitytimes.com). A magazine that features artwork.

Resource Library Magazine (www.tfaoi.com/resourc.htm). Devoted to American representational art. Includes articles, news, and information.

A View from the Edge of the Universe. (http://chromogenia.typepad.com/artatlanta/ art_in_atlanta_news_comments_reviews/index.html). Blog of art collector Erik Schneider that covers exhibitions in Atlanta, Georgia, and Portland, Oregon.

Also see "Career Management, Business, and Marketing" and "Interior Design and Architecture."

PHOTOGRAPHING ARTWORK
Publications

How to Photograph Works of Art by Sheldan Collins. New York: Watson-Guptill Publications, 1992. Covers all aspects of photographing art, including lighting and lighting techniques, film, filtration, and more.

Photographing Art by Jim Chambers. Visual Arts Ontario, 1153A Queen Street West, Toronto, Ontario M6J 1J4, Canada. A step-by-step guide to photographing two-dimensional and three-dimensional artwork. www.vao.org

Photographing Your Artwork: A Step-by-Step Guide to Taking High-Quality Slides at an Affordable Price by Russell Hart. Cincinnati, Ohio: North Light Books, revised 2000. Provides examples of the results of various types of lighting and camera angles; discusses the photographing of challenging artwork, including three-dimensional pieces, miniatures, and installations, and the masking and cleaning of slides.

Photographing Your Craftwork: A Hands-On Guide for Crafts People by Steve Meltzer. Wilmington, Del.: The Crafts Report, revised 1997. Gives the basics of photographing craft objects for those who are not professional photographers. Advises on equipment and film selection, processing, making prints, and care of cameras and slides. Also provides valuable hints for dealing with special situations and materials that are difficult to photograph.

The Quick & Easy Guide to Photographing Your Artwork by Roger Saddington. Cincinnati, Ohio: North Light Books, 2003. Describes how to take satisfying photos of artwork without spending a lot of time or money.

Taking the Leap. Building a Career as a Visual Artist by Cay Lang. San Francisco: Chronicle Books, revised 2006. See "Photographic Equipment" and "Basic Photographic Procedures."

Web Sites

Art Link Swap (http://artlinkswap.org/photographing_art.shtml). Photographing Your Art: A Short Tutorial.

Artist Help Network (www.artisthelpnetwork.com). Founded by Caroll Michels, career coach and artist-advocate, this site is devoted to all aspects of career development. See heading "Presentation Tools" and subheading "Photographing Artwork."

The Artists Web (www.theartistsweb.net/wiki/How_To_Photograph_Artwork#). Article on "How to Photograph Artwork."

PRESENTATION TOOLS
Publications

Alleviating Prepress Anxiety: How to Manage Your Print Projects for Savings, Schedule and Quality by Ann Goodheart. Mountainview, Calif.: Leaping Antelope Productions, 2000. Includes information on how to plan a project, prepare a budget, evaluate a printer, and how to select paper, envelopes, and typefaces.

The Artists' Survival Manual: A Complete Guide to Marketing Your Work by Toby Judith Klayman with Cobbett Steinberg. San Francisco: Klaman and Branchcomb, revised 1996. Desktop edition. See various chapters on "What to Bring to a Viewing."

Getting It Printed: How to Work with Printers and Graphic Imaging Services to Assure Quality, Stay on Schedule and Control Costs by Mark Beach and Eric Kenly. Cincinnati, Ohio: North Light Books, revised 2004. Includes tips and advice from industry experts, checklists, and helpful illustrations.

Perfect Portfolio. Visual Arts Ontario, 1153A Queen Street West, Toronto, Ontario M6J 1J4, Canada. An analysis of basic presentation concepts including what galleries and juries want to see, what to put in your portfolio, and when to change it. www.vao.org

Presentation Power Tools for Fine Arts by Renée Phillips. New York: Manhattan Arts International, revised 2006. Provides ideas and tips on writing résumés, biographies, business letters, and more. Samples are included.

The Relatively Pain-Free Artist Statement by Alyson B. Stanfield. Stanfield Art Associates, P.O. Box 988, Goldon, CO 80402. An ebook that provides tips for developing an artist statement. www.artbizcoach.com

Taking the Leap: Building a Career as a Visual Artist by Cay Lang. San Francisco: Chronicle Books, revised 2006. See "Creating Your Artist's Packet."

Writing the Artist Statement: Revealing the True Spirit of Your Work by Ariane Goodwin. Infinity Publishing, 2002. Guides artists through the process of writing an artist statement and building a psychological bridge between art and audience by tapping into the exact words that portray the singular spirit of your work.

Web Sites

Artist Help Network (www.artisthelpnetwork.com). Founded by Caroll Michels, career coach and artist-advocate, this site is devoted to all aspects of career development. See heading "Presentation Tools" and subheadings "Photographing Artwork" and "Presentation Media."

Digital Photography Resources for Artists (www.art-support.com/digital.htm). Resources include image-editing software, Photoshop Web sites, online digital processing, and more.

Also see "Career Management, Business, and Marketing," "Internet Art Marketing," and "Photographing Your Work."

PRESS RELATIONS AND PUBLICITY

Publications

Bacon's Media Directories. Chicago: Cision US, Inc., revised regularly. Publishes various media directories with contact information, including *Internet Media Directory, Newspaper/Magazine Directory, Radio/TV/Cable Directory, Metro California Media Directory,* and *New York Publicity Outlets.*

Complete Guide to Internet Publicity by Steve O'Keefe. New York: John Wiley, 2002. Provides information on vehicles for obtaining Internet publicity, including search engine optimization, newsletters, email merge programs, syndication, and more.

Complete Publicity Plans: How to Create Publicity That Will Spark Media Exposure and Excitement by Sandra L. Beckwith. Avon, Mass.: Adams Media Corporation, 2003. Includes information on developing pitch letters, press releases, press kits, and more.

Critics List, compiled by Caroll Michels, career coach and artist-advocate. 1724 Burgos Drive, Sarasota, FL 34238. The names and street addresses of art critics, primarily in the New York City area. Some email addresses are included. Updated on an ongoing basis. Formatted printout for reproduction on labels.

Editor and Publishers Annual Directory of Syndicated Services. New York: Editor and Publisher Company, revised annually. Lists syndicates serving newspapers in the United States and abroad with news and feature articles.

Encyclopedia of Associations. Farmington Hills, Mich.: Gale Group. Revised regularly. Offers the following editions organized by speciality: International Organizations; National Organizations of the United States; Regional, State, and Local Organizations; and Women's Associations Worldwide. Indexed by title and subject. Each entry includes address, purpose, programs, and publications.

Fine Art Publicity: The Complete Guide for Galleries and Artists by Susan Abbott. New York: Allworth Press, revised 2005. Explains how to organize an effective public-relations plan. Includes sample forms, letters, and press releases.

Fine Artist's Guide to Marketing and Self-Promotion by Julius Vitali. New York: Allworth Press, revised 2003. Covers effective techniques for generating publicity. Describes guerilla tactics for using the media to build a successful art career.

Interior Design and Architecture Press Contacts, compiled by Caroll Michels, career coach and artist-advocate. 1724 Burgos Drive, Sarasota, FL 34238. The names and street addresses of writers, editors, and publications covering interior design, architecture, landscape architecture, and gardening. Some email addresses are included. Updated on an ongoing basis. Printout formatted for reproduction on labels. www.carollmichels.com

International, National & Regional Art Press Contacts, compiled by Caroll Michels, career coach and artist-advocate. 1724 Burgos Drive, Sarasota, FL 34238. The names and street addresses of arts writers, editors, and international, national, and regional publications. Includes arts, general interest, and arts-related radio and television programs. Many email addresses are also included. Updated on an ongoing basis. Formatted printout for reproduction on labels. www.carollmichels.com

The New Rules of Marketing and PR: How to Use News Releases, Blogs, Podcasting, Viral Marketing and Online Media to Reach Buyers Directly by David

Meerman Scott. Hoboken, N.J.: John Wiley, 2007. Provides the technical novice with an accessible guide to cutting-edge media arenas and formats.

New York Area Art Press Contacts, compiled by Caroll Michels, career coach and artist-advocate. 1724 Burgos Drive, Sarasota, FL 34238. The names and street addresses of art press contacts in the New York area. Also includes "listing columns" in New York and guidelines for preparing a listing news release. Many email addresses are also included. Updated on an ongoing basis. Formatted printout for reproduction on labels. www.carollmichels.com

Power Up with PR: A Publicity Guide for Artists by Jackie Abramian. Nevada City, Calif.: Artnetwork Press, 2008. Covers how to write an effective press release and make the most of free publicity opportunities. Includes more than 200 national media contacts.

Presentation Power Tools for Fine Arts by Renée Phillips. New York: Manhattan Arts International, revised 2006. See chapter "The Publicity Campaign."

The Publicity Handbook by David R. Yale and Andrew J. Carothers. New York: McGraw Hill, revised 2001. One hundred journalists and public-relations pros provide tips, guidance, and advice on how to organize a publicity and public-relations campaign, with tips on writing press releases.

Self-Promotion for the Creative Person: Get the Word Out About Who You Are and What You Do by Lee Silber. New York: Crown Publishers, 2001. Filled with ideas to successfully get the word out quickly, easily, and inexpensively about who you are and what you do.

Sell Yourself Without Selling Your Soul: A Woman's Guide to Promoting Herself, Her Business, Her Product, or Her Cause with Integrity and Spirit by Susan Harrow. New York: Harper Collins, 2003.

Six Steps to Free Publicity by Marcia Yudkin. New York: Career Press, revised 2008. Provides tips and information for generating media coverage.

Writer's Guide to Queries, Pitches & Proposals by Moira Allen. New York: Allworth Press, 2001. Provides advice for approaching publications through effective queries and proposals, and writing a synopsis. Helpful to artists interested in initiating feature articles about their work and career.

Writer's Market. Cincinnati, Ohio: Writer's Digest Books. Published annually.

Web Sites

Artist Help Network (www.artisthelpnetwork.com). Founded by Caroll Michels, career coach and artist-advocate, this site is devoted to all aspects of career development. See heading "Career" and subheadings "Art World Mailing Lists" and "Press and Public Relations." Also see heading "Other Resources" and subheading "Periodicals."

Free Press Release (www.free-press-release.com). A free email press release distribution service.

I-Newswire.com (www.i-newswire.com). A free email press release distribution service.

Mediafinder.com (www.mediafinder.com). A database of more than 70,000 U.S. and Canadian magazines, journals, newsletters, newspapers, tabloids, catalogs, college publications, and directories. Available by subscription.

NewsDirectory (www.ecola.com). Links to more than 6,500 English-language print and broadcast media from around the world.

PR.com (www.pr.com). A free email press release distribution service.

Ulrich's Periodical Directory (www.ulrichsweb.com). Provides access to thousands of international newspapers, periodicals, and ezines. Available by subscription.

Organizations

International Association of Art Critics (AICA), 32 rue Yves Toudic, 75010 Paris, France. Membership organization. Web site provides links to regional chapters throughout the world. www.aica-int.org

Also see "Mailing Lists" and "Periodicals."

PRICING ARTWORK

Publications

The Artists' Survival Manual: A Complete Guide to Marketing Your Work by Toby Judith Klayman with Cobbett Steinberg. Originally published by Charles Scribner's Sons, the book is now being published by Toby Judith Klayman and Joseph Branchcomb, revised in 1996. See chapter "Getting Ready: Pricing Your Work."

The Basic Guide to Pricing Your Craftwork by James Dillehay. Torreon, N.Mex.: Warm Snow Publishers, 1997. Suggests formulas for setting prices to achieve maximum profits. Includes a step-by-step record-keeping system and sample forms.

The Big Picture: The Professional Photographer's Guide to Rights, Rates & Negotiation by Lou Jacobs Jr. Cincinnati, Ohio.: Writers Digest Books, 2000. Addresses the pricing of photographs and the art of negotiation. Includes sample contracts and resource lists.

Graphic Artists Guild Handbook: Pricing and Ethical Guidelines. New York: Graphic Artists Guild, revised 2007. Contains essential information on business, pricing, and ethical standards for nearly every discipline in the visual-communications industry.

InformArt: The Limited Edition Art Price Journal, Westown Publishing Company, Inc., P.O. Box 147, Easton, CT 06612. Publishes information online about market values of limited edition prints, including the names of artists, titles of print, and high and low selling prices. Subscription required. Published monthly. www.informartmag.com

Pricing Photography: The Complete Guide to Assignment & Stock Prices by Michal Heron and David MacTavish. New York: Allworth Press, revised 2002. Although geared for commercial photographers, this book will be very helpful to fine artists for establishing fees when photographs of your artwork are used in such media as newspapers, magazines, annual reports, books, posters, and calendars.

Pricing Your Artwork with Confidence by Alexandria Levin. Painted Jay Publishing, P. O. Box 2234, Jenkintown, PA 19046-0834. www.paintedjay.com

Talking Prices: Symbolic Meanings of Prices on the Market for Contemporary Art by Olav Velthuis. Princeton, N.J.: Princeton University Press, 2005. A highly praised book that provides an analysis of how prices are set in the contemporary

art market and discusses the tension between art and commerce that character-
izes the art world.

Web Sites

Artist Help Network (www.artisthelpnetwork.com). Founded by Caroll Michels,
career coach and artist-advocate, this site is devoted to all aspects of career
development. See heading "Money" and subheading "Pricing Artwork."
Empty Easel (http://emptyeasel.com/2006/12/11/dont-sell-yourself-short-price-your-
art-for-what-its-worth). "Don't Sell Yourself Short: Price Your Art for What It's
Worth."

PRINTS AND PRINTMAKING
Publications

Art on Paper. 150 W. 28th Street, Suite 504, New York, NY 10001. Covers information on a range of paper-based media, including limited edition prints. Six
issues per year.
The Complete Printmaker: Techniques, Traditions, Innovations by John Ross,
Clare Romano, and Tim Ross. New York: The Free Press/Macmillan, revised
1990. Practical, nuts-and-bolts information gleaned from the authors' thirty-
five years of teaching and printmaking.
Contemporary Impressions. The American Print Alliance, 302 Larkspur Turn,
Peachtree City, GA 30269-2210. Includes articles, reviews, and interviews
related to printmaking. Published semiannually. www.printalliance.org
The Fine Artist's Career Guide by Daniel Grant. New York: Allworth Press, revised
2004. See section "Developing a Print Market."
Guide to Print Workshops in Canada and the United States. The American Print
Alliance, 302 Larkspur Turn, Peachtree City, GA 30269, updated every two
years. Lists more than five hundred places to make prints, paperworks, and
artists' books. www.printalliance.org
How to Profit from the Art Print Market by Barney Davey. Scottsdale, Ariz.: Bold
Star Communications, 2005. Written to help artists understand the world of
prints. Covers a wide range of issues, including the economics of self-publishing,
examples of successful self-published artists, finding and working with a publisher, marketing and selling self-published prints, and more.
InformArt: The Limited Edition Art Price Journal. Westown Publishing Company,
Inc., P.O. Box 147, Easton, CT 06612. Publishes information through an online
subscription about market values of limited edition prints, including the names
of artists, titles of print, and high and low selling prices. Published monthly.
www.informartmag.com
*Mastering Digital Printing: The Photographer's and Artist's Guide to High-Quality
Digital Output* by Harald Johnson. Muska & Lipman, 2002. A guide to mas-
tering the art of digital printmaking. Includes instructions in the latest digital
printing techniques.
Monotype: Mediums and Methods for Painterly Printmaking by Julia Ayres. New
York: Watson Guptill Publications, 2001. Includes a brief history of the mono-

type, a comprehensive chapter on materials, and step-by-step instructions, accompanied by examples of monotype prints.

Printmaking: History and Process by Donald Saff and Deli Sacilotto. London: International Thomson Publishing, 1997. An encyclopedia of information on printmaking, including "how-to" information, and the history and development of printmaking.

Printworld Directory: Contemporary Prints and Prices, edited by Selma Smith. Printworld International, Inc., P.O. Box 1957, West Chester, PA 19380, revised 2008.

Producing and Marketing Prints by Sue Viders. Marketing Solutions, 9739 Tall Grass Circle, Littleton, CO 80124-3108, revised 1997. A guide to getting started in the print market. Covers preprinting decisions, information on how a print is made, and marketing suggestions.

Web Sites

Artist Help Network (www.artisthelpnetwork.com). Founded by Caroll Michels, career coach and artist-advocate, this site is devoted to all aspects of artist career development. See heading "Other Resources" and subheading "Prints and Printmaking."

Baren Woodcut Forum (www.barenforum.org). An organization established to exchange information about woodblock printmaking.

Book Arts Directory (www.bookarts.com). Primarily a resource for artists working in the book-arts field, it also includes information for printmakers.

Fine Art Giclee Printers (www.fineartgicleeprinters.org). A site devoted to information about giclée sponsored by FLAAR, a nonprofit organization that has prepared forty reports about various printers, including tips, product comparisons, reviews, evaluations, and more.

Giclee Information (www.giclee-information.org). Devoted to information about giclées, including marketing and criteria for selecting a printer.

International Print Center New York Directory of North American Print Workshops (www.ipcny.org/info/workshops/Frameset_Workshops.htm). A directory that lists workshops alphabetically and by state.

Woodblock (www.woodblock.com). A forum for woodblock printmakers that includes information on tools, materials, suppliers, technical tips, information exchange, and printmakers' Web sites.

Organizations

The American Print Alliance, 302 Larkspur Turn, Peachtree City, GA 30269-2210. Not-for-profit alliance of artists' organizations involved in printmaking. Publishes *Contemporary Impressions* and *Guide to Print Workshops*. www.printalliance.org

Boston Printmakers, c/o Emmanuel College, 400 The Fenway, Boston, MA 02115. Membership is awarded by a jury. www.bostonprintmakers.org

Honolulu Printmakers, Academy Art Center, 1111 Victoria Street, Honolulu, HI 96814. Membership organization. Publishes a newsletter and sponsors exhibitions, workshops, and classes. www.honoluluprintmakers.org

International Print Center New York, 526 W. 26th Street, Suite 824, New York, NY 10001. A nonprofit institution devoted solely to the exhibition and understanding of historical and contemporary fine-art prints. Publishes the *Directory of North American Print Workshops* online. www.ipcny.org

Londonprintstudio, 425 Harrow Road, London W104RE, United Kingdom. A nonprofit organization that provides services to artists and the public, including exhibitions and educational programs, open access to printmaking facilities, and digital services. Also offers a summer residency program. www.londonprint studio.org.uk

Los Angeles Printmaking Society, 2928-A Santa Monica Blvd., Santa Monica, CA 90404-2414. Sponsors exhibitions, publications, catalogs, and special programs. www.laprintmakers.com

The Lower East Side Printshop, Inc., 306 W. 37th Street, 6th Floor, New York, NY 10018. A not-for-profit contemporary art and printmaking center. Offers professional workspace, residencies, and educational opportunities to artists at all career levels. http://printshop.org

Maryland Printmakers. Membership organization. Sponsors educational programs, exhibitions, publications, and an artist's registry. www.marylandprintmakers.org

Mid America Print Council. C/o Kristin Powers Nowlin, 2800 Woods Blvd., #307, Lincoln, NE 68502. Membership organization. Sponsors exhibitions, publications, and educational programs. www.midamericaprintcouncil.org

Monotype Guild of New England, P.O. Box 134, Sharon, MA 02067. Dedicated to furthering the art of monotype and monoprint through educational programs, exhibitions, seminars, and workshops. Open to all New England artists. www.mgne.org

Northwest Print Council, 416 NW 12th Avenue, Portland, OR 97209. Juried membership organization for printmakers throughout the Northwest United States and Canada. Sponsors a newsletter and other programs. www.printartsnw.org/nwpc_web/

Pittsburgh Print Group. Affiliated with the Pittsburgh Center for the Arts. Provides vehicles for local printmakers to exhibit and sell their work. Sponsors educational programs. www.pittsburghprintgroup.com

The Print Center, 1614 Latimer Street, Philadelphia, PA 19103. Sponsors exhibitions, workshops, and residencies. www.printcenter.org

Printmaking Council of New Jersey, 440 River Road, Somerville, NJ 08876. Nonprofit membership organization that sponsors exhibitions, educational programs, and studio-rental programs. www.printnj.org

Also see "Artists' Books."

PUBLIC ART

Publications

Along the Way: MTA Arts for Transit by Sandra Bloodworth and William Ayres. New York: Monacelli Press, 2006. A tour of works commissioned by New York's Metropolitan Transit Authority (MTA) Arts for Transit program, initiated in 1985. A collection of more than 150 site-specific public-art projects.

Art in Other Places: Artists at Work in America's Community & Social Institutions by William Cleveland. Amherst, Mass.: University of Massachusetts Arts Extension

Service, revised 2000. Features accounts of artists working in the community, addressing social ills, or bringing creative solutions to everyday environments. Topics include projects that focus on the elderly, prisons, people with disabilities, hospitals, and youth at risk.

The Art of Placemaking: Interpreting Community Through Public Art and Urban Design by Ronald Fleming. New York: Merrell Publishers, 2007. A presentation of site-specific public art that engages the popular imagination through common references to history, folklore, culture, and geography, and demonstrates how the integration of approachable art with local landscape, architecture, and urban design can facilitate identification with locale. Includes case studies of spectacular and innovative works accompanied by practical information, artist interviews, examples of failures and major controversies, and strategies for the future.

Art Opportunities Monthly. P.O. Box 502, Benicia, CA 94510-0502. A listing of opportunities for artists, including public-art commissions. Published monthly. Available via email and by subscription. www.artopportunitiesmonthly.com

The Artist's Guide to Public Art: How to Find and Win Commissions by Lynn Basa. New York: Allworth Press, 2008. Provides guidance on how to start and build a career in public art. Includes information on how to find, apply for, compete for, and win a public-art commission. Interviews with experienced public artists and arts administrators and a chapter on public-art law, written by Barbara Hoffman, a public-art-law attorney. Shows the way to cut through the red tape and win commissions that are financially and artistically rewarding.

Competitions Magazine. Louisville, Ky.: The Competitions Project, Inc., published quarterly. Devoted to articles on public art, architecture, and landscape architecture competitions in the United States and abroad.

Creative Places + Spaces NewsJournal. 171 East Liberty Street, Suite 224, Toronto, Ontario M6K 3P6, Canada. Published three times a year. Contains articles on people, places, projects, and organizations that are exploring and advancing the discussion of the relationship between creativity and place. www.torontoartscape .on.ca/cpsnewsjournal

Critical Issues in Public Art: Content, Context, and Controversy. Edited by Harriet F. Senie and Sally Webster. Washington, D.C.: Smithsonian Institution Press, 1998. Artists, architects, historians, critics, curators, and philosophers explore the role of public art in creating national identity.

Designing the World's Best Public Art by Garrison Roots. Victoria, Australia: Images Publishing Company, 2002. A collection of public artworks in the United States evincing a real desire to delight and engage. Shows how public-art projects can transform mundane or ugly urban fixtures.

Dialogues in Public Art by Tom Finkelpearl. Cambridge, Mass.: M.I.T. Press, 2001. Interviews with people active in the American public-art movement. Includes a history and overview of public art in the United States.

Directory of Percent-for-Art & Art in Public Programs. compiled by Rosemary M. Cellini. Mailing Lists Labels Packages, P.O. Box 1233, Weston, CT 06883-1233. The most up-to-date and comprehensive directory of percent-for-art and public-art agencies. Lists public-art programs sponsored by city, county, state, and federal agencies, including transit and redevelopment agencies, private and not-for-profit organizations, colleges and universities, and sculpture gardens and parks. The directory, related mailing labels, and postcards for contacting the programs are available as packages or separately. Available in diskette, CD-ROM, and DVD formats, and email transmission. http://home.att.net/ ~mllpackage/package_information.htm

Mapping the Terrain: New Genre Public Art. edited by Suzanne Lacy. Seattle, Wash.: Bay Press, 1994. In this anthology of twelve essays, eleven artists, curators, and critics forge a critical framework for understanding and interpreting the new public art that has emerged over the last two decades.

Public Art Commissions. Chicago Artists' Coalition, 70 E. Lake, Suite 230, Chicago, IL 60601. Provides information on public-art commissions throughout the United States and describes how artists can apply. Available online to Chicago Artists' Coalition members. www.caconline.org

Public Art Review. St. Paul, Minn.: Forecast Public Artworks. Published twice a year. Provides a wealth of practical information on public-art programs. Also lists opportunities in public art and competitions.

Web Sites

Aesthetic Grounds (www.artsjournal.com/aestheticgrounds). A blog penned by curator Glenn Weiss on public art and public space.

Art in Cities (www.artincities.com). Documents the work of artists who are using cities as outdoor exhibition spaces throughout the world.

Artist Help Network (www.artisthelpnetwork.com). Founded by Caroll Michels, career coach and artist-advocate, this site is devoted to all aspects of career development. See heading "Exhibitions, Commissions and Sales" and subheadings "Competitions and Juried Shows" and "Public Art."

Art-Public (www.art-public.com). A membership organization that documents thousands of public art projects throughout Europe.

Public Art on the Internet (www.zpub.com/public). Includes various types of information about the field of public art: essays, articles, projects, links to other related sites, and an email group for those interested in public art.

Public Art Online (www.publicartonline.org.uk). Comprehensive and well-thought-out site. Includes advice, opportunities, and dialogues about public art. Hosted by Public Art South West.

Public Art Web Links (http://public-art.shu.ac.uk/weblinx.html). Public-art resources provided by Sheffield Hallem University in England.

Organizations

Art and Community Landscapes Program, New England Foundation for the Arts, 145 Tremont Street, Boston, MA 02111. Supports site-based public art as a catalyst for environmental awareness at the community level. Administered in conjunction with the National Endowment for the Arts, the New England Foundation for the Arts, and the National Park Service. www.nefa.org/grantprog/acl

Art Production Fund, 299 West Houston Street, Ground Floor, New York, NY 10014. A nonprofit organization dedicated to producing ambitious public-art projects, reaching new audiences, and expanding awareness through contemporary art. www.artproductionfund.org

Art-in-Architecture Program, Office of the Chief Architect, PBS, U.S. General Services Administration, 1800 F Street NW, Washington, DC 20405. A federal public-art program. Sponsors an artist registry. www.gsa.gov

Arts for Transit, Metropolitan Transit Authority, 347 Madison Avenue, 5th Floor, New York, NY 10017-3739. Some artists are selected from the Percent-for-Art Registry sponsored by the New York City Department of Cultural Affairs. Residency requirements vary by project. www.mta.info/mta/aft/index.html

Arts in Transit, 707 North First Street, 4th Floor, St. Louis, MO 63112. Program is open to all artists. www.artsintransit.org/pages/organizational.html

Chicago Public Art Group, 1259 South Wabash Avenue, Chicago, IL 60605. Maintains a registry of public-art artists. www.cpag.net/home

Community Arts International, 15 Douglass Street, San Francisco, CA 94114. Develops visual- and performing-arts programs in nonconventional settings and public environments. Work with clients to collaboratively plan and create programs that humanize public spaces and engage diverse audiences. Programs have included exhibitions and public-art projects. www.community-arts.org

Creative Time, 59 E. 4th Street, #6E, New York, NY 10003. Helps visual artists, architects, and performing artists bring their new work to a wide of public spaces in New York City. www.creativetime.org

FORECAST Public Art Works, 2324 University Avenue West, Minneapolis, MN 55114. Nonprofit organization that supports the development and appreciation of public art by creating opportunities for artists and communities to explore the public realm in the Twin Cities area. Sponsors grants for Twin City–area artists, workshops, and competitions, and publishes the *Public Art Review*. www.forecastart.org

MTA Metro Art, Los Angeles Metropolitan Transportation Authority, County of Los Angeles, One Gateway Plaza, 19th Floor, Los Angeles, CA 90012-2952. Sponsors a registry. Residency requirements vary by project. www.metro.net/about_us/metroart/default.htm

Precita Eyes Muralists, 2981 24th Street, San Francisco, CA 94110. Educates communities about the history of public and community mural art. Initiates mural projects and sponsors workshops. www.precitaeyes.org

Project for Public Spaces, Inc., 700 Broadway, 4th Floor, New York, NY 10003. Specializes in public-space planning, design, and management; assists city agencies, community groups, private developers, and planners in selecting and placing art in public spaces. Maintains a registry and offers workshops and conferences on public-space planning. www.pps.org

Public Art Fund, 1 East 53rd Street, New York, NY 10022. Promotes the integration of art into the urban landscape. Sponsors art installations in public spaces throughout New York City and provides educational and informational services. www.publicartfund.org

Public Art Network (PAN), Americans for the Arts, 1000 Vermont Avenue NW, Washington, DC 20005. Provides professional services and networking opportunities for public-art professionals, visual artists, design professionals, and organizations planning public-art projects and programs. www.artsusa.org/networks/public_art_network/default.asp

Social and Public Art Resource Center (SPARC), 685 Venice Boulevard, Venice, CA
   90291. Sponsors exhibitions, workshops, and mural production. Preserves public artwork. www.sparcmurals.org
TriMet Public Art Program, 4012 SE 17th Avenue, Portland, OR 97202. Incorporates artwork in various transit stations, bus shelters, and the commuter line that
   connects passengers to Portland's airport. http://trimet.org/publicart/index.htm

STUDIO INSURANCE

Publications

The Business of Art, edited by Lee Caplin. Englewood Cliffs, N.J.: Prentice Hall
   Direct, revised 2000. See "Insuring Artwork and the Artist" by Huntington T.
   Block.
Caring for Your Art: A Guide for Artists, Collectors, and Art Institutions by Jill
   Snyder. New York: Allworth Press, revised 2000. Provides information on insur-
   ing art in the studio, home, or gallery, while in transit and when on display.
Insurance: A User-Friendly Guide for the Arts and Nonprofit World. Texas Accoun-
   tants and Lawyers for the Arts, 1540 Sul Ross, Houston, TX 77006. Covers
   general insurance issues, including special considerations for the performing arts
   and visual arts. Provides advice about buying insurance. www.talarts.org
Insuring Your Artwork. CARFAC Ontario, 401 Richmond Street West, Suite 440,
   Toronto, Ontario M5V 3A8, Canada. Available online to CARFAC Ontario
   members. www.carfacontario.ca

Web Sites

Artist Help Network (www.artisthelpnetwork.com). Founded by Caroll Michels,
   career coach and artist-advocate, this site is devoted to all aspects of career development. See heading "Creature Comforts" and subheading "Studio Insurance."
Square Feet Chicago: An Artist's Guide to Buying and Renting Space (www
   .chicagoartistsresource.org/?q=node/591). A manual published by the Chicago
   Department of Cultural Affairs. See chapter 20, "Insurance."

Organizations

American Craft Council, 72 Spring Street, 6th Floor, New York, NY 10012. Offers
   members discounted property and casualty insurance, work-in-transit insurance, and while artwork is at shows. www.craftcouncil.org
Fireman's Fund Insurance, 777 San Marin Drive, Novato, CA 94998. Offers a fine-
   art policy that provides coverage for individuals in the fine arts and entertainment fields. www.firemansfund.com
Fractured Atlas, 248 W. 35th Street, Suite 1202, New York, NY 10001. A nonprofit
   organization that offers many support services to artist-members throughout
   the United States, including liability insurance. www.fracturedatlas.org
Huntington T. Block, Washington, D.C., office: 1120 20th Street NW, Suite 600,
   Washington, DC 20036; New York office: 199 Water Street, 30th Floor, New
   York, NY 10038; San Francisco office: 199 Freemont Street, 14th Floor, San
   Francisco, CA 94105. Offers individual artists various forms of insurance,

including domestic and international transit insurance, and insurance for the studio, equipment, materials, and furnishings, and business operations. www.huntingtonblock.com

K&K Insurance Group, Inc., P.O. Box 2338, Fort Wayne, IN 46801-2338. Provides liability insurance for artists. See the "Concessionaires, Exhibitors & Vendors" section of its Web site. www.kandkinsurance.com

Ontario Crafts Council, 990 Queen Street West, Toronto, Ontario M6J 1H1, Canada. Members are eligible for business and liability insurance. www .craft.on.ca

Notes

Introduction: An Overview

1. *The Artist's Guide to the Art Market*, 4th edition, by Betty Chamberlin, 18. Copyright 1970, 1975, 1979, 1983. Watson-Guptill Publications, New York.

Chapter 1: Launching or Relaunching Your Career: Overcoming Career Blocks

1. From *A Life in the Arts* by Eric Maisel, 83. Copyright © 1994 by Eric Maisel. Reprinted by permission of the Putnam Publishing Group/Jeremy P. Tarcher, Inc.

2. Excerpts from *The Painted Word* by Tom Wolfe. Copyright © 1975 by Tom Wolfe. Reprinted by permission of Farrar, Straus & Giroux, LLC.

3. Ralph Charell, *How to Make Things Go Your Way* (New York: Simon & Schuster, 1979), 149.

4. Ronald H. Silverman, "Art Career Education: The Third Imperative," *School Arts*, vol. 79, no. 6, February 1980, 42.

5. Comment by Barbara Price, academic dean and vice president for academic affairs, Maryland Institute, College of Art, Baltimore, published in "Support for Artists by Institutions: Comments and Discussion," *The Modern Muse: The Support and Condition of Artists*, ed. C. Richard Swaim (New York, 1989), 126. Reprinted with permission by Americans for the Arts.

6. Jo Hanson, *Artists' Taxes, the Hands-on-Guide: An Alternative to "Hobby" Taxes* (San Francisco: Vortex Press, 1987), 24.

7. Suzi Gablik, *Has Modernism Failed?* (New York: Thames and Hudson, 1984), 68.

8. Professor Leslee Nelson, University of Wisconsin-Madison, email message to author, January 10, 2008.

9. Stephen Driver, "Teach Them to Swim . . . ? How Long Can They Tread Water?," presented at the panel "Teach Them to Swim or Let Them Sink,"

Southeastern College Art Conference and Mid-American College Art Association, October 18–21, 2000, Louisville, Kentucky. Unnumbered.

10. Ibid.

11. Associate Professor Stephen Driver, Brescia University, email message to author, January 11, 2008.

12. Gary Keown, "Packaging the Art Student for Life," presented at the panel "Teach Them to Swim or Let Them Sink," Southeastern College Art Conference and Mid-American College Art Association, October 18–21, 2000, Louisville, Kentucky. Unnumbered.

13. Raphael Rubinstein, "Art Schools: A Group Crit," *Art in America,* May 2007. Interview with Bruce Ferguson, 104.

14. Raphael Rubinstein, "Art Schools: A Group Crit," *Art in America,* May 2007. Interview with Dave Hickey, 106.

15. Annette Lieberman and Vicki Lindner, *The Money Mirror: How Money Reflects Women's Dreams, Fears, and Desires* (New York: Allworth Press, 1996), 56.

16. Ibid., 54.

17. Carol Lloyd, *Creating a Life Worth Living* (New York: HarperCollins, 1997), 103.

18. Ibid.

19. Tad Crawford, *The Secret Life of Money: How Money Can Be Food for the Soul* (New York: Allworth Press, 1996), 42.

20. Ibid.

21. Carol Duncan, "Who Rules the Art World?," *Socialist Review,* vol. 70, July–August 1983, 111.

22. Ted Potter, "Introduction," *The Modern Muse: The Support and Condition of Artists,* ed. C. Richard Swaim (New York, 1989), 9. Reprinted with permission by Americans for the Arts.

23. From *THE PRACTICAL HB FOR THE EMERGING ARTIST,* 1st edition, by LAZZARI. 1996. Reprinted with permission of Wadsworth, a division of Thomsom Learning. www.thomsonrights.com. Fax: 800-730-2215.

24. Ibid.

25. From *Art & Fear* by David Bayles and Ted Orland, 47. Copyright © 1993. Reprinted by permission of the Image Continuum Press, Santa Cruz, California, and Eugene, Oregon.

26. From the book *Work with Passion.* Copyright © 1984, revised 1995 by Nancy Anderson. Reprinted with permission of New World Library, Novato, California. www.newworldlibrary.com.

Chapter 2: Launching or Relaunching Your Career: Entering the Marketplace

1. Jo Hanson, *Artists' Taxes, the Hands-on-Guide: An Alternative to "Hobby" Taxes* (San Francisco: Vortext Press, 1987), 26.

2. Ibid.

3. Judith Appelbaum and Nancy Evans, *How to Get Happily Published* (New York: Harper & Row, 1978), 12.

4. Tad Crawford, *Legal Guide for the Visual Artist* (New York: Allworth Press, 1999), 1.

5. Patrick Moore, *Future Safe: The Present Is the Future* (New York: The Estate Project for Artists with AIDS, The Alliance for the Arts, 1992), 2.

6. Crawford, op. cit., 205.

7. Ibid., 205–6.

8. Hanson, op. cit., i.

9. Barbara A. Sloan, email message to author, February 2008.

10. Maximum contributions for IRAs and Roth IRAs for the year 2008.

Chapter 3: Presentation Tools and Packages

1. Artist statement by William Hanson.

2. Shannon Wilkinson, "The Art of Self-Promotion: The Hum Below the Radar: News from the Art Front," *Art Calendar,* April 1996, 6.

3. Ibid.

4. Chicago Artists Resource, Cultural Planning Division, Department of Cultural Affairs, "Artist Story: Lynn Basa," www.chicagoartistsresource.org/visual-arts/node/350 (accessed Feburary 13, 2008).

5. From *Conquering the Paper Pile-Up* by Stephanie Culp (Cincinnati, Ohio: Writer's Digest Books, 1990), 2. © Stephanie Culp. Used with permission of Stephanie Culp. All rights reserved.

Chapter 4: Art Marketing and the Internet

1. William Lombardo, telephone interview with author, May 13, 2008.

2. Ibid.

3. William Lombardo, "How to Choose a Web Designer." Copyright © William Lombardo, 2004.

4. Ibid.

5. William Lombardo, email message to author, June 21, 2008.

6. http://nadinerobbinsportraits.blogspot.com.

7. http://tondro.com/blog.html.

8. www.tondro.com.

9. Cassandra Tondro, email to author, June 22, 2008.

10. Ibid.

11. www.susankapuscinskigaylord.com.

12. www.ingoodspirit.blogspot.com.

13. http://thecreativeyear.blogspot.com.

14. www.makingbookswithchildren.blogspot.com.

15. Susan Kapuscinski Gaylord, email to author, June 24, 2008.

16. Ibid.

17. Ibid.

18. http://iheartphotograph.blogspot.com.

19. www.lesliefry.com/articles.php4 (accessed June 22, 2008).

20. Schomburg Gallery, Bergamot Station, Santa Monica, California, November 17–December 15, 2007.

21. www.atanaskarpeles.com

22. Wikipedia contributors, "Social Network Service," *Wikipedia, The Free Encyclopedia,* http://en.wikipedia.org/wiki/Social_networking (accessed June 28, 2008).

23. Ibid.

24. www.merrillk.com.

25. Merrill K. Kazanjian, email to author, April 11, 2008.

26. www.dailymotion.com/video/x51mip_art-slave-gallery_creation.

27. http://artists.cecicasariego.com.

28. http://adriennefritze.com and From *The Mind of A* posted on www.working artistsonline.com.

29. Adrienne Fritze, "How to Use Social Networking Sites to Help Your Business Grow," www.ehow.com/how_2289008_networking-sites-help-business-grow .html (accessed June 30, 2008).

30. www.constantcontact.com/anti_spam.jsp.

31. Ellen Lupton, "Indie Publishing," Design Blog, Cooper Hewitt National Design Museum, January 5, 2007. http://blog.cooperhewitt.org/2007/01/05/indie -publishing (accessed June 30, 2008).

Chapter 5: Pricing Your Work: How Much Is It Worth?

1. Lloyd, *Creating a Life Worth Living* (New York: HarperCollins, 1997), 3.

2. Ibid.

Chapter 6: Public Relations: Keep Those Cards and Letters Coming In and Going Out

1. "Lester Hayes Selected Work, 1962–75." Press release issued by Triple Candie and posted on ArtCal, The Opinionated Guide to New York Art Galleries. www.artcal.net/event/view/12/3771 (accessed February 26, 2008).

2. Ibid.

3. Daniel Grant, *The Business of Being an Artist* (New York: Allworth Press, 1996), 195.

4. From a press release issued by the Integral Consciousness Institute for Synthesis, regarding an exhibition at the Soho Center for the Visual Arts, New York, N.Y., June 1979. (N.B., the Soho Center for the Visual Arts no longer exists.)

5. From a press release issued by Xavier Nuez in conjunction with exhibitions at the Stanford Art Spaces Gallery, Stanford University, Stanford, California, and the L. C. Horton, Jr. Gallery, San Joaquin Delta College, Stockton, California, dated August 8, 2008.

6. From a press release issued by Laura Breitman and Michael Needleman in June 2006 regarding an exhibition "Seeing Double" at the Port of Call Gallery in Warwick, N.Y.

7. From a press release issued by the Gulf Coast Museum of Art, Largo, Florida, August 29, 2005, regarding the sculpture *Big Dress* by Leslie Fry.

8. From a press release issued by the Bruce R. Lewin Gallery, New York, N.Y., for a one-person exhibition by Peter Anton, *Chocolate Throughout the Land,* April 1996.

9. "Barbara Rose," interview by Eva Cockroft, *Artworkers News,* April 1980, 13.

10. Interview with Nina Pratt, New York, N.Y., 1990.

11. Excerpts from *The Painted Word* by Tom Wolfe. Copyright © 1975 by Tom Wolfe. Reprinted by permission of Farrar, Straus and Giroux, LLC.

12. From interview with Ingrid Sischy in the article "Profiles: A Girl of the

Zeitgeist—II," by Janet Malcolm, *The New Yorker*, 51–52. Copyright 1986 Janet Malcolm. Originally in the *New Yorker*, October 27, 1986. Reprinted by permission of The Wylie Agency, Inc.

13. Nancy Stapen, "The Thorn in Culture's Side," *Art New England*, July–August 1988, 9.

14. "John Perrault," interview by Walter Weissman, *Artworkers News*, April 1980, 19.

15. "Rules for Specialized Departments," *Ethical Journalism: A Handbook of Values and Practices for News and Editorial Departments*, The New York Times, 2004, 134–39. www.nytco.com/pdf/NYT_Ethical_Journalism_0904.pdf (accessed March 7, 2008).

16. Tyler Green, "Q&A with VV Art Critic Christian Viveros-Faune, Part III," *Modern Art Notes*, Arts Journal. www.artsjournal.com/man/2008/01/qa_with_vv_art_critic_christia_2.html (accessed July 12, 2008).

17. Ibid.

Chapter 7: Exhibition and Sales Opportunities Using Those That Exist and Creating Your Own

1. Edit de Ak and Walter Robinson, "Alternative Periodicals," *The New Artspace: A Summary of Alternative Visual Arts Organizations*, prepared in conjunction with a conference held April 26–29, 1978 (Los Angeles: Los Angeles Institute of Contemporary Art, 1978), 38.

2. Suzanne K. Vinmans, *On Opening an Art Gallery* (Madison, Wis.: Suzanne K. Vinmans, 1990), 30–31.

3. Donna Marxer, "Report from New York: A History Lesson—and a Primer on Vanities," *Art Calendar*, April 1995, 13.

4. Joan Altabe, "They Should Change the Audience, Not the Artists," *Sarasota Herald-Tribune*, April 10, 1994, 2G. Copyright © 1994 *Sarasota Herald-Tribune*. Reprinted by expressed permission of the *Sarasota Herald-Tribune*.

5. Ibid.

6. Ibid.

7. *Declaration of Artists' Rights of the National Artists Equity Association (A.E.A.), USA, 1974.* Center for the Study of Ethics in the Professions of IIT, Illinois Institute of Technology. http://ethics.iit.edu/codes/coe/nat.artists.equity.assoc.dec.html (accessed March 12, 2008).

8. Guidelines for Professional Standards in the Organization of Juried Exhibition, CARFAC Ontario 1988. www.carfacontario.ca/images/guidelines_for_professional_standards_juried_exhibitions.pdf (accessed March 13, 2008).

9. Ibid.

10. Altabe, "They Should Change the Audience, Not the Artists."

11. Letter from Richard S. Harrington to executive director of NoBIAS Gallery in Bennington, Vt., dated May 19, 1998.

12. Ellen Baum, "The Whitney: Acquisitions Policies and Attitude Toward Living Artists," *Artworkers News*, December 1980, 13, 19.

13. Ibid.

14. www.atelierliz.com.

15. Sydney Delson, letter to author, October 5, 2007.

16. Guidelines and Standards, International Association for Professional Art Advisors. www.iapaa.org/guidelines.html (accessed March 16, 2008).

17. "Commissioned Artwork in the Mid-1990s: A Survey of Guild Users," The Designer's Sourcebook II: Art for the Wall, Furniture & Accessories (Madison, Wis.: The Guild, 1996), 201–2.

18. Anne Barclay Morgan, "Getting Better: Art and Healing," *Sculpture*, September–October 1994, 26.

19. Brian David Dennis, "Venue Viewer," Visual Art Management Project: Vam-p. www.vam-p.com (accessed March 23, 2008).

20. Elizabeth Bram, *Zero Gravity: Diary of a Travelling Artist*, Baldwin, N.Y., 87.

21. From an undated press release issued by Pratt Institute, Brooklyn, NY, for an exhibition, *Empty Dress: Clothing as Surrogate in Recent Art*, 1996, curated by Nina Felshin and organized by Independent Curators, Inc., New York, N.Y.

22. From a press release for an exhibition entitled *A, E, Eye, O, U, and Sometimes Why*, May 5–June 20, 1980, curated by Deborah Gardner and Karen Loftus and organized by the Organization of Independent Artists, New York, N.Y.

23. An exhibition held at Ronald Feldman Fine Arts, New York, N.Y., March 1981.

24. From a press release issued by Ronald Feldman Fine Arts, New York, N.Y., for an exhibition entitled *Top Secret: Inquiries into the Biomirror*, March 1981.

25. Kathy Borrus, "Museum Stores: Your Next Market," *The Crafts Report*, October 1995, 14.

26. Ibid.

27. Ibid.

28. Nina Pratt, *How to Sell Art: A Guide for Galleries, Art Dealers, Consultants, and Artists' Agents* (New York: Succotash Press, 1992), 6.

29. Nina Pratt, *How to Sell Art*, 9.

30. Ibid.

Chapter 8: Dealing with Dealers and Psyching Them Out

1. Grace Glueck, "Old Business, New Name: Behold the Gallerist," *New York Times*, December 24, 2005. www.nytimes.com/2005/12/24/arts/design/24gall.html?pagewanted+print (accessed December 24, 2005)

2. Dennis Christie, "Dealer vs. Gallerist," Rubberbandlazer. http://rubberbandlazer.blogspot.com/2005/12/dealers-vs-gallerist.html (accessed April 3, 2008)

3. Glueck, "Old Business, New Name."

4. Delahunt, Michael R, "Gallerist," *ArtLex Art Dictionary*, March 23, 2008. www.artlex.com (acessed April 3, 2008)

5. Interview with Nina Pratt, New York, N.Y., 1990.

6. Ivan C. Karp, "The Artist and the Dealer: A Curious Relationship," *Art in America*, March 1989, 51.

7. Ibid., 53.

8. Interview with Nancy Hoffman, "How to Succeed (By Really Trying)," by Paul Gardner, *ARTnews*, February 1990, 134.

9. Edward Feit, "Securing Gallery Representation, *American Artist* business supplement, June 1989, 69.

10. Jana Jevnikar, "An Incredible Journey: The Search for a Gallery," *American Artist*, September 1989, 12.

11. Interview with Walter Wickiser, "Artists' Career Development," by Daniel Grant, *American Artist*, September 1989, 12.

12. Interview with Judy Levy in *Artists Observed*, edited and photographed by Harvey Stein (New York: Harry N. Abrams, Inc., 1986), 61.

13. Interview with Tony Delap in *Artists Observed*, edited and photographed by Harvey Stein (New York: Harry N. Abrams, Inc., 1986), 70.

14. Renée Phillips, *The Complete Guide to New York Art Galleries* (New York: Manhattan Arts International, 2004).

15. Mark I. Rosen, *Thank You for Being Such a Pain: Spiritual Guidance for Dealing with Difficult People* (New York: Three Rivers Press, 1998), 39.

16. Nina Pratt, *How to Sell Art: A Guide for Galleries, Art Dealers, Consultants, and Artists' Agents* (New York: Succotash Press, 1992).

17. Ibid.

18. Ibid.

19. Ibid.

20. Ibid.

21. Interview with André Emmerich in *The Art Dealers: The Powers behind the Scene Tell How the Art World Really Works*, by Laura de Coppet and Alan Jones (New York: Clarkson Potter, 1984), 62.

22. Dorothy Spears, "The First Gallerists' Club," *New York Times*, June 18, 2006. www.nytimes.com/2006/06/18/arts/design/18spea.html?partner=rssnyt&emc =rss (accessed June 18, 2006)

23. Missy Sullivan, "Artist Power," Forbes Best of the Web, May 22, 2000. www.forbes.com/best/2000/0522/036.html (accessed April 9, 2008).

24. Grace Glueck, "Gallery Etiquette: A Duel of Dealers and Browsers," *New York Times*, March 8, 1991, C1.

25. Hilton Kramer, "The Case Against Price Tags," *New York Times*, March 20, 1988, Sect. 2, 33.

26. Letter to the editor by Alvin S. Lane, *New York Times*, April 24, 1988, Sect. 2, 15.

27. Letter to the editor by Roy Bohon, *New York Times*, April 24, 1988, Sect. 2, 5.

28. Renée Phillips, *The Complete Guide to New York Art Galleries* (New York: Manhattan Arts International, 2004).

29. Prepared by the Task Force on Discrimination in Art, a CETA Title VI project sponsored by the Foundation for the Community of Artists in conjunction with Women in the Arts, 1979.

30. Nancy Jervis and Maureen Shild, "Survey of NYC Galleries Finds Discrimination," *Artworkers News*, April 1979, A7.

31. Ibid, A8.

32. "Rules for Specialized Departments," *Ethical Journalism: A Handbook of Values and Practices for News and Editorial Departments, The New York Times*, 2004, 134–39. www.nytco.com/pdf/NYT_Ethical_Journalism_0904.pdf (accessed March 7, 2008).

33. Alice Goldfarb Marquis, *The Art Biz: The Covert World of Collectors, Dealers, Auction Houses, Museums and Critics* (Chicago: Contemporary Books,

Inc., 1991), 3–4. Copyright © 1991 by Alice Goldfarb Marquis. Reprinted by permission.

34. "Richard Lerner," interview by Jean E. Breitbart, *Artworkers News,* March 1981, 29.

35. Dan J. Martin, ed., *Guide to Arts Administration Training and Research 1995–97* (San Francisco: Association of Arts Administration Educators, 1995), 11.

36. Association of Arts Administration Educators. http://www.artsadministration .org/graduate.cfm and www.artsadministration.org/undergraduate.cfm (accessed April 11, 2008).

37. "Lucy Lippard," interview by David Troy, *Artworkers News,* April 1980, 16.

38. Dianne Lawrence, "John Baldessari: The Coagula Interview," *Coagula Art Journal,* Issue #32, March–April 1998, 26.

39. Benny Shaboy, "Ask studioNOTES," *studioNOTES: The Journal for Working Artists,* August–October 2000, 30–39.

40. Ibid.

41. Ibid.

42. John Biederman, editor, *Artists' Gallery Guide: Chicago and the Surrounding Area* (Chicago: Chicago Artists' Coalition, 2005).

Chapter 9: The Mysterious World of Grants: Fact and Fiction

1. Jane C. Hartwig, "Betting on Foundations," in C. M. Kurzin, J. B. Steinhoff, and A. Bonavoglia, *Foundation Grants to Individuals* (New York: The Foundation Center, 1979), xiii. (A 16th edition of *Foundation Grants to Individuals,* published in 2007 is available.)

2. Ibid.

Chapter 10: Generating Income: Alternatives to Driving a Cab

1. *Artists in the Workforce: 1990–2005,* Office of Research and Analysis National Endowment for the Arts, Research Report #48, May 2008.

2. From a press release, "National Endowment for the Arts Announces *New Artists in the Workforce* Study," issued by the National Endowment for the Arts, June 12, 2008. www.nea.gov/news/news08/ArtistsinWorkforce.html (accessed June 13, 2008).

3. Ibid.

4. *Artists in the Workforce: 1990–2005,* op. cit., 2.

5. Michael Woodward, "The Licensing and Publishing Industry Today," copyright 2007. www.licensingcourse.com/article1.shtml (accessed May 24, 2008).

6. In-person interview with Michael Woodward, May 22, 2008.

7. Caryn R. Leland, *Licensing Art and Design* (New York: Allworth Press, 1995), 95.

8. Ibid.

9. From exhibition proposal by Molly Heron, New York, N.Y.

10. From artist statement by Molly Heron, New York, N.Y.

11. Annie Dillard, *The Writing Life* (New York: HarperCollins Publishers, 1989), 33.

12. From artist statement by Molly Heron, New York, N.Y.

Chapter 11: Rationalization, Paranoia, Competition, Rejection, and the Overwhelm Factor

1. Excerpted from *The Twelve Secrets of Highly Creative Women,* by Gail McMeekin, © 2000 with permission of Red Wheel Weiser and Conari Press. 800-423-7087. www.redwheelweiser.com.

2. Email to author dated March 28, 2008.

3. Ibid.

4. Ibid.

5. From a press release issued by Eden Maxwell announcing his book, *An Artist Empowered: Define and Establish Your Value as an Artist—Now,* Fall 2007.

6. Jane Madson, *The Artist's and Critic's Forum* 1, 1, 1982.

7. Billy Curmano, "Rejecting Rejection," *Artworkers News,* January 1981, 34.

8. Ibid.

9. Ibid.

Index

About the Author

CAROLL MICHELS has helped hundreds of emerging and established visual and performing artists and writers develop their careers. She has served as a career coach and artist-advocate since 1978.

Her artwork has been exhibited in museums in the United States and abroad, including the Georges Pompidou Museum in Paris; the Kunsthalle in Vienna; the Walker Art Center in Minneapolis; and the Institute for Contemporary Art, the Clocktower, in New York City.

Caroll Michels has received numerous grants, including those awarded by the National Endowment for the Arts, the New York State Council for the Arts, the New York Council for the Humanities, and the International Fund for the Promotion of Culture/UNESCO. She has also received a fellowship from the Alden B. Dow Creativity Center in Midland, Michigan.

She was the chairwoman of the Fine Arts Advisory Board of the Fashion Institute of Technology in New York City. She conducts career workshops for artists throughout the United States and in Canada that are sponsored by arts councils, arts organizations, and colleges and universities.

Michels offers in-person and phone consultations to artists and writers in all disciplines. She is now based in Sarasota, Florida, and can be reached at the following address:

Ms. Caroll Michels
1724 Burgos Drive
Sarasota, FL 34238
Telephone: 941-922-5277
Fax: 941-922-5278
E-mail.carollmich@aol.com
Web site: www.carollmichels.com
Web site: www.artisthelpnetwork.com